CRICKET'S

SILVER · LINING

1864-1914

THE 50 YEARS FROM THE BIRTH OF *WISDEN* TO THE BEGINNING OF THE *GREAT WAR*

CRICKET'S
SILVER · LINING
1864-1914
THE 50 YEARS FROM THE BIRTH OF *WISDEN* TO THE BEGINNING OF THE *GREAT WAR*

David Rayvern Allen

Willow Books
Collins
8 Grafton Street, London W1
1987

Willow Books
William Collins Sons & Co Ltd
London · Glasgow · Sydney · Auckland
Toronto · Johannesburg

First published 1987
© David Rayvern Allen 1987

British Library Cataloguing in Publication Data
Allen, David Rayvern
Cricket's silver lining.
1. Cricket—History
I. Title
796.35'8'09   GV913

ISBN 0–00–218204–1

Set in Garamond by Ace Filmsetting Ltd, Frome, Somerset
Printed and bound in Great Britain by
Robert Hartnoll (1985) Ltd, Cornwall

Contents

CONTENTS

CONTENTS

Acknowledgements

The publishers and compiler would like to thank the following for permission to use the articles mentioned herewith:

Gerald Pawle and *Blackwood's Magazine* for 'Cricket Writer' and 'A Cricketer of the Past' (J. C. Masterman); Stephen Green for 'Aboard the *Great Britain*' (*Playfair Cricket Monthly*), and also extracts from the diaries of George Anderson and Vernon Royle which are held in the library at Lord's; the Royle family for the latter extract; *The Cricketer* for 'Some Notes on Early Cricket Abroad' (F. S. Ashley-Cooper) and 'Cricket Surnames' ('Historicus'); Barry Wilson and the *Sunday Times* for 'The Private Test Match'; Celia Davies and *Country Life* for 'Eleven Maids Dressed All in White'; the Blunden Estate for 'Cricket Won't be Druv" (Edmund Blunden); and John R. Hung for his poem 'A Collection of Words on E.B. the Cricketer'.

They would also like to acknowledge the following sources for the illustrations:

The Illustrated London News
The Illustrated Sporting and Dramatic News
Marylebone Library for *Strand Magazine*
MCC Library for *Cricket* and *The Cricketer and Hockey Player*

Newspaper Library, Colindale for *The Cricketer* (1869)
The Sphere
St. Stephen's Review
University Library, Birmingham for *Harmsworth Magazine* and *Windsor Magazine*

Every effort has been made to trace the holders of copyright material used in this anthology. We apologise for any omissions in this respect, and on notification we undertake to make the appropriate acknowledgement in subsequent editions.

Introduction

It is easy to drift into the assumption that everything that needs to be said about cricket in the late nineteenth and early twentieth century has already been said. The rich store of documentary evidence available in book-form would seem to support that view; after all, one might argue, even if the period was the most important and significant in the game's development, surely there is nothing new to be learned. And yet . . . we should pause for reflection.

A crucial demarcation point between then and now lies in the enviably relaxed and unpressured way of living – or so it would appear – enjoyed by the educated classes. During the Victorian and Edwardian age, there were no hordes of multi-media competing to devour leisure time. Consequently, the written word ruled unopposed and with it was encouraged the circulation of a host of journals and magazines that catered for the tastes of 'town and country gentlemen'.

Usually, of course, these cultured folk had extremely catholic taste and therefore, their post-kedgeree repasts could, and did, consist of indigestible pieces on such delicate issues as penal reform in the Andaman Isles made palatable by the juxtaposition of pre-mortem prospects for grouse on the Yorkshire moors.

Praise be to the sagacious editors though, who, adjacent to these examples of investigative journalism, found room for an article on cricket, because it is there in the likes of *Longman's*, *Blackwood's Magazine*, *Temple Bar* and *All the Year Round*, that are to be found a few rare gems that tend nowadays to be left neglected in the vaults of libraries.

A first reading of some of these colourful effusions can support the cynical view that nothing alters so much, that it does not stay the same. We find 'W.G.' in 1895, being concerned that cricket would become 'too much of a business like football' – ironically enough, you may think, for one with his commercial instincts. Then there is Colonel Philip Trevor declaring that: 'The keenest cricketer would not travel from the "back-blocks" to Sydney, sit in the grandstand, watch it rain for three days, and then go home again. You have no alternative, but to give that man the certainty of seeing the match played out.' He goes on: 'Assuming that you agree with me, I return fortified to my main contention that cricket is a time-limited affair, and that matches are won by the side which gets the greatest number of runs.' Another instance is when 'Archie' MacLaren states unequivocally that 'thirteen players were quite enough for a tour abroad'. So many chords reverberating the present day.

A further study of a number of the articles, however, does surely reveal aspects that are not standard issue in the books on the era. One comes across names that were not 'household', anecdotes that have not been met elsewhere and nuances that are free of cliché. There is an element of surprise in noting anxieties over the proposed introduction of the tea interval and almost unguarded disbelief when reading the contribution that Alec Waugh made to the *London Mercury* in 1922, which bemoans the lack of cricket literature. What would he say today, I wonder? Probably, something not too dissimilar to Gerald Pawle's comment, when, in relatively recent times, ringing-in with copy for his 'paper. 'Yes, I expect things have changed a bit since Lord Hawke's day.'

But these apparently contradictory and thought-provoking early reactions are as nothing compared to the residual impression, for any collection of writings within and of a period leaves a heightened awareness of the underlying feelings that were prevalent. One experiences a strange kind of transportation in time to another existence and can enjoy the flavours of the day permeating the pages. Conversation is mannered and language verbose. We smile at moments of quaintness and pomposity, at the noble sentiments and the lordly style. We become engrossed in the journalists' dissertations and are wafted back unconsciously a century ago to the over-furnished drawing-rooms of the landed gentry. For fleeting seconds, we capture the sight of a bewhiskered figure reclining on a *chaise-longue*, idly thumbing through his favourite periodical, port and pipe by his side. And then, suddenly, the time-warp is shattered. The rude realities of the late twentieth century super-impose with an insensitive sentence from a Victorian that now would be regarded as a flagrant example of racial prejudice.

It is, however, an expression of a bygone era. The words on the pages that follow, whether blinkered or enlightened have been left practically as printed, for only by doing so can we fully appreciate the motivating forces at work.

The same applies to an occasional unevenness in the standard of writing, which is more than justified by a wider range of windows on their world. Players, reporters and trained craftsmen do not necessarily possess the same literary skill and it is just as rewarding in its way to read the untutored, idiosyncratic report from the secretary of the Hudson Bay Cricket Club or the private jottings from the diaries of pioneer tourists as it is to admire the deft turn of phrase of P. G. Wodehouse or Arthur Conan Doyle. Each to his own and much from many, including several anonymous offerings.

A random choice might find Ashley-Cooper's staggeringly knowledgeable global survey; George Giffen reminiscing on battles won and lost; Lord Tennyson rating captaincy; an analysis of Ranji's incomparable batting technique; C. B. Fry on his contemporaries; an American exposition of the Bard's unwitting contribution to cricket in his plays; curious facts and extraordinary fiction; the umpire and his art and the village game from 'The Gaffer'.

There are also contained retrospective looks at the past from the present and a look at the present from the past. Naturally enough, in the era on which we are concentrating, the same thing was happening. The writers of the day were taking as their theme, the conquests of the giants from yesteryear; in reality, therefore, the threads of our silver lining cover, at least, a century of cricket. It is time to let them speak for themselves. . . .

David Rayvern Allen
June 1987

Lord's-and Players

A noble game, sir, eh?'
'It is more than a game; it is an institution,' said Tom.
'Yes,' said Arthur, 'the birthright of British boys, old and young, as Habeas Corpus and trial by jury are of British men.'

'The discipline and reliance on one another which it teaches are so valuable, I think,' continued the master, 'it ought to be an unselfish game. It merges the individual in the eleven; he does not play that he may win, but that his side may.'

And so think all the readers of *Tom Brown's School-days*. Whatever praise may be given to football, the palm amongst athletic sports is undoubtedly borne off by cricket. To these two fine games the rivalry must be confined; others — not to say can't bear competition with them — do not even approach them; fives, rounders, rackets, prison-bars, trap-ball, hockey, are all very well in their way; they develop the muscles, and involve a certain amount of skill. They do not, however, require the same nerve, the same discipline, the same agility, which both football and cricket demand. There is no room, no opportunity, for that fine play which is so frequently and spirit-stirringly displayed by the bowler and the batsman, whilst they fail to excite a tithe of the interest and enthusiasm. The appeal, therefore, lies between football and cricket. And what does football admit of? It is true troops on either side must be well marshalled, and kept under thorough control by the captain; it is true that he has his skirmishers, his main body, and his reserves, whom he wields, or ought to wield, with judgment and intelligence; but, after all, when the *mêlée* takes place, when the strife grows hot, when the shock of 'kicking' multitudes is felt, what is it all but a confused and meaningless struggle, affording but small opportunity for gallantry of exploit, evoking no applause, but rather creating a certain amount of alarm, lest in the clumsy collision of opposing forces irreparable damage to shins and ankles might ensue? 'It is meter for laming than making able the users thereof,' quoth the learned James I.

In cricket, on the contrary, the uninitiated even become at once interested. The cricket lawn is a veritable battle-field. The lookers-on behold a contest, bloodless indeed, but not less exciting than a Blenheim or a Waterloo. Look at that double regiment of players, stalwart men marshalled out in their several positions. What a picturesque feature they present on the plain! What order, what regularity, what symmetry in the plan of their arrangements! Dressed in simple but harmonious uniforms, their manly frames display strength and prowess. There is an activity even in their attitude of waiting. Their whole bearing, physical and mental, indicates the agonistes. Then, when the game commences, how the interest becomes intensified; how every faculty becomes strained; how every eye brightens up to watch the incident of the moment! The bowler, with steady, measured, though it may be rapid step, advances to the goal, the ball poised between his skilful fingers. Swift as lightning he discharges it, as from a catapult; the leathern missile shoots across the intervening space, touching the ground only to fly off it with terrific velocity, and at a perilous tangent. Who knows where it will strike? On the other side, the batsman, with calm and quick eye, has marked its approach, be it a bail ball, or a fast shooter, or a wicket ball; and he plays forward or back, gives an off cut or a leg hit, with marvellous presence of mind, according to the necessity of the moment. Sometimes it is a slow tice ball he has to guard against; the whole field traces the treacherous path of the insidious enemy, and with breathless expectation anticipates the block or the drive. Perchance the defendant strikes hard, and sends the ball flying off to the distance; again the spectators become silent, with a conflicting sense of hope and fear, as long-stop pounces upon the winged toy, and with Herculean swing whirls it back home to the wicket-keeper. Or perhaps it is point or short-leg whose skill and activity at stopping and catching are called into requisition; whilst now and then long-slip has a glorious opportunity of displaying his prowess. All these several and soul-stirring duties have to be performed, and that too with rapidity yet calmness, and before a multitude who appreciate the *finesse* of every throw, of every catch, in fact of

2

every movement of the ball and of the bat, of the hand and of the foot. The acclamations which greet the bowler who so skims the wicket that the bails fly off in branching directions, or the wicket-keeper who stumps his adversary, or the fielder who is lucky enough to get a capital catch, are not meant to disparage the luckless fortune of the batsman who has to surrender his weapon. In the game of cricket, where all enter chivalrously into the game, neither is greater nor less than the other. There is no monopoly for a gifted few; it affords scope for every diversity of talent – bowling, fielding, wicket-keeping, free hitting, safe and judicious play, and good generalship; in one of these points many a man has earned an honourable distinction, though he may be inferior in the others. A long innings bespeaks good play, but 'out the first ball' is no disgrace.

But who invented cricket? When was it invented? Where was it invented? Or perhaps 'it growed,' like Topsy, claiming no parentage. Not improbably this may have been the case; for though the name of cricket it not to be found earlier than the second half of the seventeenth century, there can be little doubt that the game itself, in some rude form, was known to the Normans, perhaps the Saxons, if not the woad-painted Britons. Archaeologists, philologists, and etymologists have been driving at the origin of the game, but have not, as yet, discovered it. Imagination, too, has been very fecund in the work, and broods of conjectures have been poured forth, like feathers and flowers from the hat of a Monsieur Houdin or a Herr Frikell. But still this question, like the law, has a glorious uncertainty about it, motleyed, however, with the prismatic hues of diversity. One person derives the name from the *chugar* of the Persians; another sees in it a likeness to the *bandy* of the Welsh; a third confounds it with the *hurley* of the Irish; a fourth fancies a resemblance between it and the *shinty* and *golf* of the Scots; whilst a fifth claims for it the honour of being a combination of all these various sports. The author of *The Cricket Field*, more bold and hazardous in his flight than the others, ventures to give a very high antiquity to cricket. He maintains that a single-wicket game was played as early as the thirteenth century, under the name of *Club-Ball*; that it is probably identical with *Handyn and Handoute*; that a genuine double-wicket game was played in Scotland about 1700, under the name of *Cat-and-Dog*; and that *creag*, or *cricce*, the Saxon term for the crooked stick or *bandy*, was the name of a game played in the year

1300. In confirmation of this he gives the following proof. 'In the Bodleian Library at Oxford,' says Strutt, 'is a Ms. dated 1344, which represents a figure, a female, in the act of bowling a ball to a man who elevates a straight bat to strike it; behind the bowler are several figures, male and female, waiting to stop and catch the ball, their attitudes grotesquely eager for the "chance." The game is called *Club-Ball*, but the score is made by hitting and running, as in cricket.' In 1740, Barrington, commenting on a statute of Edward IV, forbidding such games as cloish, ragle, half-bowle, queekeborde, and handyn and handoute, says: 'This is the most severe law ever made in any country against gaming; and some of those forbidden seem to have been manly exercises, particularly the handyn and handoute, which I should suppose to be a kind of cricket, as the term hands is still retained in that game.' Dr Jamieson, in his dictionary, published in 1722, in his definition of cricket, leaves little doubt that the game played in Scotland as Cat-and-Dog is analogous to cricket. It is a remarkable fact, however, that none of our early poets, who drew their images and illustrations so largely from the pastimes and occupations of men, makes the slightest allusion to the game. The word is to be found neither in Shakespeare, Massenger, Shirley, Marlowe, Jonson, or Beaumont and Fletcher; and even in the schedule of sports drawn up by the authority of James I for the nurture and conduct of an heir-apparent to the throne, and addressed to his eldest son, Prince Henry of Wales, under the title of the *Basilicon Doron; or, a King's Christian Dutie towards God*, there is no allusion to it. Tennis, palle-malle, and suchlike other fair and pleasant field games are mentioned, with special commendation, in the royal catalogue. Burton, in his *Anatomy of Melancholy*, specifies the pastimes of 'great men' and those of 'base inferior persons' of his time, being zealous to particularize the 'rocks on which men lose themselves' by gambling, and to show how 'wealth runs away with their hounds, and their fortunes fly away with their hawks'; he gives us, moreover, a description of the 'sights and shows of the Londoners,' and the 'May games and recreations of the country folk'; and though he narrates rope-dancers and cock-fighting as among the sports common both to town and country, and describes 'winter recreations' separately, naming even 'foot-balle and ballowne,' and would see the common people play at 'ball and barley brakes,' we find no mention of cricket; and though the great John Locke, in 1679, described 'the sports of England for a curious stranger to see,' mentioning amongst them horse-racing, hawking, hunting and bowling, wrestling, bear and bull baiting, shooting with the long bow, stob ball, cudgel playing, and hurling, we do not catch the sound of cricket.

We are, however, now very close upon the heels of the word; for Edward Phillips, a nephew of John Milton, in his 'Mysteries of Love and Eloquence, or the Arts of Wooing and Complimenting, the Treatments of Ladies at Balls, Sports, Drolls, the Witchcrafts of their Persuasive Language, &c., 1685,' has this passage: 'Will you not, when you have me, throw stocks at my head, and cry, "Would my eyes had been beaten out of my head with a cricket-ball the day before I saw thee!"' This appears to be the dawn of the sun of cricket in the hemisphere of literature, and day by day he gathers new strength, attracting increasing brightness. Stowe, in his *Survey of London*, takes notice of cricket, though he places it – perhaps he was a bilious, crotchety, *il penseroso* sort of an individual, and didn't like the game – amongst the amusements of the lower classes. Would not this, however, indicate that it had already become *popular*? 'The modern sports of the citizens, besides drinking,' he writes in this curious passage, 'are cock-fighting, bowling upon greens, backgammon, cards, dice, billiards; also musical entertainments, dancing, mask-balls, stage-plays, and club-meetings in the evenings. They sometimes ride out on horseback, and hunt with the Lord Mayor's pack of dogs when the hunt is going on. The lower classes amuse themselves at foot-ball, wrestling, cudgels, ninepins, shovel board, *cricket*, stow ball, ringing of bells, quoits, pitching the bar, bull and bear baiting, throwing at cocks, lying at ale-houses.' May we not again infer that this description belongs appropriately to London and its neighbourhood, and does not apply to the provinces, nor embraces the sports of squires and country gentlemen? From this time cricket becomes frequently mentioned. The facetious Tom D'Urfey, in his *Pills to purge Melancholy*, writes thus:

'Of noble race was Skinking,
The line of Owen Tudor,
Thum, thum, thum,
But her renown is fled and gone
Since cruel love pursued her;
Fair Winny's eyes bright shining

And lily breast alluring,
Poor Jenkin's heart, with fatal dart,
Have wounded past all curing.
Herr was the prettiest fellow
At football or at *cricket*;
At hunting chase or nimble race,
By heaven, how Herr could prick it!'

Duncombe, the poet, who had a living in Essex, sings:

'We have not any cricketer
Of such account as he.'

And again, laying the scene of a match near Canterbury,

'An ill-timed cricket-match there did
At Bishop's Fall befall.'

About the same time Jenyngs, in his *Horatii Epistolarum imitated*, alludes to it thus:

'England, when once of peace and wealth possessed,
Began to think frugality a jest;
So grew polite: hence all her well-bred heirs
Gamesters and jockeys turned, and *cricket-players*.'

Whilst Pope, in one of his Satires, alludes to the game thus:

'The judge to dance his brother-sergeant call,
The senator at cricket urge the ball,' —

which, by the by, seems a confutation of Stowe's remark — imputation rather — that cricket was confined to the lower classes.

What's in a name, however! The question is, after all, Was a game such as we understand cricket known to our early ancestors, and played by them? Was *club-ball*, or *handyn and handoute*, the same as our modern cricket? and was it known, so early as the 13th century, under either of these appellations? Certain it is that a game was played with a ball and a bandy, or crooked stick, in a way similar to that in which cricket is played now, even if wickets were not used. The great point of the game was to place the ball in a hole dug in the ground; and this was equivalent to striking the bails off. Leaping, however, a gap of three centuries, we find, according to Lisle Bowles, that Bishop Ken used to wield the cricket-bat at Winchester School. If this be correct, cricket was played, nearly as we understand the game, about the year 1650.

6

Half a century later there can be little doubt that it was played in Scotland, as we have already mentioned; and within a very short time subsequently it was a general favourite at our public schools. The fourth Earl of Carlisle learned cricket at Eton, and, in a letter to George Selwyn, boasts that even at Mannheim he was up with the dawn practising with the bat; and Walpole, alluding to his career at the same school, about the year 1726, says: 'An expedition against bargemen and a game of cricket are very pretty things; but, thank my stars, I can remember things that are very nearly as pretty.'

The game at this time was only in a crude state compared with what it is now. The wickets were pitched at the same length, it is true, but were only one foot in height and two feet apart. Between the stumps a hole was made in the ground, as in club-ball, large enough to contain the ball and the butt-end of the bat. If in play the wicket-keeper could receive the ball from the field and place it in the hole before the striker, in running home, could place his bat there, he was out. The frequent collision of the bat with the wicket-keeper's hand eventually suggested the convenience of a line rather less than four feet from, but parallel to, the wicket, now called the popping-crease. This was a first step towards reform; a second soon followed. In a match of the Hambledon Club, played in 1775, it was observed, at a critical point of the game, that the ball passed three times between the stumps without knocking off the bail. It was then determined that a third stump should be added. Again, perceiving that the new style of balls which rose over the bat rose also over the wickets, then but one foot high, the wicket was increased to the dimensions of twenty-two inches by six, at which measure it remained till about 1814, when it was raised to the height of twenty-six inches by eight, and again, to its present dimensions of twenty-seven inches, in 1817, when, as one inch was added to the stumps, two inches were added to the width between the creases. Some old rules mention one variety of measure more – twenty-four inches by seven. The game was won by notches, every run constituting a notch.

The laws for the governance of the game were made as circumstances dictated, and were, of course, originally very brief and crude. With the destruction of old Lord's Pavilion, in Marylebone, many valuable documents relating to cricket were lost; but we have a few curious regulations, published a century ago, which are interesting as throwing some light on the batologic wisdom of our ancestors. The manuscript from which we take the following extract, given *verbatim, literatim, et 'punctuatim'*, is undated, although evidently written with great care and clearness.

The Game of Cricket as Settled by ye Cricket Club at ye Star and Garter in Pall Mall

'The pitching ye first Wicket is to be determined by ye cast of a piece of Money. When ye first Wicket is pitched and ye Popping Crease Cut which must be exactly 3 Foot 10 Inches from ye Wicket ye other Wicket is to be pitched directly opposite at 22 yards distance and ye other popping crease cut 3 Foot 10 Inches before it. The Bowling Creases must be cut in a direct line from each stump. The Stumps must be 22 Inches long and ye Bail 6 Inches. The Ball must weigh between 5 and 6 Ounces. When ye Wickets are both pitched and all ye Creases Cut, the party that wins the toss up may order which side shall go in first at his Option.'

At first it was feared the alteration in the height and width apart of the stumps would render the game a hopeless one. Between the optimists and the pessimists there was a regular battle; the pessimists maintaining that the batsman would have no chance against the bowler; the optimists — the men of skill — on the other hand, asserting that the innings would be not a whit the shorter, but that the game would be better played. *Sapientia non arma defendit* — science, rather than the weapons, would be relied on. It would henceforth be a game of brain no less than of hand. At the same time, however, to aid science, it was found necessary to improve the bat. The long-pod and curved form of the cricce or bandy, then little better than a huge wooden butter-knife, was only made for hitting, reaching in most instances up to the elbow. As, however, the bowling of length-balls progressed, the form of the bat necessarily underwent a material change. Instead of the curved form of the pod, it was made straight, and reduced in length. This, with the introduction of the third stump, made a great revolution in the character of the game, and may be considered a great epoch in its history.

The earliest record we have of cricket is a score of Kent against All England, played in the year 1746, at the Artillery Ground, London, in which the highest number obtained by any one player was eighteen. These were gained by a player called Newland, on the side of England;

in the second innings he carried his bat through. Kipps, on the side of Kent, made the greatest number of runs on their side, which, however, only amounted to twelve. In 1771 a match was played off, the North *versus* the South, at Nottingham, in which the contest seems to have been a drawn one, inasmuch as the Sheffield players left the field, when the Nottingham men were sixty ahead. The compliment, however, seems to have been returned in the following year; for another cricket tournament took place between the same combatants. On this occasion Nottingham gave in.

But it was not in the Midland or Northern counties that the game was destined to become most patronized and most played. Kent and Surrey acquired far greater celebrity; the little district around Hambledon having for a time boasted of its capability to resist all England. But this supremacy, according to Beldham, did not last very long.

'When I was a boy, about 1780, the Hambledon Club could beat all England,' he says; 'but our three parishes, around Farnham, at last beat Hambledon.'

The author of *The Cricket Field* says: 'It is quite evident that Farnham was the cradle of cricketers; Surrey in the old scores means nothing more than the Farnham parishes.'

This corner of Surrey, in every match of All England, was reckoned as part of Hampshire. Beldham, who was a great authority on these matters, says, 'Kent in early times was not equal to our counties. Their great man was Crawk, and he was taken away from our parish of Alresford, in Hampshire, by Mr Amhurst, the gentleman who made the Kent matches. In those days, except around our parts, Farnham and the Surrey side of Hampshire, a little play went a long way. Why, no man used to be thought of more than Yalden; when Yalden came amongst us, we soon made up our minds what the rest must be. If you want to know the time, sir, the Hambledon Club was formed, I will tell you this: when we beat them in 1780, I heard Mr Paulet say, "Here have I been raising my club for forty years, and am I to be beaten by a parish?"'

From this it is inferred that there must have been a cricket-club which played every week regularly so long ago as 1750. In fact it is not possible to understand how the devotees, we will not say could acquire proficiency without regular practice, but how they could abstain from seizing every opportunity to wield the bat. Indeed we know George

9

Selwyn to have been so passionately fond of it, that he was out of bed early in the day to be 'at it'; whilst the enthusiasm inspired by a contest is happily described by our excellent gossip Beldham:

'We used to go as eagerly to a match as if it were two armies fighting. We stayed at nothing if masters allowed the time. From our parish to Hambledon is twenty-seven miles, and we used to ride both ways the same day, early and late. At last I and John Willes were about building a cart. You have heard of taxed carts, sir? Well, the tax was put on then, and that stopped us. The members of the Hambledon Club had a caravan to take their eleven about. They used once to play always in velvet caps. Lord Winchelsea's eleven used to play in silver-lace hats; and the fashionable dress was knee-breeches and stockings.'

When this old Beldham, a veritable gossip and an amusing one too, began to play, Nyren, the celebrity of the day, was fifty years old, and captain in the Hambledon matches; 'but not half a player,' says the sly Beldham, 'as we reckon now.' 'The law for leg before wicket was not passed, nor much wanted, till Ring, one of our best hitters, was shabby enough to get his leg in the way, and take advantage of the bowlers; and when Tom Taylor, another first-rate hitter, did the same, the bowlers found themselves beaten, and the law was passed to make leg before wicket out. The law against jerking was owing to the frightful pace Tom Walker put on; and I believe that he afterwards tried something more like the modern throwing-bowling, and so caused the words against throwing also. Willes was not the inventor of that kind of round bowling; he only revived what was forgotten.'

Cricket was played in Sussex very early. However, its laurels were not very thick or blooming, if the strength of Sussex was to be measured by the play of Newland: 'a second-rate man of our parish,' said Beldham, 'beat Newland easily.'

To one Small belonged the reputation, at least among the old players of the Hambledon Club, of having invented cricket, or brought it to any degree of perfection. In a match of Hambledon against All England, he kept up his wicket for three days, and was not bowled out after all. It is said of another player, David Harris, of the same date, that he had once bowled to him 170 balls for one run. Sparkes, Bennett, and Parry were first-rate players in those days; but above them all shone out the name of Fennex.

Matches against twenty-two were not uncommon in the latter part of the last century.

The Hambledon Club broke up in 1791, though in this year, the last of its existence, its eleven all but beat twenty-two of Middlesex at Lord's. Its dissolution, however, only served to scatter first-rate players amongst the different clubs of England, and improve the play generally throughout the cricketing counties. In the last century, Kent against England was as good an annual match as in the present. The White Conduit Fields and the Artillery Ground then supplied the place of Lord's, though in 1787 the name of Lord's is found mentioned in Bentley's *Book of Matches*, implying of course the old Marylebone ground, now Dorset Square, and not the present in St John's Wood Road, which more properly deserves the name of Dark's than Lord's. Next in importance to the Kent matches were those of Hampshire and Surrey, in each of which counties the Hambledon men used to play according to their predilections, or rather according to the gentlemen who engaged them. T. Assheton Smith, Lord Frederick Beauclerk, the Earl Darnley, Mr Paulet, the Earl of Winchester, were great patrons and players in these days. Middlesex, exclusively of the Marylebone, also had its club in these days, although it required twenty-two of their number to enable them to make a creditable stand against the disciplined forces of Hampshire, Kent, or England. In 1791 the eleven yeomen and artisans of Leicester played the Marylebone club, and were ignominiously beaten, as were also the men of Nottingham, who, a month later, threw down the gauntlet to the same famous club. Essex and Herts, emulous of the fame of Kent and Surrey, played All England in 1793, but were defeated in one innings; and so far had the game penetrated westward, that in the same year eleven yeomen at Oldfield Bray, in Berkshire, were able to accomplish that which neither the Leicester nor Nottingham men could achieve, for they fought and beat the Marylebone Club.

Cricket had by this time, that is, at the commencement of the present century, taken general hold upon the nation. Everywhere it was played. It was encouraged at our public schools; gentlemen's parks were lent to it; the village-green resounded with it; noble and peasant, the clergyman and the layman, the lawyer and the doctor, the lawyer's clerk and the doctor's lad, the artisan and his master, took part in and enjoyed it. Lord Byron in 1805 played in the Harrow Eleven against

Eton, and we know that the excellent and philanthropic William Wilberforce was laid up by the severe blow which he received on the leg whilst playing at the game with his sons. Tom Walker, Beldham, John Willes, Fennex, Hammond, Lambert, Sparkes, Bennett, and Freemantle, were the best professionals of the day; though within four or five years Budd, Brand, Osbaldeston, Parry, Ward, Howard, Beagley, Thumwood, Thaldercourt, Slater, Flavell, Ashby, Searle, and Saunders, appeared upon the scene; and before two decades had run out, the ball had been handed over to Broadbridge and Lillywhite, Mynn and Fuller Pilch. The Dukes of York, Richmond, Bedford, and Hamilton, the Earls of Thanet and Darnley, Lord Derrymore, and many others of the nobility, not only patronized, but enjoyed it heartily; whilst even the Prince Regent on several occasions played in the White Conduit Fields. When Lord's Fields existed where Dorset Square is now, a mark was set up which was long known as 'the Duke's strike,' for it recorded a hit of 132 yards in the air from the famous bat of his Grace the Duke of Hamilton.

Cricket had also become a profession, and Farnham supplied London with many of its best men; hence it was that the finest play was always to be witnessed amongst the members of the Marylebone Cricket Club. It was on their ground—a well-kept velvet-field, smooth as a bed of glass—that the principal matches came off, and the greatest science was exhibited. Many were the clubs which threw down the gauntlet to the Marylebone; it was a kind of graduating in the game to go up and contend with its redoubtable Eleven.

Many changes were introduced about this time in the style of batting and bowling. Clarke was remarkable for his round-arm delivery, and Lambert for a high under-hand play, slow, but rising very high, which was pitched with great accuracy, and turned in upon the leg stump. Mr Budd was the best hitter, as well as one of the best fieldsmen of the day. At Woolwich he is said to have hit a volley to long-field for *nine*, though Parry was here to throw it in. Robinson and Saunders were brilliant players, cutting the balls clean away from the bails. Just before the establishment of Willes's round-hand bowling, says the author of *The Cricket Field*, as if to prepare the way, Ashby came forward with an unusual bias, but no great pace. Sparkes bowled in the same style, as also did Mr Matthews and Mr Jenners some years later; still the batsmen were as powerful as ever, numbering Searle,

Beagley, Ward, Kingscote, and Knight. Suffolk again was very strong, with Fuller Pilch, the Messrs Blake, and others of the famous Bury Club; whilst later, Lillywhite, King, and the Broadbridges raised the name of Midhurst and of Sussex.

Let us glean a few of the curiosities of the cricket field. On the 24th of August 1815 a match was played at Lord's between the Epsom Club and the gentlemen of Middlesex. On that occasion Epsom scored 473 and 108; Middlesex, 92 and 72; making an unprecedented gross total of 745. In 1820 a match was played on the same ground between the Marylebone Club and the County of Norfolk, in which Ward kept possession of his wicket the greater portion of two days, and scored 278 runs in one innings. Four years later the same county played against the eleven of Pattiswick in Essex, when the latter went in first and obtained four runs. In a match played at Leicester in 1836, the North *v.* the South, Mynn obtained a giant success. He carried his bat through in both innings, and in the latter made 125 runs, against Redgate's bowling. Wisden, in one of his happy efforts, bowled ten wickets in one innings. Alfred Adams, in a match played on the 11th of July 1837, on Walden Common, Essex, between the Saffron Walden and the Bishop Stortford Clubs, scored 279 runs. This is one more than the celebrated score of Ward, and must therefore bear the palm of being the largest on record. The first innings occupied nine hours. In August 1844 eleven of Surrey and eleven of Middlesex contended at the East Surrey Ground. Middlesex scored 110 runs in the first innings; nine of the Surrey wickets fell for nine runs; the tenth, however, was very obstinate, for it defied the efforts of its adversaries to put it down till the score of Surrey exceeded that of Middlesex by nineteen. A three days' match was played at the Surrey Ground, Kennington Oval, three years later, between the counties of Kent and Surrey, when, strange to say, each side scored 272 runs in the two innings, thus making a tie. In July 1850 the North of England played their annual match against the South at Lord's. In the second innings John Wisden, known also as 'Little Wisden,' bowled every wicket of the South; and on the 8th of August the same year, twelve Caesars, natives of Godalming and members of the same family, played a match in Broadwater Park, the seat of A. Marshall, Esq., with eleven gentlemen of the county of Surrey; the former lost by sixteen runs. About this time a match was played in which eleven men were out for a run each. An innings without one run was played in Lord Wineston's park in 1856, when Challis bowled; the side that scored nothing in the first innings scored, however, 100 in the second. The gentlemen of Kent and Sussex played against the gentlemen of England in 1857, the latter scoring 342 in one innings, of which Mr Walker contributed 90 and Mr Haygarth 81. In the Surrey Club *v.* Southgate, another Mr Walker made 170 runs, and ran no fewer than 257 times. In this wonderful innings he made a drive for seven. In the United *v.* sixteen of Oxford University, played the same year, Wisden bowled fourteen maiden overs in succession; and Grundy, who went in first, carried his bat through. This against sixteen crack players, as the University men were supposed to be, was considered a marvellous feat. The principal features of 1859 consisted in the matches played by Surrey *v.* Notts, in which Parr made 130. This number, however, was surpassed by Caffyn's 157 in the Surrey *v.* sixteen of Cambridge University; and in a match, England *v.* Surrey, a third Mr Walker made 108 out of 390. His prowess, however, did not consist simply in batting, for he also took ten wickets in one innings. These large numbers were exceeded by T. Hayward, who scored 220 in the University *v.* the County of Cambridge, played in that town on the 12th of May. After a grand match at Lord's, in the year 1850, Sir F. Bathurst pitted a guardsman against George Parr, of Nottingham, to throw a cricket-ball; Parr threw 109 yards, the soldier only three yards less.

These were true and scientific games, fought with all the prowess and the skill at the command of players well trained, well disciplined, and alive to all the *finesse* requisite to ensure victory. But from time to time some eccentric games have been played. For example, on the 16th of September 1850, eleven Greenwich pensioners with one arm played eleven with one leg, in which the latter beat — with a leg to spare. And farther back, in 1811, eleven females of Surrey played against eleven females of Hampshire, at Newington, for five hundred guineas a side. Hants won. A similar match was played, in strict order and decorum, on Lavant Level, Sussex, before three hundred spectators. Robert Southey, in his *Commonplace Book*, mentions a match played at Bury between the matrons and the maids of the parish; the matrons vindicated their superiority, and then challenged any eleven petticoats in the county of Suffolk. A similar match, it is noted, was played at West Darling in 1850.

Cricket is not, be it said to the honour of mankind, confined to the tight little island which we inhabit. Wherever Englishmen have migrated to, there wickets have been pitched and the bat wielded, as in the 'old country.' Our transoceanic kinsmen, whether in America, or in the Cape, or in Australia, or even in tropical India, seem to be equally enthusiastic in the game. Ambitious are they too; for they have aspired, at least in two instances, we cannot say to cross swords with us, but at least to try their skill with us in the game. The result has of course terminated in favour of Great Britain; but we can easily imagine that these defeats will but stimulate the defeated to greater exertion, and create a spirit of emulation in their hearts only to be quenched by future success.

Hence we shall most probably hear of international matches, until they become in men's mouths as familiar as international exhibitions. For several years past, a desire had been expressed on the part of the clubs of the United States, as well as of Canada, to join issue with the Eleven of England, and gather what bay-leaves they might from contending with the elect of the old country. It was not, however, until 1859 that the final arrangements were perfected. Eleven of England, and another to act as umpire, were selected from the All England and the United Elevens, who, it was agreed, should play four matches against different twenty-twos in America, two matches in Canada and two in the United States. The twelve upon whom the suffrages of the committee fell were, Julius Caesar, Wm. Caffyn, R. Carpenter, G. Owen, J. Grundy, T. Hayward, J. Jackson, John Lillywhite, Thos. Lockyer, Geo. Parr, H. H. Stephenson, and J. Wisden. These brave champions left England in the *Nova Scotia* on Wednesday, the 7th of September, and reached Quebec on the 21st. They were enthusiastically received, and throughout their tour hospitably entertained; public dinners being given in their honour, conveyances provided to take them to and from the various grounds, and thousands of people flocking to see them exhibit their prowess. Instead of the four matches, however, five were played. The first at Montreal, when England won by eight wickets; the second at New York, when she gained victory by sixty-four runs in one innings; the third at Philadelphia, when she had seven wickets in store at the end of the game; the fourth at Hamilton, in Upper Canada, when she had ten wickets to spare; the fifth at Rochester, when she triumphed gloriously, winning in one innings and by sixty-eight runs. During these contests the six United players obtained 336 runs and destroyed 104 of the transatlantic wickets; whilst the six All England men obtained 303, bowling down 86 of the enemy's wickets. On this occasion the Britishers shone out conspicuously for their great play. The victory of the English champions was brilliant and complete; and the memory of their achievements on the occasion will remain ever a bright spot in the annals of cricketing.

Fired by the example of the Americans, our Australian brethren threw down the gauntlet likewise. The English clubs were not slow to take it up. It was no impediment, no obstruction to their ambition that one half the globe was to be traversed, that they were to visit the very antipodes, to encounter a two months' voyage, to lose sight of the old familiar constellations, and to bivouac beneath new clusters of stars. The arrangements and conditions were soon definitively settled, and in the autumn of last year the *Great Britain* sailed with the Eleven for their destination at Melbourne. Great was the excitement and enthusiasm of the whole colony at beholding this brave and plucky little band disembark at Sandbridge after their long and tedious voyage. The reception they met with exceeded all anticipation; thousands of persons had crowded on the quays to give them a joyous welcome when the steamer that was bringing them hove in sight. A triumphal arch was reared, and they were conveyed to Melbourne in a coach drawn by eight splendid greys; in fact the Victorians were determined to make it a great 'sensation' day. Stephenson and Caffyn had already contended for the honour of Great Britain in Canada and the United States, and now they were to contend for our supremacy in the science of cricketing in a new and a far more distant field. The others who were selected as their companions in, we might almost say, arms, were, Mudie, Griffith, Bennett, Iddison, Lawrence, Sewell, Mortlock, Hearne, and E. Stephenson.

Immediately upon their arrival no time was lost; the ground on which they were to play, smooth and glossy as a billiard-board, was inspected; and on the first day of the New Year the contest commenced. Every preparation had been made to give *éclat* to this great event. A grand stand, capable of holding 5000 people — a mimic Coliseum — was erected, overlooking the arena. More than 17,000 persons paid for admission to the ground upon which the match was played, and untold numbers of spectators lined the adjacent hills, or mounted trees, or posted themselves wherever a sight could be obtained of the game. To do still greater honour to their visitors, the Governor of the colony and his court attended, together with the upper ten thousand, including the Protestant and Catholic bishops, the clergy of all denominations — Church, Wesleyans, Independents; merchants, tradesmen, professional men, artisans, all flocked to the scene. Never had there been a more brilliant gathering. At twelve o'clock the Eleven of England appeared upon the ground, and were received with a tremendous ovation, which seemed to burst forth spontaneously from the breasts of all present. As the moment arrived for commencing the game, the excitement became intense on every side. At last the toss was won by George Marshall, who had been appointed captain of the eighteen, and is in fact the leading professional player of the colony. The Victorian eighteen went in, and by five o'clock that same afternoon had all their wickets demolished, for 118 runs. The Eleven then commenced their innings, and before the stumps were drawn Bennett and E. Stephenson had scored six runs. When the sun set on the second day, the All England were still in, and it was feared that they would never be out. They felt, perhaps, that great things were expected of them, and they were determined to show that great things could be done by them. Griffith, the lion hitter, who had given the field plenty of fatigue, was at last caught out, after he had made 61 runs. This, however, could have no great influence on the game, for there were yet seven wickets to go down. On the third day, Caffyn proved that Griffith had a worthy successor, topping the score with 79 before he was caught at mid-wicket by O. Mulling, one of the colt players. It is unnecessary, however, to particularize further; with these figures and other sundries the Eleven notched 305. No way intimidated, however, by this large and overwhelming array of figures, the Victorians went pluckily in for their second innings, and covered the fourth day. The batting was not efficient, and the wickets fell like reeds, the All Englanders winning in one innings, with 96 runs to spare.

A few days afterwards the British champions pitched their tent at Beechworth, twenty-two of that district having thrown down the gauntlet to them. It was intended to carry the match over three days; but owing to the rapid manner in which the Beechworth players were disposed of, the balance of the third day was occupied by a single-wicket match, in which Griffith, with three fielders, played eleven of their Beechworth antagonists. Finding themselves defeated in this manner, the Victorians sought and affected an alliance with the clubs of New South Wales. The united elevens, it was thought, would be a match for the single Eleven of England; and it must be confessed that, so far as they played, they behaved themselves creditably. The allies went in first and notched 153, whilst the Englanders' score only amounted to 111. In the second innings the twenty-two made 144, the Eleven having 186 to tie them; but owing to previous engagements the match unfortunately could not be played out. After this the British corps entered upon what might be called a tour of engagements, visiting Sydney and Tasmania, as well as various towns in the interior of Victoria. Everywhere they triumphed; everywhere British skill and British prowess were made apparent. Only on one occasion did the All England Eleven sustain a defeat, and that was at Castlemaine. But what of that? Cricket is not only a game of skill, but it is, as we have already observed, a game of chance, and even the best players must be prepared for occasional reverses. In this instance, when the fortune of the day went against our fellow-countrymen, their play was not at fault. It is not a pleasant thing to plead excuses, but there can be little doubt that the ground at Castlemaine was rough and coarse, and ill adapted to that *finesse*, on which the calculations of the scientific bowler and the scientific batsman are based. It is no discredit to a billiard-player that he is defeated by an inferior 'wielder of the cue' on an old rude table; and in this instance, if the Castlemaine men encountered the English Eleven on a smooth and well-kept field, they would have been signally defeated – and this with no discredit to themselves.

The time, however, for the departure of these guests of the Victorians was drawing near; but before they could leave another ovation must be given them, another demonstration of brotherly feeling take place, another demonstration of enthusiasm – on this occasion the enthusiasm of regret – had to be made. Accordingly benefits were given for them at the Theatre Royal and the Royal Lyceum, both of which were fully attended; whilst showers of testimonials and addresses were presented to them by the various cricket-clubs of the colony. No wonder, then, after the hearty and gratifying treatment they received, the Eleven felt a pang at quitting those hospitable shores. 'It was somewhat difficult to get us here,' observed Stephenson, the captain of the All Englanders, on their arrival; 'but I am sure it will be more difficult to get us back.' However, they at length bade adieu to the colony, having played twelve matches, of which six were won, four were drawn, and two were lost.

Long may cricketing flourish in Great Britain! It is truly an Anglo-Saxon game, thriving best on malt and hops. Its home is in the land of beer. Its great ally is John Barleycorn. Witness Kent and Surrey, the nursery of our best players. Neither your Rhine wines, nor your clarets, nor your Burgundies nourish it; they make the blood too thin. Spirits are as bad; they make the blood too hot. No; cricket relies on a cool head, a quick eye, a supple wrist, a swift foot; all the nobler attributes of the man, mental and physical, are brought into play by it. It admits of no Dundrearies or Gantiers. It is a healthy and manly sport; it trains and disciplines the noblest faculties of the body, and tends to make Englishmen what they are – the masters of the world. We would not overlook the pleasures and advantages of boating and yachting, and we admire the Volunteer Movement as a noble and important institution. But neither of these should be allowed to interfere with the natural development of cricket, which is the sport *sui generis*, and has its own characteristics, its own sources of gratification, its own causes of excitement. There must be something in a game which creates for itself such intense devotion and attachment. Whilst, then, the French exclaim, *'Vive la Bagatelle!'* let every Englishman cry, *'Vive le Cricket!'*

Temple Bar 1862

19

Cricket under Queen Victoria

C. W. Alcock

Cricket in the Victorian era! The history of cricket since the Queen's accession has been of course a record of its gradual development from the primitive sport, or at least its steady advance from comparative obscurity, or at best the amusement of a certain favoured few, to the majesty of a national recreation, and more than that — the recognized sport of the English-speaking race. These are brave words, no doubt; but will any one seriously attempt to refute them? There was cricket, and plenty of it, Heaven be thanked! What there was, too, was for the time at all events of good quality. The Marylebone Club was already a power in the land. It was, when the Queen ascended the throne, nearing or within measurable distance of, the celebration of its Jubilee. But Lord's had not as yet begun to assume the air of venerable respectability destined for it in the not very remote future. Cricket was not *de rigueur* even on the sacred soil in Dorset Square. At least one reads of balloon ascents and *fêtes* which would, no doubt, terribly shock the cricket fathers who have looked over and on Lord's through the ages, some of them; all honour to their devotion for the whole period of the Queen's reign, or very near it. Still, even in 1837, Lord's was the Mecca of the cricket pilgrim, attracting the bulk of the best players of the day. Sussex — with the Broadbridges, Tom Box, William Lillywhite — was quite to the front, so much so that it was able to defeat England. Kent, with Fuller Pilch, Alfred Mynn, Wenman, and others of only slightly lesser ability, had also a very strong side, and one able to defeat Sussex twice in 1837. In the north, Notts had already begun to assert itself, notwithstanding that in this particular year its eleven went down before both Kent and Sussex. Round London the game was gaining ground rapidly; just at the moment Surrey was — speaking in a Pickwickian sense, of course —

under a cloud. The heroes of the old Hambledon Club had most of them passed away, leaving a blank apparently difficult to fill. At all events, as a county, Surrey was for the time dormant, waiting for the revival which was to come within a few years. Sixty years ago the Brighton ground, then in the occupation of the great wicket-keeper, Tom Box, was in its way as famous as its successor, on which 'Ranji', Murdoch, Brann, Newham, Marlow, and Bean have scored so largely of late years. Top hats were the recognized headgear of the cricketer of the period. Our illustration of Fuller Pilch, as he played for Kent against Sussex, gives not only an idea of the player as he was at the time, but will also recall to those who can go back so far, at least an idea of the old Sussex ground. Mention has already been made of the growth of Notts, the nursery of a continuous succession of great players able to keep the county for a long period at the very summit of cricket. The best exemplar of Notts was Redgate, the forerunner of a brilliant array of all-round players, among whom George Parr, Jackson, and Daft—a name one is glad to see perpetuated in the cricket of to-day, Tinley, the Shaws, Morley, Shrewsbury, Gunn, and others too numerous to name. A little later George Parr was a name to be conjured with as a batsman; something as W. G. Grace has been for the last quarter of a century—a brilliant batsman all round, but as a leg-hitter without a rival before or since. The accompanying illustration conveys a good idea of a player of many parts, certainly one of the greatest of his time, about 1845. But in attempting to sketch the leading cricketers we are perhaps getting far ahead and overlooking the game itself. At the end of the 'thirties, in many respects the arrangements were still in a comparatively primitive state. The skilled groundsman had not yet arisen to devote all his time and skill to the preparation of wickets carefully shorn and worked to the perfection of a billiard table. To make runs even at Lord's was a liberal education, and generally the scoring was ridiculously slow to our modern ideas, notwithstanding the sensation created at the time by Alfred Adam's remarkable innings of 279 for Saffron Walden against Bishop Stortford. But all the same the bowlers were treated with scant respect compared with their more favoured descendants of to-day. The Queen had indeed been on the throne for several years before the bowler had even the satisfaction of getting the credit of every wicket he secured. In a general way, unless the batsman was actually bowled, he had not the reflected glory of a mention on the score sheets. There were a few exceptions, it is true, but they were rare. In other ways, too, cricket was without form and void. With a view apparently to handicapping the sides players were transferred in many cases, so that it was not infrequent to see a southerner representing the north or a leading player given to a county other than his own to give the game a more even appearance. Surrey, as already stated, was for the moment disorganized. Still Reigate and Mitcham were even then rearing cricketers whose names have been perpetuated in latter-day cricket. The Montpelier Club at Walworth was attracting the best of the players on the south of London. It was the old Montpelier indeed which laid the foundation of the Surrey County Club of today. Bound to seek a fresh home on the demolition of the Beehive Tavern, it found a new habitation, converting for the purpose of a cricket ground what had previously been a market garden. There, within a few hundred yards of Kennington Church, the Montpelier settled to merge in the course of a year or two into the full-blown glory of a county club. At all events, in 1845 'the Oval' was established as the home of Surrey cricket. How in the course of a few years it acquired all its old glories, how it was able to play England, and successfully; how under the management of Mr William Burrup it encouraged county cricket, is familiar to every reader of cricket literature. Then came a long and apparently almost interminable succession of bad cricket and ill-luck to be again redeemed by a glorious revival of the good old days, and a continuance of prosperity which has enabled it to take and retain the highest honours of county cricket during the greater part of the last decade. The early days of the Queen's accession were noteworthy too for the commencement, practically, of the Oxford and Cambridge match. It had been played twice before, with the result a double first for Oxford. But in 1838 was begun the series which has continued up till to-day with only the break of one year. Amateur cricketers were then unable to cope with professionals on even terms. 'The Barndoor match,' which was a product of the cricket season of 1837, clearly shows the relative strength of the two classes. To equalize the sides, Mr W. Ward, who had been one of the most conspicuous figures in cricket for nearly a quarter of a century, conceived the idea of giving the Players four stumps instead of three to defend. But still, in spite of this disadvantage, the Players won easily by more than an innings. The match was not inappropriately called 'Ward's folly', and the experiment was proved such a failure that there was no idea of repeating it. As a matter of fact, the authorities reverted to the old system of pitting eleven Players against sixteen Gentlemen. For a long, long time this superiority of the professionals remained practically undisturbed. But the 'forties, as it happened, brought to the light of day a cricketer who was destined to change, or help to change, the whole order of the game. Born on July 18th, 1848, W. G. Grace was already recognized as one of the greatest players of the day long before he was out of his teens; as early as 1864, indeed, he was representing the Gentlemen, and the successes they were able to achieve against the Players for the next twenty years and more were, it is not too much to say, due in a very great measure to his phenomenal ability as an all-round cricketer. The latter half of the Victorian era has produced nothing more wonderful in the world of sport than the remarkable achievements of the Grand Old Man. It is difficult indeed to determine which is the more remarkable, his wonderful retention of form as a player, or the physical vitality which has kept him without a rival, certainly without a superior, for thirty-three years. But the history of cricket is, happily, not the history of an individual or of individuals, however brilliant he or they may be. Still W. G. Grace's career has been after all the notable feature of a great development of cricket, not only in England, but in the Colonies. How much he himself has contributed to it is hardly necessary to add. But still the fact remains. Thirty years ago there was little county cricket of any real quality. Surrey and Notts were doing their best to encourage the game, and Cambridgeshire, with Tom and Dan Hayward, Carpenter, and Tarrant, was for a short time able to hold its own with the strongest. But imperceptibly the tendency towards a better class of cricket was spreading. Kent and Sussex in the south were coming up again, and Middlesex in turn organized a county club. Yorkshire cricket had always been in evidence in Sheffield and in some of the other big towns. Lancashire very soon caught the infection, with Derbyshire following not long after. The three Graces had meanwhile brought Gloucestershire to the front, and then came another revival with Hampshire resuscitated, and Somersetshire, Leicestershire, Essex, all coming rapidly up to the level of the best of the old counties. The visit of the first Australian team to England in 1878 had meanwhile done incalculable good, in giving a new impetus to the game, which, just at the time, it may be stated, it wanted somehow. That English cricket has benefited materially by the periodical appearances of Australian cricketers will be generally and ungrudgingly admitted. Besides Australians, too, there have been Parsees, Americans, Canadians, and South Africans, at one time or other over here, perfecting or at least improving their education in cricket. The gradual extension of county cricket and the enlargement of the number of those reckoned as first class, has stimulated the ambition of counties for the time of lesser influence, to the undoubted benefit of the game. That cricket was never more popular than it is at the time is certain. The public interest was never keener; the game is played in the spirit of true sport, and on the whole the tone is good in all ways. The history of athletics cannot, indeed, show anything more gratifying from the standpoint of public interest or of public morality than the record of cricket during the Queen's reign.

Diamond Jubilee Number of the
Illustrated Sporting and Dramatic News 1897

3

Great Batsmen of All Time

Colonel Philip Trevor, C.B.E.

My title is one which should frighten the writer rather than the reader, and I expect the retort: 'You have bitten off more than you can chew.' That is as may be. At the same time I shall counter-retort that, as far as I know, no definite attempt has yet been made to classify in any kind of order the great batsmen which the game of cricket has produced. If that be so, I get a kind of consolation: I am not up against competition. Now, it is obvious that if we are to measure, we must first be agreed upon a common standard of measurement. I will state, therefore, as definitely as I can what I conceive to be a correct standard of measurement. And though I do not put it, Euclid-like, in the form of a definition, I hope nevertheless to express the general idea plainly enough.

What is a Great Batsman?

Cricket in general is a positive game, and in particular batting is a positive art. Cricket was never intended to be a negative game, and temporary negativism is only tolerable as a necessary though melancholy prelude to positivism. It follows, therefore, that the less negativism and the more positivism you display in your performance, the better player you are. Moreover, a game of cricket (that is to say, a match at cricket) was always intended to be a time-limited affair. It was never meant to last less than half a day (unless the match should be over sooner) or more than three days. True, the Australians have for about a quarter of a century or more indulged in their own land in the unlimited time match, but that innovation was brought in solely and entirely for financial reasons. In Australia big matches are still few and travel distances are long. And as it is essential that big matches should be made to pay — they will no longer be undertaken when they do not—

it is also essential that you give the man who expends much time and money in order that he may see them a reasonable return for his expenditure. The keenest cricketer would not travel from the 'back blocks' to Sydney, sit in the grand stand, watch it rain for three days, and then go home again. You have no alternative, then, but to give that man the certainty of seeing the match played out.

Assuming that you agree with me, I return fortified to my main contention that cricket is a time-limited affair, and that matches are won by the side which gets the greater number of runs. Consequently, the greatest batsman is he who makes the greatest number of runs in the shortest possible time. I proceed to state the personal case, or, if you like to put it so, to give it away. I am only offering to you five batsmen for consideration, and concerning two of them I am in considerable doubt. The first three on my list are 'W.G.' – the Grand Old Man of Cricket – 'Ranji', and Victor Trumper (in that order), and I have also to consider the peculiar but distinct claims of Gilbert Jessop and Jack Hobbs.

The Coming of the 'G.O.M.'

It should be hardly necessary to premise (at the same time, I am afraid it is) that context is everything. And so if it is not a case of the Grand Old Man first and the rest nowhere, it is certainly a case of the Grand Old Man an easy first. Until W. G. Grace burst upon the cricket world, took it by storm, and became the best batsman in it at the age of nineteen, the bowler was the wild beast of the field – a murderous, devouring wild beast. Or, to take another analogy, the batsman was the 'bull' destined to be butchered to make a Spanish holiday. Some bulls last longer than others and put up a better fight in the ring. But in the end they are all dragged out of the arena dead. 'W.G.' was the first bull to send his bowler tormentors scuttling into the funk holes and to change the attitude of the spectators. Their applause was no longer for the matador: they shouted in ecstasy, 'Bravo the bull!'

At this time of day we can scarcely realize the extent of the revolution which this boy of nineteen practically, but all unconsciously, brought about. Prior to his coming, an occasional batsman would make a score of a hundred runs. That was a feat indeed, and was acclaimed as such. When 'W.G.' was in his zenith, say from 1869 to

1879, no one would lay you level money that he would not make a hundred runs in the match in which he was about to take part. And as he was a great athlete with a big heart and a constitution of iron, it was always regarded as a reasonable possibility that that hundred would grow into two hundred or even into three. No one, I fear, will ever have the chance again of becoming the great batsman which W. G. Grace proved himself to be. He was the best because he had the best bowling to meet, and because he was not content merely to 'defy it,' as the jargon of that day used to run. He pulverized it. In the common phrase, he used to 'wipe the floor with 'em'. There was much indiscipline in those days in the cricket field, and we have it on record that these bowlers would go up to their captains and decline to bowl to the chap any more. Many an amateur did that, also the few professionals who felt themselves important enough players to be able to afford insubordination.

I feel as I write that I shall be taken severely to task for making the unreserved statement that 'W.G.' (who, by the way, had no predecessor) had better bowling to meet than any of his successors. I hear some moderns say: 'Freeman, Lillywhite, Hill, Shaw, Morley, etc. That for a tale!' And not without apparent reason will some of them raise the counterblast of 'Spoff, Lohmann, Turner, Trumble, Peel, Rhodes, Barnes, etc.' What right, they will ask me, have I to assume that any of the old-timers were better bowlers than these? I will make the moderns a concession. Given equal conditions, I shall allow, man for man, that the moderns are intrinsically better bowlers than the older men. But in the matter of bowling the state of the wicket is everything, absolutely everything. In a few, in a very few, parts of this land there are village green wickets to-day which are as bad as the wickets on which 'W.G.' made his huge scores.

Take any of your modern batsmen, especially those who hold that discretion is the better part of valour, and make them play half-a-dozen Saturday afternoons running on these village greens opposed only by the village bowlers. Select men whose averages are about fifty odd runs per innings in first-class cricket. At the end of their village course I doubt if any one of them would have a double figure average, and I should expect those of them who have insisted on 'seeing it through' to demand the institution of a civil V.C.

The Bowler and the Wicket

You can put this case in a nutshell. The bowler who can keep a consistently good length and change his pace without change of action is an infinitely better bowler on a really bad wicket (that is to say, he is far more likely to get the best of batsmen out) than any of the great bowlers of the last twenty-five years are upon these impossibly perfect wickets, which, in my opinion, threaten to ruin the science of batting, because they automatically eliminate from it the qualities of daring and enterprise.

Quite unconsciously and unintentionally, the Australians have done us a disservice by their high art achievements in the making of wickets. We have copied them, and whether you play to-day at Melbourne, Sydney, Adelaide, or the Oval, or Leicester, or Lord's, you get in continuous fine weather a wicket out of which all the life has been rolled. If the ball bowled gets up more than stump high, the players, fieldsmen as well as batsmen, congregate round the spot which has done the accursed thing, in sorrow or in anger, according to their temperaments. They are the more perplexed when a minute inspection of the turf fails to reveal the wicked secret. Should the thing occur again, there is a longer stoppage of play and much wagging of heads; while a further repetition will cause the groundsman some uneasiness. He may be hauled before the county committee for dereliction of duty, especially if the home side were batting when the unfortunate instances happened.

No, never again except by some uncommon freak of Nature shall we see first-class cricket matches played on the kind of wicket on which the great 'W.G.' gained his most signal triumphs. And because that is so he can never have an equal. Only in one particular are we left in the least doubt as to the supremacy of W. G. Grace's batsmanship. Could he have dealt with the 'googly,' and how could he have done it? Would the 'googly' bowler have got from the greatest of all batsmen the same unceremonious treatment that was meted out by him to all other bowlers? I am afraid you and I must be left to guess. On the evidence available, I come to the conclusion that 'W.G.' would have mastered the 'googly' as he mastered every other wile of any and every bowler. But that is only my opinion. Still, if he had been no better or no worse than all the other great batsmen in their treatment of the 'googly', his place on the list does not suffer in consequence. He is first — easy first, and must remain first for all time.

Ranji the Wizard

I put second on the list the wizard 'Ranji'. He is a very old friend of mine, and even if he were not he would not accuse me of cheek. You may call him 'Ranji', too, if you like (you probably do), and he will not mind. Courteous as he is to all comers, he is apt to be a little impatient of time-wasting and time-wasters. I was talking to him at Lord's a couple of summers ago when a pompous old gentleman pushed himself between us and without apology of any kind introduced himself to the wizard. He had a question to ask, he said, and it took him an eternity to ask it. He added to its length by introducing the word 'Maharajah' at two-second intervals. Boiled down, it all came to this: Which is the easier to play, fast bowling or slow? Ranji was about to reply when the pompous one 'pomped' on. He expatiated in his own best vein on the difficulty of an immediate reply. He would be prepared to give the Maharajah notice of the question. Then at last Ranji spoke. 'I've great pleasure in answering you at once. Slow, undoubtedly; we can all of us make a mistake if you give us time to think.' The pompous one retired bewildered, and I murmured to Ranji that I supposed that exception proved the rule. Ranji had understood me all right and grinned. And yet I was wrong. Ranji never gave himself time to think. With him instant action came with instant thought, except when action was delayed on account of instant thought.

Consciously or unconsciously, Ranji himself explained the secret of his own unique success when he laid down his wonderful batting rule: 'First see where the ball is going to pitch; then go to it; then hit it.' But Ranji's pupil who means to follow that rule must first come to me for a bit of advice before he tries to do so: 'First have the eye of a hawk; then train it.' How does the vulture know the whereabouts of the dying beast? Not by smell, certainly, but by eye. Although the bird itself is beyond the reach of human sight, he is there at the business moment to do the job in hand for all that. So was Ranji's bat.

It is impossible to explain to the modern generation the wizardry of Ranji's batting. It is even difficult to inspire belief when in simple words, but with elaboration of context, you tell the young man of to-day what it was that Ranji actually did. Indeed, comparatively

29

recently a young man who has played for England, after paying me the compliment of assuming that I was on the side of the moderns, said: 'Tell me honestly, could this Ranji really compare with all our swells to-day, or is it just a tale?' I did not convince him, for later he said to someone else, 'I take it that this Ranji, if he had had to play against the swing stuff we have to deal with to-day, would not have got a run.' That slander, of course, is laughable, but there is another slander on Ranji which is cruel because it is insidious. I must bring Tennyson, not the England captain, but his grandfather, to the rescue:— '. . . *a lie which is part a truth is a harder matter to fight.*'

Ranji Extends the Field

Ranji is held responsible for the attitude of the 'stand-in-front-of-your-wicket-on-purpose' brigade. Quite true; but it was then the attack brigade. Now it is the funk brigade. Ranji only stood in front of his wicket to score. Until he invented and perfected his wonderful leg-glide stroke, more than one-third of the area of the cricket circle was uncultivated waste. It was no man's land; no man was put to field there. Ranji altered all that, and he made the opposing captain tired of sending expeditions there. Ranji caused him to garrison the place, and to do that of course he had to weaken other vital points of the defence.

Then Ranji, dropping the glide shot, would attack the position thus weakened. Let it never be forgotten that even if he had not invented the glide shot Ranji would have successfully challenged comparison with the best of his contemporaries. He had all the ordinary strokes of the admittedly great batsman, and these he would use after he had made the opposing captain man the defences in the leg segment of the circle.

I have indulged in one speculation about 'W.G.' – the 'googly' speculation. I will indulge in one about Ranji. If he had played when 'W.G.' was in his zenith, where would he have ranked? I honestly believe that Ranji might possibly have ranked even above 'W.G.' I once saw Ranji (at the very beginning of his career) play in a 'holiday' match on an absolutely wicked wicket. It was certainly the most dangerous wicket on which I have ever seen a decent match played. Lilley was standing a very long way back to Woodcock's fast bowling, and even then now and again the ball went over his head. Ranji, if I remember rightly, made forty-nine out of seventy-one. His colleagues nearly all declined to stand and face the bowling, and I think they were perfectly right. Woodcock, in my opinion should not have been allowed to bowl on that wicket, and even if all bowling except slow bowling had been barred on it, there was even then distinct physical danger to the batsmen. Ranji stood there and took 'fours' off his face. He did not always stand — sometimes he dashed in and drove the fast bowler to the ropes. Woodcock was not pitching the ball short on purpose, and indeed I have reason to believe that he did not like bowling on that wicket. Ranji was not then qualified by residence to play for Sussex, but by courtesy of the other side he took part in this 'holiday' game. It was the first time I had seen him bat, and I went away dazed, as one who has seen a miracle performed.

'Oh, help!' I said to my father and brother; 'if he can carry on like that on a cart-track, what will he do on the lawn at Hove?' In vain my father talked to me of 'W.G.' I could only reply, 'What can be more wonderful than what we have just seen?' No, Ranji comes second all right, but if he had been a contemporary of 'W.G.' he might have stood first.

The Grace of Victor Trumper

My number three, as I have said, is Victor Trumper. Of course, like 'W.G.' and Ranji, he was self-made. Was he as good a batsman as he looked? He was, of course, an absolute joy to watch at the wicket, for he was the last word in gracefulness. Not even a beautifully-made woman skating superbly could rival the grace of Trumper batting. I knew Victor pretty well; he was the most extraordinary mixture of modesty and confidence that I have ever encountered. He could never be lured, although many tried to lure him, into any expression in words of his belief in himself. Yet he was appreciative enough when you talked to him of the batting of others. Still, the self-confidence was obvious enough when he faced the bowler, whom he literally treated as of no consequence. Neither 'W.G.' nor Ranji made the bowler look quite so foolish as Victor Trumper did.

Trumper, of course, made thousands of runs in his short career, but the reason I rank him so high is that he could have made tens of thousands more. He was an artist, and he loathed repeating himself. Once, in a match at Lord's, Schofield Haigh, then the best bowler of the day on a rain-damaged wicket, bowled Victor three balls in succession, each one of which was a perfect length, and all three pitched practically on the same spot. They were the opening balls of the match. Trumper put the first into the gallery of the hotel. The second he lay back and cut for four behind point. He danced into the third and lifted it into Q stand with a fine on-drive. This one illustration will suffice. If you had bowled 'W.G.' a series of half volleys on the off, and he found that he could get each one of them through the covers for four, he would have gone on getting them through. And even Ranji would have resisted the temptation to do the original thing better than Victor. But I repeat that Trumper just could not repeat himself. His artistic cricket temperament fought against repetition.

Jessop the Revolutionary

It is with unassailable confidence I put first, second, and third in my list of batsmen of all time W. G. Grace, Ranji, and Trumper. I come to number four on that list prepared to meet stout opposition. My man is Gilbert Jessop. And before the opposition begin to cry: 'The noes have it!' I would refer them to my definition of great. At the risk of wearying I must insist that the high standard which comes of high endeavour is essential to justify the application of 'great' to any batsman. As I have already maintained, both Ranji and Trumper set themselves a higher standard of batting than the great 'W.G.' A simple illustration of this contention will, I hope, make a universal appeal. 'W.G.' could hit sixes with the best of them, but his practical batting code was always success, long-sustained success. So, times out of number he hit a four when he could have hit a six. For nothing was 'W.G.' more remarkable than for his shrewd 'horse sense.' You could not be caught when you carpeted the ball, and his instinctive art, for he never learnt it, I think, of placing the ball enabled him to get a four almost every time.

On the delicacy of the touch of Ranji, and on the unique variety of the stroke-making possessed by Trumper, I have already insisted. In high endeavour, Gilbert Jessop went one better still. He must needs thrash the ball. Indeed, there ought not to have been anything of it left when it reached its destination. And here I will stop to tell the opposition that Jessop knew where that ball was going and meant it to go there. He was bitterly, indeed continuously, assailed by the orthodox for many seasons, nor were these people ashamed to bring in the so-called argument of luck to their aid. All the old stories about the blacksmith on the village green were trotted out to prove that the greatest hitter who ever lived was a mere country cricketer. For he was the greatest hitter who ever lived, easily and absolutely. Stubborn as the stubbornest of political Tories were the drawing-room batsmen, and the drawing-room critics were even more stubborn when they declined to admit Jessop to the inner circle of the elect. But, like Disraeli, he lived to rule the elect. With him sheer record of fact won in the end.

If I said that Jessop tried to punish severely seven-tenths of the balls bowled to him, I should be considerably under the mark. Jessop got only fifty-three hundreds in first-class matches. But no fewer than four times did he get two hundreds in the same match, a performance which has only twice been equalled and once surpassed. And I would add that his more successful rivals in this matter were all careful players. To get a hundred runs at all on Jessopian lines is to achieve something of a feat. If that is so, what must it mean to get on those lines two two-hundreds in one match against first-class bowling? A charmed life, indeed, but to live it a man must make his own charm! And remember, please, that Jessop always had appearances against him. He did everything in the way in which all teachers of cricket agreed it should not be done. He had neither gracefulness nor style, nor was it always brought home, even to the observant, that he had method.

Jessop was not merely the greatest hitter who ever lived, but also the finest firm-footed strokesman. Even Ranji and Trumper realized that there were certain batting impossibilities. Jessop no doubt realized what he would have called practical impossibilities, but he refused to recognize them. The ball bowled had to be smashed; it is all summed up in that. Relying on the unique value of the setting of a supreme standard in batting, I place Jessop fourth on my list, and, like Warren Hastings, I stand aghast at my own moderation.

Where Does Hobbs Stand?

And what about Jack Hobbs? He is not my number five, because if you do not class him first of all I do not know where you are to class him. Here you come to refining and super-refining. What would have happened had Jack Hobbs been an amateur? That is to say, had he been in a position untrammelled in any way to play for himself and bat for his own reputation. I do not wish to be misunderstood. I am not accusing 'W.G.', Ranji, or Trumper of batting for themselves and not for their sides, whilst obviously to make such an accusation against Jessop would be merely laughable. By batting for themselves these men were most clearly batting for their sides. Generally speaking, Trumper got better support than the others, but, with this exception, the side for which they played regularly wanted all the runs they could get from them. Suppose Hobbs in a position to attempt, for the mere fun of the thing, to make the strokes in which Ranji, Trumper, and Jessop delighted. Hobbs has got sixty, and his Surrey partners are proving to him regularly and conclusively that they are 'rabbity'. Tate bowls Hobbs his best ball. Hobbs allows himself to attempt a fancy stroke and his middle stump cavorts. Hobbs retires and mounts the pavilion steps, amused and smiling. An anxious Surrey committee-man, almost in tears, groans to the great batsman as he passes:—

'What happened, Jack?'

'Oh! I thought I'd try the pull shot on that one of Maurice's and put it on to the gasworks. I'll do it the next time.' Imagine Hobbs trying to carry out his threat and failing! Surely all the Surrey committee-men would be summoned by wireless! To waste money may be forgiven a professional batsman, but to waste runs never. Further illustration is unnecessary.

A professional batsman cannot bat as he likes, and the man who does not bat as he likes does not bat as well as he can. Every now and then when I see a real Hobbs innings played I find myself murmuring: 'I wish you and "W.G." and Ranji and poor Victor Trumper and Jessop had all been contemporaries in those bad old days. I mean those good old days, when the ball took the delightful liberty of misbehaving itself. Whatever had happened to you five, the rest would have been practically nowhere.'

Hobbs scores one remarkable point in batsmanship. He deals with the 'googly' bowling better than any man who ever lived. Here he is supreme because 'googly' bowling is already a thing of the past. Its inventor, B. J. T. Bosanquet, only learnt his own alphabet. Ernest Vogler and Aubrey Faulkner became past-masters of the thing. Neither of them troubled Jack Hobbs on turf or matting, and here I dare to ask: Is not the man capable of descrying and detecting the 'googly' also capable of descrying and detecting any wile of any bowler?

I come, then, to the definite conclusion that Jack Hobbs must rank very high in the list of great batsmen of all times. Narrowed down to its most practical limits, I take it that the era of great batsmen was roughly the last ten years of the nineteenth century. For during those ten years the powers of 'W.G.', despite his amazing performance in 1895, were on the wane, and Hobbs had not yet appeared. Other batsmen with historical claims to fame were in their zenith, for the contemporaries of Ranji, Trumper, and Jessop were Archie Maclaren, Charles Fry, Tip Foster, Johnny Tyldesley, and Tom Hayward. I put severe restraint on myself when I decline to add to that list. No; since that period I can only put Hobbs confidently among the elect, though I lay myself open to severe cross-examination were the claims of Aubrey Faulkner and Charlie Macartney to come up for consideration.

Hobbs, Macartney, and Faulkner are all over forty years of age. For some time past I have been scanning the cricket horizon. I do not see a ghost of a sign of the coming of the real 'young 'un' thereon, except Hammond, the young Gloucestershire batsman, or, if his health does not fail him, young 'Duleep'.

Strand Magazine 1928

crocodile tears over the two batsmen, restraining with difficulty a tendency to laugh like hyenas. Thus is the courtesy of the modern cricket-field observed. *'Toujours la politesse!'* And were I present at the performance I should vacate my seat in the gallery and go behind the scenes to warn my excellent old friend Martin, the custodian of the Oval, that all was lost save honour, and that he had better slip away while the going was good and drop unostentatiously into the Thames over the Embankment at Vauxhall Bridge.

Result of Too-Perfect a Wicket

If anyone has at this time of day the least doubt as to the effect of the too-perfect wicket upon even the best of bowlers, let him year by year study the score-sheets of the matches played in Australia in the annual competition for the Sheffield Shield. He is a stout-hearted man who reads on undismayed the wearying iteration of mammoth scores. And he is a particularly superficially-minded cricketer who murmurs as he reads, 'Where are the bowlers?' They may make a fleeting appearance during a Christmas rain at Melbourne or Sydney. Otherwise they are beaten out of sight. They are beaten by the too-perfect wicket, which makes the three-quarter-stump-high ball an almost invariable rule. And they are beaten by the unlimited time match system, which provides the only justification in any land or in any conditions of the Asquithian policy – 'Wait and see!'

The present time is eminently suitable for making a list of the great bowlers who have appeared, and it is regretfully that I say so. I trust that I am the extreme reverse of a pessimist, but I own that I find it difficult to see how another great bowler is going to arise. Wickets get better and better, and they will possibly get better still. With first-class cricket, both in England and Australia, finance is the supreme consideration, and it is batting and not bowling which ninety-nine out of every hundred spectators pay their money to see. Also 'century-itis' has become incurable. If some peculiar chance of weather should be responsible for creating a really difficult wicket and Hobbs made forty-odd runs on it in the course of a quarter of an hour, not a tithe of those who watched would appreciate the brilliance of the performance. And even the appreciative minority would say: 'What a pity he did not tone down until he had got his hundred!'

What kind of bowler is he, then, who is likely to defeat the conjunction of the too-perfect wicket and the too-careful batsman? My answer to my own question is, 'The "googly" merchant or the very fast bowler.' To-day we are without either of them. Still, the possibilities of both are as illimitable as they ever were. There are any number of men to-day who can deliver a googly; but they find the price prohibitive. More than any other ball, the googly has to be a perfect length in order to be dangerous. It is just what the modern batsman wants when it is not. The most wary of batsmen should be able to treat himself to a four off a short-pitched googly.

Great Googly Bowlers

As every cricketer knows, B. J. T. Bosanquet invented the googly, but there have been only two great googly bowlers, Ernest Vogler and Aubrey Faulkner. Their day is over. Worst of all, there is no prospect of the reappearance of a very fast bowler. And for this strange phenomenon I am utterly at a loss to account. Even if we admit that we have not improved on the physical excellence of the Greeks of two thousand years ago, that admission does not account for the physical lapse in bowling in the last twenty years. In the 'eighties and the 'nineties there was not a first-class county eleven which did not own a really fast bowler of sorts. Since the War I have not seen a really fast one in county cricket, good, bad, or indifferent, and from careful inquiries I gather this person is not to be found on the village green either. I must perforce, then, confine myself to the 'have beens'.

I put Sydney Barnes very high indeed on my list. When Barnes appeared wickets were appreciably as good as they are now, and he had to bowl against great batsmen, *i.e.*, batsmen who were not afraid to try definitely to conquer the bowler, as well as against careful batsmen. Nature had not given Barnes the stamina of Tom Richardson, nor, to be quite candid, had she given him Tom's big heart. Otherwise, I should have placed Barnes at the top of my bowling list with the same confidence that I placed 'W.G.' at the top of my batting list.

It is to the credit of Barnes, and not to his discredit, that he brought no new factor to the art of bowling. He did practically everything that a bowler should do just a shade better than any bowler had done it before. His great asset lay in the fact that the most observant of batsmen opposed to him could not foretell from the bowler's preliminary moves what the ball was going to be like. Nor when he had been defeated by it could he honestly say that he had detected the exact difference in that ball from the preceding one which he had played. You could not detect Barnes's leg-turner.

We talk glibly to-day about flighting; Barnes could flight the ball. Scientific cricketers who bring mathematics to bear upon the practice of bowling know the importance of the parabola. An absolutely perfect camera used during, say, three consecutive overs bowled by Barnes would have given us records which might have helped us to understand the reason of his success when he defeated the great batsmen. Needless to say, his change of pace was accomplished without perceptible change of action. But Barnes needed nursing — very careful nursing. Also by temperament he was largely dependent for effectiveness upon initial success. Tom Richardson and Wilfred Rhodes indulged themselves in the suppressed chuckle when the batsmen went for them; they knew it was the beginning of the end. And Tom was a very fast bowler and Wilfred a very slow one. Sydney Barnes was neither; he was medium pace.

When you try to pass in review the great bowlers of all time, you cannot possibly escape consideration of Tom Richardson and Wilfred Rhodes. It is essential here you confer the title 'great' on any one person in any undertaking that he should have proved himself great during some considerable period of time — and in the Test Match arena. Applying that maxim to the cricket-field, you cannot justly speak of Henry Martyn as one of the greatest of wicket-keepers. He had too short a career. And yet during that brief career I myself saw Martyn do feats of wicket-keeping which I deliberately define as amazing. The same reason precludes me from putting Frank Foster in the list of the world's greatest bowlers.

Foster, like George Hirst, was a fast left-handed swinger; he swung both ways, and his in-swinger was a positive beast. His most difficult ball was more difficult to treat than George Hirst's most difficult, and yet I am not putting George Hirst in the inner circle of the elect. Hirst has modestly described himself as a county rather than a Test Match cricketer, and he came very near greatness in doing so. For surely a great man is he who knows his own limitations, unwise though he be in regard to his own reputation to admit them. (By the way, I would remark that George Hirst was perhaps the greatest county cricketer who has been seen or will be seen.) Still, whether we like it or not, we have the Test Match standard at the back of our heads as we talk about the great cricketer, be he batsman or bowler.

Tom Richardson's Lone Hand

Tom Richardson so often played a lone hand, and superbly he played it. And Tom was a county cricketer as well as a Test Match cricketer. It may be remembered that in four consecutive seasons for Surrey he took more than a thousand wickets, a feat that has never been equalled. And when you remember that he bowled practically his fastest all the time, you are made to realize that cricket in any of its departments is, after all, a nice amalgam of skill and physique. The googly was unknown in Tom's day. Consequently, the only help he could get in a Test Match, where, by the way, he was the only fast bowler on the side, had to come from the slow leg-turner (he likes a fast wicket), and, far oftener than not, there was 'no sich person' in the eleven. So it was Tom versus the enemy – a long, fierce frontal attack, a kind of Horatius on the Bridge, only with Horatius doing the attacking.

A famous Test Match was once played at Manchester, in which 'Ranji' did all our batting and Tom all our bowling. Ranji conjured away until he had made over one hundred and fifty runs, and Tom bowled unchanged for three hours and ten minutes (we did not have in those Spartan times the tea interval for lady cricketers), and bowled his fastest too! The Tom-Ranji combination did not quite come off, but the Australians only just got home by ten runs. You could not break Tom's heart even if you stone-walled him, while if you went for him he could not, as I have said, control the smile that spread over his face. The experts will tell you rightly that Bill Lockwood could bowl a more difficult ball than Tom, and they are right. But Lockwood also wanted nursing. Tom would, so to speak, put any nurse in any pram and push it. He was always a forward child.

Rhodes, of course, has lasted far longer than Tom, and not mainly because he was a slow bowler and not a fast one. The most perfect labour-saving device I have ever seen is the bowling action of Wilfred Rhodes. It is so ridiculously easy. Only it is so ridiculously easy that a few hundred-thousand bowlers in the last thirty years have tried to copy it, and have tried in vain. There is not the least necessity for Rhodes to take out a patent for it. There is no fear of it being infringed. Rhodes, however, has had one advantage which in the case of a really great bowler I believe to be unique. He has never been compelled to bowl. When in his essentially undramatic way he made his dramatic entry into the Yorkshire eleven, there were several good bowlers in it, and there always have been several ever since. Not in an England side has the brunt of the bowling been made to fall on him. Yet call on Rhodes to perform on a 'sticky dog' (when you can get one) and the modern big batsman is in as much trouble with him as the big batsman of thirty years ago used to be. Rhodes 'puts 'em where he likes', and he knows where they ought to be put. He had the instinct of a veteran when he came out; he knew where to put them even then.

There is another unique feature about the bowling of Rhodes. His bowling was practically in abeyance for about fifteen years, and it may be, had he been an amateur, he would not have bowled at all at that time. In an evil hour he learnt to bat, with the result that he was promoted from number eleven on the Yorkshire batting list to number one on the England list. When Hobbs and others came along Rhodes was wanted to bowl again. He complied, and at the age of fifty or so stood once more at the top of the bowling list. Here again the experts make the same comparison between Peel and Rhodes as they made between Lockwood and Richardson. To Peel they gave the credit of bowling the more difficult ball. I can only retort: 'He laughs loudest who laughs last!'

We are beginning to get at what we want by the processes of elimination and exhaustion. I do not stop to mention George Lohmann, A. G. Steel, Old Jack Hearne, while Shaw, Morley, Tom Emmett, etc., belong to the fairy-tale period. Also I even put ruthlessly out of the running the great 'Spoff', Charlie Turner, Hughie Trumble, while fast bowlers will rise in their graves in resentment if I give the Australian Jones preference over them.

Age of Great Bowlers

It is, I repeat, the period during the close of the nineteenth and the beginning of the twentieth century to which I look to find my great bowlers. I do not think I shall be asked to allow any post-war products to sit in the seats of the mighty. The natural, yet desirable, wave of optimism which happily pervaded the cricket-field when the game went on again subsequent to the great upheaval strove to carry Maurice Tate on its crest. That he was the best of them, easily the best, I frankly and gladly admit, but I was always unfortunately sure that his action was not, and could not be, the action of a laster. It did not display the happy and healthy energy of a Tom Richardson or the no-energy-at-all of a Wilfred Rhodes. Even if you had conscripted Tate and made him do four-fifths of his soldiering at physical drill, I doubt if you would have so lubricated his joints and loosened his muscles as to make you think the machine was working because it could not help working.

It comes, then, to this: The passport for the entrance of a bowler into the land of great of all time must bear on its visa the words, 'Perennially fit and always available'. A lot of bowlers may get as far as 'Ellis Island' unchecked and revel there for a while in its doubtful notoriety. Only those whose papers bear the special label will get into the land, not of promise, but of recognized performance. I would try hard to get Sydney Barnes, as it were, out of pawn and pass him on even if I had to forge his ticket. He would not fail me on the big occasion, and we know that it is the big occasion that counts. But as I have been at great pains to make my own weapons, I must be content to be hoist with my own petard. I wave him a sorrowful good-bye and I go on in the humble capacity of courier with Wilfred Rhodes and Tom Richardson.

Final Choice

So I have reduced my candidates to two, and if I am asked for the supreme test of the pluck of my opinions I must laconically reply: 'Tom'. Then, no doubt, I shall be put into the witness-box and subjected to severe cross-examination. 'D'you tell m'Lud and the members of the jury that as a bowling artist Tom Richardson should rank above Wilfred Rhodes?' I decline answer and throw myself on the Bench for protection, claiming that this is not cross-examination in the legal sense of the term, but introduction of new matter. The Bench upholds my objection, and all the reply my cross-examiner gets is: 'That, everything and everybody considered, Tom was the more constant, and consequently the greater, bowling force'. Swells as well as rabbits were by him discomfited on good wickets and slaughtered by him on bad ones.

Thus my final answer to the problem I have set myself to solve is Tom Richardson. I shall not get a jury of experts to agree with me, or at any rate of those who rank in the public estimation as experts. But the end is not now and the decision of the supreme and final Court of

Appeal has not yet been invoked. The uncomfortable but inexorable claims of Anno Domini will not allow me to hear the final decision. I can only look to 'Father Time' to protect my reputation.

Strand Magazine 1928

5

More Great Bowlers

Peel and Briggs

A. C. MacLaren

Bobby Peel has always seemed to me the greatest left-hander of my time: playing against or with him, I held the same opinion. His action was peculiar, in that he used to bring his arm well behind his back with the suspicion of a flourish, and then fairly whip the ball down. If there was anything in the wicket to help him, few batsmen indeed lived long at the crease against him. No one spotted a batsman's weakness more quickly than he, and the batsman thus found out got short shrift. Bobby never wasted any time. He was like a terrier on a rat.

In that duel of brains, strategy, bluff — call it what you will — between batsman and bowler, Bobby seldom, if ever, came off second best. He knew how to bowl under any conditions, and of how few bowlers can that be said? If the wicket was too slow he would speed up his action; and, by making the ball turn more quickly than ninety-nine out of a hundred bowlers would do, he would cause the batsmen to believe the pitch a difficult one. If the wicket was — from his point of view — 'real jam', or was breaking up, his accuracy of length and natural spin would finish off most sides for something short of three figures. He knew that a good batsman on a perfect wicket would play his length and spin ball, so he would bowl instead a ball that swung into the batsman very quickly at the last. Or, again, he would send along a higher ball, cleverly held back. The highest in the land had to confess themselves nonplussed by the Yorkshireman's many wiles.

It always amused me to watch Bobby's every expression when he knew he was there, and that the batsman had no chance against him. A rare plucked one, he came off with the bat against the best, when runs were wanted.

45

Add to this the fact that he was a clinking cover-point, and his qualifications to be considered the greatest of all-rounders few would care to dispute. If there were more Bobby Peels to-day some of the batsmen wouldn't be quite so tall.

Bobby thought nothing of getting up at five o'clock in the morning to witness a gallop on the racecourse, and later go to the ground and bowl a side out, as he did more than once or twice in Australia. At shooting he is distinctly interesting. He generally claims everything that falls. I remember once how, after a match in which he had assisted Prince Ranjitsinhji's side in Yorkshire, he was entertained by the Prince to some shooting. A hare got up and had a very thin time of it. After receiving at least eight barrels from Bobby and his brother pros., it managed to crawl — minus a few legs and an ear or so — beyond the Prince's boundary. To the keeper's warning of that fact, Bobby, vaulting over a stile, replied that they paid no heed to that sort of thing in Yorkshire. He proceeded to entertain us with a combination of hunting and shooting, the ultimate outcome of which was luckily the death of poor puss.

There was always something doing when Bobby was about. He had a keen sense of the ridiculous; and as I write, I can see him swaying from side to side with laughter over the capers of an old apple-woman who had got into the way of our coach and four as we were driving from the station at Sydney. I really thought he would fall off his perch.

I shall always remember Bobby's kindly words of encouragement to me in Australia in 1894, when, before the second match, against Victoria at Melbourne, he heard that it was not possible for the skipper to find a place for me, and replied that he would stand down then, for he considered that I was batting better than anyone else at the nets. It was in no small measure due to him that I got my place, and had the good fortune to be still in at 6 o'clock on the first day, with 220 not out to my credit.

When there was mischief afoot, Bobby was usually at the bottom of it. On the voyage out in '94 one of his brother pros. had a hammock that was the envy of all. The quarter-master used to rig it up nightly for its proud possessor. One night, after the ladies had gone below, and the proud possessor snored sublimely 'midst the gentle zephyrs of the Indian Ocean — behold! a figure clad in striped pyjamas that crept nearer and yet nearer to the envied hammock; then one vicious slash

46

with the borrowed carving-knife, and down came Humpty-Dumpty, hammock and all! Then it was: 'Bobby, where art thou?'

In those days it was not customary for our professionals to wear dress clothes at dinner. But the proud possessor of the hammock had also dress clothes, and turned up in them at the professionals' table the first night on board. On the second night the dress trousers were missing. The owner, nothing daunted, appeared in dress coat and waistcoat and grey flannel bags. Of course, he did not suspect Bobby – oh, no! But he entertained wrongful suspicion of an innocent individual on a later occasion. For it was Bobby who did wittingly lock up, with intent to burn, the same Mr Owner, in the engine-room (temperature 300 in the shade, or thereabouts); and it was the writer who did rescue the victim, after a long struggle and almost on the point of death – to get no thanks whatever, but to be held guilty of the locking-up! But Bobby had always a wonderful way of covering up his foot-tracks.

Peel and Briggs – the names go together on the lips of most who speak them, for these two men were the great left-hand bowlers of their day. For cheery, honest graft, commend me to poor Johnny. Ever merry and bright, worth his weight in gold on a dull day; the sun seemed always shining when Johnny was with us. When a thunderstorm stopped play in the Test match at Adelaide in 1894–5, who, for the hour we had to spend in our dressing-room, entertained us with a fine rendering of Macbeth, but Johnny? How we laughed! But on he went, as if it was going to rain until Doomsday, never pausing for a word or even to take breath. We told him he had missed his vocation, and had thrown away a Cesarewitch. He still went on. For a long time it puzzled me why Johnny should have committed to memory so much Shakespeare. Did he contemplate chancing his arm on the stage later, when it had lost its cunning on the cricket field?

Poor fellow! How keen he was to play one more Test match, just to make up a certain number to which he attached great significance. I used my interest on his behalf with the Selection Committee, and got him chosen for the game at Leeds in 1899 when he had almost given up hope; and it is not pleasant to think that, however indirectly, my action had a result that no one could have foreseen. The excitement proved too much for him and sent him off his head.

This was on the night of the first day of the match. I went to see him before it was over; and it struck me as very odd that, though he had

47

failed to recognize his brother, he knew me. I have always thought that we should have won that match on the second day but for the catastrophe of his breakdown. As it was, rain on the last day made a draw of it.

There was one marked difference between Johnny and Peel. When the wicket was plumb, especially, Briggs used to bowl up into the air, whereas the other great left-hander was always whipping the ball down. As will be readily understood, on a good pitch Johnny was the easier to hit. Hit for four into the country, he would often send down an exactly similar ball — with a similar result — to follow, and then, wiping his forehead with his handkerchief as he walked to his place in the field, would remark: 'It's a fine day, Mr MacLaren.'

World of Cricket 1914

6

Interview with
Mr A. C. MacLaren

Fred W. Ward

It is a generally accepted fact that, like a poet, a cricketer is born, not made. The art of batting, or of bowling, generally runs in the family: 'like father, like son'. If this should not be the case, the schoolboy gives promise of the man. The lad who scores freely, or performs the hat trick with the ball, passes on to his county eleven. Sometimes he comes off, as they remark in cricket parlance; more frequently, however, he fails to do himself justice, and is, perhaps, relegated to the second eleven before he is permitted again to pit his strength against his compeers.

There are exceptions to every rule, however. Mr W. G. Grace never looked back after he had once secured county honours. Mr A. C. MacLaren may fairly say he has done likewise. He played a great innings for his county when he was first included in the team, and beyond a doubt Lancashire is weakened by more than I care to say when the Old Harrovian is missing from her ranks.

Mr MacLaren, although he has visited the Antipodes twice, is yet under thirty. To be exact, he was born on December 1st, 1871, so that at the present time he is but twenty-eight years of age. As a schoolboy he displayed remarkable aptitude for the game, but did not come before the public prominently until the Eton v. Harrow match of 1887. Even at that early date Mr MacLaren displayed all the finish of an experienced batsman: possibly he possessed even more polish then than now, but he lacked generalship and hitting power. Be that as it may, he was the top scorer for his side in either innings with 55 and 67, but despite these individual efforts, Harrow lost by five wickets.

In 1888, however, his school defeated Eton by 156 runs. Curiously enough, Mr MacLaren had very little to do with this result, for he made but 0 (that dreaded duck!) and 4, while his ill-fortune pursued him a twelvemonth later, Harrow gaining an easy victory, while he scored but 17 and 16.

Still, every cloud has its silver lining, and this form was far too bad to be true. In 1890 Mr Maclaren captained the Harrow eleven against Eton. He was the first to go to the wickets, but he was also the seventh to leave. He hit the bowling to all parts of the field; the spectators of this ultra fashionable fixture were never provided with better value for their time spent round the ring; the young batsman had made 76 before he returned to the pavilion.

This performance naturally placed the seal of excellence upon his play, and he was asked to represent Lancashire in her county fixtures. Mr MacLaren came, saw, and conquered, for against Sussex at Brighton on August 14th he hit up what was practically a faultless 108. How many players are there who have effected a similar performance, coming into county cricket from a public school style of play? I can recollect no other.

Following Mr Hornby and Mr Crosfield, Mr MacLaren was elected captain of the Lancashire team, and in 1895 scored the highest individual innings yet made in first-class cricket. Playing against Somerset, at Taunton, in July, he compiled 424 runs, thus beating the 344 standing to the credit of Mr W. G. Grace by no uncertain margin.

Prior to this, however, Mr MacLaren had toured through Australia as one of Mr A. E. Stoddart's eleven. He was a success, for he secured the second place in the batting averages: 47.4 for twenty innings in eleven-a-side matches, and 40.9 for thirty-three innings, all matches played being considered. More than that, he was also busy amongst the 'centurions' — if I may be pardoned for the use of the word. Against Victoria, on November 16th, he placed 228 — his highest total for the tour — against his name, this being followed by 106 v. Queensland and New South Wales on February 15th, and 120 against Australia, at Melbourne, on March 1st.

Mr MacLaren's performances for his county need no comment from me, but I may just touch briefly upon his last Australian tour. He wooed and won his bride 'down under', and he never played better cricket in his life than when last at the Antipodes. We were fairly and squarely beaten in the Test Matches, I am ready to admit that; but Mr MacLaren can look back upon the visit with feelings of unalloyed satisfaction.

In the five Test Matches he was at the head of the batting averages with 54.22 runs for ten innings, 124 being his highest contribution. In the eleven a-side matches his average was 54.57 for twenty innings, and in all matches 54.34 for twenty-eight innings.

These figures speak for themselves, but I may add Mr MacLaren was also responsible for exactly half-a-dozen centuries during the tour: 181 *v.* Thirteen of Queensland and New South Wales; 142 *v.* New South Wales; 140 *v.* New South Wales (the return match); 124 *v.* Australia, at Adelaide; 109 *v.* Australia, at Sydney; and 100 *v.* New South Wales, also at Sydney.

Returning home, the Lancashire captain could only take part in six of the county fixtures. In these he secured an average of 23.30, with 76 as his highest contribution. But he was as dashing as of old while at the wicket, and even smarter in the field. At slip or at cover-slip he appears to judge the flight of the ball unerringly, while boundary after boundary is saved by the manner in which he picks up the fastest cut, snick, or drive with either hand. I was ruminating over these things as the South-Western express whirled me away over the gleaming metals to Wokingham, where, in a delightful old countryside mansion, Mr MacLaren has established himself in the heart of as delightful scenery as may well be met with within a hundred miles of London.

There, in his study, he sat and chatted over cricket matters. The Lancashire eleven, the great scene at the Oval after the finish of the last Test Match there – these and kindred pictures reflected the ruddy fireglow from the walls. Outside, the sun was throwing its rays athwart the gravelled drive; there was the indefinite hum inseparable from the country, the missel-thrushes and the blackbirds disported themselves among the trees, just budding into life; while, stranger still, the red coat and bushy tail of a squirrel could be seen just at the edge of the copse that ran down to the lawn.

But this is not cricket. I must drag myself away. The memory of the Harrow *v.* Eton match I have already referred to was crossing my mind. I lost no time, but, plunging directly into my subject, wondered what the Lancashire captain thought of public school cricket of these days. Did it compare favourably with days that are past and gone? Mr MacLaren hesitated slightly ere he replied. But there were no signs of hesitation when he was once induced to talk.

'No,' he remarked; 'I really do not think public school cricket, as cricket, has advanced since a few years back. I can naturally only speak of Harrow personally; yet what do we find? That year by year these public school matches remain drawn; they are not finished in the time allowed for their decision.

'And why? That is a difficult question to answer. My own opinion is, gained by watching the boys at the game, that their batting is as good as, or maybe better than, ever, but there is a marked falling off in the class of bowling. Bowling is very moderate, to say the least of it.

'Of course, it is much easier to teach a boy how to bat than to teach him how to become a successful bowler. It is quite possible to make a batsman, provided the boy is willing to listen to the hints, and possesses some idea of the game; but the best coach cannot make a successful bowler.

'In saying this, I may explain that you can give a boy hints in bowling, but he must be born, not made. He may be told a few things, how to place his feet as he delivers the ball, and what length of run is best to take; but he cannot be made a real bowler under these conditions unless he has an inclination for that kind of work. Unfortunately, too, a schoolboy does not, as a rule, take so kindly to bowling as to batting. There is not the same pleasure in bowling from his point of view: he has not the same inducement in attempting to secure wickets, and as a natural consequence, public school bowling, I am sorry to say, is becoming worse, instead of better, every year. I am sorry to say this is the case, but it is a fact.

'As regards University cricket, I am a little diffident in touching this, seeing that I have only played about twice against Cambridge. But I think the same criticism will apply as in the public schools: that batting is advancing, while the bowling is at least standing still, if not falling off in quality.

'We get very few real bowlers from the 'Varsities now. Yes, we have had Mr C. L. Townsend, Mr F. S. Jackson, Mr S. M. J. Woods, and Mr Kortright, men who are worth their places in a county team for this department alone; but what I complain of is, that we get no new blood.

'As a matter of fact, I cannot say who is their best real bowler. No, I fear they cannot produce anyone approaching the stamp of the late Mr A. G. Steel. Of course, Mr C. M. Wells is a good bowler, but he has left his University for a long time now. He was the last of the bowlers to come from either Oxford or Cambridge; since he left, they have produced none that might be termed really first-class.'

After this expression of opinion upon what are generally looked upon as the training grounds for county cricket, it was difficult to muster up courage sufficient to enable me to suggest amateur cricket as a whole.

But Mr MacLaren reassured me at once.

'Amateur cricket,' he opined, 'is improving, and in this way there are more good cricketers now than there were in the past. But' (and here he qualified it) 'the players of the present day are no better than they were twenty years ago. There are more of them, that is all. There are more good batsmen to-day than there were at the time I have mentioned, but that may be explained by the growth of the game. The bowling, I think, must have been better then than now, and when the best elevens are contrasted there is very little difference to be discovered, the improvements in the grounds also being taken into consideration.

'Briefly, our batsmen now are as good as the old ones, but there are more of them; the class of cricket is just about the same, but the All England eleven of 1879 was about as good as we could place in the field now, possibly better.

'Yes, I feel constrained to admit that the class of all-round bowling in county cricket is to-day much below the average. Indeed, there are not so many good bowlers now as there were five years ago. It is impossible, or it appears to be, to discover new bowlers of any degree of excellence, Rhodes, of Yorkshire, being the exception. Of late years, what have we found? That a young bowler of more than average form is a *rara avis*. Look at Lancashire, for instance. She hasn't discovered one really good bowler during the past five years.

'Yet what a contrast we find in Australia. They *have* got some bowlers; it will take our very best All England side to beat them this coming summer. They will, of course, be without poor Harry Trott, the finest captain and one of the best fellows I have ever met. But it will be found, I think, the best eleven Australia has ever sent across to this country, and one that will require considerable beating.'

'That is consoling,' I remarked; 'but cannot we expect something from our professional players?'

'Well,' was Mr MacLaren's rejoinder, 'we are certainly getting more professionals every year. My idea is that the amateurs are steadily decreasing in numbers, while the professionals are becoming much finer players. Yes, it is very difficult to say whether they are better in bowling or in batting.

'It is more like an all-round improvement, but I will say this, there are more professionals capable of getting a hundred runs against the best bowling than was formerly the case.

'Certainly; the professional bowlers are far in advance of the amateurs. Why? I suppose it must be that they take more trouble over it. A large number know that their livelihood depends upon their ability to get wickets, so they try their hardest to reach the highest standard of excellence. That is how I judge matters, my opinion being formed from the men I play against.

'Bowlers are of two classes: head bowlers, men who bowl with their heads; and mechanical bowlers. Which is better? The former, without a doubt.

'This is where the Australians are so much ahead of us in their own country. Their wickets are dry and hard, and it is useless for a man to keep on bowling dead on the wicket. He must perforce use his judgment, and as a natural consequence the bowler at Sydney, or Adelaide, or any other of the Australian grounds, is obliged to try experiments in the attempt to secure a wicket. They try far more of these experiments and dodges than our bowlers here — they must do so in order to justify their reputation.

'When a batsman goes in, the bowler is continually trying some device in order to get him out, or to tempt him in some fashion. This style of play is strange to a new-comer, and he falls into the trap laid for him. Then he wonders why he could not have seen what was likely to happen. But a new man possesses very little chance of becoming a success upon Australian wickets: he has too much to learn to be able to crowd all his experience into the beginning of one tour.

'English bowlers are also at a considerable disadvantage upon an Australian wicket. The condition of the ground does not assist them, and then there is the difference in the game to be considered. The English batsman plays in a free and dashing style; the Australian will not be tempted. He knows the game will be played to a finish, he need not hurry himself; so he is cautious in every stroke he plays. Visiting bowlers would be far more successful were the home batsmen to play the game to which they had been accustomed, *but they won't.*

'The conditions of bowling are altogether different in the two countries, and a strange team will discover the change in either. Here in England the climatic conditions, the wet weather, frequently assists the bowlers to a no uncertain extent. They are enabled to get far more work upon the ball – McKibbin discovered that, when he was last here, he broke back far too much. It is a dangerous thing to prophesy about Australian bowlers, I am aware, but I fully expect them to show their real form.

'Their best performer with the ball? Hugh Trumble, without a doubt. He knows our wickets well; he is remarkably good upon his own wickets, and he uses his judgement to the best advantage. Upon a wicket that suits him he is practically unplayable, while he is a man who can be always relied upon. McLeod, again, is another man who may be a very good bowler for them, while his performances with the bat are well-known features in his play.'

It was evident Mr MacLaren possessed a high opinion of the calibre of our visitors. No doubt he recollected the last of the English tours. To test him, however, I brought the conversation round to the subject of Australian cricket, and asked him what he thought of the all-round conditions at the Antipodes.

'We were beaten, fairly and squarely,' he admitted; 'but after all, we had a far more formidable task than that faced by any of the earlier elevens. On the former occasions cricket had not secured such a hold upon the Australian public. They had not been educated up to it – the game was in a transitory stage, so to speak.

'Now the case is vastly different. Cricket has been improved all round in Australia, while, as I have said before, a new man must almost entirely alter his style of play if he wishes to be a success. And some men cannot do that, consequently they fail.

'Even when he does make this alteration, it takes a very long time before he can feel at all at home under the different conditions. It is always the same, and it by no means follows that because a man is a great player here in England he will prove an equal success in Australia.

'Far from it. First-class batsmen might prove harmless; it would take time to conform to the new order of things, and it is only natural that a player should be a greater success upon a second visit than during his first. The Australian bowling was a great factor in their success against us in the Test Matches. You may recollect only three centuries were scored against them, yet there are men here in England, not in the front rank, who I feel confident would get any amount of runs off their bowlers.

'But it does not follow that, because the Australians have scored hundred after hundred upon their own wickets, they will be equally successful here. They, under altered conditions, last time they were here, were dismissed cheaply on occasions, and I should like to see them get thirty runs apiece, instead of the centuries, should the pitch prove suitable for our bowlers.

'Australian cricket, taking it right through, is not on a par with county cricket here, but it is good enough, and they will be a very great side this year. If they get fair luck, we shall need to be at our best to beat them; but should they get soft wickets, they may not be able to play upon them.

'In speaking of Australian cricket at home, it must not be forgotten that four years ago they were a very young eleven, and almost inexperienced. That is quite different now. There is twice the number of players, and they have gained a greater knowledge of the game, and how to play it to the best advantage.

'Up-country cricket during the tour of an English eleven is not looked upon in a serious light at all, I can assure you. These matches are simply considered in the nature of a picnic. The names of the players are placed in a hat, and every man determines upon having a day out.

'Still, there is this to be said of the matches we played in the country during our last tour in Australia: the matting wickets put many of our batsmen right off their game. They had, perhaps, almost recovered from the effects of the long voyage. They would practise upon turf and then go upon matting. That would upset their form at once, and entirely.

'It is a fearful drawback to any visiting team, this playing first on turf and then on matting. If I have anything to say about the arrangements of another team and its tour in Australia, I shall most strongly deprecate the custom of playing under these conditions. We should never play upon matting at all.

'Upon the average, during our last tour, we played three of these matches in a fortnight. We found the ball came in at a lightning pace, and regulated our style accordingly.

'Then we would play another match upon the turf. That is fast enough, but not nearly so fast as matting. The Australians may smile when they read this, but I am absolutely certain several of our batsmen's failures were caused by the exchange of surface. Yes, I hope when England plays Australia again, on their own ground, it will be stipulated that turf wickets must be provided for all the fixtures entered upon, both Test Matches and up-country contests.

'These matches, played far away from the usual grounds, of course do a great deal of good from a cricket point of view; that is to say, locally. But our batsmen did not attempt to do their best. Many of them got out as soon as they could. When they had made thirty or forty runs they would become reckless, simply because they did not like, playing against odds, to make too big a score. The curious thing, though, is that we met many good bowlers in these matches. That and the wicket-keeping were their strongest points. There were one or two of these up-country bowlers whom I should like to see playing for Lancashire. Their batting, on the other hand, was not of a very high-class order. But these matches were very enjoyable, after all.'

After this I was a bit chary of suggesting 'spectators' as a topic for discussion, but Mr MacLaren plunged into the matter at once.

'I regret to say the spectators behaved very badly on occasions,' he admitted. 'There was a great deal too much of the "barracking" humour about then, especially at Sydney, on the occasion of our last Test Match there. At Melbourne, however, the crowd behaved much fairer to us. There is a great difference between an Australian and an English crowd. The former are not nearly so generous: they do not like to see you winning. As long as they are on top they are satisfied; but if there is a prospect of their being beaten, then they commence to "boo" and yell at the visiting players.

'There are too many critics in Australia, and, as is generally the case, those who know least have the most to say. As regards the umpiring while we were there I have nothing at all to complain of. It was perfectly fair.'

'But what about the number of players taken out?' I hazarded. 'There was something said about too small a reserve. Was that the case?'

'No, certainly not,' was Mr MacLaren's rejoinder. 'If you are forming a cricket team to tour abroad, you cannot take more than thirteen. When you play your first match upon Australian soil, let us suppose the side makes a total of 400 or 500 runs. That is not at all improbable, seeing the scoring that has occurred during the progress of the recent inter-Colonial fixtures. Every man of the side makes from 55 to 56 runs apiece.

'Whom are you to leave out? Why, you cannot take a batsman out of the team who can score to the extent I have mentioned, and the result is that you have about four men looking on, match after match, with but a very slight chance of their being given a trial.

'Very frequently a man may be in Australia, under these circumstances, for four or five weeks before he is asked to get into his flannels. Look at Mr Philipson when he was taken out as a reserve wicket-keeper. How frequently were his services required? No, a side comprising thirteen members is quite large enough for all practical purposes.

'It was not the paucity of our numbers that upset us in Australia. It was the heat. During the day we would be beneath a broiling sun; then at night, up would come the hot wind, and we could not sleep. That in itself was enough to put a man off his form. However, the Australians will be at a disadvantage should they experience any cold weather during their visit here, so we must not complain upon that score.'

The winter payment of professionals proved a good subject, and Mr MacLaren spoke up decidedly in the matter of rendering the closing days of a good old servant a little easier than is sometimes the case.

'I think,' he suggested, 'that winter payments to professional cricketers should be made the general rule. But in this connection there should be a universal law: one man should be paid as well as another. It is hard that one man should be paid £2 or £1 a week and that another should get nothing.

'Professionals are underpaid at the best of times, for it must not be forgotten they soon get old. After they have reached the age of thirty-five, they are not much good for county work. The great cricketers, the idols of the public, are all right — they may depend upon a rousing benefit; but what of the smaller men?

'They have wives and families, and they are put to the same expense as a more successful member of the team. Yet what have they to look forward to in their old age? A few secure posts as coaches at the public schools, but they are exceptionally fortunate. Time after time I have seen professionals upon the cricket-field looking as miserable as possible. Wondering where their next sovereign was coming from, very likely. Is this fair? Can a man show his real form when he is overburdened with responsibilities?

'Certainly not. The professional player is a sober, honest, hardworking servant of the club or county, and he deserves better all-round treatment. The big man can go to the secretary or treasurer and say, "Oh, if you won't pay me at a certain rate, another county will", and he gains his point. What chance has a little man of making a similar bargain? None at all.

'A fast bowler? No; why should it make a greater difference to him? The public must not forget that he does not generally last as long as a medium pace or slow bowler. That fact explains more than one failure on previous form.'

Then Mr MacLaren cried 'enough', and refused to be drawn farther. But I may add he is equally at home with his gun as with his cricket bat, and that if he has a weakness it runs in the direction of greyhounds.

Strand Magazine 1899

7

Interview with Mr W. G. Grace

Fred W. Ward

Throughout the extent of the British Empire, be it north, south, east or west, more this season, perhaps, than in any other, has the name of Mr William Gilbert Grace become a household word. Be it peer or peasant, all unite in doing homage to the hero of a hundred 'centuries' — the man who has done more to further the progress of the grand old English game than any other man of this or any other time; and, although he reached the age of forty-seven in July last (a period when a cricketer is generally supposed to become superfluous upon the field), Mr Grace is yet the man who is considered the most dangerous of any side, not alone by our English teams, but by visitors from the Antipodes. No matter what the ground may be, hard or soft, when the champion walks to his place at the wickets, who is to say when he will be again sent back to the pavilion?

And this is the position which he has occupied since so long ago as 1866, when, at the age of eighteen, he set the cricket world a-wondering by his innings of 224 not out, for England *v*. Surrey. From then until now he has stood head and shoulders above all other contemporary batsmen; he has seen younger blood infused into the county teams, and go again, yet he is now capable of as much endurance upon the grassy sward as any.

But the place he holds in first-class cricket may, perhaps, be shown best by a brief *resumé* of his performances on the pitch. In 1866 he was at the head of the batting averages, then being, as already mentioned, but eighteen years of age, a feat which has probably been accomplished by no other player. In 1868, 1869, 1870, 1871, 1872, 1873, 1874, 1876, 1877, 1879 and 1880 he occupied the same position, and then, taking no account of his performances during the intervening seasons, this year we find him only deposed from what may be best described as

60

the premiership amongst wielders of the willow for a single fortnight until the end of June, when he possessed an average of 83.50 for twenty innings, while he had scored 1000 runs before the season had become a month old. In 1868 his best average was 65 per innings, 57 in 1869, 54 in 1870, 78 in 1871, 57 in 1872, 71 in 1873, 53 in 1874, 62 in 1876, 43 in 1885 and 54 in 1887. To calculate the number of runs he has scored during all these years would be an impossible task, yet it would be well within the mark if we place the number at 70,000, and to-day he is playing as consistent a game as at any period of his career. Well, indeed, may one of the verses of an earlier song be repeated:

> There's a name which will live for ever and aye,
> In the true-born cricketer's mind —
> A name which is loudly re-echoed to-day,
> And borne on the wings of the wind.
> Britannia may gladly be proud of her sons,
> Since who is more famous than he,
> The stalwart compiler of thousands of runs,
> 'Leviathan' W.G.?*

From the figures which have already been quoted, it may be rightly judged that Mr Grace in reality inaugurated high and rapid scoring in cricket. In 1859, the highest average was the 30.21 of Mr V. Walker. But how would these figures strike a critical observer of the play of to-day? And yet, fêted and honoured on all sides, the Gloucestershire captain is as simple and unaffected at the present time as at the period when he was just commencing to be a power in first-class cricket.

I was fortunate enough to meet him as he stepped off the field at Lord's a few weeks back with the plaudits of the spectators, in recognition of his innings of 125 for the MCC against Kent, yet ringing in the air. But with kindliness and good-fellowship beaming from every line of his bronzed and bearded face, the champion grasped my hand with a grip which made me wince again, and acceded to my request for a few minutes' chat on past and present cricket. With the kindly 'burr' of the West Country tongue lingering on every sentence, he told me how he was born at Downend, near Bristol, on July 18th, 1848, and, plunging at once into the thread of his story, went on to speak of the first match he recollected watching, at that time a wee lad of six, seated upon his father's knee.

* From the *All England Cricket and Football Journal*.

'That was when I saw the All England Eleven play against Twenty-two of West Gloucestershire, at Bristol,' he remarked, 'and I remember that two or three of the elder players at that time wore tall hats. That, as I was telling you, was the first match I can remember seeing, but as years went on I believe that I was present at every match I possibly could get at. And all the time my brothers and myself were being coached by my uncle, Mr Pocock, into the rudiments of the game.

'He was a great enthusiast in the game, you know, and taught us the correct style, and when I was old enough I used to play for the West Gloucestershire Club, of which my father was the manager. Unfortunately, however, we had no ground at Downend, and had to play upon the common, about a mile away; but we lads when at home used to pitch our wickets in the orchard. That was where I first got a knowledge of the game.

'The first match I played in? Well, that was when I was nine years old, and I scored 3 not out. I played three more innings that year, I remember, and scored only another single. That wasn't exactly great, was it? Nor were my records exactly as I wished for the next few years. In 1858, I played six innings for 4 runs; 1859, nine innings for 12 runs; 1860, four innings for 82; 1861, ten innings for 46; and 1862, five innings for 53.

'But all this time, you must remember, I was still practising under Uncle Pocock's eye, while beyond cricket we boys also went in for the kite carriages, of which he was the inventor. Of course, this is really outside the game, but I may mention that we used to beat the carriages drawn by horses frequently, while on one occasion he raced and defeated the Duke of York's carriage on the London Road. That was his recreation, you know; but to get back to cricket again. I left school in 1863, and after a very severe illness I was placed under the charge of a tutor by my father. That season I played nineteen innings, and hit 350 runs, being not out on six occasions, and securing an average of 26.

'By this time, as you may imagine, I was getting pretty well known as a cricketer in the neighbourhood of Bristol, and had scored 18 and 1 in the match Gentlemen of Gloucester v. Gentlemen of Devon. But it was not until '64 that I accomplished my first great performance. I was only fifteen at that time, mind you, but a big boy for my age, and playing for the Gentlemen of South Wales against the Gentlemen of

Sussex made 170 and 56 not out, and took two wickets in the first innings. This success led to my being requested to play in the following year for the Gentlemen *v.* the Players both at Lord's and the Oval. I did fairly well, but the first century I ever hit up in first-class cricket was made in 1866. England was playing Surrey, at the Oval, and, going in fifth for the former, I did not come out again until I had made 224, and then was not out.

'Since then I have been playing continually in first-class cricket whenever I have been available and eligible, although at times my duties precluded all idea of my donning the flannels. In the field I used to prefer being placed at long leg, but I much prefer point now. Eighteen stone, for that is what I have weighed for a good many years past, is quite enough for me to carry when batting, and I can tell you I don't care for sprinting to the boundary in the attempt to save a four as much as I did in my younger days.

'What was my best year with the bat? Well (with a laugh) I have had so many that I almost forget, but I think you may be safe in saying that I was most successful in 1870. In that season I had 35 innings, scoring 2739 runs, and having an average of 78 at the close. With these figures you may perhaps think I had a little luck with the bowlers. But I don't think I had. I know I had to face J. C. Shaw, Alfred Shaw, Southerton, Martin McIntyre and Wootton, and they were all good men.

'Then my best season with the ball, I think, was in 1867. I took 39 wickets at a cost of 6.21 each; in 1874 I secured 129 for 12; 1875, 192 for 12; and again in 1877 the same average, 179 for 12. My highest innings, I may add, was that scored in 1876 against Twenty-two of Grimsby and District for a United South of England Eleven. When we went on the ground they grumbled because we had brought a weak team, but there wasn't much said after I made 400, not out, out of 681, and was at the wickets until nearly four o'clock on the third day. But this performance was never an actual record, you know. A few weeks after I had made the runs I have just mentioned, I made 344 for Gentlemen of MCC against Kent, followed with 179 *v.* Notts, and 318 not out *v.* Yorkshire.

'Beyond these performances, I have three times scored over a hundred in each innings, and, with Mr B. B. Cooper, made a record of 283 for the first wicket for Gentlemen of the South against Players of the South. This stood as a record until it was beaten by Messrs. H. T.

Hewett and L. C. Palairet at Taunton, playing for Somersetshire *v.* Yorkshire. As to what I should call the best of my innings – well, you must judge that for yourself.

'And now to present-day cricket. Well, I think myself that the players who were known when I first came out would fairly hold their own now, while in many cases I fancy they might be better. Of course, we hadn't the pitches then that we have now, and every hit was run out. The consequence of this was that perhaps a batsman would get excited in trying to get a six, with a short run as the last, and the field had a better chance of running him out than they have at the present day.

'Why, there were no boundaries at the time I am speaking of, and at Lord's and the Oval, if the ball didn't go inside the pavilion we had to run it out. This is what makes me think that it is easier to get a hundred now than it was then. The only remedy that I know for this would be to put a wooden fence right round the playing ground, say some 2 feet high. If a ball should be sent over, it should be a boundary, and count the regulation four; if not, it should be run out.

'Of course, the reason these boundaries were established had nothing to do with saving the batsmen. It was the crowd who had to be considered, for I have seen a fieldsman knock down four or five spectators when going after a ball. We used to go right in, and let everybody take care of himself. As regards the question whether batting and bowling are improving, of course, there are a great many more players now than there were twenty and twenty-five years ago, but I don't think there is much difference.

'The players, I am bound to admit, are stronger in bowling than the amateurs, but I think I can explain that. An amateur does not appear to care for bowling so much as for batting. And then, again, a professional does not go on for so many years. You hear of them, as a general rule, for a few seasons, and then they give up the game and go into business. But with amateurs the case is very different. They play solely for the love of the thing itself, and keep on year after year, and season after season.

'Not much difference in University cricket? No, I can't say that there is, although taken as a whole it is better now than it used to be. And the same may be said of public school cricket, although with the latter I should like to point out one thing. That is this: there is a tendency to keep a boy down to a certain style in his play. He must play the "correct game", it is said; but suppose a lad has an ugly style, and yet is a hitter who can get runs, why should he not be coached up in that? Instead of that, however, he is taught how to hold his bat by the regulation rule, and the result is that instead of being a fearless slogger he is to a great measure spoilt. These remarks, I may as well say, apply equally to the bowling as to the batting.

'My opinion is that, provided a lad is able to keep his wicket up and to get runs, although his style may not be a pretty one for a spectator to watch, he should be allowed to play his own game, under certain not too strict conditions, of course. When at the Universities the style of a young player has been practically formed, but it would be as well if the men were to practise bowling more than they do just now. But I suppose the reason why the ball is not so favoured as the bat is by reason of the wickets being much easier now than was the case when I first remember them. Now, almost every college at both Oxford and Cambridge has grounds of its own, and there is ample opportunity for them to turn out good teams. I should not say that upon the average there is much difference between either 'Varsity eleven, but you must remember that Fenners is much easier for the batsmen, and correspondingly more difficult for the bowlers, than the Parks at Oxford. I should say that is why the Cantabs are not so very strong as a rule in the latter department, for it takes all the heart out of a man to send down over after over, day after day, without getting a wicket. As regards the best bowlers I have met at Cambridge, I might mention W. N. Powys, A. G. Steel, S. M. J. Woods, and F. S. Jackson.

'But it is not exactly fair to judge the capability of a team from their display upon a London ground. For one thing, the batsmen are far from being at home under the altered conditions. The men are nervous, too, especially if it should be their first appearance in London.

'And as regards the admission of additional counties into the championship series: this I do not think is exactly an improvement. With so many teams engaged it will be found impossible to play home and away matches with each county. The consequence of this may be that, perhaps, some strong counties will only meet some of the weaker ones; and then again, matters may get so complicated when the points come to be calculated that there will be a difficulty in really finding out who are the champions.

'Then there is another thing I am afraid of. That is, that cricket will be made too much of a business, like football – with the consequence that none but professionals will be seen playing. That, I hope, will not come in our times; but there is that probability to be faced. Should such a condition of affairs occur – well, betting and all other kindred evils will follow in its wake, and instead of the game being followed up for love, it will simply be a matter of £. s. d.

'And then there is another thing that militates against the well-being of a team. That is the behaviour of the crowd. If a batsman is unfortunate, there is always a section of the public which starts jeering as soon as he may come in. That takes all the confidence out of a man, and if he should be an amateur, he would not stand it for long. Then, again, if a fieldsman fails to take a difficult chance, or is slow in a return, the crowd set about him again. But I can tell you a man feels quite bad enough when he knows he has missed a chance of sending an opponent back, without having the spectators howling at him. You can't expect anyone to stand too much of this kind of treatment, and if things should reach a climax, the gentlemen always have a remedy in their own hands. All they will have to do will be to give up the county games, form clubs, and decide fixtures amongst themselves.

'How do I think the alteration in the rule of follow-on will affect the game, you ask. That all depends; and as it has been afforded such a short trial, I prefer not to say too much upon the subject; but I think it may make the game a little fairer for the fielding side. Say their opponents complete their first innings, and then have to follow on. Well, the chances are all in favour of a big score being knocked up. The bowlers and fieldsmen are fatigued, while the batsmen have had an opportunity of resting themselves. With the margin enlarged to 120 runs, however, it should tend to make the game of a more equal character, for it is not often that an eleven would fall so far in the rear as that figure.

'Then you mention the "retired hurt" question, that has provoked such a discussion since the pronouncement of the secretary of the MCC. Of course, if a batsman is hurt he retires, and then may come out again and finish his innings if an arrangement is made with the opposing captain. As for saying that a player might retire under what practically would mean false pretences for the sake of his average, that cannot be taken into serious consideration for a moment. A man would never do that – that is my experience of the game; and if he should do so by any chance, well, he wouldn't be played again, you may depend upon that.

'Now, that is hardly a fair question to ask.'

This in reply to a question of mine respecting which ground in England was the best, in Mr Grace's opinion.

'All county grounds are good; some are naturally slower than others, but no fault can be found with the manner in which they are kept. But if you want to know which is the easiest ground from a batsman's point of view, I should certainly pitch upon that at Brighton. There is a very small boundary there, it is fast, and a team ought to be able to score a hundred a day there in advance of the figures they might obtain upon some other grounds.

'But I think that on the whole Australian wickets are better, as a rule, than ours. They have all the climatic advantages necessary to make a pitch something like what we were getting in May and June of this year. At Melbourne, Adelaide and Sydney the grounds are as good as ours, as level as a billiard table, and much easier to score upon owing to their being so fast. But it doesn't follow from this that a player who has made a big reputation home here would do well in the Antipodes. For one thing, the climate is liable to upset a visitor, and then the glare of the sun exercises a dazzling effect upon one, which you are a considerable time in getting used to.

'In America they also have fairly good grounds; that was how I found it when I was across there, and I dare say they have improved matters considerably since then. But the cricket is only about as good as that of the weakest of our counties, although the clubs are so enthusiastic over the game, that negotiations have been opened for the visit of a couple of our teams some time during the present season. But there is really no comparison between English and Colonial cricket. Why, here, at home, we ought to beat Australia every time, although when you take a team out there, there is a certainty that it would not be a really representative one. The matters I have already mentioned would militate against its success, while the hospitality is too much for good play.

'There is, however, one feature of the Australian cricket which I may perhaps mention. They have had a really wonderful succession of first-class bowlers in a short time. The batting, when the number of players is considered in proportion, is not nearly so good; but as they have so very few professionals, the amateurs are forced to handle the leather themselves. In the big matches and club fixtures, the latter more especially, I have found that the trundling is better there than in England.

'But I have met some capital bowlers in the past. I should class them in two sections, the slows including A. Shaw, Peate, Southerton, Mr A. G. Steel, Watson, Mr Buchanan; and the fasts — Freeman, Tarrant, Jackson, Hill, Willsher, Morley, J. C. Shaw, Mr Tonge and Mr Appleby.

'I think myself that the bowling was quite as difficult when I came out in first-class cricket as at the present time; but amongst the most successful of the present time with the leather, I should put Peel, Briggs, and Mr C. L. Townsend as the slows, and Mr S. Woods, Mr Kortright, Mold, Richardson and Lockwood as the fasts.

'The consideration of the various degrees of excellence amongst the bowlers takes you, as a matter of course, to the consideration of throwing. I must admit that some of the very fast bowlers (I need mention no names) are looked upon with suspicion; but I really do not think they are any worse now than they were in years gone by. There was always a certain percentage of suspicion, and so, I suppose, it will have to go on. There is one thing certain, and that is, you will never get an umpire to no-ball a suspicious bowler who is allowed to take part in present cricket.

'The only remedy I can suggest would be for a dozen umpires and a similar number of captains of the best county teams to meet together. The names of all the bowlers who were suspected of throwing should be placed upon a slip of paper. Then they should be marked, as by ballot, whether they were considered to throw or not, the decision of a two-thirds majority to be final, and if a man were convicted of throwing he should not be allowed to bowl again. That is the only way in which the evil could be coped with, in my opinion, and when a man knew that he might be debarred from further play — well, it would make him much more careful.

'Then another thing that is often asked me is, whether I think football improves a man for cricket. No, I do not. A man cannot do well at cricket unless he has followed the game up all his life, while I could mention Rugby forwards who really run away from fast bowlers. A cricketer, however, should take plenty of exercise to keep himself fit during the winter. But people have much over-rated the methods I

Two forerunners of the cricket magazines of today, *The Cricketer* of 1869 and *The Cricketer and Hockey Player* of 1907, together with a contemporary advertisement for cricket equipment

above Practising in the nets at Lord's, 1894
below Winter cricket for women on the indoor pitches at the St Bride's Institute

top left, centre and **below right** 'W.G.' demonstrating the art of batsmanship
top right Ranji, Prince of cricket, in native costume
below left England captain (and author) A. C. MacLaren at the wicket

SHAKESPEARE ON CRICKET.

Drawn by S. T. Dadd.

How the Bard might have seen the noble game

pursue. You read of all kinds of means, but you may take it from me that they are, in the majority of instances, untrue.

'Last winter I was certainly out once or twice a week with the Clifton Foot Beagles, but I commenced practising much later this year than usual. But it doesn't follow that even if a man is in training he will do equally well at all times. A spell of bad luck may unsettle him, or a biting east wind may take all the suppleness out of his joints. A man who plays cricket, and cricket alone, though, is not likely to make a shining light. Exercise is what you require. If you can't run you can ride, and if you can't ride you can walk.

'This reminds me that I was never defeated over hurdles at 200 yards, while my favourite distance on the flat was a quarter of a mile. But I have been credited with covering 100 yards in $10\frac{4}{5}$ sec., and clearing 5 feet in the high jump, while I remember one instance in which there was an amusing dispute with my brother, E.M. You must know that he could beat me in a 100 yards sprint, but we both entered for the event and got on the mark. I kept one eye upon the starter and, poaching a couple of yards at the pistol shot, won by a foot. E.M. wouldn't speak to me after this for a time, but the coolness soon wore off with the dear old fellow. But I never possessed any style in my running. When I came out at sixteen I was unmercifully chaffed at the way I threw my legs and arms about, but I persevered, and at last, two years later, won the 300 yards strangers' race at Clifton College sports.'

Upon turning up the records, it may be mentioned *en passant* that in 1869 he had gained the reputation of being one of the fastest quarter-mile runners in England, and in 1870, when giving racing up, had gained over seventy cups and medals. In 1866 Mr Grace secured eighteen 1sts and two 2nds; 1867, one 1st; 1868, six 1sts; 1869, seventeen 1sts, nine 2nds, and one 3rd; and in 1870, five 1sts, one 2nd and one 3rd. His best times were: 100 yards upon grass, $10\frac{4}{5}$ sec.; 150 yards (with 5 yards start), $15\frac{1}{2}$ sec.; 200 yards hurdles, 28 sec.; 440 yards flat race, $52\frac{1}{5}$ sec.; long jump, $17\frac{1}{2}$ feet; high jump, 5 feet; hop, step and jump, 41 feet; pole jump, 9 feet; and throwing the cricket ball, 122 yards. These figures will give an idea of what he was capable of at his best.

'How should I advise a young beginner to start learning the game? That is a somewhat difficult question, for every player possesses a style more or less distinctive. But the great thing for a youngster to secure is a good coach, who will teach him the correct way in which to hold his bat and take up his position at the wickets. Perhaps a lad may say that the hard and fast rules may make him feel cramped and stiff at the wicket, but you may depend upon it that he will soon adapt himself to the various conditions. Then, in taking his place against the bowler, the batsman should be particular in seeing that he plays with a perfectly straight bat, while his toes should be just outside an imaginary line drawn from the leg and off stump of each wicket respectively. This will enable him to get well over his work, while he will stand less chance of being bowled off his pads.

'As for the position in which to stand, there is no hard and fast rule, but what I generally favour is the placing of the left leg about 12 inches in front and at right angles to my other. The right foot should come inside the crease, and as a general rule should not be moved. Shift your left foot as much as you like when batting, but upon the right depends the stability of your defence. If you are continually shifting it, you will get out very soon.

'And now for the bat. No doubt you have observed the peculiarity of many players in respect of the length of the handle. Some have long, others again have them shorter. I myself prefer a handle of the ordinary length, and hold it about half-way up. Then you must keep your eye upon the bowler until the instant when the ball leaves his hand, for you can generally tell by this in which way he intends to break. Then you should make the bat hit the ball, not let the ball hit the bat.

'If you make up your mind to hit, hit hard, half measures are of no use; and when you block, put just a little power into your strokes. You should not be content to stop the ball by simply interposing the bat, but play it in such a manner that runs may be secured. Hit hard, then: that is my advice to a young player; but get well over the ball and never spoon it up. A hit travels much farther when it is kept down than when sent high in the air; while it is but seldom found that a slogger, who skies all his hits, scores many runs.

'With regard to the various styles of play, it is difficult to advise. You see, each player generally has a different method, and a long-reached man will be able to get forward and smother a ball that shorter-reached batsmen can only play by getting farther back. There is consequently much that must be left to individual judgment, but I should most strongly caution a player against betraying a tendency to play across the wicket, or to pull balls. A leg ball that is a leg ball should be hit to leg, but young players are only too apt to attempt to pull almost every ball sent down. The result of this is that they fail to do much in the game owing to their faulty style.

'In cutting, you should never fail to keep the ball down, patting it down, if I may use the expression, although nothing but practice will bring the familiarity necessary for the playing of the game. You should practise frequently and play as carefully at the nets as in an actual match; while many useful hints may be learnt by watching the best players. A beginner, mind you, should not be a copyist, but there is more to be learnt in half an hour's actual practice than can be taught in a week of theory.

'And now we come to bowling. In this department too much attention cannot be given, although the young beginner should not attempt to bowl fast at first. If he does, possibly he will sacrifice pitch and straightness. Commencing, say, at 18 yards instead of 22, he should gradually work his way back to the longer distance, and by placing a mark, easily seen, upon the pitch at a certain distance from the wicket, he will soon be able to vary his length at will, and bowl somewhere near the spot aimed at. Trying to twist the ball should only come after a man has learnt to bowl straight. To accomplish this the ball should be held firmly in the hand, with the fingers grasping it well over the centre and resting over the seams. Then in leaving go, the fingers should relax their grasp, imparting the twist so destructive to the unwary batsman.

'But there is more to be gained by altering your pace and length than by bowling dead upon the wicket time after time. Many batsmen will simply play maiden after maiden if the bowling is straight, but if you give them a few balls on either side of the wicket, it is probable that they will give a chance and be out. Of course, this does not apply to a poor batsman. He cannot play straight bowling for any length of time, and is bound to let the ball beat him eventually.

'Which is the better bowling, fast or slow? Well, that depends upon the ground. Although a fast bowler upon a good wicket is easier to score from, my eye is not so sure as it was at one time, and I think I prefer a medium-paced ball myself. Considering the two styles of bowling, however, slow is generally the better upon a soft wicket, and fast upon a hard, difficult pitch.

'Now, in conclusion, we come to the fielding. It is as much by activity in this department that a match is won as with the bat, for, if catches are missed, returns muffed, and runs allowed to be stolen – well, the bowlers will be sadly handicapped. Each man in the field should be intent upon the game, and nothing else. Talking during the over should not be allowed. A fieldsman should invariably run in to a ball, and not wait for it to come to him, while he can never tell what catches he may bring off unless he makes the attempt.

'One curious thing that is sometimes seen is that a poor field may take a catch coming off the bat at a tremendous pace, while he may miss an easy one. When making a catch off a swift ball, the hands should "give" a few inches involuntarily, but with a slow the ball is apt to jump out of your grip before the fingers can close round it.

'Then there is another point worth attention. Suppose you miss a ball. The best do this at times, but never lose a moment in vain regrets, but sprint off and save the runs. Then in returning the ball, unless you have an excellent reason, never throw to the bowler's end. When returning from the long field send the ball low and straight. The greater the curve, the longer it takes to reach the wicket, and the less chance is there of running the batsman out. By the due observance of these rules, there is no reason, if a young player is possessed of a good eye and head, why he should not prove a successful exponent of our noble game.

'There is one thing, however, in addition to these I have already enumerated, that has been discussed considerably; that is, upon either a wet or drying wicket, if you are successful in the toss, should you put your opponents in or have first knock yourself? The latter, most decidedly, I should say; for in this climate of ours you can never be certain of the weather for two days in succession. In fact, I may safely say that only about once in thirty or forty times does the experiment of putting your opponents in first prove successful.'

Strand Magazine 1895

8

W. G. Grace: A Memory

A. Conan Doyle

To those who knew W. G. Grace he was more than a great cricketer. He had many of the characteristics of a great man. There was a masterful generosity and a large direct simplicity and frankness which, combined with his huge frame, swarthy features, bushy beard, and a somewhat lumbering carriage, made an impression which could never be forgotten. In spite of his giant West-of-England build, there was, as it seemed to me, something of the gipsy in his colouring, his vitality, and his quick dark eyes with their wary expression. The bright yellow and red cap which he loved to wear added to this Zingari effect. His elder brother, the Coroner, small, wizened, dark and wiry, had even more of this gipsy appearance. I speak, of course, only of the effect produced, for I have no reason to think that such blood was in his veins, though, following Borrow, I am ready to believe that there is no better in Europe.

There was a fine open-air breeziness of manner about the man which made his company a delight and added a zest to the game. He was, of course, a highly educated surgeon, but he had rather the fashion of talk which one would associate with a jovial farmer. His voice was high-pitched, considering the huge chest from which it came, and it preserved something of the Western burr. 'Hullo, young 'un, a bit too good for you, that one!' 'Never mind, my lad, you're not the first good man that has dropped an easy catch.' 'Shut your legs to it before you try to pick it up.' These were the scraps of advice or consolation which he would shout – the voice was loud though high – to the youngster who needed admonition or sympathy.

His style and methods were peculiar to himself. In his youth, when he was tall, slim and agile, he must have been as ideal in his form as in his results. But as this generation knew him he had run to great size

73

and a certain awkwardness of build. It was amazing that a man who was capable of such exertions should carry such weight. As he came towards the wicket, walking heavily with shoulders rounded, his great girth outlined by his coloured sash, one would have imagined that his day was past. 'He may make his twenty or thirty,' one thought, 'and then Nature will dismiss him if the bowler fails.' Never was there a greater fallacy. He seemed slow, stiff and heavy at first. When he had made fifty in his quiet, methodical fashion, he was somewhat younger and fresher. At the end of a century he had not turned a hair, and was watching the ball with as clear an eye as in the first over. Younger batsmen might tire and grow ragged in their strokes, but never the old man. It was his advice to play every ball as if it were the first – and he lived up to it. There was no feeling for the ball, no half-hits or wild slogs. Everything that he did was firm, definite and well within his strength.

I have had the privilege of fielding at point more than once while he made his hundred, and have in my mind a clear impression of his methods. I do not know if he took the centre or the leg guard, or the point between them, but he actually stood very clear of his wicket, bending his huge shoulders and presenting a very broad face of the bat towards the bowler. Then as he saw the latter advance he would slowly raise himself to his height and draw back the blade of his bat, while his left toe would go upwards until only the heel of that foot remained upon the ground. He gauged the pitch of the ball in an instant, and if it were doubtful played back rather than forward. Often he smothered a really dangerous length ball by a curious half-cock stroke to which he was partial. He took no risks, and in playing forward trailed the bottom of his bat along the grass as it advanced so as to guard against the shooter – a relic no doubt of his early days in the 'sixties, when shooters were seen more often than on modern grounds.

The great strength of his batting was upon the offside. I should not suppose that there was ever a batsman who was so good at controlling that most uncontrollable of all balls, the good-length ball outside the off stump. He would not disregard it, as is the modern habit. It was, indeed, seldom that he let a ball pass without offering at it. He did not flinch from it as a foe, but rather welcomed it as a friend, and stepping across the wicket while bending his great shoulders he watched it closely as it rose, and patted it with an easy tap through the slips. In vain with a fast bumpy bowler pounding them down did three quivering fieldsmen crouch in the slips, their hands outstretched and eager for the coming catch. Never with the edge of the bat, but always with the true centre, would he turn the ball groundwards, so that it flashed down and then fizzed off between the grasping hands, flying with its own momentum to the boundary. With incredible accuracy he would place it according to the fields, curving it off squarely if third man were not in his place or tapping it almost straight down upon the ground if short-slip were standing wide of the wicket. In no shot was he so supremely excellent, and, like all great things, it seemed simplicity itself as he did it. Only when one saw other great batsmen fail did one realize how accurate was the timing and the wrist-work of the old man. When he was well on towards his sixtieth year I have seen him standing up to Lockwood when man after man was helpless at the other wicket, tapping those terrific expresses away through the slips with the easy sureness with which one would bounce a tennis ball with a racket. Nor was he ever to be frightened by the most dangerous bowler. Poised and firm, he never flinched, but turned the rising ball to leg or patted it to the off. The fastest bowler in England sent one like a cannon-shot through his beard, with only a comic shake of the head and a good-humoured growl in reply.

It was in this command of the off ball and in his perfect defence that his great merit lay, but there was no stroke at which he was not adept. With his true eye he hit a larger proportion of leg balls than any other man. He stepped back and struck them off his legs not with a whole-hearted swing, but with a sharp, decisive turn of the wrists, watching the ball to the last instant. The only shot which he produced less frequently than his contemporaries was the big sixer, beloved of the crowd. He seldom ventured that great effort, which has an equal chance of ending on the pavilion or in the hands of cover-point. His batting was always well within his strength, and though an analysis of his scores will show that he found the boundary as often as anyone, he never gave the impression that he was hitting hard.

I think that when he was well set the best chance of getting rid of him may have been to serve him up with something so delectable that he might be tempted into a liberty. This theory occurred to me after watching him play seven professional bowlers of all paces and types until he had topped the hundred. Since the best had failed, I thought I would try the other variety — I was captaining an MCC team upon that day — so I ventured upon an experimental over. It succeeded to a marvel. A half volley upon the off with all the fielders upon the off side tempted him to sweep it round to the on. For once he got it on the edge and it went an amazing height perpendicularly into the air, and then down into the hands of Storer, the Derbyshire wicket-keeper. The old man laughed and shook his head at me. He was thinking probably that it was the worst ball that ever got his wicket, but he was too polite to say so. He was not always polite, however. I can remember that in the second innings of the same match he was given out leg-before to Cranfield, a left-handed bowler, bowling round the wicket. I forget who the umpire was, but the old man was very angry. I can see him now with his thick, padded, and somewhat bandy legs, marching towards the pavilion, but his face and beard turned over his right shoulder while he glared back and rumbled all sorts of comminations. His temper grew somewhat shorter, I fancy, during his latter days. It is not surprising when one considers the strain of a succession of three-day matches upon a man of his age. At his normal he was a cheery, boyish-hearted and boisterous man, the jolliest of playmates.

Of his bowling I have very clear recollections. He was an innovator among bowlers, for he really invented the leg theory a generation before it was rediscovered and practised by Vine, Armstrong and others. Grace's traps at leg were proverbial in the 'seventies. His manner was peculiar. He would lumber up to the wicket and toss up the ball in a take-it-or-leave-it style, as if he cared little whether it pitched between the wickets or in the next parish. As a matter of fact this careless attitude covered a very remarkable accuracy. His command of length was absolute, and he had just enough leg spin to beat the bat if you played forward to the pitch of the ball. He was full of guile, and the bad ball which was worth four to you was sent, as likely as not, to unsettle you and lead you on. Never shall I forget three successive balls which I received from him, the graduated stages of a trap which was my undoing and my ruin. The first was a dropping half-volley which no one could help hitting for four. The next looked exactly the same, and I had pranced out to it before I realized that it was really somewhat shorter. I hit at it none the less, and with some luck and a sidelong shot scored another four. The third seemed far the most tempting of the three. No child could have lobbed up anything more seductive. Only when I was ten feet down the pitch did I realize the effect was produced by a higher trajectory, and that the ball was really so short that I could not get at the pitch of it. It shot past me with a little top spin to put devil into it, and I heard the squawk of 'How's that?' as Lilley put down my wicket. There was the old man rubbing his great brown hands and wagging his beard in laughter as I marched sadly home to the dressing-room.

Those who know him will never look at the classic sward of Lord's without an occasional vision of the great cricketer. One can see him in many typical attitudes. Most clearly perhaps he appears coming down the pavilion steps, with ten thousand people clapping as the red and yellow cap, the huge stooping shoulders, and the famous black beard emerge from the open door. Very clearly also can one recall him when he was dissatisfied with the wicket and had detected some danger spot which the roller had missed. He would squat out on the pitch, sitting on his heels, and slapping away with his bat to flatten out the trouble. Most clearly of all, however, one sees his big figure in the centre of an after-luncheon group, and as one approaches one hears again that jolly voice and roar of infectious laughter. He was and will remain the very impersonation of cricket, redolent of fresh air, of good humour, of conflict without malice, of chivalrous strife, of keenness for victory by fair means and utter detestation of all that were foul. Few men have done more for the generation in which he lived, and his influence was none the less because it was a spontaneous and utterly conscious one.

Strand Magazine 1927

9

Interview with Prince Ranjitsinhji

Fred W. Ward

When the time arrives for cricket history to be written, the name of Prince Ranjitsinhji, the young Indian player, will be inscribed upon the roll of fame. Several things will conduce to such an event occurring. In the first place, the Prince has rapidly played himself into the hearts and favour of the British public. At the present time it would be difficult to discover a more popular player throughout the length and breadth of the Empire. The roar of welcome that goes up from the throats of the assembled thousands as 'K.S.' steps upon the field is equal even to the outburst of enthusiasm that greets the champion, the immortal 'W.G.'. It may be explained that 'K.S.' stands for 'Kumar Shri', meaning 'Prince'.

Another thing is that, although known to first-class cricket for barely two seasons, Prince Ranjitsinhji, after having been unaccountably passed over by the executive sitting at Lord's in the first of the Test Matches against Australia this year, attained the summit of a cricketer's ambition by being requested to play for the mother country, at Manchester, when the second of the international fixtures was decided.

His performance upon that occasion is now a matter of history, but I must be pardoned for referring to it. After the failures of such men as Mr W. G. Grace, Mr A. E. Stoddart and others, with the bat, an easy victory for the Colonials appeared within measurable distance. But the Prince came to the rescue of his side. He treated the Antipodean bowlers with indifference. Jones sent down his express deliveries; Giffen, the wily, sent up full tosses for catches; Trott tempted him to hit, but every ball was met and dispatched, clean and hard, far out of the reach of the fieldsmen.

At the end of the second day's play, Prince Ranjitsinhji was not out, and it appeared as though he might even then retrieve the fortunes of his side. Unfortunately, however, he was unable to secure a partner who could stay with him, and when the last of the English wickets fell, he was not out for a grand contribution of 154, made at a time when even the bravest heart might have been pardoned had it quailed at the stupendous task before it.

Reverting now to county cricket, the Prince qualified for Sussex last season. The batting of the county had, previous to his inclusion in the eleven, fallen considerably from its former high estate, although there were still men remaining who, upon a good wicket, might generally be relied upon to make runs. The inclusion of the young Indian, however, strengthened the side considerably, although the fact that he was qualified to play took most people by surprise. Doubts were also expressed concerning the wisdom of the inclusion of the young Cantab, but he soon set these at rest by a remarkable performance effected upon his first appearance for the county. Playing against the MCC at Lord's, he scored 77 not out in the first innings and 150 in his second.

After this brilliant display of batting against some of the best bowlers of the day, the Prince continued in a scoring vein. He rapidly accustomed himself to his new surroundings, and secured runs against all classes of bowling. His strokes were, perhaps, not quite those usually seen upon the field, and there were those writers who referred to 'patents' of his own invention. One stroke, upon the leg side, was an especial feature of his play, and bowlers, time after time, saw their best balls neatly turned aside from the wicket, and dispatched to the boundary. Still, these strokes brought runs, and early in the present season the Sussex player deposed Gunn, Abel and 'W.G.', heading the list of the first-class batting averages.

Bearing these facts in mind, I buttonholed the Prince upon the cricket field a few weeks back, just as he had returned to the pavilion after another of his clean-hit and stylishly-compiled contributions.

With a hearty grasp of the hand and a pleasant smile, I found him an interesting subject. Of medium height, and apparently not powerfully built, he yet carries a considerable amount of muscle, lying beneath the skin as tense and as powerful as steel.

'Can you give me a few particulars of your cricket experiences?' I queried.

'Certainly,' was his reply, as he led the way to a seat. 'I suppose you want something about my early life?'

'Yes.'

'Well, I was born in India on September 10, 1872, at Sarodar, in the province of Kathiaward. I was always very fond of athletics, and, I should say, commenced playing cricket when I was about ten or eleven years of age. Of course, you must understand that it was a — well — a very "illiterate" sort of game I played then; while I was at school, of course. We students, however, had an advantage in attending a school presided over by Mr Chester Macnaghten, an old Cambridge University man. He, of course, was very keen upon the summer game; had brought bats, wickets and other things to his school, and gave his students many useful hints.'

'And I suppose a school eleven was formed?' I queried.

'Yes', was Prince Ranjitsinhji's reply. 'We had a school eleven, and played two other large schools every year. What sort of team did we have? Very fair indeed. The fielding was very good, although it naturally varied at different times. An eleven is never at the same pitch of excellence in the field for two matches in succession. The batting and bowling were also very fair, although I think the fielding was the best of the three.

'How did we proceed at practice? We had batting and bowling at the nets, and we also formed a couple of rival elevens in the school itself. You see, it was like this: we had a north side and a south side. Some of the students boarded in one, and the remainder in the other. We formed an eleven at each, and played matches between ourselves. Near the college we had a cricket ground with a very pretty pavilion, presented to the college by the late Maharajah of Bhownuggur. In front of this we used to practise regularly in native costume. The name of the school? The Rajkumar College, Rajkote. I spent eight years at it. Of course, there were only a limited number of students, about forty, the sons of princes and chiefs, at school with me, but the rivalry when we played the High School at Rajkote and the Girassia School at Wudwan was very keen indeed. Other matches? Yes, we generally played several during the season, with the other elevens near, of course.'

'But had you no coaches?' was my natural question. 'How were the principles of cricket taught?'

'Oh,' was the Prince's laughing answer, 'we had no coaches in the regular acceptation of the term as understood in England. We had to learn the game ourselves, with Mr Macnaghten's hints of course. That was how matters stood while I was at school.'

'And when you came to England?'

'I was about sixteen when I first arrived in this country. No, I did not proceed to Cambridge at once. I remained in London for about six months under the care of a private tutor, preparing for my exams. During that time I played a great deal of lawn tennis, a game I am very fond of, and a little cricket with a private club.

'When I went to Cambridge, however, I was very keen upon the game, and practised assiduously. Naturally, I found a great difference in the Indian and English styles, and I had, if I may say so, to "unlearn" the former before I could do much with the latter.

'I found English cricket very different from what I had been accustomed to, although I had the advantage of being coached by some of the Surrey professionals, such as Sharpe, Richardson, Lockwood, Watts and others. They come down to Cambridge every year, I may explain, to coach the undergraduates.

'Did I not find the new game hard to learn? Yes, I did, for it was almost two years before I was capable of doing much with it. I should say that I was not able to play it properly until 1891. Of course, I did not go into the University eleven until 1893. That was, in fact, my first and last years, as I came down at the end of the season.'

These remarks brought the conversation round to the subject of University cricket generally.

'Cricket at both Oxford and Cambridge', Prince Ranjitsinhji explained, 'is generally very good. County cricketers, I am aware, do not invariably look upon the play as first-class; yet when we are pitted against them we generally give them a good game – often as not beat them. Judged by that test I think, myself, a more serious view should be taken of the play. The batting of a University team, however, is invariably better than the bowling, although we have brought out some very good men. Why such is the case, however, may be readily explained. A man takes his place at the nets with the bat, and as he finds he can get a professional to bowl to him, he does not worry himself about the matter.

'The fielding of a University team is also invariably good, although I am afraid there has been a tendency of late years to overlook, in a measure, this department of the game. The reason for this, perhaps, is that there is too much practice at the nets, and, as a result, there is no opportunity of fielding the ball.

'What about a player securing his Blue? Of course, the first trial means everything to a man. If he should not come off, there is not much chance for his being included in the team, for that year at least. Yes, he is afforded another chance in the trial matches, but he is generally so anxious then that he is unable to do himself full justice. A player "funks" it, if I may so express myself. Then the captain remarks: "What use would it be to play that man? He's too nervous." The result is he has to wait for another year.

'No, I cannot say there is much to choose between Oxford and Cambridge as regards the play generally. The batting, however, is very different, although, personally, I prefer that shown by the Light Blues. It appears to me to possess more taking style. Why is that? Well, I really cannot say, unless it is in consequence of there being less coaching at Oxford than at Cambridge.

'There are better bowlers produced at Oxford. Why is that? I suppose the ground at Fenner's is better adapted, and is easier than the Parks at Cambridge. The bowlers meet with greater success at practice, and consequently do not lose heart, and persevere. That is the only explanation I can give of the matter.

'County cricket? Oh, I think that is very good indeed, as a rule; although there is a proviso to be added. That is, that I consider it is beginning to be looked upon in a too serious manner, and is being made too much of a business character.

'The counties? On their season's all-round form, I think that Surrey is the best team. Here, also, I might add — upon a good wicket. Yorkshire, on the other hand, are the best team upon a bad wicket. Another thing is, that I consider if Richardson were taken out of the Surrey team, they would drop back considerably. Richardson is a grand bowler, and in his absence the county eleven would suffer an almost irretrievable loss. Of course, the same may be said of others beyond Surrey. For instance, if you were to take Mold out of the Lancashire team, the result would be the same. No, I do not think Yorkshire would be affected in the same manner if any one particular bowler was withdrawn. They have a first-class reserve to fall back upon, and are in fact a finer, all-round batting, bowling and fielding side.'

Australian cricket was then touched upon by the Prince.

'The Antipodean eleven playing in England are a very good side,' he remarked. 'They are very good all round, but their batting, as a whole, is superior to their bowling. Still, they have been very successful in their engagements, haven't they? Yes, I should say they are a better team than any other I have seen with one exception, that of the bowling of the 1888 eleven. At that time C. T. B. Turner and Ferris were at their best.'

'Let me see, I think G. H. S. Trott coached you a little when you first came to England?' I remarked.

'No,' was the smiling reply, 'there's not an atom of truth in that report. Yes, I see it has been stated as a fact in certain quarters, but you may deny it *in toto*. What really happened was this: when I came across from India, I visited the Oval in company with my tutor. The match then being played was Surrey *v.* the Australians. We were invited into the pavilion, and Mr Alcock very kindly introduced several members of the Colonial eleven to me. Percy McDonnell, C. T. B. Turner and G. H. S. Trott were amongst the number. They chatted to me upon cricket matters for a few moments, but I received no hints whatever. How the idea first gained ground I am unable to say; but it is utter nonsense to imagine for a moment that I was then assisted in any way by Trott.'

So a very pretty romance woven round the appearance of the young Prince against his former mentor at Manchester was exploded in a moment. No doubt a chance remark first started the story, and other details were supplied as it went the round.

Then, as a recollection of the incident at the University match crossed my mind, I questioned the Prince upon the subject; whether he thought the tactics of the Cambridge captain were justified under the conditions governing the play, and so on.

'No,' he opined, 'I cannot say that I think it was necessary to pursue such a course. They did not require to prevent the follow on, and, I think, would have done better had they allowed the Oxonians to continue batting. It was, however, simply an error of judgment, for no doubt the Cambridge captain was of the opinion that the wicket would crumble as play went on, and the side having the fourth innings would be at a disadvantage.

'Instead of that, however, I believe the wicket improved, and was better on the third day than the second. So you see their only excuse for sending down wides and no balls was gone. No, I cannot say I think a larger number of runs to render a "follow on" necessary is required. The present number (120) I think is quite sufficient for all practical purposes, and I would not recommend its increase to 150, 180 or 200.

'Public school cricket? Yes, I think it pretty fair when taken upon the average. Of course, I only know of Dulwich, Harrow and Uppingham. Harrow is, undoubtedly, the superior school out of the three I have named. Why? Because they are well coached there, and many of the masters are very fine players. Take Mr A. C. MacLaren for instance. He is a master at Harrow, and no doubt his example and style exercise a good effect upon the boys.

'What style of batting should I recommend? I should advise any young player to follow up the style, under capable coaching, that comes to him naturally. I cannot say I am an advocate for stonewalling, but every player finds it necessary to exhibit a certain degree of caution at times. There is no reason why a batsman, however, should try to score at the expense of getting out, and simply to earn the applause of a certain section of the public.

'The showy player may be cheered by those who simply visit a match for the express purpose of witnessing rapid scoring, and who do not care or know anything about the more delicate side of the game. I certainly do not believe in "playing to the gallery", neither do I believe in making the game unnecessarily slow. A player should endeavour to strike the happy medium.

'The method of the county championship? I think it was a right and generous recognition of merit when the new counties were included in the running, and it has made the struggle keener. Oh, yes, I have heard that several advocate some of the older counties being dropped, but I do not favour such a suggestion.

'Sussex, for instance, has a very dangerous side. For one thing, we never know when we are beaten, and we have this season accomplished some very fine performances — some that other counties would find difficult to surpass. In the Whit-week we were set over 200 when we followed on against Gloucester and Hampshire. Yet, at the finish, we were only robbed of victory by the call of time.

'Again, when we met Oxford University we had over 380 runs to get, and only about three hours and three-quarters to do it in. Still, we were within 18 of the required number when stumps were drawn. Unfortunately, we have been afflicted this year by an epidemic of bad fielding, easy catches being missed time after time. I am unable to say why this has been the case; a team cannot maintain one standard of excellence in each of their engagements; but when you find the best men offenders in this respect, you can put it down to sheer bad luck for the side.'

From county cricket we then passed to play generally, in India.

'There was not much good cricket there while I was at home', said the Prince. 'It has, however, greatly advanced of late, judging by the statements of Lord Hawke and Lord Harris. The Parsees have improved considerably in particular. Naturally, the visits of English elevens have given in the past, and will give in the future, a great impetus to the game. But there is a great disadvantage which the native players have to contend against — that is the absence of professional bowlers or coaches. J. T. Hearne, I believe, is the only player who visits India at the present time, although I think a Surrey man went out a few years back to coach the Parsees.

'Why are there no professionals there? One reason is that the whole of the grounds there are more or less public. Then there is a little coaching obtainable from any amateur player of English nationality near, although I am afraid that is not worth much in the majority of instances.

'Another matter that retards cricket in India is that it is impossible to play much during the rainy season, and not at all during the height of the summer. During the season I first mentioned it is impossible to know when heavy rain may fall, and although we, as schoolboys, played at any time, adults do not take the same view of the situation.

'Cricket is played, as a rule, during the winter. It is just comfortable then, something like a warm English spring day. It is, however, chilly in the morning up till about ten o'clock, when the sun commences to make itself felt, then hot up to six o'clock. At night it is really quite frosty. So you may judge from that that cricket in India has to be played under considerable disadvantages.'

A recollection of seeing the Prince in football costume while at Cambridge next provoked a question from me upon the subject.

'Yes,' he replied, 'I played football at Cambridge until I hurt my knee, then I thought it time to give it up. Association at first, and

Rugby afterwards, as I cared for it much more than the dribbling game; my knee gave way, however, at Association.

'Which do I consider the better game? Rugby, certainly. It is possible to get up your interest in even a bad game under that code; but under the other, the play must be very good indeed to repay watching it.

'Another thing is, I consider Rugby far safer from a player's point of view. You may get a scratch of a bruise, but in Association, if you are kicked or thrown, the injury is of a far more lasting character.

'Do I go in for athletics? Not much now, but I am very fond of shooting. Cycling? Yes, I cycle a little, and I have two American bicycles in the pavilion now. I am very fond of tennis and racquets. In fact, at one time I played the former very much better than I did cricket. Yes' (in reply to an incredulous smile on my part), 'I assure you it is a fact.'

'And I believe you bowl a little?' I remarked, as I rose to leave the Prince.

'Yes, I can bowl a little. In fact, I was very successful when I first commenced playing for Sussex. Now, however, Mr Murdoch does not care to put me on, as he is afraid I should spoil my batting. Mr Stoddart, of Middlesex, is not put on to bowl, I believe from the same cause, so we sympathize with each other for the harsh treatment of our respective captains. My style? I should describe it as being a slow medium, with a break from the off.'

Then, as a final question, I asked the Prince if he could tell me how he had been so successful at such an early period of his career.

'Luck,' was his laughing response. 'I commence my practice very early. I am shooting through the winter, and so keep myself fit, and in April I am at the nets. But luck is everything with a cricketer. If he has that — and a little skill — he has little to fear.'

The following interesting letter from Prince Ranjitsinhji will bring this interview to an appropriate conclusion:

To the Editor of the *Strand Magazine*   August 1st, 1896

Dear Sir,

I think it only right to inform you that my late principal and friend, Mr Chester Macnaghten, was the first and chief agent in making me fond of English outdoor sports — cricket and racquets principally. I have always been grateful to him for it, and I take this the first opportunity of correcting statements in several papers of my having commenced playing these games in England in 1888. I was much pained to hear of his untimely death some months ago, or else I should have been able to get much interesting information about the Rajkumar College and my early schooldays. I take this opportunity also of thanking the British public for the very kind way in which they have always received me on all grounds, and that has in no small measure conduced to my success in cricket. Trusting that I have not encroached too much on your valuable space, I remain

       Yours truly,
       Ranjitsinhji

               Strand Magazine 1896

10

Cricket Etiquette in India

Clement Scott

'Ranjitsinhji.' There ! after several fruitless efforts, I have spelt the Indian Prince's name at last. It cost me some trouble, but the task which has weighed on my mind for some time is now fairly accomplished. And what, you will ask, have I to say about this splendid cricketer? Only this, that the recent discussions in which Prince Ranjitsinhji's name has occurred as to whether he should play in this match or that, whether he should represent the English gentlemen against the players, and so on, remind me that I have something very serious to say on the subject of the etiquette of cricket as practised in India. When I arrived in Bombay in the winter of 1892, I found that gloriously beautiful city literally cricket mad. Bombay is celebrated for its wide stretches of grass or common land between the city and the sea, and every square patch of the common not occupied by the residents who camp out during the hot weather, finding it more convenient to be dwellers in tents than to be lessees of furnished houses, was seized upon by the little Indian boys in order to practise cricket. The sight delighted me, and my cricket-loving heart went out to the smart little natives, who had at any rate learned something from their rulers in the England far away, and one of the fruits of our power in commercial Bombay was an evident love of our manly games. It is well, thought I, that England has induced the rich natives to send their sons to be educated in England, to persuade them to take degrees at Oxford and Cambridge, to go up to the Bar, to walk the hospitals, and so on, and it is as well also that the cricket mania has extended to 'beautiful Bombay'.

I was lucky enough to be in Bombay when Lord Hawke's team played against the Parsees, and I was present on the Gymkhana ground when the Parsees gave the Englishmen a good beating. I have seldom seen a better eleven than that of the young and active Parsees who beat Lord Hawke's team in the first match at Bombay. They batted well, they bowled well, and in the field they were as active as cats. But the match between the Englishmen and the Parsees revealed to me a very curious social code existing in Bombay, and doubtless all over India, in connection with the game of cricket. In England at any local cricket match, whether on a village green or in the squire's park, if the squire happened to be playing, or the squire's son, or an officer resident in the neighbourhood, or the parson, or the local solicitor, it would surely be considered very snobbish if all classes in the cricket field did not sit down together at one common meal in the cricket tent. It is no more 'infra dig.' for the gentry to break bread with the artisan, or the tradesman, than for the lady of the house to 'lead off' with the butler, or the Lord of the Manor with the lady's maid at a servants' ball.

But such customs as these do not prevail, I am sorry to say, in India. On the occasion of which I am speaking the captain of the Parsees' eleven happened to be a Cambridge graduate. His father was one of the wealthiest merchants in Bombay. In England and at college he had freely mixed with the best and most aristocratic people, but at home, in his native town of Bombay, this Cambridge graduate and all his companions in the cricket field were not allowed to break bread with the Englishmen or to enter any English club, merely because their skins were dark, and they were descended from the ancient Persian stock known as Parsees.

Here were these Parsee gentlemen and cricketers invited to play with Englishmen on the ground of an English athletic club, but were not allowed to enter the doors of the club on any consideration whatever. In fact the cricket field was divided into two sections, one for the Europeans and one for the natives, and no native dared to be seen in the European Section. Joking apart, it was a case of black and white. When the luncheon hour arrived, the English team went into the Gymkhana club-house, and the Parsees went off to their own tents and messed alone. The inconsistency of this proceeding fairly astonished me. In England the whites and blacks of every creed and nationality would dine together in college hall, or in the halls of the various inns of court as students. In England, Indians and Parsees would not be shunned in any kind of society, and yet in India a wide line of distinction is drawn between the native and the European.

But the anomaly did not end here. During the cricket festival a splendid entertainment was given to the cricketers, and all the distinguished Europeans resident at, or visitors in Bombay, by a wealthy and distinguished Parsee lady who lives in a palace on Malabar Hill. On this occasion the Governor-General of Bombay (Lord Harris, a celebrated cricketer), with all the English cricket team, was present, and decorated with garlands of Tuber roses by the Parsee ladies. I had the honour of an invitation also, and I remember well that to me was presented a specially constructed necklet of sweet-smelling flowers, with which I was invested by some very handsome Parsee girls in token of their admiration for some compliment I had paid in print to their courteous and highly-gifted race. And yet you will scarcely believe me when I say that although our hostess and her husband who invited us all, from the Governor-General downwards, to Malabar Hill, though sometimes invited on formal occasions to Government House, were not permitted to enter the doors of any club-house in Bombay, and I can assure you that the lawn of the Bombay Yacht Club by the side of the sea is the rendezvous of all rank and fashion in Bombay! Nay, more! Our kindly hostess told me that although when in London during one celebrated season she entertained right royally the best people and the most aristocratic in the land, at home in Bombay not one of those she entertained in London was allowed to return the compliment by asking her even as a guest to tea in the Bombay Yacht Club.

But even this was not all! The father of this same highly-educated and distinguished Parsee lady had, out of his own pocket, bought some valuable land, and devoted it to an English club for athletic purposes on one of the loveliest spots in Bombay. But though bought, built and furnished by him, his own daughter and his other children were not allowed to enter the grounds that their father had purchased, because it was an English club, and they were Parsees.

When I expressed my astonishment at this grave inconsistency to Anglo-Indians, they told me that I knew nothing about the subject, that it was far more important than I imagined, and 'that a line must be drawn somewhere'. I was equally astonished when I was told that it was 'very bad form' to be seen driving about Bombay with a Parsee gentleman, one of the most intellectual companions I have ever met in any country. For that, however, I cared nothing. With my Parsee friend I went to the Towers of Joy and Silence, to a Parsee wedding, one of the most beautiful sights I have ever seen, and to a Parsee funeral, one of the saddest, particularly when we came to the 'corner of farewells', and the contents of the bier entered with the priests and attendants through that awful door, and the grim vultures swept down from the Tower of Silence, as the mourners were left alone weeping in the lovely flower garden. I was a 'passenger', no doubt, but I was a student of manners, and customs also, and some of the happiest hours I spent in Bombay were at the hospitable tables of my Parsee hosts, who before I left their splendid city, gave me a banquet at their own Parsee Club House, where I enjoyed a most delightful and memorable evening. Some day, perhaps, in the distant future the obstinate Anglo-Indian Conservatism will break down, and it will dawn upon the Anglo-Indian mind that a Parsee gentleman who can dine or lunch at Trinity College, Cambridge, with his fellow graduates and under-graduates, or at the Inner or Middle Temple, or Gray's Inn, with his fellow-cricketers in the Gymkhana Club at Bombay, and that similarly a gifted lady who has entertained Royalty and the highest aristocracy in London, and welcomed the Governor-General of Bombay at Malabar Hill, would do no dishonour to the afternoon teas and pleasant social gatherings at the Yacht Club at Bombay. Why should not social law bend in India as elsewhere? We have won India, we have Anglicized India; let us live with India.

Wheel of Life 1899

11

Lord's and its Literature

Alec Waugh

Rather wistfully on a late summer afternoon, at the close of the last match, we walked down the pavilion steps at Lord's. For eight months Lord's would be shut; we should pass by it on the 'bus, and the white seats of the mound would be empty. A few groundsmen would be pottering about; someone would be rolling the practice pitch. We should stand up on the 'bus as we go by, for one always does stand up on a 'bus as one passes Lord's, but no longer should we crane our necks to read the figures on the telegraph, or peer eagerly to distinguish the players, to see whether it is Hearne or Hendren that was still not out. The season was not over, of course; there was still the Scarborough festival, and the champion county had to meet England at the Oval. But these games were, after all, an anti-climax; for the true cricketer the season is at an end when the last ball is bowled at Lord's.

At first we were not too sorry. Four months is a long time at even the best of games, and it was pleasant to think that in a fortnight's time we should be getting out our football jerseys and putting new bars upon our boots. It would be great fun going down to the Old Deer Park for the trial games and meeting our old friends. Soon the season would be really started, and every Tuesday morning would bring the yellow card: 'You have been selected to play for "A" XV *v.* Exiles or Harlequins "A" or Old Felstedians.' And then on Saturday we should let the District Railway carry us out to strange places — Northfields and Boston Manor — places whose names are familiar to us on the tubes, but are distant in the imagination, like Chimborazo or Cotopaxi, places where we never expect anyone to live. For members of an 'A' XV life is always an adventure; and then, when the game is over, and we sit back in the carriage lazy and tired, it is amusing to read through the soccer results in the evening paper and learn that at Stamford Bridge 40,000 people saw 'Cock outwit the custodian and net the ball in the first three minutes'. And afterwards we go on to Simpson's and meet our friends from the other games, and eat a great deal of roast beef, and drink a great deal of beer. Oh, yes, there are many compensations for the loss of summer! The autumn passed quickly and pleasantly, but towards Christmas there came, as there always must come, an evening when we sat over the fire and remembered suddenly that it was four months since we had held a cricket bat, that May was still a long way off, and the procession of Saturdays seemed endless. On such an evening we take down *Wisden* and pore over the old scores long after our usual bedtime.

For *Wisden* is the cricketer's bible. The uninitiated make mock. 'What is it,' they say, 'but a record? We can understand your wanting to look at the scores of matches that you have seen, that will recall to you pleasant hours in pleasant company. But what possible enjoyment can you get out of reading figures and accounts of matches that you have never been to? It is no doubt an admirable work of reference for the statistician, but as literature, as a thing that is read for pleasure! Why, it reminds us of the half-pay major who spent his evenings reading the Army List of 1860!'

It is hard to explain. In the same way that the letters x and y possess a significance for the mathematician, so for the cricketer these bare figures are a symbol and a story. We can clothe the skeleton with flesh. We can picture the scene. We know exactly how it happened. We know what the score-board looked like when that seventh wicket fell, we can gauge the value of Strudwick's 5 not out, and when we read 'Ducat lbw b Woolley 12' we know exactly the emotion of the man sitting at the end of the free seats below the telegraph. 'If only Ducat can stay in,' he had thought, 'Surrey may win yet. There are several people who might stop at the other end while he gets the runs.' But the umpire's finger rose, and we know the depression with which he wrote on the thumb-marked score-card 'lbw b Woolley 12', and then pulled himself together and prepared to watch in a dream 'untroubled of hope' the inevitable end delayed for a few minutes by Smith and Rushby.

And, as we study the figures of Warner's many centuries, we are sitting again on the mound, looking into that haze which covers the ground shortly after five o'clock in August, with the sun blazing on to us from the left of the pavilion, and to shield our eyes we have bent the match-card beneath our hats.

How many hours during the year, I wonder, must we spend over our *Wisden*? A great many surely, so many indeed that we cannot help thinking how small is the literature of cricket. Only two shelves in a whole library. There are one or two novels, *Willow the King*, A. A. Milne's *The Day's Play*, a few of Mr Lucas's Essays, the complete works of P. F. Warner, W. J. Ford's *Middlesex Cricket*, Lord Harris's *Lord's and the MCC*, a few volumes of reminiscence, one or two textbooks, P. G. Wodehouse's delightful *Mike*, and *The Hambledon Men* — very little, really, when one thinks of the literature that hunting and fishing have produced.

Hardly any poetry has been written about the game. There is a quantity of verse, pleasant jingly stuff of the drinking-song variety, the best of it valedictory, such as Andrew Lang's *Beneath the Daisies Now They Lie*. But the few attempts that have been made at serious poetry have not been fortunate. Edward Cracroft Lefroy, for example, to whom cricket appealed chiefly as an aesthetic spectacle, included in his catalogue of the physical attributes of a bowler the

> Elbows apt to make the leather spin
> Up the slow bat and round the unwary shin,

which is not only poor verse but proves on the part of the author an inadequate knowledge of the no-ball law.

But perhaps verse is not a happy medium through which to express an enjoyment of cricket. Phrases like 'unwary shin' will intrude themselves, and, although Pindar used to celebrate with equally appropriate ardour the feats of generals and of athletes, the very idea of commemorating in heroic couplets Woolley's two great innings at Lord's seems ridiculous. We have grown so accustomed to reading accounts of cricket matches in the prose style of the sporting press that any other treatment is impossible. Perhaps Mr Masefield will one day attempt an epic of the fifth Test Match at the Oval, but I doubt if it would be a success. It would be a quaint performance, as though one were to walk down the Strand in court dress of Jacobean cut. The jargon of a cricket report is unsuited to heroic verse, but it is indispensable. If, for instance, we were informed that Hendren,

Snared into over-confidence, stept back,
Swinging his bat as though he would eclipse
The thundered violence of Albert Trott.
Yet had he not correctly judged the flight
Of the quick spinning ball. Aghast he heard
Behind his back the rattle of the stumps,

we should not be very much the wiser. We should prefer to learn of such a tragedy in straightforward narrative: 'Hendren hooked Mailey to the on-boundary twice in succession; but, in an attempt to repeat the stroke to a ball that was pitched further up to him and that went away with the arm, he was clean bowled.'

Indeed, A. E. Housman's *On an Athlete Dying Young* is the best serious poem that can be said to interpret any side of cricket, and that poem is written to a runner. But it is universal, for it contains the tragedy of all professional sport:

Now you will never swell the rout
Of lads that wore their honours out,
Of runners whom renown outran
And the fame died before the man.

Contemporary reference to any cricketer no longer playing is made in the past tense. 'Tarrant was . . .'; and how many of the enthusiastic Ovalites who recall so eagerly the great days of 'Locky and Brocky' pause to consider that their hero is still alive?

The lack of prose literature dealing with cricket is, however, as surprising as it is deplorable. For a hundred years ago the game must have been able to supply an intriguing background for a novel. Lord's was like Paddington recreation ground, and, when there was no match, the public were allowed to hire a pitch there for a shilling, a sum that included the use of stumps, bat and ball: there were no mowing machines then, and the grass was kept down by a flock of sheep, which was penned up on match days. On Saturdays four or five hundred sheep were driven on to the ground on their way to the Smithfield Market. And then half a dozen small boys would run out and pick out any long grass or thick tufts that were still left. It is not surprising that there were shooters then. And never since the days of the gladiators can there have been such wholesale bribery and corruption as there was in the days of Lord Frederick Beauclerk.

Enormous bets were made. Matches were played for stakes of one thousand guineas a side – in those days no small sum, and professionals found it hard to live on their pay; indeed, they made little effort to; and in big matches where a lot of money was at stake it was not uncommon to find one side trying to get themselves out while their opponents were trying to give them easy balls to make runs off. And Lord Harris tells a story of how two professionals had a dispute at one of the annual general meetings at Lord's, and in the presence of the noble lords of the MCC such questions as 'Who sold the match at Nottingham?' and 'Who would bowl at anything but the wicket for Kent?' were bandied about to the consternation, Lord Harris says, 'of some of those present who had lost their money contrary to all calculation on the matches referred to'! There were few newspaper reporters then, and things could be done at Old Trafford news of which would come tardily to Lord's.

The only persons who appear to have remained incorruptible during these early days are, strangely enough, the umpires. Perhaps they put too high a premium on their honesty, and the bookmakers found it cheaper to have dealings with the players, or perhaps there was a general conspiracy of silence, no one being sufficiently without blame to cast a stone. At any rate, the interpreters of the law seem to have given satisfaction, and they can have had no easy time. For it was during these years that the code of laws under which we play to-day was compiled. And it was compiled in a most haphazard fashion. No committee sat over a table and weighed every possible contingency and interpretation of the laws. The authorities were worthy fellows, but lazy and unimaginative. They drew up a rough code and waited for things to happen. If any particular practice began to cause a nuisance they were prepared to put a stop to it. In the meantime let the wheel turn.

It did turn, and often with uncomfortable complications. At one time, for instance, in the days when there were only two stumps, a hole was cut between and beneath the wickets, and when a batsman completed a run he had to pop his bat into this hole. If the bowler succeeded in popping the ball there before the bat the batsman was run out. It was found, however, that bat and ball would often arrive in the hole simultaneously, with sad results to the bowler's fingers; and often enough, when a fieldsman had anticipated the bat, the defeated player would take what revenge he could by driving his bat upon the knuckles of his conqueror. After a certain number of fingers had been broken the authorities thought fit to substitute for the hole the present popping-crease.

Much the same thing happened in the case of leg-before-wicket. As pads were not then invented, and as the ball was delivered with much rapidity, it had never seemed likely that any batsman would, with deliberate intention, place his unprotected legs in the path of a hard ball. But one day the cricket world was thrown into consternation by the tactics of one Ring, who placed his body in front of the wicket in such a way that it was impossible for him to be bowled out. His shins became very sore, but his score became very large. This gallant act of self-sacrifice for the good of his side did not win the admiration it deserved; it was described by a contemporary writer as 'a shabby way of taking advantage of a bowler', so that when Tom Taylor adopted the same tactics the bowlers 'declared themselves beaten': a leg-before-wicket rule was drawn up, and another opportunity for Spartan courage was lost to an effeminate age.

The laws were altered to suit each fresh development. And when we remember the manifold and barbarous practices of that day, we cannot but shudder when we try to imagine what fearsome and horrible atrocities must have taken place before the law about 'obstruction of the field' was invented. Cannot we picture some burly butcher skying the ball to point and then, in order to save his wicket, rushing at the fieldsman and prostrating him with his bat? Cannot we see the batsman at the other end effecting a half-nelson upon the bowler who was about to catch his partner? The laws of Rome were not built up without bloodshed, nor were the laws of cricket. What opportunities for humorous narrative have been lost!

If only there had been some naturalistic writer who would have collected laboriously all these stories and made a novel of them! If Zola had been an Englishman we could have forgiven him his endless descriptions of gold-beaters and agricultural labourers, if one of the Macquarts had been a professional cricketer and one of those interminable novels had reconstructed the cricket world of his day. If only the caprice of things had allowed George Moore to spend his early years near a cricket field instead of a racing stable!

But even those few novelists who have included cricket in their panorama of the period appear to be woefully ignorant of the management of the game. What a sad mess Dickens made of it, and how well he might have done it! How entertaining Mr Winkle might have been behind the wicket: what sublime decisions he would have given as an umpire! But, no; Muggleton play Dingley Dell and the great Podder 'blocked the doubtful balls, missed the bad ones, took the good ones and sent them flying to all parts of the field', which is surely the most quaint procedure that any batsman has ever followed; and as a climax Dingley Dell give in and allow the superior prowess of all Muggleton, apparently before they have had their own innings – an action without precedent in the annals of the game.

And so it has happened that our one complete picture of the Homeric days has come to us not from the novelists, the official recorders of the hour, but from John Nyren, who wrote without any thought of posterity a guide book for the young cricketer. There are some books that, like wine, acquire qualities with the passage of time, and for us to-day *The Young Cricketer's Tutor* possesses a value that it did not have for those for whose service it was written. To the young blood of 1840 it was merely a manual, a sort of field service regulations; to-day it is a piece of literature; it interprets a period; it reveals a personality.

As we read John Nyren's advice we can see how the game was played in 1820 on rough pitches, without pads, in top hats, and with a courage the depth of which may be gauged from the instructions that he gives to long-stop:

> When the ball does not come to his hand with a fair bound, he must go down upon his right knee with his hands before him: then in case these should miss it, his body will form a bulwark and arrest its farther progress.

In those days we learn that spectators were patient folk who sat on backless seats, drank porter, smoked long pipes and made bets about the match. There was leisure then, and John Nyren believed that the batsman should wait to make his runs till bowler and fieldsmen were exhausted:

> I would strongly recommend the young batsman to turn his whole attention to stopping: for by acting this part well, he becomes a serious antagonist to the bowler; who, when he sees a man coming in that he knows will stop all his length-balls with ease, is always in a degree disheartened. He has no affection for such a customer. Besides, in this accomplishment lies the distinction between the scientific player and the random batsman.

The random batsman: it is an adjective we find often in *The Young Cricketer's Tutor*. For Nyren had an intense hatred of unskilled success. Cricket was to him an art the technique of which could only be mastered after an elaborate apprenticeship. He distrusted the short cut, and we find him the most bitter opponent of the young idea. He is the eternal Tory of yesterday, of to-day and of tomorrow. And he is very human to us as he stands on the brink of change uttering his solemn warning. For it was towards the end of his career that round-arm bowling was introduced, and it is hard to realize the revolution this caused in the world of sport. It made as much stir and roused as many bad feelings in its own province as its contemporary the Reform Bill. This bowling was described as the 'new march of intellect—style', and in 1827 three matches were played between Sussex and England to test the merits of the two methods. The county won the first two matches, and the nine professionals on the England side were so incensed that they signed a formal petition 'that we, the undersigned, do agree that we will not play the third match between all England and Sussex unless the Sussex bowlers bowl fair — that is abstain from throwing'. And the great Mr Ward, when asked his opinion, said, 'I can only say cricketers are a peaceable class of men. With this bowling I never see a match that might not end in a wrangle.'

John Nyren was its most fierce opponent, and it is rather pathetic to read his violent and ineffectual protest. This invention would ruin cricket. He saw a new game that would lack the grace and skill of the game as he and his friends had played it. The ball would come so fast that the batsman would not have time to prepare for it.

> The indifferent batsman possesses as fair a chance of success as the most refined player. And the reason for this is obvious, because from the random manner of delivering the ball it is impossible for the fine batsman to have time for that finesse and delicate management which so peculiarly distinguished the elegant manoeuvring of the chief players who occupied the field about eight, ten or more years ago.

And he goes on to state his belief that if the present system persisted a few years longer 'the elegant and scientific game of cricket will develop into a mere exhibition of rough, coarse horseplay'.

What would he say if he could return to the pavilion at the Oval, and see Hitch bowling at how many miles is it an hour? and Hendren hooking him to the square-leg boundary? And the last paragraph of his protest is that of every man since the beginning of time who has seen his day pass, his heroes overthrown, and a rash, irreverent generation in their place.

> I can use my eyes [he writes], I can compare notes and points in the two styles of playing, and they who have known me will bear testimony that I have never been accustomed to express myself rashly.

A forlorn figure, trusting so simply in the permanence of a static world.

It is sad to think how quickly that world has passed, and how effectively the machinery of our industrial system has already taken cricket to itself. Nyren's game is no longer an entertainment for a few. It has become part of the national life, and probably, if the Bolshevists get their way here, it will be nationalized with the cinema and the theatre and association football. It is hard to find much in common between the old men who smoked long pipes and drank strong porter and watched Mr Haygarth bat three hours for sixteen runs, and the twenty thousand who flock to the Middlesex and Surrey match because the newspapers have told them to, and who barrack any batsman who plays through a maiden over. Indeed, on those big days, I do not think that you find there the survival of the old enthusiast. You will find him rather on a cold morning shivering at the back of the mound, on the third day of a match that is certain to be a draw, when there are only a couple of hundred spectators. No one knows why he goes there. He will be very cold. He will not see particularly good cricket. Professional batsmen will play for a draw in the most professional manner. The fielding towards four o'clock will grow slack, and half an hour before the end the captains will decide that it is no good going on, and that they might just as well draw stumps. Your old man in the mound knows that this must happen. But he goes there all the same, and at three o'clock he buys an evening paper to read an account of the match and he sees that the reporter says, 'Hardstaff was beaten and bowled by a yorker'. And the old man will chuckle, knowing that it was a half volley and that Hardstaff hit over it. And in January, when he reads through his *Wisden*, he will put a tick against that match, with the others that he has seen, and he will add them up and find that he has spent five more days at Lord's this year than he did the year before. He will remember how his grandfather used to talk to him about Fuller Pilch; and he will smile, knowing the superiority of Hendren. And he will continue to watch cricket as his grandfather watched it on cold days as well as warm, when a draw is certain and when there is a chance of a great finish. One day he believes that the professional batsmen will fail, that there will be a collapse and a sensational victory, and only two hundred people will have seen it. He knows that many matches are played in the year and that very few of them yield great finishes, and he knows that the only way to make sure of the big occasion is to go there whenever stumps are pitched. And it is of him that we must think when we would reconstruct the cricket world of 1830.

For Nyren was the Homer of cricket and the Homeric days have passed. In 1922 the soil is no longer virgin. Cricket is a different game, and for the novelist it is less intriguing. There is no betting, there is no dishonesty, and, though we hear whispers of the questionable diplomacy of the northern leagues, it would hardly be possible to invent a cricket story with a credible villain. Nat Gould found no difficulty in writing a hundred novels of the racecourse; it is extremely difficult to write one of the cricket field. No scope is provided for dramatic narrative. Cricket in the lives of most of us is a delightful interlude — pleasant hours in pleasant company; and we do not take our success or failure very seriously. At school it is important: caps and cups are at stake, positions of authority go to the most proficient; and it so happens that the only great cricket book of recent times is a school story, P. G. Wodehouse's *Mike.* But apart from school it is hard to find in cricket a motive of sufficient strength to allow of the development and presentation of dramatic action. On the racecourse large sums of money are at stake. On the success of a horse may depend the future happiness of the hero and the heroine. But I doubt if the result of a cricket match has in recent years ever involved much more than the temporary loss or gain of personal prestige. In *Willow the King* J. C. Snaith chose a cricket match as the setting for a summer idyll, but the author of *Brooke of Covenden* would hardly rank that story highly among his other very considerable achievements. The moment for the great cricket novel has passed: irrecoverably perhaps. And in the winter months we find ourselves returning as of old to a few books of reminiscence and to our long yellow-backed, tattered row of *Wisden*, and of the two we find *Wisden* the more companionable.

London Mercury 1922

12

Cricket Writer

Gerald Pawle

At precisely five minutes to eight in the morning, my father would leave the house to catch his train to London, and soon after five o'clock another train would deposit him back at Bishop's Stortford. On summer evenings I used to wait impatiently for him to come and bowl to me in the net on our lawn. He spent most of the day in a gloomy building in Copthall Avenue where men on high stools entered figures in large ledgers. As a naturally inquisitive small boy I tried to discover what he actually did there from Monday to Friday, and whether he enjoyed it. According to my mother the Stock Exchange was not a place for enjoyment. The work, it appeared, was mainly mathematical and concerned stocks and shares, which you bought or sold. Enjoyment was something entirely reserved for the evenings and the weekends.

I decided that when I grew up I would work at something I enjoyed all the time, and from the moment when I had an article accepted by my prep-school magazine my mind was made up. 'I am going to be a journalist,' I announced.

My father, who regarded all journalists except those employed on *The Times* and *Horse and Hound* as a rather raffish lot, socially several stages below stockbrokers and jobbers, did his best to discourage me. 'You are going on to the Stock Exchange', he said firmly, but any possibility of being press-ganged into the family firm was dramatically removed by Mr Clarence Hatry.* When the smoke and flames of that spectacular intrusion into the life of the City had cleared away, the Stock Exchange counted its casualties and my father was among them.

* An ingenious and over-confident financier. In 1930 he was sentenced to fourteen years' imprisonment for forgery and frauds which cost municipalities and individuals some £13,500,000.

I was then at a public school in Yorkshire. Soon after I went there I began bombarding the local daily newspaper with reports of the school's activities. For over a thousand years St Peter's, York, had been a centre of learning, but I arrived in an era when it was better known as a famous cricket nursery. The academic imbalance was partially redressed by contemporaries like C. Northcote Parkinson and Christopher Hill, but the readers of the *Yorkshire Herald* were reminded of this only on speech day. For the rest of the year the name of St Peter's figures mainly in the sporting columns, and when the *Herald* gave me my head I branched out with reckless confidence, supplying them in the summer months not only with reports of my school's cricket matches but, much more presumptuously, with outspoken comments on England's Test teams and the chances of Cambridge in the Varsity match. In the winter, bereft of cricket, I had to cast my net wider, and the East Riding farmers, who formed the main part of the paper's readership, had to put up with long dissertations on squash rackets. On one occasion, when the sports editor was faced with an ugly double-column gap on the back page, they were even regaled with a review of the origins of real tennis, which was not played anywhere in the East Riding – or any other Riding, for that matter. When the Hatry crash came and there was no more money with which to pay the school fees, I bundled up my precious press cuttings and sent them to the *Yorkshire Post* with a request for an interview.

By today's standards the *Yorkshire Post* had a tiny circulation but its influence and standing in the industrial community it served – and far beyond the confines of the West Riding – were immense. Arthur Mann, its distinguished editor, who summoned me to Leeds, was an austere and alarming figure who spoke in a quiet, chilling voice. As he cross-examined me about my hopes and ambitions my self-confidence drained away.

'I see you are the editor of your school magazine. I have a copy here. It does not seem a very intellectual journal,' he said severely. 'Your own interests would seem to lie chiefly in the sporting field.' I had discovered that Mr Mann himself was not greatly interested in sport apart from racing, but his board included several eminent figures who were keen on cricket, including a former Yorkshire and England batsman, T. L. Taylor. Now uneasily aware of my intellectual deficiencies, I thought it was no good offering myself as a budding literary or art critic. Like most schoolboys in those days sport was the only subject on which I could write with any personal experience, and cricket was my favourite game.

'Cricket?' said Arthur Mann. 'That could be useful. We are short of people who understand about cricket at the moment. Are you agreeable to joining my staff at one pound a week? You are a fortunate young man to get an opportunity like this.'

In nearly ten years on his staff I saw him only once more, when he fractionally increased my salary to counter an offer from the *Morning Post*. 'It is a mistake to imagine, as so many young men like you do, that you would be better off in Fleet Street,' he said magisterially. 'There are many advantages in working for a newspaper like the *Yorkshire Post*.'

The advantages were certainly not financial, but in retrospect I led an idyllic existence. In those days the company published the morning paper, which boasted the impressive slogan 'Twixt Trent and Tweed'; an evening paper with a flourishing circulation which was alleged to pay most of the bills; a 'popular' daily, the *Leeds Mercury*, which just about paid its way; and a weekly paper, which definitely did not. I learned the craft of sub-editing on the evening paper, rising long before dawn when England were playing in Australia to 'sub' the splash story from Sydney or Melbourne. When the sports editor was satisfied that I was well grounded in all the more tedious chores inside the office, I was set free to serve my apprenticeship as a sports writer, covering cricket in the summer and Rugby football in winter.

As the fledgling second string at cricket I travelled with Yorkshire's second eleven to strange, uncompromising places like Castleford and Brighouse, Walsall and Chester-le-Street; to pleasant seaside grounds like Redcar, Colwyn Bay and Skegness; and to the vast empty arenas of Headingley, Bramall Lane (now only a stirring memory) and Old Trafford. There a handful of true enthusiasts would gather to inspect the budding Huttons, Washbrooks, Yardleys and Cranstons in their novice days. Occasionally they would get a glimpse of great players of the past still soldiering on in Minor County sides – like the immortal Sydney Barnes, bowling fast leg-breaks for Staffordshire well after his sixtieth birthday.

Since the appetite of Yorkshiremen for cricket news was insatiable, and the *Yorkshire Post* was their bible, they expected special coverage of many attractive fixtures which would receive scant attention from a provincial paper today. Gentlemen *v.* Players, the Varsity match, and Eton *v.* Harrow widened my field, but most of all I looked forward to Yorkshire's Championship games, which fell to me when the Test matches came round.

The procedure for covering a Yorkshire match differed widely from present-day methods, inevitably restricted by trade-union regulations, shortage of newsprint, and the falling value of the pound. Champion county year after year in the 'thirties, Yorkshire drew large and vociferous crowds; a far larger public in mill and dale waited eagerly for news of their achievements, and this was relayed by a posse of cricket writers who travelled with the side from May to September.

They had room to spread themselves, for nothing sold more papers than a Yorkshire cricket contents-bill. From noon onwards the newsboys invented fresh sensations daily. 'YORKSHIRE – AMAZING COLLAPSE!' they would proclaim if two wickets fell quickly; or 'SUTCLIFFE FAILS', if the idol of Pudsey was out for 49.

Writers from the national papers might arrive late at the ground, weave their elegant essays, and depart early, but most of the Yorkshire press party faced a far more arduous day. First they had to turn out a lengthy report for their evening paper, dictated every hour or so up to tea. After completing at least a column of this running commentary it was time to turn to a far more demanding task. With play still in progress one was expected to write a further column and a half of detached and critical comment for the morning paper. Ideally the last sentence of this would be finished as the final over was bowled.

This imposed few problems if the day's play drew peacefully to its close. If, however, the game suddenly came to life, possibly changing the whole balance of the struggle, everything already written might have to be recast.

In one respect we were luckier in those days. We were not personally responsible for the actual transmission of our 'copy', for perched at the back of the press-box, like sparrows on a branch with beaks wide open, were the messengers. As the typewriters clattered they waited to pounce and bear off to the nearest telephone the news of another Sutcliffe century, another bowling feat by Verity. When play ended for the day at, say, Sheffield, a messenger would snatch my morning paper story, enclose it in a large blue envelope labelled 'NEWS INTEL-LIGENCE – NOT TO BE DELAYED', and cycle to the railway station, where he would hand it to the guard. When the train reached Leeds it would be met by another messenger who would grab the envelope and pedal back to the impressive red-brick building in Albion Street where the sub-editors were waiting for it. If Yorkshire were playing farther afield, on some foreign ground like Hove or Bristol, one's report was typed on a Press Telegram form, franked with a yellow pass guaranteeing deferred payment, and entrusted to the local General Post Office. The GPO rarely let us down. Occasionally folio 10 would reach the office before folio 2, but a provincial morning paper went to press so late in those days that there always seemed to be time in hand.

Nowadays no union would allow a staff writer to produce two different reports for his employer for the same salary. It was, however, a form of slavery which I, for one, thoroughly enjoyed. Sometimes, when we were provided with a particularly decrepit telephonist, I used to wonder anxiously whether my graphic account would ever reach its destination. I comforted myself by reflecting that a predecessor, Mr A. W. Pullin ('Old Ebor'), must have had much more to worry about. Often he had to rely on pigeons to deliver his contributions. How many pigeons managed to get off the ground when shackled to one of Old Ebor's weighty commentaries I have never understood.

There was a glamour about the Yorkshire team of the 'thirties which set them apart from their opponents. Technically armed at all points, and reinforced by an unrelenting determination to destroy their enemies, they were the complete attacking machine. Often there were eight Test players in the side, all superb performers, and all characters in their own right. In undisputed command of this combative and brilliantly equipped force was Brian Sellers, spectacular fielder close to the wicket, and as great a character as any of them.

One of my special favourites was that great left-hander, Maurice Leyland. Cap at a jaunty angle he was, like Eddie Paynter from the other side of the Pennines, a batsman unmoved by disaster. He could bowl a Chinaman with deceptive innocence, and he was a beautiful mover and thrower in the deep field.

Maurice was also a humorist. On one occasion he and Herbert Sutcliffe shared a mammoth partnership against Worcestershire which defied constant bowling changes. Eventually the Worcester captain, Charles Lyttelton — later Governor-General of New Zealand — seized the ball. 'I'll show you how to break this stand,' he announced. With his very first delivery, which bounced twice and then shot to hit the base of the middle stump, he clean-bowled Sutcliffe.

To Leyland, standing amazed at the bowler's end, he said, 'What do you think of that, Maurice?'

'Well, skipper,' said Leyland drily, 'I reckon Herbert's a bit short of practice against your kind of bowling.'

Wherever Yorkshire played they made news. Their standards were so consistently high that if they lost a match in a fit of absentmindedness elderly members of the County Club would write indignant letters to the papers. In the nine years I spent in that great nursery of the game they won the Championship seven times, their final success being clinched on the very brink of war by Verity's brilliant bowling in the last two Championship matches of his life.

A few days later I walked through the red-brick archway in Albion Street for the last time, bound for Portsmouth and the lower deck of the Navy. Instinct told me that, whatever the course of the war, my pleasant days as a sporting journalist had come to an end. I never expected to write about cricket again.

A world war and thirty years later, during which I had been fully and diversely occupied with other forms of writing, the telephone rang at my home in Cornwall. It was E. W. Swanton. 'I wonder,' he said in his persuasive way, 'whether you could fit in some cricket reporting for us?'

I put forward a number of half-hearted excuses — that I was writing a book on Gibraltar; that Cornwall was far removed from the first-class cricket scene; and that, anyway, I would never be able to master all the changes in the game, particularly the new-fangled bonus points scheme which had just been introduced. A week later I found myself at Taunton for Somerset's match against my former heroes, Yorkshire.

Even in that friendly environment I felt I was in a different world from the one I had left behind in 1939. The laws of cricket had altered. So had the attitude of players, officials and spectators. On and off the field the dress and demeanour of the average county cricketer reflected a subtly changed society. It was, however, in the press-box that the march of time was most apparent. To my dismay the sturdy race of telephonist-messengers, with their flat caps and bicycle clips, had vanished without trace; nobody in the brave new world was anxious to do a day's work of this kind for a pound. So at half-past three on that first afternoon I dialled Fleet Street and introduced myself to a brisk, businesslike voice called 'Sports Desk'. 'Pawle at Taunton . . . Yorkshire versus Somerset,' I said defensively.

There was an ominous pause before the Voice said apologetically, 'Can you ring back in half an hour? We haven't quite worked it out. Space is a bit tight.'

This seemed odd. No one on the *Yorkshire Post* had ever told my messenger that space was tight. They merely cleared the decks by spiking anything which might have come in about Association football, bowls or speedway racing; they were not considered gentlemanly pursuits, anyway.

When I rang back, the anonymous voice issued a stream of meaningless directions. 'You'd better top and tail it today. Can you give us three-seven-two? Don't forget to let Manchester have it. Oh, and by the way, we'd better have a check-call, just in case.'

Not liking to mention that I did not understand a word of this I sought out Eric Hill, who was working in a semi-detached cubby-hole of the ramshackle, spider-infested region which still serves as Taunton's press-box. A former Somerset batsman, Hill was now a sports journalist of great experience and versatility, and he quickly converted my instructions into intelligible English. It appeared that *The Daily Telegraph* wished me to supply them with the middle of my report first, dictating precisely 245 words at the tea interval. At the close of play they wanted a general introduction of 105 words, followed by a further 70 which had to cover the last $2\frac{1}{2}$ hours of the day.

This complicated formula allowed the bulk of my report to be set in type before the pressure on the copy-takers, sitting in their cubicles in London with headphones at the ready, became really acute. When I had finished my last call to Fleet Street I then had to telephone my 'top-and-tail' to Manchester, where a different staff of sub-editors fashioned their own headlines for the Northern editions.

From the correspondent's point of view this ingenious system, made necessary by modern pressures on the paper's communications network, seemed fraught with alarming possibilities. What if the early hours of play were completely lacking in incident, and my precious 245 words had to be squandered on mediocrity? With only 70 words left, what would happen if Trueman did the hat-trick, and Yorkshire, going in late in the day, lost half their wickets for 29 before the close?

On that first evening of my return to cricket writing I finished my 'middle' story and sat despondently waiting for a bowler or batsman to perform some extraordinary feat which would wreck all my calculations. To my wonder and relief the hills beyond the ground were suddenly cloaked by a grey, weeping haze which rolled relentlessly forward, and the umpires brought proceedings to an end. I dictated my unsinspiring 'top-and-tail' to London. When I turned to Manchester I found to my alarm that I was dictating to a woman; but not only did she seem to know the names and initials of every player and every position on the field, she even knew all about bonus points and check-calls. 'You just ring up to see if they've lost your report,' she explained consolingly.

An hour afterwards I rang the sports desk in London and the same brisk voice asked if I had enjoyed my day. 'It's a bit different since I last did this sort of thing,' I ventured. 'I never had to write a report backwards for the *Yorkshire Post*. They didn't go in for this topping and tailing ...'

'Yes, I expect things have changed a bit since Lord Hawke's day,' he replied unfeelingly. 'You'll soon get used to it, though.'

Now, some 250 matches later, I am resigned to the social and technical reasons for changes which have made the cricket writer's task more demanding. I accept also the plethora of limited-over cricket and, less philosophically, the mindless uproar which so often debases Test Matches, Gillette Cup finals and even the peace of a Sunday afternoon at Glastonbury. It is a changed world, but in a County Championship match spread over three days, when a batsman has time to build an innings on firm foundations, and even a leg-break bowler can be given a chance to practise his enthralling craft, the essential character of the game still survives.

It still attracts men of sterling quality to its service, rewarding them far better for their efforts than in the days when the legendary Alec Skelding of Leicestershire risked all his meagre benefit money on a horse. It is still for the most part played in pleasant surroundings. And, best of all for the scribe returning to the field late in his days, there are friendships to be renewed — with spectators who were famous players in their time, and with umpires, scorers and groundsmen.

Checking on essential facts and figures the cricket reporter inevitably spends much time with the scorers, whose task, like our own, has become infinitely more complex with the arrival of commercial sponsorship, cash awards, and financial penalties. They work with electric calculators to determine over rates and run rates; they record the weather and the state of the pitch, the number of sixes hit, and the duration of individual innings and partnerships.

Several of them no longer use conventional scorebooks, relying instead on graph paper and innumerable dots and dashes. Practitioners of these arcane methods, of which Ted Lester of Yorkshire is a notable exponent, claim that more information can be extracted from their hieroglyphics. As far as I am concerned they might just as well set it down in Mandarin Chinese or Amharic. I often wonder what that great Glamorgan bowler, Jack Mercer, still a County scorer for Northants at over eighty, thinks of such innovations, but he keeps these reflections to himself and discourses instead on his duels with Jack Hobbs long ago.

Writers reminiscing about their youth habitually claim that there are no characters left, no glorious eccentrics, and I must admit that the modern cricket press-box has no one quite like C. B. Fry or Robertson-Glasgow, 'Beau' Vincent of *The Times*, or the blunt and uncompromising correspondent who once grew so tired of a messenger entering the box at Lord's and calling in stentorian tones for Colonel Philip Trevor of *The Daily Telegraph* that he told his own messenger never to appear without loudly demanding the attention of Able Seaman B. J. Evans of *The Star*.

The working routine of Fry, whose distinctive commentaries set a new style in cricket writing — erudite, witty and often wildly inconsequential — never ceased to fascinate me. He would dash off an instalment of his random reflections for the *Evening Standard* and beckon his chauffeur to bring his alarm clock. Having set this for the time of his next telephone call he would then fall asleep, the clock ticking away loudly in his overcoat pocket, or occasionally on his head, where he would anchor it with his hat.

There was much gaiety and laughter in the press-box of those days. Now frivolity is curbed by the new statistical school of cricket writers, grimly intent on recording every mathematical triviality, and alarming the rest of us by suggestions that we might have missed some peculiar landmark like Boycott's 6000th boundary or Underwood's 3000th maiden over. Immortals like 'Crusoe' and Cardus showed a proper disregard for figures, concentrating instead on artistry, technique and the human foibles paraded daily before them. What would the statistical school have made of Skelding, Richard Tyldesley, or Emmott Robinson?

Perhaps, however, one should count oneself fortunate in writing about the game before evolution becomes even more pronounced and cricket is transformed by the showmanship of Mr Packer into a different pastime altogether. If the time should come when, almost universally, white flannels are exchanged for track suits of many colours; synthetic pitches, prepared in the laboratories, are delivered each evening to floodlit arenas surfaced with plastic grass; and computerized robots take the place of umpires and scorers— then the image of Broad-Halfpenny Down will fade away under the arc-lights, and the ghosts of John Nyren and Silver Billy Beldham will return to the village green, which is cricket's natural setting.

Blackwood's Magazine 1978

13

Report of a Cricket Match

William Shakespeare

MEDIUMISTIC—Shakespeare interviewed; he gives a full report of the great match in advance.

It has been denied by some writers that the game of cricket had been developed in the time of Shakespeare, and Mr Charles Box, in his otherwise excellent book on *The Theory and Practice of Cricket*, goes so far as to say (p. 9) that 'no one has yet been able to produce any evidence from his plays of his knowledge thereof.'

With a view to determine this question for ourselves, we spent an hour or two the other evening *en rapport* with some celebrated Shakespearian mediums. We greatly regret that want of space debars us from giving in full the communications we then received from the Immortal Bard. We have, in fact, been obliged to strain a point, and omit some other interesting *Cricketana*, to make room for the following report of the great match soon to be played at Philadelphia.

It seems that the Bard of Avon, having accidentally met the crowds of cricketers *en route* to the cricket field, politely inquired,

> 'What work's, my countrymen, in hand? Where go you
> With bats and clubs? The matter speak, I pray you.' (*a*)

One of the number, surprised at his ignorance, replied,

> *1st Cit.* 'Our business is not unknown to the SENATE! They have had inkling, this fortnight, what we intend to do, which now we'll show 'em in deeds. They shall know we have strong arms too.' (*b*)

Perceiving that everybody who was anybody was bound for the cricket match, it struck the immortal dramatist,

(*a*) Coriolanus, Act i., Sc. 1.
(*b*) Ibid.

'Here is like to be a good presence of worthies.' (*a*)

And he said,

'Nay, I'll come; if I lose a scruple of this sport, let me be boiled to death with melancholy.' (*b*)

2nd Cit. 'It will be pastime passing excellent.' (*c*)
3rd Cit. 'Sport royal, I warrant you.' (*d*)

Arriving at the enclosure, he asked,

Shaks. 'Is this Moor-fields to muster in?' (*e*)
1st Cit. 'Aye, my lord.' – 'And with her Sovereign [Majesty's] GRACE,
Here on this grass plot, in this very place,
To come and sport.' (*f*)

On being introduced to the committee, he remarked,

'I wish your enterprise to-day may thrive.' (*g*)

And on presentation to our visitors he addressed them thus,

'And you, good yeomen,
Whose limbs were made in England, show us here
The mettle of your pasture; let us swear
That you are worth your breeding, which I doubt not;
For there is none of you so mean and base,
That hath not noble lustre in your eyes.' (*h*)

He admired the match ball, exclaiming,

'A carbuncle entire, as big as thou art,
Were not so rich a jewel.' (*i*)

Glancing over a copy of the 'Official Hand-Book', he, at first, blanched our cheeks with fear, premising,

'I am nothing if not critical,' (*k*)

(*a*) Love's Labour's Lost, Act v., Sc. 2.
(*b*) Twelfth Night, Act ii, Sc. 5.
(*c*) Taming of the Shrew, Ind. 1.
(*d*) Twelfth Night, Act ii, Sc. 3.
(*e*) Henry VIII, Act v, Sc. 3.
(*f*) Tempest, Act iv, Sc. 1.
(*g*) Julius Caesar, Act iii, Sc. 1.
(*h*) Henry V, Act iii, Sc. 1.
(*i*) Coriolanus, Act i, Sc. 4.
(*k*) Othello, Act ii, Sc. 1.

but presently reassured us a little, adding,

> 'There are some shrewd contents in yond same paper.' (*a*)

To one of the players, just attired in his cricket costume, he hinted,

> 'Costly thy habit as thy purse can buy,
> But not expressed in fancy; rich, not gaudy:
> For the apparel oft proclaims the man.' (*b*)

Of another he remarked,

> 'How oddly he is suited! I think he bought his doublet in Italy, his round
> hose in France, his bonnet in Germany.' (*c*)

But he added,

> 'He seems to be the more noble in being fantastical: a great man, I'll
> warrant.' (*d*)

The committee soon found he was *au fait* with the game, and claiming him as a native of Philadelphia (he having already claimed them as 'his countrymen'), they invited him to fill a vacancy on the Twenty-two; having accepted, he immediately became excited over the prospect, and burst out,

> 'O, that a man might know
> The end of this day's business, ere it come!' (*e*)
> 'O, let the hours be short
> Till fields, and blows, and groans applaud our sport.' (*f*)

Before leaving the club-house, one of our players (a nervous man) muttered,

> 'I have not that alacrity of spirit
> Nor cheer of mind that I was wont to have,' (*g*)

and asked Shakespeare,

> 'What say you now? What comfort have we now?' (*h*)

(*a*) Merchant of Venice, Act iii, Sc. 2.
(*b*) Hamlet, Act i, Sc. 3.
(*c*) Merchant of Venice, Act i, Sc. 2.
(*d*) Winter's Tale, Act iv, Sc. 3.
(*e*) Julius Caesar, Act v, Sc. 1.
(*f*) Henry IV Part I, Act i, Sc. 3.
(*g*) Richard III, Act v, Sc. 3.
(*h*) Richard II, Act iii, Sc. 2.

Whereupon he delivered the following little lecture to a gradually increasing audience,

'Because you want the GRACE that others have,
You judge it straight a thing impossible
To compass wonders.' (*a*)

'When Fortune means to men most good,
She looks upon them with a threatening eye.' (*b*)

'Things out of hope are compass'd oft with vent'ring,' (*c*)
'By how much unexpected, by so much
We must awake endeavour for defence,
For courage mounteth with occasion.' (*d*)

'But wherefore do you droop? Why look you sad?
Be great in act, as you have been in thought;
Threaten the threatener.' (*e*)

'To fear the foe, since fear oppresseth strength,
Gives, in your weakness, strength unto the foe,
And so your follies fight against yourself.' (*f*)

'Did I but suspect a fearful man,
He should have leave to go away betimes;
Lest, in our need, he might infect another,

And make him of like spirit to himself.
If any such be here, as God forbid!
Let him depart before we need his help.' (*g*)

'Perish the man whose mind is backward now.' (*h*)

Passing from the pavilion, he glanced at the grandstand, and observing that

'Our greatest friends attend us,' (*i*)

he indulged in the following soliloquy:

(*a*) Henry VI, Part I, Act v, Sec. 4.
(*b*) King John, Act iii, Sc. 4.
(*c*) Poems.
(*d*) King John, Act ii, Sc. 1.
(*e*) Ibid., Act v, Sc. 1.
(*f*) Richard II, Act iii, Sc. 2.
(*g*) Henry VI, Part I, Act iii, Sc. 1.
(*h*) Henry V, Act iii, Sc. 3.
(*i*) Coriolanus, Act i, Sc. 1.

'''Tis ten to one this play can never please
All that are here. Some come to take their ease!
For this play at this time, is only in
The merciful construction of good women;
If *they* smile,
And say 'twill do, I know, within a mile,
All the best men are ours; for 'tis ill hap,
If they hold, when their ladies bid them clap.' (*a*)

All being ready, he assumed to himself a good deal, saying to the captain of the English Eleven,

'Prepare you, generals!
The enemy comes on in gallant show,
And something's to be done immediately.' (*b*)

And to our captain and fielders,

'Call forth your actors by the scroll. Masters, spread yourselves.' (*c*)

The umpire having given the word,

'The Play's the thing,' (*d*)

and the batsman having returned,

'Aye, boy, ready,' (*e*)

Shakespeare thus:

'Make you ready your stiff bats.' (*f*)

'Fight, gentlemen of England, fight, bold yeomen.' (*g*)

Turning to the bowler, he exhorted him with one word,

'Now be a FREEMAN!' (*h*)

Just then the band struck up, and Romeo and Juliet (who were among the spectators), seeking out a retired spot, looked,

(*a*) Henry VIII, Epilogue.
(*b*) Julius Caesar, Act v, Sc. 1.
(*c*) Midsummer Night's Dream, Act 1, Sc. 2.
(*d*) Hamlet, Act ii, Sc. 2.
(*e*) Romeo and Juliet, Act i, Sc. 5.
(*f*) Coriolanus, Act i, Sc. 1.
(*g*) Richard III, Act v, Sc. 3.
(*h*) Julius Caesar, Act v, Sc. 3.

'Here will we sit, and let the sounds of music
Creep in our ears.' (*a*)

But the batsman (whose attention was so attracted by the waltz that he lost his wicket) swore,

'May those same instruments, which you profane,
Never sound more!' (*b*)

Meantime Shakespeare was making signs to Romeo,

'She is a woman, therefore may be woo'd;
She is a woman, therefore may be won.' (*c*)

And now the champion batsman of the world, the inheritor of cricket,

'Propped by ancestry, whose GRACE
Chalks successors their way,' (*d*)

had taken his stand and commenced,

'A very good piece of work, I assure you, and a merry.' (*e*)

Shakespeare thought to flatter him with this compliment,

'An excellent play — an honest method, as wholesome as sweet, and by very much more handsome than fine.' (*f*)

Grace (*aside*). 'Why, what a candy deal of courtesy
This fawning greyhound then did proffer me!' (*g*)

He does me double wrong
That wounds me with the flatteries of his tongue.' (*h*)

(*aloud*) 'Sir, praise me not,
My work hath not yet warmed me.' (*i*)

By which he clearly intended to go in for a long innings.

(*a*) Merchant of Venice, Act v, Sc. 1.
(*b*) Coriolanus, Act i, Sc. 9.
(*c*) Titus Andronicus, Act ii, Sc. 1.
(*d*) Henry VIII, Act i, Sc. 1.
(*e*) Midsummer Night's Dream, Act i, Sc. 1.
(*f*) Hamlet, Act ii, Sc. 2.
(*g*) Henry IV, Part I, Act i, Sc. 3.
(*h*) Richard II, Act iii, Sc. 2.
(*i*) Coriolanus, Act i, Sc. 5.

Somewhat later in the game.

> 'When Fortune, in her shift and change of mood', (*a*)

had sent more than one to the tent, chanting this dirge,

> 'No reckoning made, but sent to my account
> With all my imperfections on my head,' (*b*)

Captain Fitzgerald came into the field, consulting anxiously with Mr Grace; and though he whispered,

> 'I will tell it softly; yond crickets
> Shall not hear it,' (*c*)

our reporter overheard this much,

> *Fitz.* 'We must do something, and i' the heat.' (*d*)

> 'Despatch
> Those centuries to our aid; the rest will serve
> For a short holding: if we lose the field,
> We cannot keep the town.' (*e*)

> *Gra.* 'Fear not our care, sir.' (*e*)

> *Fitz.* 'It makes us or it mars us; think on that,
> And fix most firm thy resolution.' (*f*)

> 'For 'tis a cause that hath no mean dependence
> Upon our joint and several dignities.' (*g*)

Whereupon Grace opened his shoulders and made

> 'A hit, a very palpable hit!' (*h*)

through the dodging heads of the brilliant assemblage, clear to the grandstand. Mr Shakespeare had just previously remarked that he feared that was a spot

> 'Where ladies shall be frighted,
> And, gladly quaked,* hear more.' (*i*)

(*a*) Timon of Athens, Act i, Sc. 1.
(*b*) Hamlet, Act i, Sc. 5.
(*c*) Winter's Tale, Act ii, Sc. 1.
(*d*) King Lear, Act i, Sc. 1.
(*e*) Coriolanus, Act i, Sc. 7.
(*f*) Othello, Act v, Sc. 1.
(*g*) Troilus and Cressida, Act ii, Sc. 2.
(*h*) Hamlet, Act v, Sc. 2.
(*i*) Coriolanus, Act i, Sc. 9.

* Thrown into delighted trepidation. – COMMENTATOR

His captain applauded,

> 'O noble fellow!
> Thou wast a soldier
> Even to Cato's wish, not fierce and terrible
> Only in strokes; but with thy grim looks, and
> The thunder-like percussion of thy sounds,
> Thou mad'st thine enemies shake, as if the world
> Were feverous, and did tremble.' (*a*)

In the excitement, the fielding became loose, and two runs were made on an overthrow. Our captain, mortified and enraged, rebuked the delinquent,

> 'Call you that backing of your friends?
> A plague upon such backing!' (*b*)

We may here remark, by way of digression, that our informant mentioned that he afterward learned that the excitement in town, during Mr Grace's innings, was intense. Among other evidences of this, he mentioned that even the august City Fathers passed the following motion to adjourn:

> 'Let's hence, and hear
> How the despatch is made; and in what fashion,
> More than in singularity, he goes
> Upon his present action.'
> *Omnes.* 'Let's along.' [*Exeunt.*] (*c*)

At this point of the game a painful accident befell one of the players. Anxious friends looked and asked,

> 'Is not that he, that lies upon the ground?
> He lies not like the living. O my heart!' (*d*)

> '*His bloody brow! O Jupiter, no blood.*' (*e*)

Then our captain gave the order,

> 'Go we to our tent:
> The blood upon your visage dries; 'tis time
> It should be looked to. Come.' (*f*)

(*a*) Coriolanus, Act i, Sc. 4.
(*b*) Henry IV, Part I, Act ii, Sc. 4.
(*c*) Coriolanus, Act i, Sc. 1.
(*d*) Julius Caesar, Act v, Sc. 3.
(*e*) Coriolanus, Act i, Sc. 3.
(*f*) Ibid., Act i, Sc. 9.

The first innings was long and tedious to the fielders.

> 'I do not bear these crossings,' (*a*)
> 'I 'gin to be aweary of the sun,' (*b*)

said one. Another pleaded,

> 'And nature must obey necessity:
> Which we will niggard with a little rest.' (*c*)

And they all agreed (more often than W.S. would tell),

> 'But we'll drink together.' (*d*)

After these indulgences, friend Will appears to have become somewhat mixed; for, on reappearing (long after the others), he admits that he articulated, in a broken manner,

> 'Another general shout!
> I do believe that these applauses are
> For some new honours heaped on Caesar!' (*e*)

Evidently confounding his veteran friend, the old professional, who distinguished himself in the 1859 matches, with his present companions. A little later ('still harping on my daughter') he yelled out,

> 'Julius Caesar, thou art mighty yet!' (*f*)

thereby attracting the attention of an obese old party outside the ropes, who responded, equally vigorously,

> 'If I could shake off but one seven years
> From these old arms and legs, by the good gods,
> I'd with thee every foot!' (*g*)

But now the innings closed, and, one and all having complimented Captain Fitzgerald,

> 'You have made good work,
> You and your apron men,' (*h*)

(*a*) Henry IV, Part I, Act iii, Sc. 1.
(*b*) Macbeth, Act v, Sc. 5.
(*c*) Julius Caesar, Act iv, Sc. 3.
(*d*) Corilanus, Act v, Sc. 3.
(*e*) Julius Caesar, Act i, Sc. 2.
(*f*) Ibid., Act v, Sc. 3.
(*g*) Coriolanus, Act iv, Sc. 1.
(*h*) Coriolanus, Act iv, Sc. 6.

'They said they were an-hungry'; (*a*)

and, approaching the pavilion, could not restrain from crying out, with gusto,

'A goodly house: the feast smells well!' (*b*)

'The Tempest' (equinoxial), 'like the tyrannous breathing of the North,' shortly after burst with such fury that Shakespeare exclaimed,

'Since I was man,
Such sheets of fire, such bursts of horrid thunder,
Such groans of roaring wind and rain, I never
Remember to have heard.' (*c*)

Further play was prevented that day. On the way home, Shakespeare asked,

'Say, what abridgement have you for this evening?
What masque? What music? How shall we beguile
The lazy time, if not with some delight?' (*d*)

But, as this only professes to be a report of the cricket match, we will 'take up the thread of our discourse', when play was resumed on the following Monday, the Philadelphians at the bat. But

'Cormorant devouring time' (*e*)

warns us to abstain from details, and, in

'Taking the instant by the forward top,' (*f*)

we must make short work of the rest.

There were the usual types of players. The determined batsman,

'Marked you his lip, and eyes?' (*g*)

The cautious runner,

'Give the word, ho! and stand.' (*h*)

(*a*) Coriolanus, Act i, Sc. 1.
(*b*) Ibid., Act iv, Sc. 5.
(*c*) King Lear, Act iii, Sc. 2.
(*d*) Midsummer Night's Dream, Act v, Sc. 1.
(*e*) Love's Labour's Lost, Act i, Sc. 1.
(*f*) All's Well that Ends Well, Act v, Sc. 3.
(*g*) Coriolanus, Act i, Sc. 1.
(*h*) Julius Caesar, Act iv, Sc. 2.

The overreaching runner,

> 'We may outrun,
> By violent swiftness, that which we run at,
> And lose by overrunning.' (*a*)

The stealthy runner,

> 'A snapper-up of unconsidered trifles.' (*b*)

The frightened runner,

> 'Stand! and go back.' (*c*)

> 'Back, I say, go; back – that is the utmost of your having, – back.' (*d*)

The uncertain runner,

> 'With every minute you do change a mind.' (*e*)

It was now William Shakespeare's turn to go in. Sublime contemplation! During a temporary absence of the umpire (at the soda-fountain) a fielder,

> 'The kindest man in doing courtesies,' (*f*)

cautioned him, round-arm bowling not having been invented in his time,

> 'Take heed, be wary how you place your [feet]' (*g*)

But he replied, firmly,

> 'I pray thee, cease thy counsel,
> Which falls into my ears as profitless
> As water in a sieve.' (*h*)

> 'Like a bold champion I assume the lists,
> Nor ask advice of any other thought
> But faithfulness and courage.' (*i*)

> 'What man dare, I dare.' (*k*)

(*a*) King Henry VIII, Act i, Sc. 1.
(*b*) Winter's Tale, Act iv, Sc. 2.
(*c*) Coriolanus, Act v, Sc. 2.
(*d*) Ibid., Act v, Sc. 2.
(*e*) Ibid., Act i, Sc. 1, etc.
(*f*) Merchant of Venice, Act iii, Sc. 2.
(*g*) Henry VI, Part I, Act iii, Sc. 2.
(*h*) Much Ado about Nothing, Act v, Sc. 1.
(*i*) Pericles, Act i, Sc. 1.
(*k*) Macbeth, Act iii, Sc. 4.

'For I am fresh of spirit, and resolved
To meet all perils very constantly.' (*a*)

The rebuffed fielder, like

'a hot friend cooling', (*b*)

muttered that he hoped he might be bowled first ball, which elicited
the observation,

'I had rather be set quick i' the earth
And bowled to death with turnips.' (*c*)

A titled member of the Eleven poked a little chaff at him, at which
Shakespeare blurted out,

'Tut, tut, my lord, we will not stand to prate;
Talkers are no good doers; be assured,
We go to use our hands, and not our tongues.' (*d*)

And now came an exhibition of cricket indeed! Grace himself
reciprocated a compliment,

'What you do
Still betters what is done.' (*e*)

'Let it be booked with the rest of this day's deeds.' (*f*)

Of Appleby he said,

'He is a marvellous good neighbour, in sooth, and a very good bowler.' (*g*)

Once William broke a bat, and 'suiting the action to the word' —
thus,

'Go, get you home, you fragments.' (*h*)

He was supplied afresh, but said,

'This is too heavy; let me see another.' (*i*)

'These are stars indeed;
And, sometimes, falling ones.' (*k*)

(*a*) Julius Caesar, Act v, Sc. 1.
(*b*) Ibid., Act iv, Sc. 2.
(*c*) Merry Wives of Windsor, Act iii, Sc. 4.
(*d*) Richard III, Act i, Sc. 3.
(*e*) Winter's Tale, Act iv, Sc. 3.
(*f*) Henry IV, Part II, Act iv, Sc. 3.
(*g*) Love's Labour's Lost, Act v, Sc. 2.
(*h*) Coriolanus, Act i, Sc. 1.
(*i*) Hamlet, Act v, Sc. 2.
(*k*) Henry VIII, Act iv, Sc. 1.

So it proved at length; the great star, and hero of the match, falling to one of Rose's 'cork-screws'. 'Thus the whirligig of time brings in his revenges'. Greatly disgusted, but remembering that

> ''Tis the CAUSE makes all,
> Degrades or hallows courage
> In its fall,'

he, gracefully bowing, and remarking to the bowler,

> 'Take my cap, – Jupiter!' (a)

retired toward the pavilion. But

> 'Matrons flung gloves,
> Ladies and maids their scarfs and handkerchers,
> Upon him as he passed: the nobles bended,
> As to Jove's statue; and the commons made
> A shower and thunder, with their caps and shouts;
> I never saw the like.' (b)

At this moment, what man's pride and conceit could resist such flattery! Alas! in an evil moment he bends over the beaming beauties, and, never doubting, asks which is the fav'rite, thus,

> 'How now, my as fair as noble ladies (and the moon, were she earthly, no nobler), whither do you follow your eyes so fast?'
>
> *Volumnia.* 'Honorable – * * ' (c)

Thus ended the innings, and the Gentlemen Eleven had to face a second innings!

But hold! one other player on the same side must be briefly noticed – the 'Cricket'. Such magnificent form did he show, that, during his innings, Mr Shakespeare was constrained to ask 'Gay Mother Cricket' how her descendant had acquired his powers, and received the following reply,

> 'When yet he was but tender-boiled and the only son of my womb; when youth with comeliness plucked all gaze his way; when, for a day of king's entreaties, a mother should not sell him an hour from her behold-ing; I – considering how honour would become such a person – was pleased to let him seek danger where he was like to find fame.' (d)

(a) Coriolanus, Act ii, Sc. 1.
(b) Ibid., Act ii, Sc. 1.
(c) Ibid., Act i, Sc. 1.
(d) Coriolanus, Act i, Sc. 3.

He replied,

> 'He hath borne himself beyond the promise of his age; doing, in the figure of a lamb, the feats of a lion.' (*a*)

But no delay between innings; Fitzgerald was heard to shout,

> 'Cut short all intermission.' (*b*)

> 'We make woe wanton with this fond delay.' (*c*)

> 'And come, young Cato, let us to the field!
> 'Tis three o'clock, and, Romans, yet ere night,
> We shall try fortune in a second fight.' (*d*)

Heu! miserabile dictu!

> 'Beaten, but not without honour!
> In this glorious and well-foughten field,
> We kept together in our chivalry.' (*e*)

> 'I shall have glory by this losing day.' (*f*)

> 'So call the field to rest, and let's away
> To part the glories of this happy day.' (*g*)

> *The Committee.* 'I will entertain them.' (*h*)

We cannot follow them to the festive board. Perhaps there was *not* formed a mutual admiration society, and perhaps Shakespeare did *not* say in the course of his speech,

> 'A braver choice of dauntless spirits,
> Than now the English bottoms have waft o'er,
> Did never float upon the swelling tide,' etc., (*i*)

any more than did their spokesman, who shall be nameless, late in the evening, address to each individual player, every member of the several committees, and a hundred miscellaneous handshakers, this, and a lot more similar stuff,

(*a*) Much Ado about Nothing, Act i, Sc. 1.
(*b*) Macbeth, Act iv, Sc. 3.
(*c*) Richard II, Act v, Sc. 1.
(*d*) Julius Caesar, Act v, Sc. 3.
(*e*) Henry V, Act iv, Sc. 6.
(*f*) Julius Caesar, Act v, Sc. last.
(*g*) Ibid., Act v, Sc. last.
(*h*) Ibid., Act v, Sc. last.
(*i*) King John, Act ii, Sc. 1.

'Since my dear soul was mistress of her choice,
And could of men distinguish her election,
Hath sealed *thee* for herself. For thou hast been
As one, in suffering all, that suffers nothing;
A man, that Fortune's buffets and rewards
Hast ta'en with equal thanks; and blessed are those,
Whose blood and judgment are so well co-mingled,
That they are not a pipe for Fortune's finger
To sound what stop she please. Give me that man
That is not passion's slave, and I will wear him
In my heart's core, ay, in my heart of heart,
As I do THEE.' (*a*)

'Something too much of this!' — We must bid you goodbye, spectators!

'Farewell to you, and you, and you,'
'Voluminous.' (*b*)

'And whether we shall ever meet again, I know not,
Therefore, our everlasting farewell take;
If we do meet again, why, we shall smile;
If not, why, then this parting was well made.' (*c*)

'The games are done.' (*d*)

P.S. Lord Campbell has vindicated Shakespeare's reputation for Legal Acquirements, and we commend the foregoing 'evidence from Shakespeare's plays' to Mr Box, with the hope that he will, in the next edition of his book, retract his imputation on the universality of Shakespeare's genius.

Official Handbook of International Cricket Fête, Philadelphia 1872

(*a*) Hamlet, Act iii, Sc. 2.
(*b*) Julius Caesar, Act v, Sc. 5.
(*c*) Julius Caesar, Act v, Sc. 1.
(*d*) Ibid., Act i, Sc. 2.

14

Charles Dickens and Cricket

To the Editor of Cricket

Sir, – In the last issue of *Cricket* the interesting subject was raised of Charles Dickens' references to the game in his published works. Cricket is mentioned in several of his books in addition to the well-known chapter in *Pickwick*. In *Martin Chuzzlewit* there are two allusions to the game. In chapter xxvii it states that within the offices of the Anglo-Bengalee Disinterested Loan and Life Assurance Company are 'green ledgers with red backs, like strong cricket-balls beaten flat' – a picturesque description.

A little further on, in chapter xxxvi, where Tom Pinch's journey by the stagecoach from Salisbury to London is related, the following passage occurs: – 'Yoho, among the gathering shades; making of no account the deep reflections of the trees, but scampering on through light and darkness, all the same, as if the light of London, fifty miles away, were quite enough to travel by, and some to spare. Yoho, beside the village green, where cricket players linger yet, and every little indentation made in the fresh grass by bat or wicket, ball or player's foot, sheds out its perfume on the night.'

In chapter xlviii of *Barnaby Rudge* poor Barnaby is inveigled into the lawless crowd who attend Lord George Gordon's 'No Popery' meeting in St George's Fields, and, whilst there, 'Barnaby had been thinking within himself that the smell of the trodden grass brought back his old days at cricket, when he was a young boy and played on Chigwell Green,' when he is accosted by Maypole Hugh.

In *The Old Curiosity Shop*, chapter xxiv, Little Nell and her grandfather arrive in their wandering at a small (un-named) village where 'The men and boys were playing at cricket on the green; and as the other folks were looking on, they wandered up and down, uncertain where to seek a humble lodging.'

Turning to Dickens' minor writings, we read in *The Schoolboy's Story* that 'Old Cheesman one night in his sleep, put his hat on over his night-cap, got hold of a fishing-rod and a cricket bat, and went down into the parlour.'

In *A Flight* occurs the following passage in a vivid description of a journey by express train from London to Folkestone: 'Now a wood, now a bridge, now a landscape, now a cutting, now a – Bang! a single-barrelled station – there was a cricket match somewhere with two white tents, and then four flying cows, then turnips – .'

In an *Uncommercial Paper, Dulborough Town*, Dickens describes his own sensations upon re-visiting Rochester, which he had not seen since he resided there as a child. He finds that the old playing field is now built over by a railway station, and says: 'Here too, had we, the small boys of Boles's, had that cricket match against the small boys of Coles's, when Boles and Coles had actually met upon the ground, and when, instead of instantly hitting out at one another with the utmost fury, as we had all hoped and expected, those sneaks had said respectively, 'I hope Mrs Boles is well' and 'I hope Mrs Coles and the baby are doing charmingly!'

The above list does not, I believe, exhaust all the allusions to cricket in Dickens' works. I was under the impression that Steerforth, when at Mr Creakle's school, excelled at cricket; and also that upon the morning of Maypole Hugh's execution, he was awakened from pleasant dreams of the green fields and his old days at cricket. Glancing through *David Copperfield* and *Barnaby Rudge* I have failed to verify these impressions, and so leave to other admirers of the immortal Boz the pleasant task of discovering his other references to cricket.

In very early boyhood Charles Dickens was too delicate and fragile a child to indulge in the pastimes of his more robust companions, but he took his favourite *Robinson Crusoe* or *Peregrine Pickle* to the playground, and there he would alternately read and watch his companions at their games. His subsequent unhappy boyhood is well-known, and unfortunately he never had the opportunity of taking part in the games and pastimes of youths of his own age.

In his early reporting days Dickens must often have posted past cricket matches on the village green. One can imagine his keen and kindly eye taking in the scene at a glance, and years afterwards, in a few graphic touches, he gives us a vivid pen-picture of his impressions in Tom Pinch's journey to London.

In his later years, when entertaining at Gad's Hill, Dickens would arrange cricket and running matches for the amusement of his guests; in which the villagers who took part were stimulated by the kindly praise and encouragement of the genial Boz, who took the greatest interest in their contests, giving small prizes to the successful players, and extending his open-handed hospitality to all.

The famous All Muggleton v. Dingley Dell match has been stated by a Dickens commentator to have been the description of an actual match played between the Cobham and Town Malling Clubs. As Dickens was born in 1812 and *Pickwick* was published early in 1836 the date would probably be between 1830 and 1835. Perhaps one may be allowed to commend to Mr Ashley-Cooper the congenial task of discovering the actual match, and of identifying in the redoubtable Dumkins some rustic Fuller Pilch who too long has blushed unseen under his *nom-de-plume.* In the account of the match itself it will be noticed that the umpires stand (to the modern eye) in an unusual position; but in contemporaneous prints they are depicted exactly as stated in the text, thus once again proving Dickens' minute attention to the smallest detail, a characteristic which is such a striking feature of all his writings.

Yours, &c.,
A. C. DENHAM

Cricket: A Weekly Record of the Game 1910

15

The Lost Bowlers

P. G. Wodehouse

We had arrived at Marvis Bay, and were to play the last match of our tour on the following morning. Marvis Bay is in Devonshire. We always take it last on our fixture-list, so as to end happily, as it were. Sidmouth may rout us, and Seaton may make us hunt leather till the soles of our boots wear though; but it is the boast of the Weary Willies that against Marvis Bay they never fail to get their own back. As a matter of fact, we hardly treat the thing as a match. We look on it as a picnic. We have a splendid time — the place is a paradise and the local curate a sportsman to his fingertips — and the actual game is a treat after the stern struggles of the earlier part of the tour. It is in the Marvis Bay match that I take my annual wicket, usually through a catch in the deep; while Geake, our leg-break artist, generally seizes the opportunity of playing his great double-figure innings, and pulling his average for the season out of the realms of the minuses. Except for the curate, Dacre, who played for Cambridge in the nineties and is a sound and pretty bat of the Johnny Douglas type, the local team is composed of unskilled labourers. They hit hard and high and in a semicircle. Geake has six men in the country, and invariably reaps a plenteous harvest of wickets. When we go in it is an understood thing among us that every possible risk must be taken, and if a batsman shows symptoms of sitting on the splice and playing himself in, his partner feels it a duty to run him out at the earliest possible moment. I remember one year Sharples, our fast bowler, said he had never made a century, and wanted to see what it felt like, so he was going to play himself in against Marvis Bay, and take no risks. His statement was coldly received, and on the scoresheet of the match you will find these words are written:—

J. B. Sharples, run out 0

The wicked never prosper.

We were gathered together in the parlour of the only inn the village possesses on the night before the match, very sociable and comfortable and pleased with ourselves. We had come flushed with victory from Seaton, and everything pointed to a delightful game on the morrow. There were no signs of rain. It had been a beautiful evening, and the glass was going up. It was pretty to see the faith we had in that glass. On our last visit, a year back, the thing had prophesied much rain, and we had been unanimous in pointing out that of course no sane man ever thought of trusting a barometer.

Geake had just finished telling us, at considerable length, how he once made twenty-three not out in a house match at Malvern (which none of us believed) when Sharples strolled in.

He wore a cynical smile.

As a rule this smile of his is the forerunner of some bad news. He is apt to come up just before the Seaton match and tell me that he has strained his heart, or a lung, or something, and cannot possibly bowl a ball. But, as the match next day was only against Marvis Bay, it seemed impossible that any bad news he might have could really matter. Even if he could not bowl for some reason it would not be particularly serious. Our changes were capable of getting Marvis Bay out.

However, I thought it was my duty, in my capacity of captain of the team, to hear all that was to be heard.

'What's the matter, Sharples?' I asked.

He shook his head pityingly.

'See,' he said – 'see how the little victims play, regardless of their fate.'

One of the little victims, Gregory, our wicket-keeper, flung a bound volume of the *Farmers' Magazine* at him.

He caught it high up with one hand.

'I'm in rare form,' he said, complacently. 'I can see anything. Good job too. We shall need good fielding.'

'Sharples,' I said, 'you've got something up your sleeve. Out with it, or get out. You're frightening Sanderson.'

Sanderson, our nervous batsman, was already beginning to quake like a jelly caught in a storm.

'What's up, Sharples?' said several voices.

Our fast bowler condescended to explain.

'As I was coming up the street just now,' he said, 'I suddenly noticed a horse shy violently. And next minute I saw the reason. A little shrimp of a man with a face like a music-hall comedian was coming towards me. Do any of you know Wix? Apollo Wix?'

'Plays for Somerset,' said Sanderson.

'He do,' assented Sharples. 'And likewise does he play – on occasion and by special request – for Marvis Bay.'

'What?' I shouted.

Sharples's smile became a grin.

'James, my gallant skipper, I speak the truth. Wix, who, I may point out, is eighth in the first-class averages, has come down here all for love of us to play against the Weary Willies.'

Our jaws fell. We had been looking forward to a gentle, go-as-you-please village game. With Wix against us we might have to go our hardest to win.

'Haven't Somerset a match?' asked Geake. 'I thought they were playing Gloucestershire.'

'Not till Monday, Gloucestershire. They are free till then. Hence,' added Sharples, calmly, 'we shall also have the pleasure of playing to-morrow against Jack Coggin and T. C. Smith.'

A perfect howl of anguish rose from all corners of the room.

'Wha-a-at?'

'Jack Coggin!'

'What on earth – '

'Who – '

'T. C. Smith!'

'Wix, Smith, *and* Coggin! Good Lord!' There followed a lull, during which I heard Sanderson murmur, sadly, 'And the last time I played against Jack Coggin he outed me in my first over!'

'Sharples,' I said.

'Sir to you.'

'Tell me you're lying and I'll forgive you.'

'You pain me, James. I am a slave to truth. Haven't you ever heard that story of me when I was a boy? My father found me cutting down a cherry tree. "Who is cutting down this tree?" he asked, sternly. "Father," I said, "I cannot tell a lie. It is probably the cat." You needn't believe what I say, of course. Wix is my authority. Oh, and, by the way – '

'Yes?'

'There is a party of public-school boys down here, reading with a coach. Winchester men. Mere lads, of course, mere lads — nothing more. Still, two of them were in the team this year, and one of the two — Shellick — knocked up seventy against Eton.'

The concentrated gloom seemed to make the room quite dark; or it may have been the tobacco smoke.

'Let's scratch,' suggested somebody, miserably.

'But look here, Sharples,' I said, 'I can't understand this. Dacre told me he hadn't got a very strong side.'

'No, poor man, he's had disappointments. You see, the Australians have got a match, so he couldn't get Trumper and Noble.'

'I believe there's something at the bottom of all this.'

'There is,' said Sharples, 'if you want to know. I got it from Wix, who seemed to think it was so good that he couldn't keep it to himself.'

'Well?'

'The man Dacre, who has got a sense of humour which strikes one as almost irreligious in a curate, is putting up a deep jest on the Weary Willies. He has collected all these celebrities, and — this is the point; you ought to laugh here — he is going to play them all under assumed names. You see the rollicking idea? The score of the match will be printed in all the sporting papers, and it will get about that an ordinary village team has beaten the club hollow. We shall never live it down.'

'We can explain,' said Geake, hopefully.

'Who would believe us?'

'Now, look here,' I said, firmly; 'this is absurd. We mustn't chuck up the sponge in this rotten way. There's no earthly sense in going into the field a beaten side. Just because they've got a county man or two—'

'Three,' corrected Sharples.

'That doesn't necessarily mean that they will win. As a matter of fact, in this sort of game a good club bat is far more likely to make runs than a county man, who's used to billiard-table wickets. They may have a few cracks, but we're far stronger all through.'

'I made twenty-three not out once,' said Geake. 'It was in a house match at Malvern.'

'And, hang it all,' I cried, warming to my work, 'you and Geake, Sharples, are a good enough pair of bowlers to bother any batsman.'

'My dear James,' said Sharples, enthusiastically, 'you make me blush. Your stately compliments embarrass me.'

'It isn't only their batsmen,' said Sanderson, despondently. 'Look at their bowlers. Jack Coggin.'

'And Smith,' said Gregory.

'Who's Smith?' I said, scornfully. 'A man who goes on second change – '

'First change,' said Gregory. 'And for a first-class county.'

'Well, look at our batting,' I urged. 'There's Sanderson, for one – '

'And me,' put in Geake. 'I once made twenty-three not out. It was in a house match at Malvern.'

'You never know what will happen at cricket,' I said. 'Buck up, and let's make these Somerset men so sick that they'll stay in their own county another year or hang themselves with the laces of their cricket boots.'

'And, in passing,' said Sharples, pouring out a measure of whisky and adding a dash of soda-water, 'let's drink confusion to the man Dacre – the Rev. Dacre, curate and serpent. May his first ball hit him on the funny-bone, his second wind him, and his third get him l-b-w.'

We drank the toast with considerable enthusiasm.

The inhabitants of Marvis Bay turned out in force to see us massacred. The curate's low plot had probably become public property, for there was an alert air about the crowd as of those who expect amusement in the near future.

'You've got some new men in your team, I see,' I said to Dacre. I wondered whether Wix had told him that he had informed Sharples of the state of affairs.

Apparently he had not, for the serpentine curate made no confession. Instead, he waved his hand airily, as if to deprecate the attaching of any importance to the changes in his side.

'One or two,' he said. 'One or two; local celebrities, you know; very keen. You may teach them something of the game.'

'Stranger things have happened.'

I looked round me. To my left Jack Coggin was bowling his celebrated leg-theory balls to T. C. Smith.

'That's one of your new men, isn't it?' I said. 'Looks a useful man.'

'A very decent bowler on his day,' said the curate.

I believed him. A week before Jack Coggin had taken five good Notts wickets for eighty-seven.

'And the man batting? He any good?'

'A tolerable fast bowler. When in form quite useful.'

T. C. Smith had been in form ten days ago. On that occasion he had bowled Fry and had Vine caught off him in the slips in one over.

'Ah!' I said. 'We ought to have a good game, then.'

'Oh, we shall do our best,' said he, modestly.

'So,' I said, with determination, 'shall we.'

Of the opening stages of that match I have no very pleasant recollections. They won the toss, and batted first on a wicket which had evidently been prepared more carefully than was generally the case at Marvis Bay. Wix, looking positively hideous, opened the innings with Shellick, the Wykehamist expert, who had that peculiarly competent look which characterizes the public-school man who is a certainty for his 'blue' in his first year.

From the moment Wix took guard, and scraped the crease with one of the bails in his cool, unruffled way, our troubles began. Nothing could have been nobler than the struggles of Sharples and Geake. Over after over the former banged them down like a combination of Brearley and Pritchard. Over and over the latter tried every trick in his repertory. But all in vain. Wix was superb. He took everything that came to him with the ease which belongs to a man who is morally certain of a place in the English team for the fifth Test Match. His driving was titanic, his cutting a dream. When he pulled, he did it with that certainty of touch which stamps the genius. It was only the fine bowling of Sharples and Geake which kept the score within anything like decent limits. After an hour's play eighty was on the board, and the pair were still together.

Then our luck turned. Geake, who had had a rest and was now bowling again, sent down a miserable long hop wide of the off stump. It was a ball that cried out to be hit. A novice could have dispatched it to the boundary. The vaulting ambition of the Wykehamist did not stop short at a mere four. He wanted six. He hit out much too wildly. There was a click, and Gregory had him behind the wickets.

Two minutes later, by that curious fatality which so often broods over the survivor of a long partnership, Wix, trying an almost identical stroke off Sharples, was caught at third man. Here, therefore, were their two best bats out, and the score under a hundred. We had still to deal with Smith, Coggin, the other Wykehamist, and the dastard parson, but, after all, these were but small fry in comparison. Smith and Coggin were first-class bowlers, but nobody had ever called them first-class bats.

However, they were far from being rabbits. They may have lacked style, but they certainly had vigour. Smith rattled up thirty-three, mainly by means of boundaries, and Coggin took forty. The other Wykehamist compiled a stylish twenty-five. Dacre, to the joy of the Weary Willies, failed miserably. Sharples shattered him with his second ball, and then and there danced a cake-walk by the side of the pitch.

The rest of the team were our old friends the un-skilled labourers. They did their best, and once or twice effected prodigious hits, but Geake got amongst them with slow yorkers, and the thing became a procession. The tenth Marvis Bay wicket fell five minutes before the luncheon interval. The scoring had been unusually rapid, even for that ground, which is small. The full total was two hundred and eleven.

Not a big score for a good wicket; but with Jack Coggin and T. C. Smith against us we were not riotously optimistic.

We had finished lunch, and I was trying to bring Sanderson to a frame of mind which would render him fit to come in first with me with any chance of surviving a couple of overs, when a motor-car puffed up to the entrance to the ground. It contained one man, who wore goggles and a cap with a peak that covered his nose.

There was a general move on the part of the two teams in his direction. A contemplative inspection of a motor-car is the very thing to round off a cricket lunch. I took Sanderson along with me to look at it, arguing as we went. Sanderson is a beautiful bat, but he has an impossible set of nerves. His flesh creeps when he goes to the wickets, but if he survives a few overs he is worth watching. I had almost succeeded in convincing him that Coggin and Smith were rather poor third-class bowlers when we joined the group round the car. Its owner had removed his goggles, but his face was strange to me.

Smith and Coggin, however, coming up arm-in-arm a moment later, recognized him and greeted him as a brother. He received their greetings calmly and replied to them precisely. He seemed a man who rarely permitted himself to become excited.

'Halloa, Charlie!' said Smith.

'How's things?' inquired Coggin.

'Middling,' said the new-comer.

'Is that the motor?'

'That is the motor,' replied he, with the precision of an Ollendorff.

Smith climbed into the vacated seat. Coggin was inspecting the rear of the machine. Its owner eyed them without emotion. The motor continued, as Sharples pathetically put it, to throb as though its little heart would break.

Coggin now proceeded to clamber carefully over the body of the car.

'Don't cut the leather with your spikes,' said Charlie.

'Right ho,' replied Coggin. 'What's this thing for?' He touched a lever with his hand.

'That sets the thing going,' said Charlie.

Instant attention on the part of T. C. Smith.

'What — this?' he said.

The owner nodded, and the next moment, without warning, the car bounded forward down the road. That same instinct which prompts a man to touch wet paint to see if it really *is* wet had induced T. C. Smith to pull the lever.

Our first impulse, on recovering from our surprise, was to laugh. The sight of Jack Coggin hanging on to the back of his seat was humorous.

Then the serious side of the thing struck us. One or two of the group made a half-hearted dash down the road, but stopped on realizing the futility of giving chase. Assistance was out of the question.

'They're all right,' said the owner of the car, without emotion, 'if they know how to steer; and it's simple enough. Yes, there they go round the corner. They're all right.'

A buzz of conversation began. We all discussed the incident at one and the same time. The only person who made no contribution to the discussion was Charlie. He lit a cigar.

Dacre pulled a watch out of the pocket of his blazer.

'We ought to be starting again soon,' he said. 'It's nearly three. When do you think those two men will be coming back?'

Charlie blew the ash off his cigar.

'That,' he said, 'I can't say. I doubt if either of them knows how to stop the car.'

'Good gracious!' exclaimed Dacre. 'Then you mean to say they will go on – '

'Till the thing runs down, I suppose.'

'And when will that be?' I asked.

'Why, I couldn't say exactly. They've got enough petrol to take them – oh, say fifty miles.'

'Fifty – miles!' gasped Dacre.

'Call it forty-five,' said Charlie, making a concession.

'Shall we start?' I asked, suavely. 'Are your men ready?'

Dacre passed a handkerchief over his forehead. 'But – but – but – ' he said.

'You had better play two substitutes.'

'But – '

'After all,' I said, gently; 'their absence cannot be so very important. As you said, they are merely local talent.'

He looked at me with eyes that were full of expression.

'Merely local talent,' I repeated.

It was shortly after the tea interval, when our score was a hundred and sixty for three wickets, that a small boy entered the field, bearing in his hand a telegram for the bereaved Charlie. It was signed 'Smith,' and had been dispatched apparently from somewhere in the middle of Cornwall.

'Motor safe,' it read. 'Returning by train. Tell Dacre not wait dinner.'

It was at that moment, I fancy, that the Rev. Joseph Dacre experienced a fleeting regret that he had ever taken holy orders.

Clergymen have to be so guarded in their speech.

And when, an hour later, the Weary Willies won the match with five wickets in hand, this regret may possibly have become keener.

Strand Magazine 1905

16

Aboard the Great Britain

Stephen Green

Many cricket lovers no doubt have followed with interest the amazing last voyage of the *Great Britain* from the Falkland Islands to Bristol. When it was built, Brunel's masterpiece in iron was the largest ship afloat and it was the first vessel of any size in which the screw propeller was used. Cricketers, however, will be interested in the *Great Britain* mainly because she carried the first two cricket teams to go to Australia. Both H. H. Stephenson's team in 1861 and G. Parr's band two years later went out in her.

By a happy chance we know quite a lot about these trips due to three sources. In the first place William Caffyn (who was also a veteran of the first overseas tour ever – the North American visit of 1859) described both voyages in his memoirs *Seventy-one Not Out*. In addition the Library at Lord's has preserved the diary kept on the 1863–4 tour by that great Yorkshire player, George Anderson. Last, but by no means least, a pirated edition of E. M. Grace's diary was published under the title *A Trip to Australia: Scraps from the Diary of One of the Twelve*.

Of these three sources, Caffyn's book is the least informative about voyages aboard the *Great Britain*. The author was obviously keener to describe the cricket than to narrate the adventures on the trip to the Antipodes. He was, however, the only one who was able to describe both trips. Not the least interesting feature of the 1861–2 tour was the fact that it was commercially sponsored by the well-known firm of restaurant contractors Messrs. Spiers & Pond. This firm sent an agent, a Mr Mallam, to seek out the best England XI which he could obtain. Each player was to receive £150 for the trip with first class travelling expenses found. In the end a good, but not fully representative, team was found.

A banquet was arranged in the team's honour prior to departure at which the following refrain was sung:

Success to the Eleven of England!
The toast is three times and one more
May they all meet with success o'er the briny
And safely return to our shore!

This last sentiment was not a trite one. Caffyn had had some nasty experiences crossing the Atlantic in 1859. He was to find the *Great Britain*, to use his own words, 'a sail down the Thames in comparison'. The only misery with which he had to contend was caused by mosquitoes. He used to get a large piece of muslin and wrap it round his head before going to bed, in addition to putting a pair of stockings on his arms.

When the team eventually reached Australia they were met by a crowd of around 10,000 excited people and a coach-and-four took the weary team to the Cafe de Paris in Melbourne where there was again a big welcome. The first of many cricket tours to Australia had begun!

In Caffyn's opinion the team which went out two years later was a far stronger one than that led by H. H. Stephenson. George Parr was the captain and, oddly enough, Caffyn was the only member of the team to have been down under two years previously. Strong though Parr's band was, it did not seem to Caffyn to be as powerful a combination as the side which went to the United States and Canada in 1859.

It is useful to have Caffyn's accounts of the two voyages but fuller and more interesting accounts of the second trip are to be found in the diary kept by Anderson and by Grace. It is remarkable that Anderson had the energy and the inclination to keep a journal since he was tormented by sea-sickness. On October 15th the *Great Britain* left the Mersey and by 6 p.m. that evening Anderson retired to bed sick. It was not until a week later, on the 22nd, that he was able to take his place again at the dinner table. Even after that he had several bad patches. One must take off one's hat to these early pioneers – life was not always very easy for them. Even the ship's captain found the voyage hazardous and fell and hurt himself. He was a popular man and greatly endeared himself to the 865 people on board the great ship.

The cricketers were clearly a merry bunch and thought up many entertainments to while away the time. Dances, concerts, magic lantern shows, games of whist, walking races, mock trials, quoits and even 'cock-fights' were all enjoyed. This latter game was played between two opponents who had a stick passed at the back of their knee-joints and held there with their arms. Whilst in this uncomfortable position each tried to knock the other over. Caffyn used to like playing the cornet whilst Anderson had a fine voice and used to sing a solo or two.

At one of the concerts the following song was sung. The composer was no Wordsworth but at least the sentiment was sincere:

> There's the Cricketers bold the Eleven of All England
> As fine a set of fellows as e'er crossed the sea.
> I hope soon to see them with bat and ball in hand
> Astonishing the natives of proud Australie.
> May success attend them in all their endeavours
> And a very good harvest I hope they may reap;
> One little suggestion may I for them whisper
> Not to hold the offspring of England a little too cheap!

The diary of E. M. Grace was eventually published and, from letters which he wrote in 1900, it is clear that the author's permission was not sought. Perhaps at this distance of time we need not be too hard on the enterprising (or unscrupulous?) publisher. If he had not published the diary we would have known much less than we do about the trip to Australia in 1863.

Grace's medical skills were much needed, apart from tending to the victims of sea-sickness. On October 24th a little child, aged only five, died of dysentery. Six days previously a sailor had cut his finger off whilst eating dinner! On November 18th George Tarrant got toothache which was cured by pulling the tooth out — fortunately Dr Grace was first time lucky. He himself felt far from well at times with sea-sickness and he had to have a painful finger lanced. To cap it all, on October 30th Julius Caesar had the gout — surely an unusual complaint for an active cricketer!

After two months at sea the passengers must have thought that the rest of the journey would present no difficulties. On December 14th, however, a great gale arose and the rest of the story is best described in Grace's own words: 'Tuesday, Dec. 15th. The gales increased in fury during the night to that extent that the Captain stopped the screw and lay to; and now we are only "drifting" about two miles an hour, it is blowing awfully hard, and so thick was the weather that it was evening ere the Captain sighted Cape Otway.

'Wednesday Dec. 16th. — When we rose at six o'clock we all expected to be going through "The Heads", but there was no pilot to take us in. It was blowing a gale, and we lay to for a couple of hours drifting towards the shore, the Captain tried to steam out again, but uselessly, wind and sea being so strong against him. So Captain Gray was obliged to do what he had never done before, i.e. pilot the good ship inside the Heads, as no pilot boat could live outside. It was awfully nervous work; as we were going in the breakers on each side were tremendous, the waves at times being twenty or thirty feet above us; one most providentially broke just behind us, or most likely it would have swept some of us overboard. When safe through the Heads, the pilot came on board and conducted us through the Bay. Captain Gray told me, "that to possess the whole of Australia he would not suffer so for two days," he never would have attempted the pilotage if not obliged to.'

The next day the team arrived in Melbourne to find that there had been extensive flooding in the district. Soon the second tour of Australia was commenced. Here we bid farewell to the *Great Britain*. Perhaps if one goes to Bristol to see her in honourable retirement one will be able to think of George Anderson feeling sea-sick, of William Caffyn playing the cornet and of Dr E. M. Grace acting as a temporary dentist!

Playfair Cricket Monthly 1971

17

A Trip to Australia

E. M. Grace

Wednesday, Oct. 21 (192 miles). – Got up queer, medicined, and was better at twelve o'clock, when a breeze was felt from the right quarter, and ship driven before the wind a trifle out of her course. About 10 p.m., a tremendous rainstorm came on; luckily it lasted only ten minutes.

Thursday, Oct. 22 (151 miles). – Sighted a great many vessels to-day; spoke the *Seringapatam*, that sailed from Liverpool twenty days back; also spoke the *Great Australia*, from Liverpool on the 7th of October, for Melbourne, with about 600 passengers on board. We are still steaming away, what little wind there is abroad being in the wrong quarter.

Friday, Oct. 23 (179 miles). – Heat quite oppressive when we rose, and getting on deck, surprised to see land on both sides of us – the Islands of Madeira. Find I can lick all the rest of 'the twelve' at quoits and bull-board.

Saturday, Oct. 24 (201 miles). – Very warm. Passed through the Canary Islands to-day; some of the passengers saw a small whale; Mr ———, while pretending to box with R. Carpenter, lost his bowler hat overboard, so lent him my red cap. Regret to record, a little child, five years of age, died of dysentery this evening.

Sunday, Oct. 25 (194 miles). – Burial service read, and child buried in the deep at 2.30 a.m. A lovely morning! Service read and sermon preached on deck.

Monday, Oct. 26 (187 miles). – Wind gradually died away to nothing, so are now steaming away, and have just got into the tropics.

Piano in the saloon wants tuning badly; lots of singing by the ladies. A beautiful sunset, lovely in the extreme, but no twilight, as in dear old England; very close, especially in my berth.

Tuesday, Oct. 27 (192 miles). — Another lovely day and beautiful sunset; and quite equal in beauty was the rising of the moon; it was splendid. Hardly any wind, and at this rate of sailing shall not get to Melbourne this side of Christmas.

Wednesday, Oct. 28 (176 miles). — Still another beautiful day, and still pace awfully slow; any quantity of flying fish, from fifty to a hundred at a time; very playful things, and very odd to see fish about the size and shape of dace, jumping out of and turning somersaults before alighting on the water. Have been going along smoothly, but low, without the screw, but wish old Boreas would blow a bit stronger, it is so jolly without the 'thump', 'thump' of the screw. Had a meeting in saloon, to form a supreme court of the *Great Britain*, to try criminal cases once a week, prisoner to choose his own counsel; five to form a committee to elect a judge for each case, get up cases, &c.

Thursday, Oct. 29 (183 miles). — Still sailing but not more than seven or eight miles an hour; have bet we do ten before the morning; capital game of whist this evening.

Friday, Oct. 30 (183 miles). — All went smooth to-day until after dinner, when down came a tremendous sheet of rain; kept on for one hour, when wind changed; lost bet about the ten miles an hour; Julius Caesar got the gout rather severely.

Saturday, Oct. 31 (193 miles). — Steaming under bare poles all day; saw several porpoises. Trial on this evening; was subpoenaed as a witness, to prove that one of the witnesses for the prosecution was a ticket-of-leave man, returned convict, or anything in that line, but was not called on, prosecutor's evidence so weak. The trial is a case of attempted murder, brought by Mr Bright (a passenger) against Mr Maguire, the late American consul at Melbourne (another passenger), who was charged with giving Mr B. some 'bitters' which he said nearly poisoned him (all humbug, of course). Judge, jury (six in number), and counsel (two for each side) having assembled, the prisoner was brought in handcuffed, holding a Chinese fan in one hand, and in the other a tremendous bowie knife, which he termed 'his toothpick'. The counsel for the prosecution objected to the prisoner retaining so dangerous a weapon, and moved that the judge instruct the officer of the court to 'take away that bauble', so the judge asked to look at it; but the prisoner adroitly changed it for a cigar (smart fellow, this prisoner), and on that 'weapon' being handed up, the learned judge pocketed it, and said all danger was past. The prosecutor, in his nightcap, and face ghastly white, then gave evidence. He pretended he was so ill that he had lost his voice, so the captain's speaking-trumpet was fetched, and through that the prosecutor shouted 'he was nearly dead'. The compound, the prisoner told him, was bitters and thar-crouse (or, as the French call it, 'cart horse', because it made every one that took it *so strong*); *he* had nearly lost his life, and was convinced the stuff was a subtle poison, criminally given him by the prisoner. To prove the poison, they called Dr Moore, who had been everywhere, seen everything, and for many a long year had studied medicine in Persia, under the celebrated 'Dr Whiskey'. Had analyzed the so-called 'bitters', and found it to consist of essence of rattlesnake, a most deadly poison when taken in small quantities, but on cross-examination admitted it was very likely to prolong life if taken by the bottle at a draught two or three times a day. Other evidence was given against the prisoner, who called Captain Grey and several ladies and gentlemen as to character; but the principal witness for the defence was a Mr Madoch, who stated that from drinking the ship's sherry he was very ill the first two days (all gammon this) he was on board, losing in that period 7lbs in weight, but taking the prisoner's 'bitters' (witness wished he had a cellarful of them) had made him all right, and had increased his weight. '14lbs in fourteen days'. There was no getting over evidence like this. The jury unanimously returned a verdict of Not Guilty. The prisoner was restored to his friends, and the prosecutor, as a warning to others, justly fined 'a bottle of champagne'.

Sunday, Nov. 1 (181 miles). – Very wet; service on deck interrupted by rain, which continued for three hours. I have never seen such rain in England, and when it ceased there was so tremendous a head wind that, although steaming under bare poles, we made very little progress.

Monday, Nov. 2 (133 miles). – Crossed the Line at 6 p.m.; all very quiet, as tarring, shaving, and all that kind of thing is entirely done away with now aboard all ships; saw more porpoises and another small whale. Captain begins to think we shall have a long passage for the *Great Britain*.

Scraps from the Diary of One of the Twelve 1864

18

George Anderson's Diary

1864. January —
1st, New Years' day. Commenced the first match at Melbourne — a very fine day and the ground filled with spectators — the largest company we ever saw — about 14,000.

2nd. A.E.E. [All England Eleven] *v.* Melbourne contd., about 10,000 people there to-day.

3rd, Sunday — Went to Dinner at Mr Farrar's — Hutchinson called for me about 5 and drove me round about the country.

4th. A.E.E. *v.* Melbourne continued.

5th. A.E.E. *v.* Melbourne concluded — The Eleven had 6 wickets to fall and about 8 runs to get — myself and Caffyn not out.

6th. Started at a quarter past twelve for Sandhurst — passed thro' the Diggings — passed Mount Macedon on our way — fine ride.

7th. Commenced the first day's play at Sandhurst — very rough ground.

8th. Went this morning by invitation to Latham & Watson's reef — did not go down the shaft. Match contd.

9th. Went to the Prince of Wales reef at Eaglehawk — a very hot dusty morning and heavy rain in afternoon, in which we played and got wet through — won our match very easily.

10th. Returned to Melbourne to-day — Parr left behind very ill from Erysipelas.

11th. Started for Ballarat this morning and commenced the match — saw Braithwaite. B. Fryer & wife here.

12th. Match contd.

13th. Match concluded and left at half past twelve at night for Ararat. Travelled all night by coach and arrived at half past nine after a tremendous jolting.

14th. Commenced the match at Ararat — saw Henry Smith and Chr. Simpson and family.

15th. Match concluded and the Eleven won easily — in one innings — 22 played like so many old women. Saw John Little and wife.

16th. Went out with John Little to the Western, saw Geo. Kay. Dined with the 22 at night.

17th. Went to Eversley with Mr & Mrs Little and stayed all night. Most of the Eleven went fishing and shooting.

18th. Left Eversley for Maryboro' in the morning — passed thro' the amphitheatre — had invitation to stay and lunch at Avoca and met a very pleasant party — went on to Maryboro'. Every one out to see our arrival.

19th. Commenced play at Maryboro'. Went to ball in honour of the A.E. Eleven this evening — nearly all there.

20th. Match at Maryborough contd. Saw Harry Court's brother.

21st. Match at Maryboro' concluded — won easily. Started for Castlemaine at night — 30 miles across the country and arrived about nine at night.

22nd. Left Castlemaine for Melbourne arriving at noon.

23rd. Recd. welcome letter from home and preparing for the mail for England.

24th. Sent letters and papers off to England. Went to St Kilda to tea with Mr & Mrs May.

25th. Started for New Zealand at 10 o'clock by the *Alhambra* and as soon as we got out of smooth water began to be sick.

26th. Very sick and ill – steamer small and sea rough.

27th. Sea rough and self very sick.

28th. Fell out of berth and hurt myself.

29th. Felt very poorly and leg lame and sore all over, but went on deck most of the day.

30th. Called at Invercargill and left mail – in smooth water and felt a little better – left again at 8 a.m. for Dunedin. coasting the whole way along a fine bold shore – sea roughish with a head wind. Arrived off Port Chalmers at night and onshore.

31st. Entered the Harbour of Port Chalmers and went up close to the town and anchored. Went out after breakfast to a Maori Settlement of about 40 natives – some very fine half caste people amongst them. On our return the water was very rough and we were all a good deal frightened, being in a small open boat – returned on board the *Alhambra* and slept there all night.

Feb. 1st. Went on shore about eleven this morning at Port Chalmers. A procession of about a dozen boats was formed, manned by the watermen of the place. We occupied the last which was gaily decked out with flags and a very great demonstration was made – guns firing, band playing. Addresses were delivered to us in the principal hotel and afterwards we all sat down to luncheon. We then started for Dunedin in a coach drawn by 6 horses and driven by the celebrated 'Cabbage Tree Red' followed by a large number of carriages and horsemen. The road is newly made across the mountains and was frightfully grand. The town was filled with people and was the grandest reception ever seen by any of us.

2nd. Commenced the match at Dunedin.

Extracts from George Anderson's Diary 1863/4

19

Vernon Royle's Diary

Went up to Horn's place in the morning and watched some of our fellows play tennis. Lunched at the club. Practised afterwards and dined at the club with Horn in the evening before going to the Assembly Ball which was given in our honour. I enjoyed myself very much. The room was very tastefully decorated. At the far-end were placed bats and wickets and tents on each side where refreshments were served. Bye the bye I met Sandeman, an old B.N.C. man, very unexpectedly, he had just arrived from the Cape, so called on me at the hotel.

First day of our Match against 18 South Australians. In fact our first match in the Colonies. They went in first and made 110. Jarvis played best for them with 28. We got 106 for 4 wickets, Webbe 35, Hornby 42 not out.

Match continued. All our side out for 185. Self run out for 2. Hornby got 78. 10 of the 18 down in their 2nd innings for 98. Had to pack up after dinner at the club in the evening.

Went to breakfast with Fitzroy at the club. Match continued at 12.30. South Australians made 37 more, total 135. Went in to get 63, lost 7 wickets in doing it. Self and Emmett not out with 20 and 5 respectively. Dined at the club in the evening and left Adelaide afterwards for the *Semaphore* where we went on board the *Victoria* for Melbourne, sailed about 12 o'clock at midnight. We had all spent a very pleasant time in Adelaide, being treated with the greatest hospitality. Was very sorry to leave.

On the sea. *'Ill all day'*.

Ill in the morning, but rather better. Arrived at Sandridge end of Port

Phillip about 4 o'clock p.m. We passed the heads entering the bay about 12 o'clock, Queenscliffe is on the left on entering. The distance of this port from the heads to the landing place is 40 miles. Thus forming an immense harbour, as the heads are only about one mile apart. Even when inside you very nearly lose sight of land. On arriving off Sandridge we were met by the Committee and several gentlemen of the Melbourne club, who had come out in a steam launch. We went on board and were landing at Sandridge. Heard of the death of Princess Alice. Were driven to the Town Hall in drags and were there received by the Mayor etc. who welcomed us to Melbourne and drank our health in champagne. Went to see the end of the match between the Australians and 15 Victorians. The former won by about 5 wickets. Murdoch got 152. We all dined at the Melbourne club with '*Black-wood*' in the evening except Manly who went to see his cousin, who is Master of the Mint. Took up our quarters at the Mistal Hotel, Collins St.

Webbe and I went to lunch with Campbell at his father's house. Practised in the afternoon and went to Col. Anderson's to play tennis afterwards. Dined with Robinson at South Yarra in the evening.

Played in a match v. 18 West of England on the Melbourne ground. Harris, Hornby, Lucas & Hone also played. We got 416. Hornby 27, Lucas 79, Hone 13. Harris and self 8. Got the 18 out in 45 minutes for 34 runs. Dined with *Fanning* at the club, a Brother of Ned Fanning who was at B.N.C. with me.

Extracts from Vernon Royle's Diary
(MCC Tour to Australia) 1878/9

20

The Australian Cricketers at Home

M. Randal Roberts

If one looks at the fixture list of the Australians, which extends without a break from the beginning of May to the middle of September, it seems almost a misnomer to speak of them as ever being at home. It is difficult to have a fixed abode when you are compelled to be at the Oval one day, at Eastbourne the next, and two days afterwards at Sheffield. However, if the exigencies of their cricketing programme deprive the Australian Eleven of the delights of hearth and home during their campaign in England, the team, like other invading armies, occasionally enjoys the luxury of head-quarters. And the head-quarters of the Eleven, as everyone knows, are situated at the Inns of Court Hotel in Holborn. The hotel is, in fact, the base of operations from which Major Wardill, the manager, directs the movements of his troops, and to which the army of invaders periodically returns after a victorious onslaught on one of the counties.

Truth compels me to admit that on the occasion of my spending a day with the Australians at their London home I was not an invited guest. It was I who proposed the visit. However, I didn't meet with the fate that usually awaits the self-invited guest. On the contrary, Major Wardill and his merry men gave me as warm a welcome as if I had been an old friend whom they had long been pressing to visit them. Probably I bored them, but at any rate they didn't show it, though for one whole day I lived and moved and had my being among them, just as if I had been a member of the eleven.

The clocks in Holborn only pointed to a few minutes past nine when I reached the Inns of Court Hotel, but, early as it was, two or three of the Australians had already finished breakfast. Major Wardill was sitting at a table in the corner of the room, with a huge pile of letters in front of him, which told plainly enough that the manager of a touring team must have the pen of a ready writer if he attends personally to all his correspondence. Hugh Trumble was reclining in a capacious saddle-bag, deep in thought, and looking as if he were devising new methods (it wanted only three weeks to the first of the Test Matches) for getting England's batsmen out. But Hugh Trumble has always a preoccupied air, so perhaps his thoughts may have been engaged on a far less interesting problem.

Presently the rest of the team began to drop in one by one. I hope I am not giving away any secrets when I state that the last to put in an appearance was Clem Hill.

I can conscientiously recommend a breakfast with the Australians as a first-rate recipe to anyone afflicted with an attack of the blues. There was a joke ready for each new-comer, and there was a general air of hilarity which one associates more with a party of light-hearted schoolboys than with a team which has travelled all the way from Australia on the serious business of trailing the flag of English cricket in the dust. As Mr Trumble moved across the room to Major Wardill and came within range of the photographer's weapon, one of his companions at the breakfast table threw an elongated bâton of bread over to him, with the remark, 'Here, Hughie, you mustn't be photographed without a bat in your hand.' Trumble caught the impromptu bat and made a fine forward stroke with it, but he declined altogether to let the tableau be preserved in a photograph.

Long before breakfast was over I descried a familiar figure in the doorway. It was the burly form of Jim Phillips, the Anglo-Australian cricketer, who can boast that for the last seven years he has never seen a winter. This pleasant feat he has achieved by the simple expedient of playing cricket in England during the summer and in Australia during our winter— a see-saw piece of work that most of us envy him. Phillips is engaged with the Australian team as official scorer, and on that particular morning had looked in to see Major Wardill on a matter of business, as he had doubtless done on many mornings before. But it at once occurred to my mind that there was quite a dramatic touch about Phillips's presence there. Here was the man whose action in no-balling Mr Jones during Mr Stoddart's last tour in Australia had caused more commotion than any event of the last twenty years in the cricket world, standing side by side and chatting pleasantly with the very cricketer whose bowling he had condemned. As a matter of fact, there was really nothing remarkable about the incident, as the Australians, like the good sportsmen they are, feel nothing but respect for an umpire who has the courage of his convictions; but not having seen the two men in the same room before, the scene struck me in much the same light as if I had found Lord Salisbury and Sir William Harcourt hobnobbing together.

The post that morning had brought to each of the team a small pamphlet, the work of some one of the multitudinous army of cricket writers whom every visit of Australians to this country brings into being giving a highly imaginative life-story of every member of the team, which proved far more interesting than the historian could possibly have anticipated. It added a relish to Mr Darling's breakfast to find himself described as the finest batsman in Australia. This was satisfactory so far as it went, and his natural pride was not abated on discovering that exactly the same terms of praise were applied to Mr Hill. Any batsman living could feel well disposed towards the writer who bracketed him with Clem Hill, but the glow of satisfaction began to cool when it appeared that the pamphleteer, in his desire to extol the merits of the team, had described each and every member of it as 'undoubtedly the best batsman in Australia.'

The quarters specially reserved for the Australians in the hotel consist of a cluster of bedrooms, all on the same floor, and a large room overlooking the comparatively peaceful wastes of Lincoln's Inn Fields which is used as a common room and dining-room by the team. On the outside of the door of this room is affixed a conspicuous placard bearing the legend, 'PRIVATE. RESERVED FOR THE AUSTRALIAN XI.' This placard is mainly intended to warn off interviewers and other irresponsible callers, and for the sake of further security a waiter is told off specially to guard the threshold.

Speaking as a mere native of the British Isles I should have called the weather warm, but the Australians evidently thought differently, for a bright fire was burning in the breakfast-room. The sight of that fire was very suggestive of the contrast between the climates here and 'down under.' There is nothing, Clem Hill remarked to me, which strikes the Australian cricketer on his first visit to this country more than the premature stiffness which is so prevalent among English players.

The everyday sight on an English ground of a man who is unable to 'shy,' and can do nothing but 'jerk,' is unknown in Australia. Even Colonials who have passed their cricket prime, and have reached the age of forty, can still throw with much the same dash as of old. Among the best English teams there is often a woeful deficiency in this essential to good fielding; the cold and damp of our Northern climate penetrates into the bones and creates a chronic and incurable stiffness often before a man is thirty.

'Major,' said Mr Noble, from the end of the room, where he was attentively examining a barometer, 'what time did you say that train of ours starts?' The Major replied that there was no need to worry about trains, as he had ordered a four-horse shay to convey the team to Leyton that morning. This was the signal for a general move. Within a couple of minutes the Major was left alone trying to solve the problem of how the team was to be at Bradford till 6.31 Wednesday evening, and at Lord's the next morning, without travelling in the night; while the said team were in their bedrooms, tumbling bats, boots, and shirts into eleven cricket bags, preparatory for their battle against Essex, which was to begin at Leyton a couple of hours later.

Mr Jones I found in his room with one hand on his cricket bag and the other on the button of the electric bell, in a state of consternation, because one of his cricket boots was missing. Finally, however, the absent boot was recovered, and the eleven came clattering down the stairs to the front hall. The Major's four-horse shay, which took the form of a remarkably smart drag, was standing in readiness at the Holborn entrance. Oddly enough, though the street was crowded at the time, it apparently did not occur to any of the passers-by that the coach contained the Australian Eleven. A couple of small boys and their smaller sister tumbled to the fact and raised a weak cheer, but, otherwise, the team passed unnoticed from the hall door to the roof of the four-in-hand.

As the story of how the Australians fared at Leyton will be stale history by the time this appears in print, the reader must now imagine, after the manner of Acts I and II in a melodrama, a period of eight hours to have elapsed.

The official dinner-hour of the team, when they are in London at any rate, is seven o'clock, but this fixture is an elastic one. However, on this particular evening, as the men returned in good time from Leyton, it was punctually observed. Inasmuch as the Australians dine on exactly the same lines as other less distinguished mortals, I am not going to describe the dinner. But it may possibly interest those who hold the creed that stimulants are necessary to sustained exertion to learn that two of the team are confirmed water drinkers.

Judging from the bushels of invitation cards which lay piled on Major Wardill's table, it seemed as if there were a conspiracy among the managers of every entertainment in London to deprive the Australians of their well-earned repose after a match. However, as luck had it, on this particular day they had an off evening. So after dinner, when cigars were produced, we still sat around the room chatting about everything in general and cricket in particular.

The conversation drifted to the comparative merits of devoting only three days to a match, as is done in county cricket, and of playing every important game to a finish, as the custom is in Australia. Gregory, Trumble, and Hill were very emphatic in declaring that they enjoy cricket far more in England than in Australia. That our three-day fixtures produce much more lively batting than the indefinitely extended matches in Australia is a fact with which every cricket spectator will agree, but it was interesting to hear the opinion of three players who have had practical experience of the pros and cons of the methods which prevail in both countries.

The visit of an Australian team to this country, I learned, is a far more formal affair than any of the tours in Australia undertaken by English cricketers. Before the present Australian team started each of the members signed an official agreement under which he bound himself to observe certain conditions. One of the most notable of these conditions was that during the tour none of the team should contribute to the Press either in this country or in Australia. I only mention this as a good instance of the serious spirit in which the tour was undertaken. The Australians have come over with the object of beating England if they can, and anything likely to interfere with their attaining that result is to be rigidly eschewed.

There is no recipe for making time fly like talking cricket gossip. Before I had heard half of what the new-comers had to tell me of their impressions of cricket in the old country the clock had struck eleven, and as there was evidently a disposition to move bedwards, I considerately took my departure.

Strand Magazine 1899

156

21

Some Notes on Early Cricket Abroad

F. S. Ashley-Cooper

It is many years since a 'poet' wrote:
No German, Frenchman, or Fijee will ever master cricket, sir,
Because they haven't got the pluck to stand before the wicket, sir.'

The falsity of the lines has long been proved, and cricket can claim to be played in almost every part of the world. Pycroft never spoke truer words than when he said: 'Every regiment and every man-o'-war has its club; and our soldiers sailors astonish the natives of every clime, both inland and maritime, with a specimen of a British game.' Did not members of the Royal Navy play 'Krickett' near Aleppo (about seventy miles east of the Mediterranean) as early as 1676, the crews of H.M. Ships 'Fury' and 'Hecla' do the same as far north as latitude 69 at Igloolik in 1822, the men of the Training Squadrons play at Recherché Bay, Spitzbergen, when

'The sun was shining brightly, shining with all his might,
And this was odd, because it was the middle of the night';

and did not our troops proceed to pitch wickets in Baghdad the day after the city was captured? Not every follower of the game is aware of the difficulties with which our sailors have had to contend in order to enjoy a game. They have even gone to the length of cleaning a ditch surrounding an obsolete fortress in Cyprus so as to play a pick-up match, and more than once boat-sails have been laid down on an African desert in order to procure a pitch which would be a billiard-table compared with the outfield.

A facetious critic once wrote: 'The game is essentially English, and though our countrymen carry it abroad wherever they go, it is difficult

157

to inoculate or knock it into the foreigner. The Italians are too fat for cricket; the French too thin; the Dutch too dumpy; the Belgians too bilious; the Flemish too flatulent; the East Indians too peppery; the Laplanders too bow-legged; the Swiss too sentimental; the Greeks too lazy; the Egyptians too long in the neck; and the Germans too short in the wind.'

The appended notes, it may be well to point out, touch only lightly on early cricket abroad, for to deal with the subject in any detail would require far more space than is at command. As a similar review has not been attempted before, it is hoped that some of the information which follows will be found useful and not without interest.

Europe

Details of the beginnings of cricket in France are lost in the mists of antiquity, for it can be said, as of many other countries, that the game was played there before details were published. Yet we know that as early as 1777 Boydell issued an engraving showing a match in progress at Belle Isle, and that within the next decade it was only the outbreak of the French Revolution which prevented the Surrey team, on the suggestion of the Duke of Dorset, then our Ambassador in Paris, going over to show the game in the Bois de Boulogne. The eleven, in fact, had journeyed as far as Dover — Yalden, the wicket-keeper, had been chosen captain — when, most unexpectedly, it was met by the Duke, who was flying before the coming storm. Soon after the Napoleonic wars the game took firm root in the country, owing largely to the presence of lace-workers from Nottingham, and before the middle of the last century clubs existed, if they did not actually flourish, at Dieppe, Calais, Boulogne, Bordeaux, St Servan, Paris, St Omer, and other places. As early as 1833 St Omer met Boulogne three times, the former team including Mr Wettenhall, sen., aged 62, four of his sons, and a grandson. Messrs. Woodbridge and Charles Beauclerk, both well-known at Lord's, were supporters of the St Omer CC, whose ground was described as 'an open plain, a fine sward, on a free-stone bottom, which makes it peculiarly elastic.' It was, therefore, evidently superior to that at Boulogne, which was stated to be 'a meadow, which was cropped last year.' An impetus to the game was given by occasional visits of teams from Nottingham, and respecting one of these events the late Dean Hole wrote:

'That England has no rival
Well know the trembling pack,
Whom Charley Brown by Calais town
Bowl'd out behind his back,'

the said Brown possessing the genius of being able to deliver the ball at a good pace round his back with astonishing precision.

Since those far-distant days several well-known clubs, including MCC and Butterflies, have played in France, and such events have almost invariably been productive of curious comments from the locals, whose views were, to say the least, generally original. Thus, when the MCC were in Paris in 1867 a Frenchman remarked to 'Bob' Fitzgerald: 'It is a truly magnificent game, but I cannot understand why you do not engage a servant to field for you instead of having so much running-about to do yourself'; and in a report of the play it was recorded in all seriousness, 'The bowler, grasping the ball in the right hand, watches for the favourable moment when the attention of the batsman is distracted, and then launches it at him with incredible force; the batsman, however, is on the alert; he strikes it to an enormous height, and immediately runs.' This quaint view of things recalls the fact that, whilst the Emperor (Napoleon III), Empress and Prince Imperial were watching a match between Bickley Park and Beckenham, long-on brought off a difficult and spectacular catch. A minute or so later a gentleman-in-waiting, hat in hand, approached the successful fieldsman with a message from the Emperor, thanking him very much for his performance, and asking him to do it again. On another occasion the Emperor asked whether a certain West Kent match was being played for money, and Herbert Edlmann answered in his most dignified manner, 'No, sire; for honour.' At least once, however, the same Napoleon proved a good friend to cricketers. He had visited the Paris CC, and had the game explained to him, and this circumstance saved the club, for a few days afterwards an old Oxford man, while making a run, tripped, fell and broke his arm. The matter was at once reported to the police, and the club was about to be suppressed as dangerous, when an appeal to the Emperor prevented so dire a calamity.

Reference to the Paris CC recalls that, in 1865, there was published a handbook of 24 pages entitled, 'La Clef Du Cricket; ou Courte Explication De La Marche et Des Principales Règles De Ce Jeu. Par An

Old Stump, MPCC.' It dealt with cricket generally, and gave the twenty rules of the Paris CC.

The unconscious humour of which the French mind has proved so prolific was never more in evidence than in a 'Guide,' in which, by means of a conversation, every word of which is most amusing, an attempt was made to explain the intricacies of the game. The performance ended thus:

'It seems very dangerous, Henri.'

'True! For me, I would rather exercise myself with diabolo or dominoes.'

The description was written in all seriousness, and to this day the author of it probably considers that he produced a valuable treatise on the game. Many years ago, I can recall, a 'Maire' of a seaside resort much favoured by English families, decided to promote a fête for the benefit of the younger visitors, in which 'Juvenile Sports,' with cricket as the chief attraction, were to be held. The good man, wishing his plans to obtain as much publicity as possible, decided to make an English translation of the French posters and handbills. The idea was sound, but unfortunately the announcements in English were headed 'Childish Games,' much to the righteous indignation of the visiting youth old enough to take part in a properly-organized match. All this notwithstanding, however, there is a serious side to the game in France, and for years there has been a cricket League in Paris. From time to time, too, France has met Belgium and Holland, and, on at least one occasion, Germany.

The recent visit of an MCC team to Cologne broke fresh ground, for never before had the premier club sent a side to Germany. Many followers of cricket may smile at the idea of the game being played in that country except by Englishmen, yet the fact remains that in 1910 the MCC were asked to send a team to Nurnberg, and that three years later attempts were made to induce an Australian side to play a series of matches in Germany in 1916. There probably was a certain amount of enthusiasm for the game there, but the standard of proficiency attained was very low, for when a Leicester team went to Berlin in 1911 it won each of its four games with an innings and over 100 runs to spare.

The modern history of cricket in Germany really dates from 1858, when the Berlin CC, which became the Anglo-American CC, was formed. One of the most amusing features of the club's early matches was the large number of accidents with which the spectators met. The natives, not understanding the game, thought that the nearer they approached the better view would they obtain, and in this belief they persisted, repeated warnings notwithstanding. Wrecked hats and parasols, contused shins, and severe bruises became of almost every-day occurrence; but it was long before these would-be spectators, realizing that a cricket ball really can hurt, decided to give the cricket-field a wide berth.

Hamburg became an early centre of the game owing to the large number of English visitors who wished to avail themselves of the mineral springs there. Thus in August, 1863, Lord Marcus Beresford, then a youth of fourteen, helped Hamburg to beat Frankfurt by an innings and six runs. In the same month an eleven of Cambridge University were seen in Dresden, where they beat the local club, in the Grosse Gehege, by seven wickets. The curious can find the full scores of both these games in Capt. W. Bayly's 'Cricket Chronicle for the Season 1863.' The greatest days of Hamburg cricket, however, were in 1865, when there was a Grand Cricket Week. Among the well-known Englishmen who participated were Mr J. Round, who kept wicket for the Gentlemen; the Rev S. C. Voules, of Marlborough and Oxford fame; and Mr Charles Alcock, for so long Secretary to the Surrey County CC. Those who played enjoyed themselves immensely, but the inhabitants, not understanding the game, looked on in stolid silence, evidently regarding cricket as hard work and not a recreation. To the German porters, too, the size and shape of the cricket bags were a source of wonder, at which they did not cease to express their aston-ishment for many a long day. The original idea was that 'England' should play fourteen of Europe, but, almost at the last moment, it was agreed that the latter side should consist of seventeen men. Although allowing such odds, the Englishmen won both games, the first after a fairly close finish, the second by an innings and 51 runs. The Festival was concluded by a match in which France, represented by the Paris CC, beat Germany. Mr Alcock captained the successful side, and as he made top score, was presented publicly with a cricket bat, which, as he declared, 'must have been made in France.' For years afterwards a favourite match at Hamburg was 'Eton and Harrow v. The World.' Several well-known players took part in these games at different times, including W. H. Long, now the first Lord Long.

The Anglo-American Club, mentioned above, used to meet on the Hippodrome Riding Ground at the corner of the Charlottenburg Road, near the Zoological Gardens. Its success, however, proved its undoing, for the Berliners, envious of its popularity, took it over, lock, stock and barrel — a high-handed action which caused no little resentment. One result of the proceeding was that more Germans became interested in the game, although the standard of the cricket was naturally not so high as before. The club, under its new auspices, used to assemble in the Tempelhofer Feld, and their chief match was with the Kjobenhaven Bold Club of Copenhagen.

Karlsruhe also was an early centre of the game, and a history of its doings was published as far back as 1874. Jena v. Weimar, too, was for long an annual match, the first meeting of the sides being in June, 1883, when, after a terrific struggle, Jena won by a single run. Mention of the book on the Karlsruhe CC reminds one that at various times several publications on the game have been issued in Germany. Strange though it may seem, some of these enjoyed quite a good sale, notwithstanding that in the majority of instances they contained but little reading matter and illustrations only of such commonplace things as cricket boots, bats, and stumps, with perhaps a few diagrams for the placing of the field. Although of little value, however, from the English point of view, these handbooks have much interest for a collector of cricket literature. One of the best of them was that issued at Stuttgart in 1893, the chief contents of which were a sketch of the game's history, an explanatory chapter on the laws, and instructions for players. The author's knowledge of his subject was fairly sound, but the same cannot be said respecting the artist responsible for the illustrations. One of the plates, showing a game in progress, is decidedly amusing, for the bats are like Indian clubs, the wicket as broad as it is high, the creases of prodigious length, while something suspiciously like a holly bush is shown flourishing vigorously about half-way down the pitch. The telegraph board, too, is a short distance behind the wicket-keeper while the fieldsmen are shown wearing knickerbockers and pads, and the bowlers using leg-guards and wicket-keeping gloves. On another page is a picture of a women's match. Here we find two of the fieldswomen standing so close in that they could shake hands with each other and the batswoman. There are apparently two wicket-keeperesses, and the umpire, a man, is shown standing so close in that nothing but an accident or Providence could possibly prevent him from being cut off in his prime.

A book which lacked such amusing blunders was published at Leipzig in 1907. From an Englishman's point of view the most valuable feature of this is the glossary of terms in English and German, with their pronunciation and the laws to which they refer. It might be worth while for some publisher in this country to expand the idea by giving a list of the chief terms used in the game with their French, Dutch, and German equivalents. That the military occupation of the Rhine has done something to popularize the game in Germany is apparent from the fact that this year alone the MCC, Gentlemen of Holland, Oxford Authentics, Butterflies, Cryptics, Hampshire Hogs, and other visiting teams have played in Cologne.

In the Iberian Peninsula the game is known to have been played over a century ago, for an officer who served under Crawford in the famous Light Division wrote in his journal to the following effect in 1810, shortly before the Battle of Busaco: 'We found things pretty slow, kicking our heels in idleness at Lisbon. So one of us got a kindly ship's carpenter to make us some cricket implements. He did very well, but the difficulty was the ball. He turned a piece of wood about the size and shape of a cricket ball, but the missile proved more deadly than the enemy's fire, and after several of us had been more or less severely wounded, we abandoned this form of amusement. Later, however, the game was resumed when proper implements had been received from England.' Lisbon *v.* Oporto has long been a regular fixture, and, considering the difficulties of travel which have to be contended with, it said much for the keenness of the players that the matches took place. Thus, when the sides met at Lisbon in 1873, it was reported that the journey of the Oporto team was 200 miles by rail, and took thirteen hours to perform 'through a sweltering sun.' This notwithstanding, however, the Oporto men won a well-contested game by 11 runs. Several teams from England have visited the country, giving a most welcome fillip to the game. So far as Spain is concerned, there is an interesting note in Capt. the Hon. D. Bingham's 'Recollections of Paris,' in which, referring to the year 1867, he wrote: 'With the aid of some artillery-men, who had come over with English guns to the Exhibition, we got up a very fair eleven, of which I was captain, and played a foreign eleven — an eleven of Spaniards or Spanish-speaking lads from the South American Republic, who were being educated in England, and had come over to Paris to see the Exhibition. . . . Alas! we lost the match by one run. The Spanish bowling was a trifle too good for us. It will be recalled that last year a team from Bilbao visited us, winning three games and losing two.'

It is always interesting to hear a foreigner's candid view of cricket, and therefore the following short extracts are taken from a Lisbon paper of over fifty years ago: '. . . an active, running, driving, jumping game, which can only be played by a person having a good pair of legs, and in a climate where warmed punch is found insufficient to keep up animal heat. . . . Sometimes it (the ball) tumbles into a thicket and the players take hours before they can get hold of it, and all this time the player does not cease running from post to post and marking points. . . . At other times the projectile sent with a vigorous arm cannot be stopped, and breaks the leg of the party who awaits it. The arrangements for the cricket-match include a sumptuous dinner in the marquee for fifty persons, an indispensable accompaniment to every cricket match.' Quaint as much of the foregoing is, it hardly surpasses in sheer drollery the following, which appeared in the 'Comercio de Portugal' in 1895, the year in which 'W.G.' received a national testimonial: 'The value of the *objets d'art* − chronometers, chains, rings, medals, etc. − which have been presented to him, are worth nearly eighty millions of reis. He earns some forty millions of reis per annum, that is to say more than the Duke of Cambridge as Commander-in-Chief, and more than most magistrates and other British functionaries receive.'

It is many years since *Punch* wrote:

> 'In matters of cricket the fault of the Dutch
> Is hitting too little and missing too much.'

Such lines would be libellous now, and would have been for long past. When the game in Holland was young the standard of play was naturally far from high, but pains were taken, and with success, to eradicate faults and effect improvement. There is a record of the existence as far back as 1855 of a club at Utrecht, formed by some gentlemen from the Cape of Good Hope, who were then at Utrecht University, but all particulars of its doings seem to have been lost. For all practical purposes the history of the game in the country may be said to date from October 13, 1875, when the first Dutch cricket club was formed, at Daventer, by Mr. Romiju, a former Consul in England who, although not a player himself, was quite enthusiastic about the game. Owing chiefly to the lack of instructors, however, the club had only a short existence, but in May, 1878, the Haageche Club was formed under the title of the Concordia CC, and it was soon followed by the institution of others at Haarlem, Amsterdam, Utrecht, Leyden, Rotterdam, etc. In fact, such popularity was there for the game that within ten years over 100 clubs were established. It was in 1881 that an English side, the Uxbridge CC, was seen in Holland for the first time, and, although not strong, it was good enough to dismiss XXII of Holland for totals of 14 and 33, there being sixteen 'ducks' in the first innings, and thirteen in the second. As it was recorded that 'many thousands must have paid for admission,' it is evident that the game must already have progressed far in the affections of the public. That tour was the first of forty which have been made from this country, among the sides which have made the trip being the Gentlemen of Worcestershire, MCC, Gentlemen of Bucks, and Free Foresters. In September, 1883, the Dutch Cricket Union (Nederlandsche Cricket-Bond) was formed, and in 1887, through the generosity of Baron Tuyll, the patron of the Haarlem Club, the services of an English professional were obtained. A red-letter day in the annals of Dutch cricket occurred in 1888, when, for the first time, a visiting team (the Dalston Albert CC) was defeated. The successful side was the Hague CC, whose victory occasioned much joy. 'Nederlandsche Sport', in its description, did not fail to do full justice to the event, its report commencing: 'Bravo den Haag! Well played! zal er zeker wel in alle', etc.

It was, of course, very slowly that the finer points of the game became recognised by spectators, and a member of one of the earlier visiting sides has told how, upon making a good hit which merited applause, he was informed in a loud voice from the ring: 'I will beg you to pay attention, for if anyone should be hit the game will have to be stopped.' But, considering the disadvantages under which cricketers in Holland have laboured, it is surprising that such good results have been obtained. The lack of sound instruction and good wickets must have combined to form a serious handicap to advancement, and even within the last twenty years it could be said with truth that there was only one ground in the country — that at the Hague — which had a good mowing-machine. Fortunately, enthusiasm was most marked, and a move in the right direction was made when, in 1892, a team came over to play a series of games in Yorkshire. Five later trips have been made to this country, and although the Gentlemen of Holland have at no time been equal to meeting the Gentlemen of England on level terms, many will be able to recall with appreciation the all-round skill of Mr C. J. Posthuma, who played not only for Dutch teams, but also for the London County CC. So far Holland's international matches have been chiefly with France and Belgium, a series of games in which their record is distinctly good. Should anyone wish to read in some detail the story of the rise of Dutch cricket he may be recommended to obtain 'Cricket', by W. Muller, a book of 247 pages, illustrated by the author, and published at Haarlem twenty-five years ago.

Belgium was accorded an early chance of taking to cricket, for the Earl of Carlisle wrote to George Selwyn from Spa on August 28, 1768: 'I rise at six, am on horseback till breakfast, play at cricket till dinner, and dance in the evening till I can scarce crawl to bed at eleven. There is a life for you.' Later – *longo intervallo* – the game was revived in the country by our Army. Col. Basil Jackson, in his 'Notes and Reminiscences of a Staff Officer,' mentions cricket being played at Brussels in 1814, whilst Capt. Gordon, as quoted by Pycroft in 'The Cricket Field', said: 'Some of our officers were amusing themselves on the 12th of June, 1815, in company with that devoted cricketer, the Duke of Richmond, when the Duke of Wellington arrived, and shortly after came the Prince of Orange, which, of course, put a stop to our game. Though the hero of the Peninsular War was not apt to let his movements be known, on this occasion he made no secret that, if he were attacked from the south, Halle would be his position, and, if on the Namur side, Waterloo.' For many seasons matches between Ostend and Bruges were played fairly regularly, such meetings dating back over seventy years, and Brussels, too, was not far behind. It was at Brussels that, in 1910, a Quadrangular Tournament took place between Belgium, England (an MCC team), France, and Holland, and the same year a Belgian team was seen in this country for the first time.

The credit of introducing the game into Denmark is generally attributed to English engineers whilst building railways, between fifty and sixty years ago, and the first club is said to have been formed at Soro. As early as 1866 an interesting booklet entitled 'Haandbog I

Cricket og Langbold' was published at Copenhagen, and that the game must have been taken up with enthusiasm is evident from the fact that during the next twenty years about seventy clubs sprang up in the country. The Boldklub, of Copenhagen, has for long occupied a foremost position, whilst in Mr Charles Buchwald, Denmark has produced at least one batsman who, in his prime, was in county form. On July 3, 1904, he established a new Danish record in the shape of an innings of 187 not out, and it was somewhat remarkable that on the very same day P. Petersen should have made 178 not out for the Boldklub. Buchwald's batting that season for the Copenhagen University team (Akademisk Boldklub) was extraordinary, for his innings were 113 not out, 65 not out, 85, 187 not out, and 82 — a total of 532, and an average of 266! Since the war a great impetus has been given to the game by visits from the British Army of Occupation on the Rhine, Leicester clubs, and the MCC. The Leicester team played seven games in 1921, and the MCC three this year, all ten being won by the visitors. At Copenhagen, against the Leicester combination, Buchwald played an innings of 113.

There is evidence to suggest that Italians owed their first sight of the game to the enthusiasm of Nottinghamshire men living in the country, for the 'York Courant,' of August 28, 1828, informs us that a Nottingham tradesman had been asked to send 'a dozen sets of cricket apparatus' to Italy, but to which district was, unfortunately, not stated. Still, we know that in December, 1839, three of the World beat two of Eton by two wickets at Naples, where 'the ground was kept by a party of the King's Guards, and the match created considerable interest and excitement.' About a year later Frederic Tennyson, brother of the poet, wrote to Edward Fitzgerald saying he had fought a cricket match with the crew of the 'bellerophon' on the Parthenopaean Hills, and had 'sacked' the sailors by 90 runs. Fitzgerald's comment was: 'Is not this pleasant? — the notion of good English blood striving in worn-out Italy. I like that such men as Frederic should be abroad; so strong, haughty, and passionate. They keep up the English character abroad.' Old Public Schoolmen 'kept the ball rolling' in the country, and when an Oxford and Cambridge team beat 'All the World' at Rome in May, 1843, in a match 'for 500 scudi a-side,' we were informed that the game 'excited the astonishment of the Romans, some of whom have termed it the game of madmen.' Still, the

Englishmen proved their sanity by dining together afterwards at Melgo's Hotel. Later a flourishing club was formed at Pau, the honorary secretary and leading spirit being the late Major Naylor Leyland.

What was said in *The Cricketer* of September 2 (page 16) respecting cricket in Turkey need not be repeated here. The chief points of interest were then enumerated, but to them may be added the fact that one Sultan at least actually witnessed a match. The fortunate sovereign was Abdul Aziz, who, after watching some English officers at play, remarked: 'Wonderful, wonderful! What exertion the game requires! But why don't you make your servants do all this?' — a point of view very similar to that expressed to Mr R. A. Fitzgerald in Paris. What was claimed to be the first match ever played in Macedonia took place, under war-time conditions, in June, 1916. It was between the Lothian and Border Horse (55) and 81st Brigade Field Ambulance (27 and 11). The bats were made on the field of play, and the ball, correct as to size, weight, and shape, was fashioned by an Army saddler.

Of cricket in Greece itself there are only occasional traces, but in Corfu, especially during the British protectorate (1815—63), many good matches have been played. Interregimental games were frequent, but of more note were the meetings between the Fleet and a combined Garrison team. In later years the Greeks there took kindly to the game, and in 1891 an English cricketer, whilst staying in the island, played in one match in which he found himself without a fellow-countryman on either side. All the expressions use were English, such as 'well played,' 'well bowled,' etc., but in the score-sheet, 'bowled', 'caught', 'stumped', etc., were entered in Greek. The Greeks were good fieldsmen, and were keen enough to practise every afternoon.

Russia is a country one does not readily associate with cricket, and probably many will be surprised to hear that at least three Tsars have been acquainted with the game. In 1814, 'upon the glorious termination of the war in Belgium', Alexander I, with George III and Blucher watched a game played by Eton boys at Frogmore; some years later Nicholas I attended a match on Chatham Lines, and, taking up a ball which had fallen near him, said to the Colonel: 'I don't wonder at the courage of you English, when you teach your children to play with cannon-balls'; while the late Nicholas II not only took a keen interest in the game, but actually had a cricket-pitch in the grounds of the

Imperial Palace at Peterhof. Even sixty years ago there were certainly two clubs in the Russian capital, the St Petersburg and the Alexandrossky, but the grounds were very rough, and extras often headed the score.

An amusing story used to be told at Oxford of a wealthy young Russian of Merton College who was invited to play in a Myrmidon match, and was advised to provide himself with the necessary implements. Determined to do the thing thoroughly, he betook himself to London and ordered, besides other things, a bat, pads, gloves, wicket-keeping gauntlets, stumps, bails, a cap, a belt (with a brass cricketer on the buckle), a bag, a score-book for a hundred matches, a ball, and — a large tent. He had the reputation of being an excellent sportsman.

When the first game was played in St Petersburg the ground was surrounded by troops, as the authorities were uncertain of the nature of the proposed display. In 'Scores and Biographies' is to be found an amusing account of a match in the capital between the English Residents and the Royal Yacht 'Osborne' on the Cadet Corps ground, in 1875. 'Great astonishment was created in the minds of the natives by the performances of some fifty bluejackets from the Royal yacht, who, with that dauntless gallantry that always characterizes the British tar, played rounders with promiscuous cricket balls through the afternoon, varying the game with leap-frog and bull-baiting. A message, indeed, arrived from the chef de police, demanding an explanation of the presence of this "force of warriors" in the midst of the Russian Woolwich. The answer was apparently satisfactory, as the "warriors" were allowed to depart unmolested, all evidently delighted with their day on shore.' Cricket was introduced into Odessa in 1881, and the first match was attended by many Russian grandees. The practice of the game, however, was confined to Englishmen and a few Americans, and in the occasional matches with Constantinople no Russian ever took part.

It seems strange to recall how readily cricket was taken to by the inhabitants of the Kola Peninsula. Home-made bats and balls were used, and a six a-side single-wicket match was played between CI (16 and 14) and All Lapland (18 and 0). The full score survives, and we are informed that the girls retired, reducing the strength of each side! 'The match was attended from beginning to end with shouts of *Horosho!*

Horosho igrali! Good! Well played! and loud laughter. Heads were out of every window: *moujiks* and women were grinning from ear to ear at each hit or blunder. When the result was made known there was cheering such as Kola had probably never heard before. Thus was Angelskaya igra introduced into Russian Lapland. It might have been the introduction of a Constitution, to judge by the popular enthusiasm. In an hour or two, after everybody had dispersed and gone to bed – that is, at one o'clock in the morning – our attention was directed to a noise in front of our windows. The members of the late CI and All Lapland Elevens were engaged in another single-wicket match. Unable to sleep, they had got up to plunge again into the fascinating game. They appointed captains, chose sides, and played as well without us as with us. Now and then a difficult question arose, and they detained me at the open window for appeal as umpire. Cricket has become the rage in the White Sea Peninsula.'

The first Swiss to become acquainted with cricket was César de Saussure, who paid two visits to England in the first half of the eighteenth century, and referred to the game in his 'Lettres et Voyages' (p. 299). But many years were to pass before cricket made any headway in his own country. It was not until 1850 that John Rankin, for many years Honorary Secretary of the Wandsworth Private CC, founded a club at Geneva known as the British and Geneva CC, and became its first President. The club flourished, and more than once played matches with Lyons. Mr Andrew Lang claimed, but erroneously, to have introduced the game into Switzerland. He certainly played it many times there in light-hearted fashion, and was fond of recalling a game in the Market-place of Zug, with a camp-stool for wicket; which came to a sudden termination owing to a tremendous slog over the bowler's head going through the Burgomaster's window.

Asia

Cricket in Persia has been known for at least seventy years, but it can hardly be said that the game there has flourished. Matches at Bushire, however, date back as far as 1856, when the British seized the town in the war regarding Herat. Although the Expeditionary Force found it necessary to bore holes for the stumps in a large flat rock, and to field in deep sand under a burning sun, they enjoyed their games. Since then cricket has been played there by the local Gymkhana, the I.E. Government Telegraphists, and teams of men-o'-war visiting the Gulf.

When was the first game played in India? The 'Pioneer' of Allahabad of June 19, 1872, stated that a hat-trick had been performed in 1743, but neither authority nor detail was given, so it is impossible for the feat to be verified. Even if that incident is rejected, however, the historian of Indian cricket will have no difficulty in tracing the game back to the century before last. There was, for instance, a Calcutta Cricket Club as early as 1792, for in that year it challenged Barrackpore and Dum-Dum; while five years later we come across the full score of a match at Bombay between the Military and the Island. Army cricket has, in fact, been a delightfully prominent feature of the game in India ever since, and it would be difficult to exaggerate the part played by it in its development and popularity. In Calcutta, cricket has been played both long and continuously, and as far back as 1840 it was said of the club's ground: 'On the cricket arena stand two spacious tents, not, however, like the paltry affairs bearing that name in England, but lined with fancy chintz, furnished with looking-glasses, sofas and chairs, and each player's wants, whether it be a light for his cigar, iced soda-water or champagne, supplied by his turbaned attendant.'

The Parsees began to take to the game in 1848, in which year they established the Oriental CC, but it was not until 1861 that a Hindu was seen at the wicket. The first Hindu club, the Bombay Union, was formed in 1866, and about a year later round-armed bowling began to supersede under-hand among the natives. In 1877 the first of the long series of meetings between the Parsees and Bombay Gymkhana took place, and in the following season a Parsee took a professional engagement for the first time, M. Framji accepting employment with the Calcutta Gymkhana. In 1883 the first Mohammedan CC, which blossomed into the Mohammedan Gymkhana in 1893, was established, and in 1885 the Parsee Gymkhana of Bombay was formed. Parsee teams, by the way, visited England in 1886 and 1888, and in 1911 an All India side came over. It was not until 1889–90 that the first English tour, under G. F. Vernon, was made through India. The Parsees *v.* Bombay Presidency match dates back to 1892, and the Triangular Tournament in Bombay to 1907. The latter developed into a Quadrangular Tournament, the Mohammedans joining the Presidency, Parsees and Hindus.

The late Canon Ainger on at least one occasion was responsible for a cricket limerick, and as it is not as well-known as it deserves, and, moreover, refers to the game in India, its inclusion here may be justified:

'There was an old man of Bengal
Who purchased a Bat and a Ball,
Some gloves, and some pads —
It was one of his fads —
For he never played cricket at all!'

It is not known generally that the late Amir of Afghanistan was fond of cricket. He cultivated slogging and often practised for a few hours on end on a specially-prepared pitch at Kabul. He would order eleven of his courtiers to take the field, ostensibly to test his skill, but woe to the unlucky man who bowled or caught him, for it was not considered etiquette or good policy to send him balls which gave him no chance of slogging. It must have been amusing, to anyone acquainted with the game, to watch the efforts of the bowlers to keep the ball just the ideal distance from the wicket. It seems very likely that the game was introduced into the country by Mr Godfrey Vigne, of the Harrow Eleven of 1818, who was not only one of the first Englishmen to visit Kabul, but was an honoured guest there of Ranjit Sing. That was in 1836.

Perhaps no country owes more to our Navy and Army, so far as cricket is concerned, than China, for wherever our Fleet has been represented or our soldiers quartered, there, almost as a matter of course, has the game been played. Thus we find matches taking place at Hong Kong in 1840, although the Hong Kong CC was not actually formed until 1851. About the same period, too, meetings between the Navy and Garrison at Chusan were arranged, that place being occupied by British troops in 1841, and held until payment had been made of the indemnity fixed by the Treat of Nanking. This readiness to adapt themselves to conditions, whatever they may be, was brought somewhat prominently to the fore when Prince Henry of Prussia visited Kiaw Chow, Port Arthur, and Wei-hai-wei on a German warship. He observed to an Englishman that at Kia Chow he saw thousands of coolies putting up fortifications. At Port Arthur he saw tens of thousands engaged in the same operation. At Wei-hai-wei all that he saw taking place was two British officers laying out a cricket pitch. 'The world is yours,' he is said to have added.

Matches between Hong Kong and Shanghai date back to 1866; those between China and Japan to 1893. Although the former fixture thus boasts considerable antiquity, there was a hiatus from 1868 to 1889 and another of five years following the loss of the Hong Kong team in the 'Bokhara' in 1892. The Chinese themselves did not take readily to cricket, and when they announced their intention of giving an exhibition of the game near Shanghai many of the English residents were much interested. 'When the game began all the fielders were gathered together in a bunch, and the gabble was deafening. The bowler gave his first bowl. When the ball was thrown a long string was attached to it, the end of which was secured to the bowler's thumb. Of course, the ball could traverse only the length of the string, thereby avoiding the necessity of any outfielder, and only two runs in all the play were accomplished. The English laugh became unlimited, but the poor Chinese looked much abashed and foolish, for they evidently expected to be praised for their ingenuity in saving bodily exertion.' In April, 1887, eleven Chinese had the temerity to challenge the Georgetown CC, of British Guiana, and were beaten by an innings and 107 runs, their totals being 20 and 23 against 150 for no wicket. Since those days, however, much has happened, and for years past there have been several Chinese cricket clubs in Hong Kong, and teams have been selected from time to time to go to Singapore, Manila, and Shanghai to play against local sides. Several Chinese have become quite expert, as was pointed out in *The Cricketer* of May 7, 1921, page 22.

Cricket seems to have been introduced into Ceylon by Englishmen who settled in the island as tea and coffee planters about sixty years ago, and it was not long before it established itself there firmly. Matches between Dimbula and Dikoya go back to 1870, and — a red-letter mark in the annals of Ceylonese cricket — the Colombo Colts CC was formed in August, 1873. The natives took to the game most readily, and there have been many who would probably have proved useful in first-class cricket. It was a splendid thing for the game that many players of note settled there and kept up their cricket, among them being B. Pauncefote, P. F. Hadow, F. L. Shand, Ashley Walker, A. O. Whiting, G. Thornton, V. F. S. Crawford, P. R. May, and W. T. Greswell. Representative English and Australian teams have played in Ceylon, as well as sides from Madras and the Straits Settlements, and also the Rev. E. F. Waddy's team. On the other hand, Ceylon has visited Calcutta, Madras, Bombay, the Straits Settlements, and Burma, and in both Singapore and Calcutta has taken part in Triangular Tournaments. The game in the island has flourished exceedingly, and the organizers there have a reputation for enterprise and thoroughness which is fully merited.

Reference to Burma invites mention of the fact that cricket of a kind was played there in 1824, when British troops took Rangoon. Subsequently, there was much military cricket in the country, and even King Thebaw came partly under the fascination of the game. In 1869 and 1870 he and eight of his brothers were at a school at Mandalay, kept by Dr Marles, a well-known missionary, and whilst there he batted fairly well, but refused to do his share of fielding, and was in the habit of using very injurious language to anyone who bowled him. Many Burmans have taken kindly to the game, but there have been times when it was dangerous to play. Major Wynyard recalls it being necessary to have outposts put all round before the game commenced, 'otherwise there would speedily have been an end of us and the match.'

The game in the Straits Settlements can be traced back to October, 1852, when a picked side, which scored 11 and 1, played the Singapore Club, who made 14 and 12. There were six players in one team and nine in the other. From such small beginnings cricket in Singapore, without ever becoming particularly noteworthy, certainly attained a very useful standard of excellence. Singapore has always been the chief centre of the game in the Settlements, and the most important event in its annals was when, during the season of 1890–1, teams arrived from Hong Kong and Ceylon, and a Triangular Tournament was played. The Settlements beat both visiting sides, and Ceylon beat Hong Kong. Three years later a Straits team went to Ceylon, winning one game and drawing two. Cricket has also been played in various other districts, such as Labuan, Malacca, Penang, Perak, Selangor, Negri Sembilan and Johor.

Africa

There is a tradition to the effect that cricket was played — one cannot say established — in South Africa the century before last by Charles Anguish, who had gained note as a player whilst at Eton, and who died at the Cape in May, 1797, at the early age of twenty-eight. It is, however, tradition, and nothing more, for, as far as one knows, no document exists actually proving that the game was introduced there by him.

But there is evidence that before the middle of the last century the game was popular in Cape Town, for records extant show that many good matches took place on the Wynberg ground. In one of them, in January, 1842, a Mr Tayler (BSC), playing for Civilians *v.* Military, carried his bat through the innings of 186 for 110, which was high scoring for those days. The Military made only 78 and 56, and were accordingly beaten by an innings and 52 runs. Nor was the Navy far behind, for Navy and Army *v.* Cape Town was a favourite match, and occasionally the latter also met the Officers of the Fleet and the Wynberg Club combined. The game Mother Country *v.* Colonial Born dates back over sixty years, to the season 1861–2. We have already seen that some Cape enthusiasts were responsible for transplanting their game to Utrecht as early as 1855.

As in the case of so many other places beyond the sea, South Africa owes much to the military for popularizing the game. Cricket was established in Maritzburg about 1843–4 by the 45th Foot, and Bloemfontein, some seven years later, was similarly indebted to our troops. Kaffraria followed suit in 1851–2, when more than one game was finished abruptly through the players being ordered out on patrol duty. The game was played at Potchefstroom (Transvaal) in 1860–1, and a club was formed there in 1863. Not until 1870, however, does Pretoria seem to have known the game, and, of course, Johannesburg was later still. Of cricket in Kimberley there are records dating back to 1874, though it is probable the game had been played there a few seasons earlier. A prominent date in the annals of South African cricket is 1875–6, for then it was that, at Port Elizabeth, the first Championship Bat Tournament was held for competition in the Cape Colony. A far more important event, however, was the visit of the first English team (Major Warton's) to South Africa in 1888–9, followed by the establishment in the following season of the Currie Cup Tournament. The first of the five teams to visit England came over in 1894, whilst in 1910–11 a side toured Australia. Three times, too, have Australians visited South Africa on their way home from this country – in 1902–3, 1919–20, and 1921–2.

So far as other parts of Africa are concerned it may be stated that at

Kumasi, in 1873—4, a few games were arranged on the occasion of the visit of Sir Garnet Wolseley's expedition, and again in 1895—6, but cricket was played there in more pleasant circumstances in 1901, when there was a large crowd of now friendly Ashantis, resplendent under their gorgeous umbrellas of state. Cricket was not a new game on the Gold Coast, even in the ant-districts, over thirty-five years ago, for in 1888 the Governor, in a report of a visit he had paid to the Western District of the Colony, stated that at Axim he saw 'on the village green native boys playing as vigorously at cricket as they do in England.' In 1893—4 cricket was said to be 'an entirely new game in Matabeleland', which, if correct, would probably make C. J. Robinson's 141 for Civilians *v.* BSA Force, early in 1894, rank as the first individual hundred obtained in the country.

At Abercorn, in October, 1899, the first attempt was made to establish the national game in British Central Africa. The game was between the BSA Co. and the African Trans-Continental Telegraph Company, and it was played fourteen miles from the south side of Tanganyika. Owing to only three members of each Company being available at the time, each team was completed by natives.

That the game was known in Egypt over half a century ago one may assume from the fact that Prince Hassan, the Khedive's brother, who was educated at Oxford, played for the Bullingdon Club whilst at the University. The score of at least one match in which he took part is to be found in 'Scores and Biographies' (xi., 335), where he is shown as having gone in last against the Butterflies and made 10. Of early cricket in Egypt itself, however, there are few records, but a short quotation respecting a tied-match played just outside Port Said in 1882 between A. and B. Cos. of H.M.S. *Agincourt* and the Rest of the Camp, must be made if only to show in what perilous circumstances enthusiasts will indulge in their favourite game. 'We were stationed a mile outside the town on a broad spit of sand extending from the town to a distance of about five miles, where there is a narrow channel, a hundred yards the other side of which is Fort Gim-el, held by Arabi's men. Our camp consisted entirely of bluejackets, 280 in all, every soul only too anxious to have a go at Arabi, but unfortunately we were not allowed, so had to relieve the monotony by playing cricket on the sand. The heat was too great to do anything before 4 p.m., so we were only able to have a single-innings match. The bluejackets insisted on playing barefooted, but luckily they sustained no damage except a few extra mosquito bites.'

North America

Probably few followers of the game are aware that cricket in the United States can be traced back to the reign of George II, for at New York, in 1751, New York played eleven of London, and won by 87 runs, scoring 81 and 86 against 43 and 37. The match was played 'according to the London method', which probably meant that the laws drawn up at the Artillery Ground in 1744 were recognised. In 1754 Annapolis played Prince George's County, and the game was certainly known in Boston by 1790, for John Adams, then vice-President of the United States, in advocating in the Senate a high-sounding title for the President, said that 'There are presidents of fire companies and of a cricket club.' Furthermore there is extant a pamphlet, published in 1809, entitled 'Bye-Laws for the Government of the Boston Cricket Club.' Ten years later, and only a few days before his death, the fourth Duke of Richmond, then Viceroy of Canada, joined in a game at Kingston with the officers of the Garrison there. His Grace will, perhaps, be remembered more readily as Col. the Hon. Charles Lennox, most enthusiastic of players, and one of the chief founders of the MCC in 1787.

It is doubtful if cricket was played in Philadelphia before 1831 or 1832, and then only in a perfunctory way. The game was introduced to Haverford in 1836 by an English gardener named William Carvell, who died in 1887 at the age of ninety. As clubs sprang into existence, so did the popularity of the game increase, until gradually matches came to be arranged between some of the leading clubs of Canada and the States. The Toronto CC came early to the fore in this manner, as did the St George's and Union of New York and Philadelphia respectively. George Anthony Barber, proprietor of the 'Toronto Herald', was one of the greatest enthusiasts the Dominion has ever known. He was a good player, too, and it is with satisfaction one can add that his portrait survives him. As early as 1844 James Turner scored 120 on the Camden ground for Union CC *v*. St George's, and thereby gained the distinction of making what is believed to have been the first century obtained in the New World. Later, in the same year, J. M. Sanderson, Secretary of the former club, wrote: 'In a few years look out for a challenge from the Gentlemen of America to the Gentlemen of England, for a home and home match. You may laugh at this, but at the same time I assure you it will be done.'

As to the subsequent development of the game in North America a few facts will suffice. In 1844, at New York, Canada and the United States met for the first time, the former winning by 23 runs; in 1853 a regular professional was first engaged in Philadelphia; in 1856 took place the initial match between Eastern and Western Canada; in 1859 an English team — Parr's — went out for the first time; in 1874 the noteworthy Halifax Tournament took place; in 1878 the first Australian team went home via America, playing a few games there; in 1880 a Canadian side was seen in England for the first time; and in 1884 the Gentlemen of Philadelphia paid their first visit to this country.

Cricket in Mexico may possibly date back a full hundred years, for we know that in Mexico City, in 1839, a match was played between Reds (46 and 61) and Blues (46 and 63 for seven wickets), 'by the Mexican Union CC, for a farewell dinner to be given to Francis Leeson Ball, Esq., the Founder and President of the Club, on the occasion of his departure for Buenos Aires as Secretary to HBM Legation.' Records of the game in the country are scarce, but League matches have been played between Reforma, Pachuca, Mexico, Orizaba, and Puebla, from which one may assume that cricket there has enjoyed a certain measure of popularity.

Central America

From the records available it would not appear that the game in Central America was known much before 1886. In that year a cricketer who had settled in Nicaragua wrote: 'I have instituted your favourite old game, cricket, among the natives, but they are such a lazy race that half an hour of it at a spin completely does them up. I, however, wrote home to our Directors, and they immediately kindly sent the officers out a complete outfit. We call ourselves the Anglo-Nicaraguan team, and I have no doubt you would manage to put us all out in half an hour, provided you escaped from your innings alive, as the native bowling is very uncertain.'

Cricket does not seem really to have flourished at any time in Central America, although in 1909 Guatemala proposed sending a team to

British Honduras. The last mentioned country has seen the game played at Belize, and has also been responsible for a pamphlet entitled 'A Concise Hint and Guide to Cricket. By Isaiah Thomas.' The nature of this publication can be gauged from the following short extract: 'As the order, aspect, and attitude, on cricket presents rather a new point of view, in such an aberrant manner, I feel moved by a degree of generosity and liberality to produce this studious, profound, and perfective treatise.'

South America

Our Navy played an important part in popularising the game in South America, and at Valparaiso, Rio Janeiro, and elsewhere took part in many an interesting match. Thus in the early part of 1842, the Rio Club (Brazil) beat the officers of HMS Southampton, although 'the thermometer on the day of the match stood at 132 deg. Far. at noon.' Ten years later, at Valparaiso (Chile), a couple of games were played between HMSs Portland and Amphitrite. The score of the second match is preserved, but that of the first 'mysteriously disappeared during the bottle-emptying process that followed the fight.' Santiago, too, was not far behind, and both that town and Valparaiso have had the pleasure of entertaining Argentine cricketers, who were obliged to cross the Andes in order to play. Iquique, too, has been the scene of many a well-contested game, and in June, 1891, a revolution notwithstanding, a match took place, although many of those who played had to journey by special train, a costly luxury in those parts. Shortly afterwards, the town was bombarded and burnt by the insurgents, and one of the cricketers was heard to exclaim, as he saw the smoke issuing from the direction of his office at Pisagua, 'There goes my best bat.' Then followed the Battle of Pisagua, which the players watched whilst sitting on a hill-side.

Our sailors played at Georgetown over eighty years ago, and the Georgetown CC itself, the chief club in British Guiana, has been in existence for more than half a century. As far back, too, as 1865, British Guiana and Barbados met at Bridgetown, the home side winning easily.

Cricket in Paraguay has a history of over thirty years, and if comparatively few games of any importance have been played there, the enthusiasm of those taking part has compensated for any such shortcomings. Support, on the whole, has been poor, even when special pains were taken to get together sides representing England and Australia. On the Plaza, at Villa Rica, in March, 1894, it was said that 'a crowd of about thirty collected, and the other Englishmen, numbering about a dozen, who could not come sent their good wishes.' The natives themselves appear to have been quite uninterested. It was at the very time mentioned, to wit, March, 1894, that the first cricket match played in Venezuela took place. It was at Caracas, and the event was well patronised, probably because M. Santana, one of the leading merchants of the country, had been induced to give his support. In a letter respecting the game it was stated: 'Of course we drank his health with musical honours, and when we struck up "He's a jolly good fellow", it was highly amusing to notice the look of astonishment, mingled with alarm, on the faces of the Venezuelans. They couldn't of course make head nor tail of it.'

In the Argentine Republic the game flourishes well, and W. E. Leach, of Lancashire, had much to do with popularizing it north of Buenos Aires. The Republic has played matches with Chile, Brazil, and, in 1911–12, the MCC. Many cricketers known in England have been associated with the game in the Argentine, among them being P. A. Foy, H. G. Garnett, J. O. Anderson, K. M. Carlisle, Gilbert Tosetti, R. F. Vibart, W. C. Millward, H. E. C. Biedermann, and C. H. Gibson. The North v. South matches date from 1891–2.

Australia and New Zealand

Cricket is believed to have been introduced into Australia by officers of the regiments stationed there about 1803–4, and the most prominent of the early clubs in Sydney were undoubtedly the Military and Civilian, between which rivalry was very keen. The Australian CC, of which Mr E. W. Gregory, the grandfather of 'SE,' was a member, was only a little later in coming to the fore. The first printed account of a match seems to have been that in the 'Sydney Gazette' and 'New South Wales Advertiser' respecting a game on the old racecourse on New Year's Day, 1830.

The game apparently took root in New South Wales earlier than in any other State, but it is worthy of mention that the Hobart Town CC, of Tasmania, was established as far back as 1832. So far as Victoria is concerned, the first wicket does not seem to have been pitched – at the foot of Batsman's Hill—until about six years later. There were really a genuine bat and ball, but the stumps and bails were improvized from the ti-ti tree. During the winter the bat and ball were greased and laid-up in lavender, there not being others to be had in the State! As the number of players increased, a further supply of implements had to be obtained from India and Hobart. It was on January 9, 1845, that the present Melbourne CC was 'finally formed', their first ground being on the south side of the Yarra. Their present beautiful ground has been occupied since 1854, and the Crown grant was issued in 1863.

The first known recorded game in Western Australia was between Perth and eleven Tradesmen and Mechanics of Perth, in May, 1846. It was announced that: 'The playing appears to have been fair, and the Perth Club were declared the winners.'

The earliest match between North and South of Tasmania dates back to 1850, when the North won, at Oatlands, by 12 runs. In the following February the first inter-State game took place, Victoria playing Tasmania at Launceston. The match resulted from a challenge sent by Victoria in February, 1850, and the meeting should have taken place a month later, but this was prevented by the gentleman deputed to forward the acceptance forgetting to post the letter in time for it to go by the steamer. The Tasmanians won by three wickets. New South Wales and Victoria did not meet until March, 1856. Grounds were then far from their present state of excellence, as may be judged from the fact that, although New South Wales required only 16 to win in the second innings, they lost seven wickets in the task. There was no grass on the ground, and all the men played with their boots off, some in their bare feet.

It is believed that a club, known as the Adelaide, existed in South Australia eighty years ago, but records of its doings have not been preserved. Certain it is, however, that in 1846 the Kent and Sussex Club was formed by John Cocker, an old Kent player, its matches taking place at the foot of the present Stanley Street in North Adelaide. The Australia and Union CC were established about 1850 and 1852 respectively, and the first hundred obtained in the State was made with a cherry-wood bat. The Adelaide Oval was formally opened in December, 1873, and the first batsman to play a three-figure innings on it was the father of the brothers Hill.

In the meantime – in 1861–2 – the first English team had toured Australia under H. H. Stephenson, and the interest centred in the event is evident from the first day's takings (on the Melbourne ground) in the opening match being sufficient to cover the expenses of the entire trip. It was not until 1878 that the first Australian team visited England. The Sheffield Shield Competition was inaugurated in 1882–3.

It has been stated on good authority that the first cricket match in New Zealand was played at Russell (Bay of Islands) in 1842, and that Wellington, Dunedin, and Christchurch followed in the order named. There must have been some keen enthusiasts among the early settlers, seeing that, although Otago was not founded until 1848, the following appeared in the 'Otago News' of the following December: 'The cricket players of Dunedin publicly challenge the Cricket Club at Wellington to a trial of skill at any point equidistant between the Port of Otago and Port Nicholson.' The challenge was not accepted, and the first inter-Provincial match was between Wellington and Auckland, at Wellington, in March, 1860. Parr's England team of 1863–4 visited New Zealand, and gave a great fillip to the game, and fourteen years later the first Australian side to come over had a preliminary tour through the Dominion. Over forty years ago – in 1878–9 – a Canterbury team paid a visit to Victoria, and, although its programme was not ambitious, the event was sufficient to prove that the spirit of enterprise was in evidence. Many teams from England and Australia, and even one from Fiji, have been seen in New Zealand, but this is no occasion for alluding to their doings, or to the institution of the various inter-Provincial games. It may, however, be noted that the New Zealand Cricket Council was formed in 1895, and that the first competition for the Plunket Shield took place during the season of 1906–7.

The West Indies

The game in the West Indies can be traced back at least eighty years in several of the Islands. Thus, the Cricket Club of the 59th Foot was formed at Antigua on New Year's Day, 1842, and played its first match on July 7 the same year against the Trinidad CC, on the Grand Savanna, Trinidad, for 50 dollars. The Regiment won by 49 runs, and it was stated to be 'the first time the Trinidad CC, which is of very long standing, has been defeated.' Looking through records of the Trinidad matches, it is pleasant to come across a name which is familiar wherever the game is played. Thus, in a description of a match between the Garrison and the Trinidad CC, in September, 1852, we find it announced that, among the three thousand persons present were Lord Harris, the Governor, and Lady Harris, respectively the father and mother of the famous Kent and England cricketer.

The military had much to do with establishing the game in Barbados, and the 7th Royal Fusiliers and the 2nd Batt. 1st Royal Regiment played a leading part in the matter. When the sides met in April, 1845, it was said: 'As the Royals had vanquished every eleven that had dared to play them, and as the Fusiliers had been equally successful at Gibraltar (having beaten an eleven picked from the whole Garrison with the greatest ease), this match was looked forward to with great anxiety.' Cricket in Jamaica, too, can boast a very respectable antiquity, seeing that the Kingston CC was formed as early as 1863 by a few boys who had returned there from English Public Schools. On the occasion of the Jubilee of the club, the Governor of the Island sent a telegram to King George and received a reply. It has already been recorded that what is recognized as the first West Indian Tournament took place in 1865, when a British Guiana team played Barbados at Bridgetown.

Referring to the lighter side of cricket in the Islands, it may be recalled that, when some Englishmen proposed playing in St Kitts, Danish Officers who were present enquired if the game took place on a table. It is this ignorance on the part of foreigners which often causes amusement to the investigator. Thus, when the game was about to be introduced into St Lucia, an old French lady sent a strong protest to 'The Voice of St Lucia.' Space does not allow the letter to be quoted in full, but her opening remarks show the nature of the view she held: 'On introduit dans ce pays une espèce de bataille meurtrière qu'on nomme, par une étrange perversité morale, un jeu. Il est vrai, grâce á Dieu, que ceux qui se tiennent à l'écart, courent relativement moins de risques, mais mêmes ceux-la sont loin d'être à l'abri du danger. D'après ce que j'ai pu comprendre, ce jeu appelle, je crois, *Criquette*, se joue de la manière suivante', etc.

Various Centres and Districts

BERMUDA. — Matches between the Garrison and Royal Navy can be traced back eighty years, the former's ground having been on St George's Island, and the latter's 'adjoining the Admiralty House.' The Hamilton Club has long been the chief cricket organisation in Bermuda, and in 1905 it played a series of seven games in America, the tour being in a measure a return to that paid to the Islands by Philadelphia Zingari in 1891. An Australian team has played a few games in Bermuda.

BORNEO. – Many Borneo natives had their first experience of the game as recently as 1921, when they took very kindly to it. They throw splendidly, but swipe at random and find it difficult to bowl properly. When told that a man is 'dead' (that is, out) they leap for joy.

CANARY ISLANDS. – The original Minute-Book of the Orotava CC for the years 1826 and 1827 is still preserved, and from it many quaint facts can be gathered. For instance, the Club could boast its own doctor and apothecary. Numerous games have been played in the Canaries by officers of the Royal Navy, the Training Squadrons, and the Channel Fleet. In 1899 Mr A. T. Kemble took a team there, which played three matches and won them all.

FIJI. – Here, again, the introduction of the game was due to the Royal Navy, and Messrs. E. W. Wallington and J. S. Udal, during their official residence in the Islands, did much to develop cricket among the natives, who have attained a good standard of proficiency. Fijian teams have toured both New Zealand and Australia. In early days one tribe would challenge another, the defeated side paying ten figs to the victors.

GIBRALTAR. – Both the Royal Navy and our Military have again played a prominent part here. As early as 1842 Private Thorn (of the 48th Regt.) took four wickets in five balls against the 7th Royal Fusiliers. Most of the matches were played 'on the Garrison Ground, outside the North Front.'

JAPAN. – For years the Fleet was chiefly resonsible for matches at Yokohama and Kobe, and what is believed to have been the first game in the country was Yokohama v. Fleet in 1863. There was so much unrest at the time that the players had to be armed. Yokohama v. Kobe has long been a favourite match, and sides from Hong Kong and Shanghai have visited Japan.

JAVA. – The Batavia CC was formed in 1844, and by its rules not more than fifteen non-British members might be elected. The matches, mostly with British men-o'-war teams, were played between May or June and Christmas, when the rainy season commences.

MALTA. — The Navy and Garrison teams have been responsible for the greater part of the cricket played here for the best part of a hundred years. Some huge scores have been made on matting, especially at Verdalo and Florian.

MANILA. — A noteworthy match, which marks the commencement of the modern history of cricket here, was that between the Residents and HMS *Immortality*, in 1898. Progress has since been made, and games have been played with Hong Kong. Furthermore, Chinese teams from Hong Kong have also been received, and have met local Chinese clubs. It was Sir William Draper (1721–87), an old Etonian and active cricketer, who captured Manila, and it would be interesting to know if he could claim to be the first to pitch a wicket there.

MAURITIUS. — Naval and military men have played the leading part in the cricket here for well over half a century.

NEW GUINEA. — Port Moresby and Samari have the best teams, and the Papuans take kindly to the game. On account of the heat, 'there is very little fielding done by the Europeans, as the natives do it all.'

NORFOLK ISLAND. — In reporting a match played here in June, 1844, 'Bell's Life' stated: 'When we consider that a brig from Sydney once in two months is the only cheering evidence of civilisation that enlivens the monotonous existence of this handful of our gallant countrymen, we are sure it must gratify all our readers to find that the manly recreations of Winchester and Sandhurst are unforgotten in every clime, and that Englishmen, even in the midst of convicts and kangaroos, must still have their Lord's.' (See also 'Solomon Islands.')

ST HELENA. — The game was introduced here by HM 66th, 20th, and 53rd Regiments during the captivity of Napoleon. Sir Basil Jackson, who accompanied Sir Hudson Lowe, records cricket being played, and the game was also mentioned by several British officers in their letters, but their remarks were only casual. Major Lorrequer, Lowe's Secretary, says the game was one of the resources of 'this damnable hole.' The games were played on the Racecourse at Deadwood. Seventy years ago, when the St Helena CC had been established 'some years', there was a good ground at Longwood, and another at

Francis Plain (about two miles from Jamestown) not quite so good. A few years ago there was, and perhaps there still is, a bat in West Brighton, made from a willow tree raised from a cutting taken by Mr. Borrer from a tree by Napoleon's grave in 1840.

SAMOA. – The game seems to have been introduced here by HMS 'Diamond' about the year 1884, and the natives, who took to it readily, at once saw there was much room for improvement. Matches of 200 a-side took place, with four or five umpires and three batsmen at each end, the contests lasting for weeks. Work was neglected, and steps had to be taken to compel the natives to return to reason. Men who played were expelled from Church, and the King had to issue a special decree. As the latter fact has been doubted, it may be well to reproduce the actual Proclamation:

THE LAW REGARDING CRICKET.
TO ALL THE DISTRICTS OF SAMOA, NOTICE.

1. It is strictly prohibited for a village to travel and play cricket with another village.

2. It is strictly prohibited for two villages to play cricket together.

3. It is also prohibited for a village to play cricket among themselves.

4. Should any village or district fail to keep this law in any respect, they will be fined a sum not exceeding forty-five dollars, or in default be sent to jail for three months with hard labour.

MALIETOA, The King of Samoa.
Residence of the King, Apia.   June 20, 1890.

This tended to produce a more reasonable state of things, and gradually the above laws were relaxed. In June, 1916, a Cricket Association was formed at Apia, consisting of two white and four Samoan teams. Many of the native women hit, field, and catch well.

SANDWICH ISLANDS. – There was a club at Honolulu as early as 1852, for in May that year it was beaten by 11 runs by the officers of HMS Amphitrite, 'on the Plains of Haikiki, at Little Britain, the seat of General Miller, HM Consul of the Islands.' The King Kalakaua was fond of the game, and whilst in England in 1881 was present at the Eton v. Harrow match, and also visited the Oval. On his return home he travelled part of the way with the Anglo-Australian team of

1881–2, and every morning called the cricketers to his cabin to hear Bates sing 'The Bonny Yorkshire Lass.'

SEYCHELLES ISLANDS. – Here again the Royal Navy has done good service, especially at Victoria, in Mahé, a coaling station. Matches between the Islands and various men-o'-war are the chief attraction during the season.

SOLOMON ISLANDS. – The game is reported to have spread here from Norfolk Island through the influence of Bishop Patteson, a former Eton captain, who educated some of the natives in his training school on Norfolk Island, and taught them the game. On their return to the Solomons they kept up their cricket, and in time inter-island matches were arranged. Good grounds, however, are almost unknown, the best being at Gavatu and Makambo.

SUMATRA. – The first match played at Madan Deli was between Langkat and Serdang. A Dutchman named Verhulst took fifteen wickets for 38 runs for Serdang – six for 10 and nine for 28.

TONGA. – George Tubow II, of Tonga, the last of the independent kings of the Pacific, who died in 1918, was very fond of the game, which he learned whilst at school in Auckland. His subjects devoted so much time to cricket that it was necessary to prohibit it on five or six days of the week in order to avert famine, as the plantations were deserted for the cricket field.

Cricketer Annual 1922/3

22

Savage Cricketers

William G. Fitzgerald

Travellers in distant countries are often amused to find homely articles of European manufacture treasured as valuables, and occasionally as gods, to be worshipped by savages in various regions. Mr Savage Landor, whose disastrous attempt to enter the sacred city of Lhassa, in Tibet, occasioned so much excitement lately, tells how, when his devoted servant Chanden Sing first made his appearance before him, his prospective attendant shouldered arms with one solitary cricket-stump, and stood at stiff attention in the doorway of the tent. Now, the thing is, how did that cricket-stump get into the wilds of the Himalayas? We suppose it must have been carried thither by traders. Everyone knows of that splendid profitable trade in old clothes which went on between certain shrewd businessmen in this country and agents in Central Africa, who disposed of various incongruous garments to the natives in return for ivory, ostrich feathers, spices, and other valuable commodities.

A curious fact about the Englishman abroad is that he takes with him not merely his own personal idiosyncrasies — which are very strongly marked — but also his sports and games, to which he has been accustomed from his youth. Wherever two or three Englishmen — and women — are gathered together in a remote and hitherto unexplored spot, there you will immediately find a tennis ground, a cricket pitch, and ultimately even a racecourse. These reflections lead up to the very interesting, amusing, and striking photographs [which are reproduced in the illustration section]. The first photograph shows us a primitive but earnestly played game of cricket in progress in one of the Solomon Islands. This photo was taken four or five years ago, when the islands were annexed to the British Crown by H.M.S. *Curacao*. Now, just observe the wicket-keeper, who is a typical South Sea Islander.

Not only is he unprovided with the orthodox leg-guards, but he is practically stark naked, his ebony skin fairly shining beneath the blazing tropical sun. It is obvious from the photo that the ground itself is hardly suitable for batting and bowling, and so a strip of coconut matting, very much home made, has been laid down from the bowler's end to the wicket. You will observe that bails are dispensed with, but it would be unfair to insist on these genial savages playing the game with that accuracy of detail which we are accustomed to expect at Lord's or the Oval. A cricket pavilion is seen in the background, and at intervals all the players leave the 'field' and retire slowly to that queer-looking structure which seems to be raised on piles above the ground. They climb the little ladder, and crawl in through the hole, and then indulge in some refreshments – perhaps palm wine and bananas. This is a happy land, and our savage cricketers may play their favourite game from morning till night without any thought of what they shall eat or drink or wherewith they shall be clothed. Certainly, there is very little necessity about the latter item.

Sets of cricket implements are carried by traders to very remote parts indeed, and sold for quite a large sum, which, however, includes some elementary tuition in the noble game itself. Travellers have often found an ancient bat doing duty which has been broken and spliced all over, until hardly a square inch of the original material remains. Or again, in the event of a bat being stolen, these dusky cricketers will carve a rude specimen out of the wood of the coconut tree, and make it do duty for years. Accidents will happen, of course, and, judging from the scanty attire of our cricketers, they must be more than usually painful.

The next photograph shows quite an important match in progress at a place which looks very similar to the one shown in the last illustration. It is not so, however, for the scene of this interesting match is Quato, in New Guinea. At this place is established one of the posts of the London Missionary Society, and it is doubtless the influence of the missionaries themselves which accounts for the European clothing seen on various members of the field. This is an extremely interesting view of a New Guinea village, and here again we see that a strip of coconut matting has had to be laid down from one wicket to the other. It is really extraordinary to see these half-naked savages playing cricket in this remote part of the earth, surrounded by their own native growths of palms and papoon houses. This sport, though possibly less exciting than head-hunting, may well be encouraged by the missionaries, since it keeps their charges out of mischief, and even tends to improve their minds by inculcating some idea of discipline, watchfulness, and science. Nothing could exceed the frantic hilarity of the field when one of their number is accidentally struck by the ball. Traders in the South Seas have described how they have seen the batsmen themselves fairly collapse on the coconut matting in a perfect delirium of merriment over the discomfiture of long-off, who has perhaps been felled to the earth with a blow that would have slain any ordinary white man.

The next photograph transports us to the northern province of the beautiful Island of Ceylon. Here we see a number of black boys playing a very serious game of cricket in the Jaffna peninsula, Ceylon. At this place the Church Missionary Society has a very large school, which is known as St John's College, and when you are told that the number of students on the books is twenty-six, you will cease to wonder at the excellent game of cricket seen in progress in the schoolground.

The scoring at some of these matches is very interesting, and in some cases it is kept by means of little sticks of wood laid upon the ground, and added to or taken away from the winning and losing sides respectively.

Talk about cricket enthusiasts! Look at the couple of East Africans depicted in the next photograph. In this case the batsman is manifestly unused to wielding the willow, but his anxiety to make a good stroke is only equalled by the strenuous alertness of the wicket-keeper, whose trepidation and agony of mind between each ball are something pitiful to witness.

Amusing to relate, all kinds of queer conceptions prevail among savages as to how the game should really be played. The game we are now considering was played not far from Mengo, in Uganda, and bowler, batsman, and wicket-keeper were fully convinced that the fundamental idea of the game was not to bowl at the wicket, but to try and brain the keeper thereof, whilst the batsman did his best to preserve the life of that functionary. At other times, bats will be found up to 'two feet in width', with a wicket rather narrower than the ordinary one. Obviously, then, it is extremely difficult to get the batsman out, so batting is simply taken in turns.

Strand Magazine 1898

23

England v. France and Germany

H. Hervey

Jugganaickpallium is a commercial seaport on the eastern coast. Beyond the usual complement of district officers – I was one – the society of the station was composed almost entirely of French *negociants* and German *kaufmanns*.

We freely intermingled; they and their womenkind took kindly to our lawn tennis, our badminton, our croquet, and our boating, while we equally appreciated their magnificent billiard tables, their open hospitality, where we would be regaled with music – at the German houses especially – such as our own fair daughters of Albion could not treat us to.

But lately – that is, about the time of my being appointed to Jugganaickpallium – some fresh blood had been infused into the English community in the person of a new district superintendent of police, a new civil surgeon, and myself. We liked the foreigners, but we missed one great desideratum, and that was cricket. We found, on inquiry, that, though we English mustered some twenty males, there was not such an article as a bat in the place. We sounded the others on the subject of starting a cricket club. The Britishers unanimously approved, but our French and German friends did not 'cotton' to the idea. At a meeting convened for the purpose, M. La Rive, the chief French resident, supported by Herr Gorlitz, the most influential of the Germans, expressed the views of the 'foreign faction' – as we termed them among ourselves – in unmistakable terms.

'It is not game, vat-you-call, intimate to French peoples,' said La Rive. 'I have seen ze Engleesh at ze play in Marseilles; thees contry it makes itself ver hot for ze creeket; we sall die, we sall suffaire of ze *coup de soleil*, vat-you-call, ze heat of ze sun. *Ma foi!* but it is dangerous. I spik for my contry peoples. We reserve ourselfs from ze vote.'

This clinched the matter; we decided to start the cricket club ourselves. We set aside every other day from two to six in the afternoon; we selected the ground; we procured a complete outfit from Madras. Every Englishman, in honour bound – whether he knew a lob from a leg-guard – joined, and the consequences were that for half the week our French and German fellow exiles found themselves deprived of our society.

Some of the original sojourners who joined us were very rusty, and Pack, the policeman (not in the home acceptation of the term, remember, but an officer drawing, all told, something like £800 per annum), Giles, the medico, and I, had hard work in licking our brethren into shape. At first, the French and Germans were conspicuous by their absence from our field; they kept studiously away – men and women. Some few of the latter, however, began turning up in our tent; but more to deride and endeavour to wean us away to the boats, than to look on and approve. But we were not to be so lured.

We intended, during the coming Christmas week, to challenge the team of a neighbouring station to a three-days'-match, and we had barely six months before us to get into form.

At last our friends began to put in an appearance – La Rive and one or two others. We hailed their presence with acclamation, and offered to initiate them into the mysteries of 'ze creeket'; but they resisted our overtures, standing apart and whispering among themselves. In due course, not a cricket afternoon passed without many of them coming to witness the play. They kept aloof, and appeared to pay the greatest attention to our proceedings; talking, gesticulating, and scrambling for a small book, which seemed to possess an uncommon interest for them all.

The introduction of cricket seemed fated to upset the doings of our community; it had already extinguished two of the boating evenings; but as this pastime was so popular with our *Mesdames* and our *Fraus*, tennis and badminton had to give way thereto. Again, hitherto our mornings had generally been spent in riding parties; now, however, we noticed a falling off at our equestrian meets on the part of French and German gentlemen riders; although their better halves showed up as usual. We sounded the fair horsewomen on the subject of this defection, but could obtain no satisfactory reply. 'Ze gentilmans are busy; zey render zemselves togezaire to talk vat you Ingleesh call "ze shop" ', they would laughingly tell us, and with which we were forced to be content. Another noticeable fact; La Rive, the head of the firm of La Rive, De la Nougerede et Cie, lived in a palatial bungalow on the extreme outskirts of the station, and it was generally there that we assembled after our morning rides; we were never invited to do so now. Further, our doctor, Giles, who had been called in to see little Félicité La Rive, remarked that the extensive lawn at the back of the house, and on which we had played many a good game of tennis, was now enclosed by a tall screen of palmyra leaves! All these little incidents taken together, though not actually proving a state of strained relationship between us and our neighbours, nevertheless rendered obvious the fact that things did *not* run so pleasantly as heretofore. However, we said nothing; we stuck to our cricket; we endeavoured to make ourselves as agreeable as possible in all other respects, and matters continued in the same semi-satisfactory manner.

Christmas drew nigh; we had knocked together a fairly respectable eleven, and we were thinking of sending our challenge to Godari, when on this particular morning at Pack's house, while discussing on ways and means, a large-sized letter was handed to our host.

'Who can this be from?' muttered Pack, opening the missive. He read for a few seconds, then threw down the paper, and chuckled unctuously. 'The murder's out!' cried he. 'Listen:

'The Franco-German Cricket Club of Jugganaickpallium will hereby cast down the gage to the English Cricket Club of Jugganaickpallium, and request the honour of the game of play at the convenient time and place while the Holiday of Christmas.

'Achille, St Cyr de la Rive,

'The Captain.'

'So that's what they've been up to,' exclaimed Moggeridge, the sub-collector. 'Deep beggars, making no sign, and bursting like a thunderbolt on us! We'll play them, of course, eh?'

'Gad! I should think so,' said Giles. ''Twill be rare fun, I bet.'

'No one has been coaching them, eh?' asked Pack.

There was no such traitor in the camp; no one had the faintest suspicion of our neighbours' intentions, so well had they masked their proceedings. The absence of the men from the morning rides; the enclosed tennis courts; their steady attendance at, and attention to, our practice games, were all now accounted for. Well, to make a long story short, the challenge was accepted, and, in due course, the day of the match came round. Our opponents were evidently in earnest, for at the hour appointed they all appeared, accurately attired in brand new flannels, with tricoloured 'blazers' and tricoloured ribbons round their 'deerstalker' hats. The tents were crowded with the beauty and fashion of the locality, and the ground was in first-rate condition. La Rive, who captained them, told us in a short speech that they had determined to try and like cricket, and had tried to learn the game. At first they were dead against it, but seeing that we were so enthusiastic, and matters as they stood being likely to cause dissension which might tend to interfere with the friendly understanding which had hitherto existed among us, they had all put aside their own prejudices, accepted the inevitable, and made up their minds to assimilate themselves with their English friends in this respect as they had done in others. He confessed he intended this as a surprise for us; he thought he had fairly succeeded, and he hoped that France and Germany combined would be able to beat England in cricket, if not in anything else! It being a purely English game, they, on their part, had decided to use nothing but the English language – even to each other – while playing it.

Now the fun began.

This being the first regular match, we had umpires, and their presence had to be explained to our antagonists. Pack and La Rive tossed. Pack won, and we elected to put them in, a proceeding which they looked on as a polite concession, for they broke out into a chorus of thanks, and only half believed us when we told them that our self-denial was somewhat qualified with self-interest. They were made up of six pure Frenchmen, two 'Pondies,' or Pondicherry creoles, and three Hamburghers. Describing the match *in extenso* would occupy too much space, so I will confine myself to recording the more salient comicalities thereof. Truly it was exquisite fooling from start to finish, and my very jaws ache from laughing as I write with remembrances and recollections of that never-to-be-forgotten day green in my memory.

'The other way, sir – the other way round!' admonished the umpire at my end – I was to take first over – to Versonne, the batsman facing me, who held his bat convex side to front!

'Ze nonsense!' ejaculated Versonne in reply.

'No nonsense, sir,' said the umpire, our head lock-keeper, and an old soldier. 'Turn your bat round, sir.'

Versonne, still incredulous, hereupon took his bat by the blade and poked the handle into the block hole.

Naturally, we were in smothered fits, and our wicket-keep, choking with laughter, explained matters to the mystified Versonne, who bowed and raised his hat in acknowledgement of the hint; whereupon, wicket-keep, in duty bound, also bowed and raised *his* hat.

Straight or wide, lob, half volley, full pitch or half pitch, slow, medium, or swift — it mattered not; they swiped at everything that came, and ran as if they were on hot bricks, encouraging each other in grotesque English the while. We laughed till we could scarcely stand; and for myself, who bowled from one end throughout the innings, often had I to wipe the tears from my eyes before delivering a ball.

Their vociferations from the tent, all in our tongue, added to our risibility; the roll they gave to the letter 'r' in the reiterated cry of 'Rron! Rron!' when their men made a hit; their vituperations when anyone bungled or got out were intense in their drollery; all enhanced by their earnestness, and the evident idea that everything they said and did was quite *comme il faut*. Whenever they did get on to the ball, they either skied or tipped it; they had the crudest notions of defence, ignored block, and often stood to receive either with all three stumps uncovered, or with their legs where their bats ought to have been. But what more could we expect? Their knowledge of the game was the outcome of a few weeks' observation and the superficial study of the rules book, only a single copy of which they appeared to have among the lot of them. It was altogether French, this undertaking of theirs; something quixotic, beyond all doubt.

At the first call of 'Over,' which the old lock-keeper delivered in stentorian tones, the two batsmen, seeing a general move on the part of the field, and not comprehending the term in its correct sense, evidently concluded that play had come to an abrupt termination, for they exchanged glances, shouldered their bats, and walked off towards the tents! We had to run after them, explain, and bring them back again.

We disposed of them in rapid succession, and La Rive came in half way down.

'Hourrrrah, La Rive! Go for ze bik score! Mak ze numerous rrons!' were the cries that helped their champion on his walk to the wickets.

'How's that?' asked Childs, after delivering the first ball.

'Out!' ejaculated the umpire. I was wicket-keep. Childs had put on no break. La Rive was plainly 'l-b-w.' The Frenchman did not move.

'You are out, La Rive,' I remarked.

'Who has said?' he asked fiercely.

'The umpire at the other end.'

'*Ze ompire*!' he echoed. 'Vy you haf said I am out?' he added, shouting to that functionary, who happened to be another soldier, employed in the Customs.

'Ne'er a doubt of it, sir,' he replied. 'You was leg before wicket.'

Hereupon La Rive left his ground, walked across, and towered over the umpire, a little sturdy old Kentish Buff. 'I vas not!' thundered the Gaul.

'Yes you was!' retorted the Briton, his choler rising.

'I vas not! I tell it to *you*!' — (*crescendo*.)

'Yes you was, and I tell it to you — there!'

'Again I tell you mine leg vas not before ze wicket.'

'Well, all I can say is you *was* leg before wicket! Ain't I got eyes?'

'Pack!' cried La Rive to our captain, who, shaking with laughter, stood amid the crowd which the altercation had attracted. 'Vat is ze nonsense zat ze old Smeed spiks? How he arrives to ze decision? Is it imperatif zat one obeys him?'

'My dear fellow,' explained Pack, struggling with his mirth, 'Smith is umpire, and his decision is final; he's there for the purpose of answering appeals. Childs' ball, you see, did not break, it hit your leg; and if your leg had not been there it would have taken your wicket. Smith also saw this, and on Childs appealing to him he gave you "out." It's all fair and square.'

Poor La Rive! He walked away crestfallen. Evidently, on getting back among his fellows, he wanted the balance yet to come in on the subject of 'l.b.w.', for now the batsmen carefully stood about a yard to the 'on', blindly slogging from that position, and, of course, getting bowled out one after the other.

They were all disposed of for twenty-three runs; but the fun, so far from taming down with the close of their innings, continued fast and furious. After the given interval they issued forth from their tent, headed by La Rive, armed with leg-guards and gloves. He was evidently going to wicket-keep; but when the whole eleven streamed out similarly accoutred we simply choked.

1. Lyttleton Waiting for a Rise.—2. Called Back : The Bobby and the Pickpocket.—3. The "Demon" Bowler.—4. "Better Not Play Any More, Blackham."—5. Grace and Steel Practice Catches at the Fall of Spofforth's Wicket.—6. "How Shall I Manage Barlow?" "Put On the Pace."—7. Well-earned Repose.—8. Lord Harris's Carriage at Lord's.—9. Behind the Screen.—10. Bigger than the Giant Bonnor.

AUSTRALIA v. ENGLAND AT LORD'S, July 21, 22, and 23, 1884

above A contemporary view of events at Lord's during the England *v*. Australia Test of 1884
below The Australian team of 1884. Left to right (standing) Percy McDonnell, George Alexander (manager), George Giffen, George Palmer; (sitting) F. R. 'The Demon' Spofforth, Jack Blackham, Billy Murdoch (captain), George Bonnor, Billy Midwinter, Alec Bannerman, 'Harry' Boyle; (in front) William Cooper, 'Tup' Scott

above Three famous cricket diarists, who wrote accounts of their tours to Australia:
E. M. Grace (left), George Anderson (centre) and Rev. Vernon Royle (right)
below The Australian team of 1899 off to a Test match by horse-drawn cab

CRICKET'S SILVER LINING

William Fitzgerald's 'Savage Cricketers', playing in the Solomon Islands (**top left**), Uganda (**top right**), Northern Ceylon (**below left**) and New Guinea (**below right**)

above The noble Lords Harris (left) and Hawke
below Tommy Marshall (left), a veteran North-Country cricketer and Robert Arthur
Thoms, celebrated exponent of the umpire's art

'Halloa, La Rive!' cried Pack, who was going in first with me. 'I say, they don't all want guards and gloves.'

'But vy? It is optional, is it not?' asked the Frenchman.

'No!' laughed Pack. 'Only allowed for wicket-keep.'

La Rive's travesty of that important post was excruciatingly funny. His imitation of us intensified in absurdity when we recollected that he and his fellows were acting in all seriousness, and that, under the impression of having mastered the game, they deemed themselves justified in making this attempt to beat us with our own weapons.

Renaud and Cardorrier, their bowlers, were very swift underhanders, and it was worth a king's ransom to watch La Rive standing boldly to his wickets during intervals, only to dodge and even hop out of the way when the ball came. Was there ever such delicious folly? I felt perfectly unstrung; Pack and I could do nothing but laugh, and we were unable to do much more than block every ball.

'How you are amused yourselfs! How ze great joke!' remarked La Rive, sardonically, during a wait.

'Can't help it, my dear fellow,' I replied hysterically. By now we were quite out of hand, and made no effort to subdue our mirth. To their credit, be it said, our opponents took our hilarity wonderfully well; but this only added fuel to the flame, and turned the whole affair into a veritable saturnalia for us; we did nothing but laugh, and our tent resembled a pandemonium from the same cause.

Gorlitz stood point; I cut a ball at him. So far as position went, he could not have been better; he copied our own point perfectly; but as the ball flew at his shins, he jumped clear of it with surprising agility; cover point also failed to stop it; so Gorlitz and he raced after it. Cover had just picked up the ball when the German got up to him, and tried to snatch it away. Cover resisted; they grappled, and the field concentrated round them to see the fun. I and Pack could not run for laughter, and there ensued a break in the game. The disputants, followed by the rest, came to La Rive, who kept his place at the wicket, growling choice French under his beard.

'The ball was mine!' commenced Gortlitz, breathlessly, on coming up.

'Zen, duffaire zat you are, vy have you permitted it to rron?' asked cover, a Frenchman.

'The ball is it not to me?' appealed Gorlitz to La Rive.

'But you let it, and Querrieux he vas correct to pursue. Go you all

197

back to your stations,' continued La Rive loftily, and the farce proceeded.

'Peetch him the more, Cardorrier,' admonished the captain, as that bowler was about to commence an over.

'No-ball!' shouted Smith.

'Vat ees zat?' asked Cardorrier.

'No ball, sir; counts one for t'other side.'

'My friend, you vill please explain to me.'

'You see this 'ere line, sir? Well, one of your feet must be ahint of it as you bowls.'

'But ze Captain, M. La Rive, vat he tell me now?'

'Told you to pitch 'em up, sir.'

'Vell, for to do so it must to approach near, is it not?'

I and Pack having made forty runs between us, he declared the innings closed. The other side did not understand this, and, with creditable sporting spirit, were anxious to continue. However, we explained the matter to them, and they accepted their defeat without more ado.

The 'match', though a burlesque from beginning to end, had the effect of reconciling our opponents to the advisability of joining us; at the same time showing them the futility of trying to master cricket without the aid of British exponents of the game. From that day forth they identified themselves with us heart and soul, and during the following season, when we did actually play Godari, our eleven – with three Frenchmen and one German incorporated therein – won the match by some thirty runs!

Twenty-five Cricket Stories 1909

24

England v. Eskimos

Captain Bruce McGregor

The above match will take place in the near future— just how near, however, the proprietors of this Journal are not going to venture to state. It is safe to assert, nevertheless, that a very powerful side from the 'Frozen North', captained by that splendid hitter, Blubberlubber (pronounced Cangle), is on its way here. The Eskimos have had considerable difficulty in securing this fixture, since, following up their successive defeats by an eleven from the 'Sunny South', England has been chary of fixing up any matches except those directly necessary for the preservation of her well-deserved title, 'Land of Hope and Glory' (with an accent on the 'Hope').

As the President of the MCC in Greenland, however, Blubberlubber has exercised his influence, and, meeting rebuff with a chilly stare, has at last succeeded. It might be of interest to give a few notes of the men who are now simultaneously chewing fat and practising leg-glides to the off.

Under the skilful coaching of Greasywilliam, these little men from Aurora-Borealis have made remarkable strides. Blubberlubber himself almost sank his hometown by cracking the ice whilst trying to make his batting crease easily recognisable, and the pace at which Lardandtallowmixed bowls is said to exceed Gregory by at least ten yards. It may be safely assumed, however, that he comes off ice far more quickly than he will come off grass. I am told, indeed, that in the Land of Snow and Ice, even the balls are fitted with skates. It would be as well for these giants from the snowy wastes, therefore, not to put too much faith in Lardandtallowmixed, as he may not come up to expectations.

Big-hitters in England, if there are any, had better beware of Drippingcumoilflow, said to be the most brilliant stumper the world has ever seen. I hear that, given a really good ice-pitch, he can, by some peculiar movement of his foot, produce a noise like an off-break. As he only does this when, from his position of advantage, he sees a leg-break is coming down, the unwary batsman is more often than not taken by surprise, deluded, thoroughly bewildered, and collapsed shortly after his wicket had undergone the same change. Of Drippingcumoilflow, therefore, beware!

Blubberlubber informs me, confidentially, that, in order in some small way to protect themselves from the intense cold so prevalent in their neighbourhood, they play in bearskins. This hardly seems to me to be a sensible thing to do. I have an idea that the appearance of a team entirely devoid of flannels at Lord's would by no means enhance their chances of success.

We might win if we try hard. At any rate, they won't know much about 'Ashes'; fires are at a premium in the White Deserts, so they tell me.

Cricket Enthusiast 1922

25

Hudson Bay Cricket Club

A. P. Turner, Hon. Secretary

Officers: Hon. President – Mr Bunbridge.
Hon. Vice-President – Mr Fugl.
President – M. S. Booth, Esq.
Vice-President – James Martin, Esq.
Hon. Secretary and Treasurer – A. P. Turner.
Captain – C. S. Parker.
Vice-Captain – J. H. Wear.

To give a report on the doings of the Hudson Bay Cricket Club for the season just ended, a proposition greater than anticipated beams ahead of the writer. As the cricketing spirit is comparatively young with the Bay employees, a very meagre margin is our lot to give a flourishing account of. Compared with older established clubs the reader can form his own judgement as to how hard a task lies before me in giving each player's abilities in any detail worthy of the success attained this past season. Our endeavour to further the interests of the game has been more our ambition than personal qualities. Towards the end of the cricketing season of 1911, it was found that little or no sports were our lot to pass the hours away during our half-holidays and it was suggested by Mr Martin, manager of the Bay sports, that a few of us get together one afternoon and go down to the Groat Estate for a little cricket practice. A bat and ball were procured for the occasion, and with the aid of tree branches as wickets some fun was had if nothing else. Here the first seeds were set of a cricketing spirit which before the season drew to an end, resulted in a friendly game being arranged with the ECC and giving us our first initiation in the game, ending in our defeat but ambition to band together, go right ahead and win out.

Talking about a game does very little to its progress; it is when real hard work and earnest work is set about that results are come by and to a few was left the proposition of how best to make the spirit of cricket a fact in our midst.

At the beginning of the present year we were approached as to what our intentions were in the coming season; an outline of what was being done was laid before us, and we decided to get to work at once and form a club. Mr Martin laid the matter before our worthy manager and father of sports, Mr M. S. Booth, who put his shoulder to the wheel right merrily and called a general meeting to decide how best we could proceed to make the game a success and what support we should have. A very enthusiastic bunch gathered together and with the election of officers, the ball was set rolling which won us out in triumph for the first season.

A league being formed in the city in conjunction with the Western Canada Cricket League we decided to be affiliated with the organization and our club was duly entered. So far we were good starters; we had the necessary enthusiasm, but of grounds we were in a fix. The question was laid before Mr Booth who took it up in his jolly spirit and it was not long before we had the satisfaction of knowing that a ground had been given us by the company's directors to be known as the Hudson Bay Athletic Club grounds. The ground being very rough and not fenced in, a grounds committee was formed to look after this, which body soon got down to work and had the ground fenced in, ploughed and sown, but being new at the game a few mistakes were made which kept us off the ground this season. Next year we hope to have the ground in first-class trim as experience is the best teacher in everything and we have certainly gained ours.

To those who have followed the game this season our success is well known, both from the sporting point and the way in which we have found everything to work so harmoniously. No trouble was ever found in getting the players together at practice or matches; they were always ready for the sport. Our first game of the season was a friendly match with the Swifts, which ended in our defeat. That word 'defeat' somehow nettled us and I feel sure it was from that we got down to real cricket, determined that no such word was to be spoken of as far as our league games were concerned. To Captain Cliff Parker we have to be very grateful for the way in which he handled the team; he was always there with his smile and good heartedness, keeping the boys together and encouraging them to keep up a good spirit. Next season we hope to have him with us again and in his usual place of captain. It is very gratifying to him to know with what success he has worked and every member of the Bay club feels that too much cannot be spoken of his abilities as captain. Cricket seems to be born in the family, as his brothers all do a little with the willow as has been shown by his brother, L. Parker. A fine batsman was secured when he decided to play for the Bay and it is hoped that he also will be with the green and white colours next season. B. Varley, our last recruit for the season, proved himself to be a batsman of cool and calculating nerve. He studied the bowlers before taking any chances and once his eyes were well concentrated on what each bowler was delivering in the way of fast or slow bowls, he made the game worth watching. Cricket to him is a hobby, he is at home on the field in any position and his cricketing career has to be traced to South Africa, too far away for us to get any details of his abilities. On passing over our other members who are batsmen, it is no slight to them to do so. To go into details as to how they gained their experience of the game would tax the best of my abilities to probe into their past and probably by doing so, lose players whose heads might be turned by other clubs. 'Get it at the Bay' is a good stand-by, but we don't wish to part with good friends and players.

In conclusion to this short history of our birth I should just like to thank each and every player for their hearty support in the past season and it is the wish of the Bay to have a full membership of old friends and players at the commencement of next season, To Mr Booth and Mr Martin we cannot say all we should care to for the way in which they have supported us with their kindness and appreciation. Instead of causing any drawbacks to the game, everything was done to further it, both financially and personally, time given up to be with us and encouraging us on to success. To the other clubs in the league we should like to extend a hearty vote of thanks for their kindness in the use of their ground.

Edmonton Cricket League Souvenir Programme 1912

26

Ode to the Philadelphians

Andrew Lang

Sons of the mighty Quaker, man of men,
Who, when the recreant Church had turned her coat,
Ousting that King who first made all faiths free,
Stood for the King and Freedom, William Penn,
Welcome you are – and I would have men note
That your most subtle bowler, even He
Who sent the Indian Prince back with a duck
(I know not if by skill, or heavenly luck),
Bears the great name of King – welcome are ye!

Not yours the art of Pitcher, or of Base,
Not yours a game we do not understand. Your fields like true-born
Englishmen you place;
You pitch not, but bowl British overhand!

Oh Philadelphians! the South Saxons yield,
Even with Ranjitsinhji, to your might.
May you make all Columbia one field,
Where men may stop the yorker, and may smite
The wan half-volley to the conscious ropes!
Such, sons of Pennsylvania, are our hopes;
These men on you depend!
Keep up your glorious end,
Till Baseball droops her shattered wings, and all Columbia,
handling the heroic ball,
Plays that great Island of the Southern Cross,
Or (if she win the toss
On a sound wicket) makes our England fall!

Then, bound once more in bands of brotherhood,
That ne'er shouldhave been broken, you and we,
English of East and West, by land and sea,
One banner shall unfold,
The shining standard of the MCC
Blazoned in red and gold,
In gules and or.
On every conquered and instructed shore,
The oriflamme of Cricket, once unfurled,
Shall dominate the world.

Longman's Magazine 1897

27

Chats on the Cricket Field

Dr H. V. Hordern

'Cricket in Philadelphia is ideal. There can be nothing more delightful. It is played very keenly, with a good healthy rivalry between the clubs, and the best of good fellowship between the players. This good fellowship of the cricket field is a grand thing. Yes, in Philadelphia, as in country house cricket in England, the game is ideal.' Thus spoke Dr H. V. Hordern, as we chatted of cricket and other things arising in his four years absence from Sydney.

As you know, Dr Hordern, who has returned to practise his profession in Sydney, had represented New South Wales once before leaving for the University of Pennyslvania. And in America he became one of the most noted cricketers of the period, his 'googly' bowling achieving marked, and, at times, sensational success against not only Philadelphian and West Indian batsmen, but against Englishmen in England as well as in America.

As we talked of the peculiar type of bowling, of which he is so able an exponent, Dr Hordern termed it the 'googly' and I termed it the 'Bosie'.

'Why "Bosie"?' said he; 'it is "googly" everywhere else.' He had turned interviewer. I explained that we in Australia, as he knew, had seen the only and original B. J. T. Bosanquet in his strongest act. And, for many years before that, we had seen what we had termed 'googlies' bowled from boyhood. The 'googly' in Australian cricket was the slow leg-break, pure and simple. And when England's exponent of the leg-break that turned the other way came along, and on his conquering day showed us something new, something differing so thoroughly from our googly, what more natural than to call it 'the Bosie?'

And in Sydney, at all events, it is as 'the Bosie' this peculiar, perplexing, villainous ball is known. Dr Hordern will soon get used to the term, for in the four years since he went forth we have discovered many imitators of the original. And 'Bosie' bowling has become, perhaps, the most general topic among cricketers themselves. I read somewhere the other day that the South African 'googly' bowlers are going to show Australians something they have never seen before, save from the originator. But 'Bosie' bowlers have come up like mushrooms in Sydney. It is our fond desire that some of them will not wither away as quickly. We hope one or two will remain to show quality as Southern Cross disciples of Bosanquet. The South Africans are sure to show us quality, but, apart from that, their 'googlies' may not surprise us.

Asked if the cricket clubs and grounds of Philadelphia are really as fine as they have been pictured, Dr Hordern replied 'Quite: Germantown, Merion, Philadelphia, and Belmont have most beautiful grounds. Frankfort have lost their ground, but are getting another. These cricket clubs are quite different from anything I have seen anywhere else. They have not only their own cricket grounds, but they have golf links, tennis courts, bowling alleys, squash courts, etc.. And there are just as many ladies as there are men among the members. There are club houses, and, of course, the ladies have their own club houses. So you see they have developed the cricket clubs on lines different from ours.'

Cricket must be an expensive game over there, I thought, and, as though he were a mental telegraphist, Dr Hordern smiled, but said neither yes nor no. But he added: 'Cricket in Philadelphia is purely a recreation for gentlemen. Though there are a few professionals connected with the grounds, the clubs will not include a professional in any of their teams.' That recalls Sydney junior cricket of some years ago. The old New South Wales Junior Cricket Association debarred professionals from its competition matches, but they are no longer barred.

'I found the cricket trips,' Dr Hordern continued, 'to Bermuda and Jamaica thoroughly delightful. You get a strong contrast in weather during February and March with that of Philadelphia. You leave town in the middle of an icy winter, and in 48 hours after setting out from New York, you reach the islands, where the temperature is about 70. It is a thorough change and a most charming way to escape from the winter. I had three tours in Bermuda.'

'Oh, no. There the black people are not allowed to play. J. R. Conyers, who was born in Bermuda of English parents and educated in England, is a very fine batsman, and would do well anywhere. The whole island is composed of coral limestone, and the matting over this did not provide very good cricket on my first visit. But the last time I was there the wickets had been improved a lot and the cricket was correspondingly better. We played three 'Tests' with All Jamaica. You see the "Test" has traversed the globe.'

'There are three very fine grounds with turf wickets in Kingston. The coloured people, descendants of the African negroes, play there. They are cricket mad. It is the only term I can use to describe the strange fascination the game has for them. To illustrate this I can tell you a peculiar experience which befell myself. In one of the matches the 'googlies' astonished them, for they had never before seen any of that kind of bowling. I was awakened very early next morning by someone taking hold of my hand and feeling it as I lay in bed. Opening my eyes, to my astonishment five bedroom boys of the hotel were there, feeling my fingers and hand, and examining them all over. They had been so mystified by the 'googly' that in their keenness they desired to find out the secret in my fingers.'

'You have had some happy cricket tours in England?'

'Yes; one way and another, I have seen a good deal of English cricket. I had three different experiences, each most interesting in itself, and all equally pleasant. It the first, I went with the University of Pennsylvania team which played against the Schools. It showed us one phase of life and one phase of cricket in old England. And very interesting it was. Then I went over with the Philadelphia team which played the counties. It showed me quite a different phase of life and of cricket. J. B. King bowled magnificently on that tour. I was in good form, too, but, unfortunately, I strained myself bowling late one day, and it put me off somewhat for the rest of the tour. More recently I spent six weeks playing cricket in Scotland, and about five weeks in England, principally at Eastbourne. The country house cricket was quite delightful, the matches being played on private grounds. In English club cricket I met many fine bats — men good enough for any team — but the club bowling was weak. Keen? I should just think they are. In my experience club cricket in England is quite keen. They are not at all slack at Eastbourne or in the Sutton cricket week, and it was a great pleasure to participate in their matches. Eastbourne has a beautiful ground, with a perfect wicket.'

'And in Scotland you had some fresh experiences?'

'Yes. I played in two charity matches in Scotland, which started at 6.15 in the evening and went on to 9.15. It may seem a funny experience to an Australian, but the light was quite good. It is the twilight of the Old Country, which we practically do not know out here.'

'In Edinburgh the Australasian Club, composed of Australians and New Zealanders at the University, played the South African Club, and I made 100. But in another match against a local team I had a different experience — much more amusing in its way, because a lot was expected of me. The batsmen hit me about, one man landing a ball clean out of the ground, and when I batted a shooter sent me back without scoring. They enjoyed it — and so did I.'

'J. B. King, of Philadelphia, is one of the finest cricketers I have ever met,' said Dr Hordern, who has seen the world's best. 'He is a first-class bat, but it is his bowling that stands out. It embraces all kinds of bowling — that is, he is several very good bowlers in one man. His stock ball is a fast medium one with variations, from very fast to slow-medium. He started as a fast bowler pure and simple, but I did not see him in those days. He in-swerves with every pace, and will do it all day, and more with a new ball, but always with any ball. Though a right hander, he swerves like George Hirst into a right-hand batsman, and is very accurate, keeping on the spot all day. His is a sharp curve, the ball turning quickly in the last yard or two. King is really an extraordinary bowler, and worth a place in any team in the world. He places the field in a peculiar manner, with four men close up to the batsman. Short square-leg is about three yards from the batsman, fine leg about four or five yards back, mid-on close in, and a man like a silly mid-on, about 6ft. away. At short square-leg I secured 16 catches off him in the English tour. His accuracy makes this extraordinary placing possible without any unusual danger. He bowls the swerve — curve, they call it in America — with a beautiful delivery. With a wonderfully easy action his hand and arm pass high over his head to the left. It is an ideal bowling action.'

'Is there not a strain in such a delivery?'

'I suppose there must be a certain amount of strain on account of the inswerve, but the delivery does not give you an impression of that sort; it is so natural and easy. Nearly every bowler in America is able to make the ball curve, but few in-curve, unless, of course, left-hand.'

The type of bowler for an Australian Eleven, I suggested. Another Spofforth to make fresh history.

'Well, I consider him good enough for any eleven in the world, for he is a wonderful bowler, and first-class with the bat and in the field. A. M. Wood is possibly the most dependable bat in America. Percy Clark, C. C. Morris, F. S. White, and P. N. Leroy are also very fine cricketers. Dr Lester has gone off somewhat.'

'The wicket-keepers of Philadelphia are splendid. Jordan is absolutely first-class. The way he takes J. B. King on the leg side is wonderful. C. H. Winter, the other wicket-keeper, is only about 20 years old, and still at the University. Both are so good that if there are two representative matches they would play one in one match and one in the other. Both are highly thought of in England.'

Asked if there is any likelihood of an American team visiting Australia, Dr Hordern said:

'I should think not. It is a very lengthy journey and, as I say, they play the game merely as a recreation. It is surprising, however, how good cricket is there, considering the comparatively few men who play. It is explained by the fact of their being very keen about it. It is only a certain class which plays, and the other people do not know much about it. One day, after I had practised, a man came along and said, "Would you mind letting me have a look at that club you are using?" That was his name for the bat; and a great many like him do not know anything about cricket. There were only 26 who played cricket out of 5000 students among the candidates for that Pennsylvania team to England. And look at the record they had! It shows you how keen are those who do play.'

'Is Canadian cricket flourishing too?'

'Yes. At Toronto and Montreal the grounds are quite good, though nothing like Philadelphian grounds, of course. They have some very good cricketers there, too.'

'And you have encountered some of the South Africans?'

'Yes, I played against R. O. Schwarz in 1907 when he did so well. He bowled only the off-break, with, of course, the leg-break action, but he made the ball come off the pitch at an extraordinary pace. It was the secret of his remarkable successes. Indeed, he had two different paces off the pitch, and could regulate it by using different finger spin. I have never seen a bowler make more pace from the pitch than Schwarz.'

Dr Hordern beamed with enthusiasm as he referred to another South African: 'Vogler is the best bowler of the slow-medium type I have ever seen anywhere. He bowls the slow leg-break, the off-break, the fast ball with a swerve, and the googly, and he mixes in all these varieties cleverly. Australians will be interested in Vogler's bowling.'

Had he met Dr W. G. Grace recently in England?

'Yes; about three months ago, near Ealing. I played in a match with "Old W.G." He made 48 in absolutely first class style, and, though he is 62 years old, I believe he would have been batting still only he had to get out to catch a train. W.G. is still a wonder.'

'One of the finest men I ever met in cricket is George Beldam, the joint author with C. B. Fry of those unique books, "Great Batsmen" and "Great Bowlers". He has a cricket pitch of his own, and, needless to say, has a rare fondness for the game.'

'In 1908 I saw Alan Marshal,' said Dr Hordern. 'It was his great year. His batting was absolutely magnificent, especially his off and on driving. I never saw a man hit harder on the off-side, but, of course, I never saw Bonnor, Massie, or McDonnell, though I do remember Lyons.'

Cricket 1910

28

A Review of the Game

W. G. Grace

I wonder how many realize the remarkable hold the game of cricket has outside England. We at home are too apt to believe it is entirely English, and think it can be seen at its best in England only; but by degrees the fact dawns upon us that an eleven of Australia has defeated more than one representative English team, and we have to admit that others can play the game nearly, if not quite, as well as we can. The time has gone past when we could look on without anxiety as to the result of a contest between England and Australia, or predict a certain win for the former. I am not going to say a word here as to the wisdom of our Australian cousins in coming to us so often: this much I know and can say, the visit of the seventh team is creating as much interest as any of those which preceded it, and before the season is over we are likely to have contests which will do honour to both countries. Before dealing with cricket in this country I propose to touch upon the growth of the game in Australia, Canada, the United States, and India, and in the order named.

In Australia

I was in my fourteenth year when the first English team, under the captaincy of H. H. Stephenson, visited Australia in 1862, and can remember how my thoughts went with the players who composed it. Some of them I had seen, all of them I knew by reputation, and their doings in the past had been a part of my education. The undertaking appealed to my youthful mind, filled with enthusiasm for the game, and I was not alone in my opinion when I said what a faint chance players in Australia would have against such a combination. Results showed that even then the game was making rapid progress outside England, but there was no doubt about the superiority of the visiting team.

Twelve matches was the total number played. The first was against Eighteen of Victoria, and resulted in an easy win for the Englishmen by an innings and ninety-six runs. The remaining matches were played against twenty-two's, and gross results showed that England had won six and lost two, while four were drawn.

Two years later a second team under the leadership of George Parr went out, when the superiority of English players was more strikingly confirmed. England on that occasion was thoroughly represented, and the results were still more decisive. Sixteen matches were played — on every occasion against twenty-two of their opponents — ten were won, *none* lost, six drawn! I very much question if a stronger team could have been found at that time, and I have only to give the names of the players to prove it, George Parr, A. Clarke, J. Jackson, R. C. Tinley: Notts; W. Caffyn, Julius Caesar, T. Lockyer: Surrey; R. Carpenter, T. Hayward, G. Tarrant: Cambridgeshire; G. Anderson: Yorkshire; Mr E. M. Grace: Gloucestershire.

The first team consisted entirely of professionals, this it will be seen was made up of eleven professionals, and one gentleman — the gentleman being my brother, E. M. Grace. Every one of them was a household name, and I need not say that their doings generally were eagerly and impatiently waited for at home, and the matches in which my brother played were carefully cut out, and inserted in the list of family performances. My brother's successful effort with bat and ball at Canterbury, in 1862, was now a matter of history, and we were proud that he should be considered worthy of a place in so notable a team. Tarrant and he played single wicket matches on two or three occasions against considerable odds, and showed that Australia was still far behind in the game.

Ten years elapsed before a third team decided to go out. A few gentlemen, who were much interested in cricket at Melbourne, and who were very anxious to see another English eleven over there, invited me to take out and captain a mixed team of gentlemen and professionals. I accepted this invitation, and in the summer of 1873 made the necessary arrangements. After many disappointments, I got a fairly good twelve together, but not so strong as I desired. The composition of this team showed the marked change which was creeping over English cricket. For years the professionals had stood head and shoulders above the gentlemen, and matches between them had been almost a certainty for the former. On this occasion the professionals still predominated, but only in the proportion of seven to five. We had heard from time to time of the great strides which were taking place in Australian cricket, but we were not prepared to be beaten in three out of the first five matches. However, as soon as we became accustomed to the glare and light, we began to assert our superiority, and we won nine out of the remaining ten matches played. Altogether we played fifteen matches, all of them against odds: ten were won, three lost, and two drawn. In ten of them we played against twenty-two of our opponents, three times against eighteen, and twice against fifteen. Messrs. B. B. Cooper and W. J. Pocock, who learnt their cricket in England, and had only been in the colonies a short time, did a great deal towards winning two of the three matches lost: at Melbourne Mr Cooper scored eighty-four, and at Sydney Mr Pocock scored sixteen not out, and twenty-seven. The Australian batting did not then appear to be very good, but the bowling greatly impressed me. I must mention Mr Frank Allan, a left-hand bowler, who was then far and away the best in the colonies. Messrs. F. R. Spofforth and H. F. Boyle were commencing their career, and played once or twice against us.

Three years elapsed before a fourth team left our shores. This time it was under the management of James Lillywhite, and made up entirely of professionals. Before the end of the tour results proved that the desired improvement had taken place in Australian cricket. Against fifteen of New South Wales the Englishmen suffered defeat twice, and experienced a similar fate at the hands of fifteen of Victoria; but the 15th, 16th and 17th March, 1877, was the crowning point of Australia's long and persevering efforts, for it was the first time Australia met an eleven of England on level terms, and beat them by forty-five runs, owing to the magnificent batting of C. Bannerman. True, they suffered defeat by four wickets a fortnight later, but that did not affect the precedent established that Australia was now worthy of playing England, the home of cricket, man to man, the result being uncertain. A. and C. Bannerman, Blackham, Evans, Garrett, Horan, Midwinter, Murdoch, and Spofforth were the names dear to Australia then. They have done greater things since with both bat and ball, but there is little doubt that that was the time they made their reputations and gave an impetus to rising talent in their own country.

We at home put little value on the defeat of Lillywhite's team, and did not fully realize the wonderful improvement our cousins had made. They thought differently; for hardly had the news of it died out when the startling information came that an eleven of Australia had decided to visit England and beard the lion in his den, and on the 14th May, 1878, the first Australian team stepped hopefully on British soil. After a day or two's practice, they made their bow before an English public against Nottingham, only to be beaten by an innings and fourteen runs. 'That is about their form,' said thousands; 'not quite up to English county cricket.'

May 20th, at Lord's, caused quite a revolution in public opinion. I had the honour of being one of the eleven of the MCC on that day – an eleven considered the equal of any batting eleven in the world, and including two of the best bowlers of the day – Alfred Shaw and Morley. Cricketers in general looked upon the match as a crucial one, the result of which would make or mar the rest of the tour. Unfortunately the wicket was a bad one, owing to rain and then a drying sun, and it was impossible to arrive at an idea of their true form. We lost the match by nine wickets. This much was clear to us: Australian cricket had wonderfully improved, and henceforth England v. Australia, both playing their full strength, would be full of interest wherever it was played. The match, it will be remembered, was finished in one day, and was the first victory of an Australian eleven on English ground.

The total scores were: MCC, first innings, thirty-three; second innings, nineteen. Australia, first innings, forty-one; second innings, twelve (for one wicket). There were thirteen ducks on the MCC side, and the bowling of Spofforth, Boyle, and A. Shaw was decidedly sensational.*

The rest of the trip was a great success, and the gross results showed that of the thirty-seven matches played, eighteen were won, seven lost, and twelve were drawn, seventeen of them were eleven-a-side matches, of which the Australians won nine, lost four, and four were drawn. Their best wins were against MCC and Ground, Yorkshire, Surrey,

	O.	M.	R.	Wks.		O.	M.	R.	Wks.
* Spofforth	5.3	3	4	6		9	2	16	4
Boyle	14	7	14	3		8.1	6	3	6
A. Shaw	33.2	25	10	5		8	6	4	1

Middlesex, Gloucestershire, and Eleven Players; their heaviest defeats by Cambridge University, Nottinghamshire, Gentlemen of England, and the return against Yorkshire.

Altogether six Australian teams have visited England, and eleven English teams have gone out to Australia; and results show that England has still more than one eleven capable of defeating the combined strength of Australia. The teams which visited us in 1886 and 1888 did not materially add to the reputation of Australia, but it must be remembered that on both occasions several players who were chosen to represent Australia were unable to join the team owing to business and other engagements.

When we make comparisons of play we have undoubted evidence that England has still a strong lead in batting, but that in bowling and fielding there is little to choose between the two countries. Murdoch, G. Giffen, McDonnell, the Bannermans and Moses have been a tower of strength in batting, but one does not require to search far in England to find a large number of players who have performed as great things as they. Spofforth, Garrett, Palmer, Evans, Boyle, Turner, and Ferris are bowling names to compare with ours, but we have only to place opposite them the names of Alfred Shaw, Morley, Lohmann, Peate, Attewell, Briggs, and Barnes to make the scales hang evenly. In fielding there is little to choose between us, although I must in fairness says that at present the Australians can throw in better than we can.

In Canada and the United States

American cricketers can boast of an earlier visit by English cricketers than Australia, but the game has not progressed at the same rate in both countries. As long ago as 1859 an English twelve under George Parr visited Canada and the United States, and had little difficulty in winning all their matches. The team was made up of six players from the United All England Eleven and six from the All England Eleven, so that cricketers in Canada and the States got a thorough insight into first-class play. The first match was played against twenty-two of Lower Canada, and resulted in an easy win for the English eleven. A similar fate befell twenty-two of Hamilton and district; and later, on October 21st, at Rochester, Upper Canada, twenty of United States and Canada were defeated by an innings and sixty-eight runs.

Nine years rolled by before a second team, under Willsher, paid

Canada and the States another visit, and results were still more disastrous. Twenty-two of Canada could only score twenty-eight to England's 310 for nine wickets. Canadian bowling did not come out favourably in this match, for forty wides appear in the English score. The Philadelphians then, as now, seemed to be the strongest club in either country, and twenty-two of them lost by two wickets only. Of the six matches played, five were won, and one drawn; and Canada and the United States were, as they still are, far behind the English standard of play.

The third team, in 1872, was under the leadership of Mr R. A. Fitzgerald, secretary of the MCC, and was made up entirely of gentlemen cricketers, who were quite as successful as their predecessors. I was one of the team, and have very pleasant recollections of the hospitality and great kindness shown to us throughout the trip. Undoubtedly we were a strong batting team, and that seemed to attract the American public; but, with the exception of the Philadelphian club, we met with little opposition, and won seven out of the eight matches played, while the eighth was drawn. A reference to a note which I made at the time gives my opinion formed at the conclusion of our visit. 'The bowling was better than the batting; the fielding generally not very good; but here and there we met with brilliant exceptions.'

The fourth team, in 1879, was a combination of Notts and Yorkshire, captained by R. Daft, and was just as successful. Twelve matches were played: nine won, none lost, three drawn. Seven of them were against twenty-two, the others against varying odds, but every match was won very easily. Quite evidently the Americans considered they had improved, for one of the engagements was: — Eleven of Young America v. The English Eleven.

The result was not encouraging, for A. Shaw, Morley, and Bates created sad havoc among the American batsmen, and England won by an innings and sixty runs, and so maintained the unbroken record of wins for England in America. Up to this date thirty-six matches had been played in Canada and the States, of which English teams had won twenty-eight; the other eight were drawn.

It was natural that sooner or later a team from Canada or the United States should pay a visit to the home of cricket, and no one was surprised when it was announced early in 1884 that the Philadelphians, undoubtedly the strongest club in either country, had made up their minds to come here. They did not come believing they could hold their own with a representative team, or even the best of our county teams: they came hoping to see the best players in England, and anxious to improve their own cricket. I need not say they were as cordially welcomed as the Australians, who were making their fourth visit that year. Every club, every player in England, extended the hand of welcome; and from their first match against Dublin University on the 2nd and 3rd of June, at Dublin, until their last match against the United Services Club, on the 1st and 2nd of August, at Portsmouth, their doings were closely watched. Eighteen matches were played: eight won, five lost, five drawn. The matches played were mostly against eleven gentlemen of the first and second class counties. They did not measure their strength against our professional or first-class bowling. Their great match was against the Gentlemen of the MCC, a most disastrous one for them. The MCC won by an innings and 171 runs, scoring 406 to the Philadelphians' 174 and 61. I had the pleasure of meeting them only once when playing for the Gentlemen of Gloucestershire, but had to bear with defeat. My friend, Lord Harris, had rather the laugh over me at the result, and said, somewhere, in Lillywhite, I believe, 'If there is magic in a name it should certainly be found in the Gentlemen of Gloucestershire and the brothers Grace; but in this match the Philadelphians did not allow apprehension to neutralize their efforts. Surely this victory went far to compensate for the disappointment at Lord's. One thing, at least, is certain, that the disappointment was lifted on to other shoulders, for so great was the wrath of the Gloucestershire captain at the result that we believe he dismissed his eleven with a parting injunction, "not to let him see them for a month".'

Twelve English amateurs visited America in 1885, not a first-class team by any means, but good enough to win every match but one; and that one, as was expected, was against the Gentlemen of Philadelphia, on September 17th, 18th, and 19th. This was the first match ever won against an English team in America. A week later the English Amateurs had their revenge, defeating the Philadelphians by 243 runs. The year after a slightly stronger team of English amateurs went out, and carried everything before them, not losing a match. The Philadelphians were still considered the strongest fixture, but the first match the Englishmen won by an innings, and the second by six wickets. Altogether they played nine matches: won eight, lost none, and one was drawn.

The Gentlemen of Canada came to us in 1887, had a very enjoyable time, but met with moderate success. I played against them at Yatton for Mr Tankerville Chamberlayne's Eleven, which was chiefly composed of the Gentlemen of Gloucestershire.

The doings of the Philadelphians in England, Ireland, and Scotland in 1889 will be fresh in the memories of most players — a strong batting team, but moderate in bowling; the fielding at times very good on hard, good grounds, but on slow grounds not so good as one would have expected. One or two of their best bowlers did not come, or they certainly would have given a better account of themselves: as it was, they were a far better team than that of 1884. They played in all twelve matches. Three of them were lost against strong amateur elevens of Gloucestershire, Kent, and the MCC; four were won against the Gentlemen of Scotland, Gentlemen of Liverpool, and Gentlemen of Hampshire, and Cambridge University Long Vacation Club. The other five were drawn; these being against the Trinity College Long Vacation Club, the Gentlemen of Ireland, the Gentlemen of Surrey, the Gentlemen of Sussex, and the United Services. I can assure my readers that if the Gentlemen of Philadelphia go on improving as they have done since their first visit, when they come again they will hold their own against county amateur teams, if they do not beat them. What I have said will show that while cricket has progressed in America since the visit of the first English team, the progress is not to be compared with that made in Australia.

Cricket and Baseball

Cricket in Australia, as in England, is considered the national game; in America it has to contend against baseball. To realize the hold baseball has upon Americans we have only to watch one of the great matches. At every important match played the attendance is as large as, if not larger than at any first-class cricket-match in England; and the fact is forced upon us that baseball, not cricket, is the national game there. Cricket clubs of importance are few in number in America: baseball clubs have a hold in every large town and city, and the doings of the professional players are followed with as much interest as the doings of every first-class professional cricketer in England.

I have been asked to account for the remarkable hold baseball has upon its followers, and to compare the two games of baseball and cricket. Frankly, I cannot. It would be presumption on my part to express an opinion on the merits of a game of which I have seen, and know so little. My experience might be summed up in a visit to the Oval, and a visit to the County Ground, Ashley Hill, Bristol, when Mr Spalding's team gave their exhibitions. I was much impressed with the smartness of the fieldsmen, their catching and throwing being almost perfection. But the batting, to a cricketer, seemed rather a weak spot; and with the crowd I was disappointed that hitting the ball was the exception instead of the rule. Of course I am perfectly well aware that the pitcher is the most important member of the team, and that what I thought was a weakness in the hitting was really a tribute to his skill.

Our American friends say that a first-class match can be played in the course of a single afternoon, and that being a busy working nation, therein lies half the charm of the game to them. They are certainly enthusiastic over it, and I know that but few Englishmen have yet realized the science and aptitude required to play it well; but I do not think it will ever take hold to any extent in England or Australia, where cricket is played to such perfection. And I hope its thousands of followers will pardon me when I say that I have too strong a love for the game with which I have been so closely associated for the last twenty-five years to wish that it should.

In India

But if we want further confirmation as to the growth of cricket outside England, we have only to turn to the progress it is making in India. It has been said that wherever you find a dozen Englishmen you are sure to find the national game played. That it should be played in India by Englishmen under the disadvantages of a climate more calculated to make one physically indolent than active is a tribute in its favour, but that it should be taken up and played vigorously by the native races, is praise indeed.

The Parsees came to us in 1886. Of them it can be said that their motive was the purely disinterested one of seeing the best exponents of the game. Their display was anything but first-class; and financially, the promoters of the trip had reason to be dissatisfied and discouraged from making a second trip: but 1888 saw them back again, and, what was most gratifying, playing in improved form.

Thirty-one matches were played on the second visit against very fair elevens, and in two or three of the most important they showed up very creditably. Their last engagement, against the Gentlemen of Surrey, was only lost by nine runs, and they could show at the finish of the trip a record of eight won, eleven lost, and twelve drawn. Their enthusiasm and pluck in playing up, whether winning or losing, was the marked feature of their play, and good judges of the game predicted good results from it.

The results of Mr Vernon's team in India have been read everywhere: thirteen matches played, of which ten were won, two drawn, and one lost. The eleven could not be considered first-class, or even representative of the Gentlemen of England, but there were in it two or three batsmen who more than once have scored heavily against the best of our professional bowling, so we need not wonder they had matters pretty much their own way. Six times they won in a single innings, and the clubs played against were the strongest in India. That makes their defeat by the Parsee Eleven at Bombay on the 30th and 31st of January all the more remarkable. It was said when the team left England that the Parsees would give them the most trouble, but after the triumphal march of the English Eleven in more than half of the matches, we at home, not unreasonably, concluded that the Parsees would have to submit to defeat also. And yet they won by four wickets.

We have no occasion to go far to find the reason. With one exception Mr Vernon's Eleven never scored less than a hundred runs in an innings, and oftener the total was nearer three hundred. The Parsees got them out for ninety-seven and sixty-one; and the opinion of Mr Vernon and every one who played was that their bowling was the best they had played against in the whole tour.

In England

It has given me pleasure to speak of Australia, Canada, the United States, and India in the way I have done, but it gives me greater pleasure to say that the game has a stronger hold in England to-day than at any time in its history. For one eleven that could draw a crowd in the past we can show half a dozen or more who can do so at the present time: and we have only to look at the averages of individual players with bat and ball to find that the deeds of twenty and thirty years ago have been surpassed.

In batting the number of players, both amateur and professional, with an average of twenty runs and over is far ahead of the number in 1860 or 1870. Scoring an aggregate of 1000 runs in first-class matches during the season was thought a remarkable feat twenty years ago; we do not think so much of it now. Nine players accomplished it in 1886, and though 1889 was one of the wettest seasons we have had for years, there were five players who exceeded that total. Scoring a hundred runs in one innings is another important feature of the play to-day. It was done by more than twenty players last year, and by some of them twice or thrice. And if we only remember how general is the improvement in bowling, the performance becomes even more remarkable. County cricket is a very fair test of a batsman's powers. Well, in first-class county cricket last year the century was scored forty times. That is surely evidence enough of the great strides we have made in batting in recent years.

Take our bowling averages. Capturing a hundred wickets in first-class matches twenty or thirty years ago was another exceptional and remarkable feat. We are not surprised at it to-day. G. Lohman captured over 200 in 1888, and repeated the performance in 1889, and six others had considerably over a hundred to their credit the same year.

Batting improvement is to be expected when we consider the change for the better that has taken place in the grounds played on. A wicket that was considered good enough ten or twenty years ago would not be tolerated to-day; and I can mention two or three of our present county grounds where in favourable weather every ball can be relied on to come true, and where the batsman plays back and forward with the utmost confidence. Twenty or thirty years ago the selection of the wicket was too often left until the morning of the match, and that was considered time enough to begin preparing it. Go to any of the principal grounds to-day, and you will find that the roller is in use every day, and all day, in the season when there is no match on: and that not one, but half-a-dozen good pitches can be obtained even if the selection be deferred until the morning of the match. Now that, while it has made large batting averages easy nowadays, has made it more difficult for the bowler to get the batsman out.

Reference to some of the principal grounds in England and the Colonies will be appropriate here. The captain of the county eleven, or of any eleven travelling from home, is lacking in his duty if he does not find out something about the characteristics of a ground before a match begins. It is of little use to win the toss if he be careless about that. Judgement before a match shows the thoughtful captain: and while I have an immense respect for the man who 'rises to the occasion', I have often found that a little forethought in examining the pitch before tossing might have prevented the occasion arising at all. It used to be said, 'What is the use of winning the toss if you do not take first innings?' You do not hear that said now: anyhow, not until a thoughtful leader has carefully examined the pitch and considered the weather, light, and other circumstances, and thinks it advantageous to take first innings.

Lord's Ground has a right to the first place. In dry weather the wicket is one of the fastest and truest anywhere: in a very wet condition, one of the easiest for scoring. In a sticky condition it is almost unplayable, and about the worst I know. The soil is clayey, and that explains it. It was on a wicket of the latter kind that the Australians played their first match there in May 1878, and Spofforth, Boyle, and A. Shaw worked wonders with the ball. A strong batting eleven was all abroad and could do nothing on it. Playing forward was out of the question, playing back dangerous, and following the ball a failure. I can recall two or three occasions when it was nearly as bad. When Yorkshire County played for the first time at Lord's in 1870 the ground was hard and rough. Freeman and Emmett for Yorkshire, and A. Shaw and Wootton for the MCC, had a high time of it with the ball, tattooing the bodies of every batsman who had the pluck to face them. Neither practice wickets nor football is allowed on the centre of Lord's Ground, so that the pitch can be trusted unless when, as I have said, the ground is in a sticky condition.

At the Oval you get some of the very best wickets in the world, and some batsmen prefer it to Lord's. It is not so fast for one reason, although, for myself, I still prefer a fast wicket as long as the ball comes true. The soil is undoubtedly different from that at Lord's, for very rarely do you get the sticky and unplayable wicket I have just mentioned.

Trent Bridge is a greatly improved ground, one of the finest county grounds in England, and entirely owing to the great care now given to the preparation of the wickets. Losing the toss there does not make such a difference now as it used to.

The wicket wears fairly well from start to finish of a match, and rarely do you now find it in a crumbling condition.

Old Trafford has the reputation of being one of the best-kept grounds anywhere, but of late the pitches have not worn well. However, we hope this year will see a vast improvement. At the end of last season the Committee set about remedying the defects, and a good coat of top dressing was put down, which should in time restore it to its former and excellent condition. The out-fielding has always been good and easy there. Liverpool, in the number of matches played, is not so much favoured by the Lancashire CC, but it is a very fine and improving ground.

Bramall Lane, Sheffield, is not quite so good as the grounds I have already mentioned, but that too has improved considerably. The Yorkshire CC play all over the county — Bradford, Halifax, Dewsbury, and Huddersfield all being visited by them; and while that is to be commended, it sometimes affects the quality of particular wickets. The acknowledged head-quarters of a county club is always well looked after, the ground in particular being carefully watched and prepared.

The Kent Eleven have had a similar experience. They, too, play all over the county. One day it is at Blackheath, the next at Mote Park, then Beckenham is visited, and we have the Canterbury week in August. Beckenham has been relaid during the winter, and ought to play well if carefully looked after, and thoroughly rolled. Blackheath is a large and good ground, but does not play so well, owing, I think, in some measure to the amount of football played over it. Canterbury is a good ground, although on a slope. The wicket in dry weather is very hard and fast. Apart from the happy associations connected with it, it is a great favourite of mine.

The Sussex Eleven have occasion to be proud of their County Ground at Brighton, in the past and to-day. The old ground at Hove and the present ground have always been good, and in my estimation about the best and easiest for scoring in England.

Gloucestershire in the past may be said to have divided their favours between Clifton and Cheltenham Colleges. Both are fine grounds, Clifton, if anything, the better. Clifton has the reputation of being the easiest in all kinds of weather, in England, and it well deserves it. A difficult wicket has always been the exception there, and it is owing entirely to the care and preparation bestowed on it. The outfield is rough, but I do not see how that can be remedied much. In the season the boys are playing, and have a right to play, all over it, and it is almost impossible to preserve that part in the condition one associates with a County Ground pure and simple. The new ground at Ashley Hill puts Gloucestershire in a more favourable position. It is certainly an excellent one, one of the finest in the world for good wickets and out-fielding. As at Lord's, all practice wickets are outside the enclosure, and football is only played outside the cricket enclosure.

There are other grounds all over England, Scotland and Ireland about which I could speak favourably, but in an article of this length those I have touched upon will show how managers of important clubs realize the need of a good ground if improvement is to be made by their players. They cannot influence the weather, but they can and have made up their minds to see that, given favourable conditions, the wickets shall be carefully prepared and as true as human hands can make them. That, I believe, is the spirit actuating the committee of every county club.

However, my remarks upon grounds would not be complete without an allusion to those in the Colonies and America. I can only speak of the time when I played on them, and as that is a good many years ago, it is possible — certain I ought to say — that changes for the better have taken place. I will just mention the leading grounds — Melbourne, Sydney, Adelaide, Ballarat, Hobart Town, and Launceston were all good when I played on them in 1873–4. There was lack of knowledge at the time of making, want of judgement in deferring the selection and preparing the wicket until the day of, or the day before, the match. I know all that is changed. We should not have had the great results which players in Australia have produced had the wickets been anything but good.

Pretty much what I have said about Australia may be applied to Canada and America. Toronto, Philadelphia, and the St George's Club, New York, have good grounds, which are carefully looked after, and as good wickets can be obtained there as at most of the clubs in England. I can say very little about India. I have not been there: but my heart is there, as it is wherever cricket is played. I know they have several good grounds, and take the greatest interest in the noble game, and although the climate is too hot at times, I believe the only reason an English team has not visited India before is that the grounds are open and free, and that no gate-money could be taken to pay the expenses.

It may now be asked: Has the improvement in the grounds everywhere in any way affected the batting, bowling, and fielding? Undoubtedly it has, and in more ways than some players think. The batsman knows that he can trust the wicket in most cases now, consequently he plays with greater confidence and hits many a ball that he would not have dared to hit in the days when the wickets were not so good. At the time I began to make my big scores writers on the game were pretty unanimous about playing the ball with a certain force when compelled to play back to it. 'Do not let it hit the bat, but play firm enough to get it away from the legs, or it may roll on to the wicket,' said a very good authority. Carpenter, Daft, Jupp, and Humphrey were the players given by the same authority as being strong in that kind of play. Back play no stronger than that would not be considered first-class form to-day, and the batsman who could not hit the ball more than a yard or two beyond his legs, would take a very long time to compile a century against the best of our bowlers.

Playing it forcibly and yards away from the wicket is now expected of the majority of first-class players, and I could name a dozen who are not content unless they play it away from the fieldsmen and hard enough to score two runs. That is due in most part to the skill of the player, and, I think, partly to the improvement of the grounds. Twenty years ago, or even ten years ago, a ball bounding breast-high was not an uncommon experience on most wickets, but if it were to occur to-day with half the frequency, the reputation of the groundsman would suffer considerably.

And so it may be safely said that the batting all round is better to-day than in the past. I do not mean to say that the giants of the past would not be giants to-day; but I do say that were those players with us now they too would play in improved form, and that for one good batsman then we have a dozen now. The public have a clear knowledge of that fact. We have only to take a stroll round the ground while a great match is being played to learn what they consider good play. I have an immense respect for the barn-door or stone-wall style, but must confess to siding with the crowd when they praise the player who times the straight good-length ball, and plays it hard and clean away from the wicket. With my brother, E. M., at his best at point, good old Jupp, in his later days, had a lively time of it when playing at Clifton for his county. Ball after ball I bowled to him which he kept playing back quietly; then the particular ball came, and E.M. rushed in and caught him almost off the bat. The disgust that crept over Jupp's face as point, slip, and short-leg crowded round him, and his helplessness under the circumstances come up before me now. And yet Jupp was considered a good back-player.

Playing forward is also more general, and that, too, owing to improved wickets. Good players know that in playing forward they are now less likely to meet with a kicking ball which would hit them on the fingers, and so play forward with the greatest confidence to balls which they used to watch carefully and in many cases play back to. And short-pitched balls which were blocked then are now pulled across the wicket owing to the same cause.

But bowling more than batting has been affected by the improvement of the grounds. How rarely do we see a real good fast bowler now? The time has gone past when pace alone could obtain a wicket. It was not an uncommon plan for a fast bowler to send in a fast short one, knowing that the half-prepared wicket would cause it to bound very high and make it dangerous for the batsman to hit. When that is done now, the bowler is not surprised to see it hit to the boundary. And so we have more head-work in the bowling, a better length, more break, but less pace. The important point the bowler must bear in mind is not to exceed his strength, or he will very soon go to pieces, and get hit all over the field. No ball can be punished so easily as the short fast one on a good wicket. All good bowlers indulge in an occasional fast one; but that is a different thing to the express pace some bowlers used to keep up for an over or two. Messrs Spofforth, Steel and Turner, among the gentlemen, Alfred Shaw, Lohmann and Briggs among the professionals, have been the most prominent bowlers for years past. Spofforth's wonderful power lies in his variety. Whether he breaks six inches or twelve he takes good care that the ball will hit the wicket, should it beat the batsman: and he keeps varying his pace till he gets the batsman in two minds, and then treats him to a fast yorker. He has been more effective with fast yorkers than any bowler I know. A. G. Steel is another of the tantalizing bowlers. Rarely do you get two balls in succession the same pace from him; and if there is a weak spot in your defence he keeps hammering at that until you make a mistake.

The same may be said of Turner. He is always well within his strength, and ever varying his pace. Lohmann and Briggs work on the same lines. Alfred Shaw had the least break of the lot except on sticky wickets, but his wonderful command of length more than compensated for it.

All of them bowled with their head. They saw that the improved wickets were adding to the batsman's chances, and that simple fast bowling would not meet the case: so they cultivated variety of pace-breaking from both sides, and only departing from a good length when the batsman had mastered them. Southerton was one of that school, and proficient at it too: but the wickets were not so good in his days and helped him considerably. He used to tell with great glee how, after trying me with dodgy breaks for an hour or two, he in despair sent up a simple, harmless straight one, with no break at all, and beat me. There was nothing in the ball, but it was unexpected, and it came off. I have seen Lohmann bowl batsman after batsman with a similar ball. The batsmen admitted it was as simple a ball as any bowler could bowl, but they expected something different from him.

I am beginning to hope that very shortly we shall have an increase of good fast bowlers. The success of Mr S. M. J. Woods and Mold last year warrants me in saying that good fast bowlers would baffle a great many batsmen who are now at home with medium-paced breaks. The day of terrific pace and careless length is at an end, but a fast bowler who could bowl a good length for a dozen overs would be invaluable to any of our county elevens to-day.

Out-fielding has also benefited by the improvement in the grounds. Years ago, the pitch was rolled carefully by some clubs, but very rarely anything outside it. As long as the grass was kept short most clubs were content; and cover-point, long-leg, and the out-fieldsmen generally, had to be very quick of eye and hand to stop the ball with certainty even when it was travelling straight to them. To-day the roller is in use all over the ground, and he would not be considered a first-class fielder who failed to pick up the ball correctly and smartly on the run before throwing it in.

The wicket-keeper is another who has benefited. He dispenses with a long-stop to bowlers who are not a bit slower than some to whom it was thought necessary to have a long-stop placed years ago, and this, in a great degree, may be ascribed to the improvement of the ground.

There is no need to compare the wicket-keepers of the present with those of the past, but I cannot help saying that the doings of Messrs Philipson, McGregor, Pilling and Sherwin in 1889, without long-stops, are worthy of the highest praise. I have no need to mention Blackham; he was not here in 1889, but he is still at the top of the tree in that part of the game.

I should be less than human were I to abstain from saying something about the future of the game. I do not lay claim to the gift of prophecy, and have too much respect for the bare and simple truth to think that my opinion will be considered of exceptional value there. What I desire to say is based on my past experience, and may be said in very few words.

There is more cricket played to-day than at any time previously, and good cricket too. We have only to look at the growth of county cricket and observe the crowds that turn out to look at the play, whether the match be between first or second-class counties, to realize that the game is played more than ever. There are counties enough to form three classes, and the classification of them is a question for the immediate future. Eight is the number of the first-class counties at present, and I do not see how that can be increased. Playing home and home matches with each other means forty-two days or seven weeks of actual play, and that is as much as cricketers can manage to play, as they have so many other first-class matches to take part in out of a season which from beginning to end lasts about sixteen weeks. Second-class counties might be limited to six in number, third-class to four; and these might fulfil engagements with each other without interfering much with other important fixtures.

The hardest nut to crack will be the promotion of the second-class to the first, and the third to the second; not an easy matter, I admit; still, in the interests of the game, it will have to be cracked. The point has been under consideration, and a sub-committee of the Cricket Council was appointed in December last; and I have no doubt it will be thoroughly and impartially weighed and some decision arrived at before the end of this season.

I cannot predict that, outside of the Australian matches, there will be more exciting contests in 1890 than there were in 1889. The weather cannot be worse for one thing, and it is not unlikely that individual and club scores may be larger. It will be a very exceptional display that will outshine the Gentlemen *v.* Players match at the Oval last year. There will be plenty of good batsmen this season, but I do not know of any rising phenomenon who will surpass the achievements of the best players of the last six years in any part of the game. There is a fine opening for good fast bowlers. I could count on the fingers of one hand the batsmen who can play a fast first-class bowler with confidence. Mr S. M. J. Woods, Mold, Beaumont and Bowley are sure to do good work in the coming season, but after you have named these there are not many fast bowlers left.

The last word to my friend and comrade of many years, Lord Harris, who is giving up the game for the sterner duties of life. He will be a great loss to his county, a greater loss to the cricket world generally. He is one of the few who has contributed with both hands and head to the history of the game, and carries the heartiest wishes of every cricketer to his new sphere of work.

English Illustrated Magazine 1890

29

Cricket

Lord Harris

In a season of comparative repose — repose at any rate compared with the hurly-burly of one marked by the descent upon the cricketing world of two foreign elevens, if we may use such a word of Australian brothers and American cousins — it may not be amiss to devote a thought to the progress that cricket has made in the last decade and is still making in the estimation of the English people, and to consider whether that progress has been for good or ill to them. Let it be granted that some out-door exercise is good for mind as well as body — and we think we can show that the progress has been for good — and indeed, we think we shall not be begging the question if without any extended argument we take that for granted. It is almost, if not quite, an axiom in England that our field sports and pastimes have done much towards teaching those who take part in them first to obey, perhaps eventually to command, and thereby helping to form those capabilities which go to make a good soldier of either the regular or citizen army. Again, pastimes serve good purpose in causing the young noblemen and gentlemen of England to rub shoulders with those who are lower than themselves in the social scale, but in the republic of the playground are, perhaps, their superiors, and so force upon the minds of the former a respect for industry, honesty, sobriety, and any other of the qualities that are necessary to produce an efficient athlete; feelings which but for these remarkable English pastimes might have never been developed, or even if so, would very possibly have been smothered under the weight of self-importance. Remarkable then we call them, and justifiably we think; for must not history take note of them? And in ancient or modern history where is there mention of pastimes? Athletic sports, as understood in England — *i.e.*, running and jumping, and the brutal contests of the arena doubtless receive the notice of the historian; but where is there mention of any pursuits of a character so innocent, one would say so insignificant, if one did not know the attractions they have for many thousands in this and other English-speaking countries, as football and cricket?

But let us confine our attention to cricket. Can the historian ignore what cricket has done towards bringing together the mother country and her Australian colonies? We think not, and therefore we think ourselves justified in calling it a remarkable game, perhaps the most remarkable the world has ever seen. This fact at least is worthy of note, that practical colonial statesmen have not ignored, and do not ignore, that cricket can be a factor in creating amongst Englishmen an interest in those great offshoots from the mother country. We are inclined to question whether the excitement in Australia has been greater over the transmission of a body of colonial troops to assist the mother country in the Sudan than it was over the successes of the first Australian Eleven that visited these shores. The theorist, however, may say, 'I grant you that some outdoor exercise is good and indeed necessary; but is there not a great waste of time over such a game as cricket – time which would be much better spent in the consideration of such economic problems as might lead to solutions having a beneficial result for mankind?' Well, putting aside altogether the difficult problem whether the circulation of capital, and consequent employment of labour, which does result from a game so universally pursued as cricket, is or is not of benefit to the community, we should be inclined to say, 'If the minds of those who take an active part in the game were devoted to nothing else, the answer might be in the affirmative.' But that is not the case. Let the theorist inquire among his friends, and not seldom will he find that some athletic pursuit has exercised its sway over his earlier days. He will find perhaps that the millionaire, who devotes much of his thought and wealth to the improvement of his estate, and is an enthusiast on the subject of church architecture, was in his University Eleven; that the judge spends his leisure evenings at Lord's; that the statesman pulled an oar in his University Eight; that the rising barrister's name is celebrated in tennis court annals; that the philanthropist, who spends his evenings with the poor, may occasionally be seen no inconspicuous figure in the football field, and that the hardest of hard-worked MPs was never beaten in the racquet court; and if he finds that answer to his inquiries, perhaps he will admit that the field of athletics need not necessarily, and indeed seldom does, prevent the man who had been able to excel there to excel also in after years in graver pursuits. And, the greater covering the less, he will find this applies also to cricket; for as the young gentleman who has been a distinguished figure in the cricket-field finds the graver duties of life forcing themselves on his attention, he leaves the former for the latter, not without a heartache perhaps, but none the worse a man that the republic of the cricket-field has given him a closer acquaintance with all sorts and conditions of men, and with probably a practical knowledge of human nature that will serve him in good stead through life, which he might have acquired with difficulty, if at all, in the classroom or the study.

So much for the effect of the national game on those who learn it at school, practise it at college, and carry their enthusiasm for it to Lord's, the Oval, or the country cricket-field. They may be numbered by tens; but what is its influence on the hundreds, nay thousands, who practise cricket on the village green, or in the neighbourhood of towns and cities seek in it a relaxation from the many toils imposed by civilization on a suffering humanity? Has cricket done good to these, and is it doing them good? Now here we have to start with an accomplished fact, which is that the English people are laying hold of the game more and more every year; and it would indeed be a serious thing if we had reason to believe that it brought them harm.

It always was an essentially English game, supported by country gentlemen, and practised on village greens; but now that has taken an extended form. The splendidly appointed grounds which are to be found in or near every large town are supported by the sixpences of the people. Ten years ago most county cricket clubs eked out an uncertain subsistence on the generosity of one or two patrons; now the more wide-spread interest in the game gives them a more than sufficient income. Where hundreds dawdled up of an afternoon to see a big match, now thousands arrive early on the ground to secure a good place. Shall we ever forget the curious sight presented to the astonished gaze of any one who chanced to pass round Kennington Oval in August, 1884, on the morning of the great match, England *v.* Australia? The backs of those standing or sitting in the outermost ring of spectators can be seen from the road that encircles the ground; and that morning it was as if each person had loaned out his back as an advertisement for one of the daily papers. They were being used as preventives against sunstroke, but one was immediately struck with the anxiety there must have been to secure a coign of vantage to induce the earliest comers to sit in so hot a place.

We can remember very well when Manchester cared nothing for cricket; now, if the crack bat of every local club, who manages to get fifty runs indifferently against moderate bowling, is not tried for the county eleven, the unfortunate committee is besieged with indignant protests, hinting broadly at favouritism, and demanding the dismissal from office of the captain and most of the committee.

Now, to some minds, doubtless, there is much that is absurd in all this; why should there be such excitement over three sticks and a bit of red leather? Never mind the why, my theorists accept it, and accept this too, that it is very much better that the teeming swarms of a city should be interested in something that will take them into the open air, than that they should spend their time in a stuffy taproom, talking maudlin politics over beer and pipes, and losing more than the threepence or sixpence it would cost them to obtain admittance to the cricket-ground over a game of all-fours, played with a dog-eared pack of cards, or than that they should lounge away their afternoon in the heated alleys of the town. Politics! let them talk politics by all means in proper season; for Heaven's sake let them study the science, for in all conscience it is very necessary that the rulers of a country should understand it; but induce them also to come out of the courts, and the alleys, and the slums, into God's air and sunshine, and they will not be worse politicians one bit; and, if you can get them out in the air, let them go and take part in, or look on at, one of our manly old English pastimes; they will get more good from it than from seeing half a dozen thoroughbreds flash by a post once every half-hour during an afternoon. Waste of time, again! Well, perhaps there is, if time is always to mean money. They will not be earning that; but will not every young aspirant to cricketing honours be treasuring up in his mind how Mr Grace keeps that bat so straight over the leg-stump, and yet always seems to get the ball away to short-leg; or how years seem to make no difference to Mr Hornby's determination always to try his hardest; or how Peate goes on pitching the ball so near the same spot that at last it begins to look quite bare; and will he not be registering a solemn determination in his mind to try his best, in the hope of some day

234

emulating these giants; and will you say that his time is wasted if he has been encouraged to try to do his best at something – play it may be – but still at something? We think not; at any rate, we believe he will be a better man for it, and that his work will not suffer because he has been encouraged to do his best at play.

Let us not be misunderstood; this is no fanciful creation of a brain diseased by monomania. The people are every day showing a keener interest in athletics; and it becomes the duty of those who lead to endeavour to direct that interest and the energy it will develop into proper channels. But to be able to do so they must be prepared to hold their own. We fancy we see signs of dilettantism coming over young England in respect to cricket – a disinclination to go through the drudgery of the game, which alone can ensure eventual excellence, and a consequent hankering after the milder excitement of lawn tennis. We trust we are entirely wrong, and that gentlemen will continue to be the equals, if not the superiors, of the professionals in the cricket-field. Whilst that continues, the game will continue to be the pure game it is, untouched by the lowering tendencies of the betting-ring and its degrading accompaniments; it will remain a simple trial of skill and endurance, honoured by those who take part in it and an honour to the country that has produced it. But once let the former class begin to lose their proficiency at it, and they will drop back into the inferior position of patrons; they will no longer lead, they will barely encourage; the betting-ring will insert its foot, will little by little gain an ascendancy, and the question, 'Has the encouragement of cricket as a pursuit for the people any advantages?' may then, when put, receive a different answer from that which it is entitled to at the present day.

Contemporary Review 1885

30

Lord Harris

The great impulse given to County Cricket of late years has been due to the personal influence of some enthusiastic amateurs who have devoted themselves unselfishly towards its advancement. The names of those good sportsmen who have worked zealously to this end are too well known to need mention, but among them a very prominent position should be given to the keen cricketer we profile this week. George Robert Canning Harris, fourth Baron of that name, or to give him his full title, Baron of Seringapatam and Mysore in the East Indies, and of Belmont, County Kent, was born at Trinidad, in the West Indies, on Feb. 3, 1851. His first appearance in a contest of any importance was at Lord's, in 1868, in the great Public School match of the season. He was then in his eighteenth year, and his debut for Eton against Harrow was fairly satisfactory, as he scored 23 in his first and 6 in his second innings. In the same match of the following year, when the late C. J. Ottaway contributed 108, and Eton won by an innings and 19 runs, he failed to score; and in 1870 was only slightly more successful, having to be content with scores of 12 and 7. It was in this last year that he first became actively associated with County Cricket, and from 1870, when he was elected to serve on the Committee of the County Club, of which his father was then President, dates his identification with Kentish cricket, of which he has been an enthusiastic supporter. His first year at Oxford (1871) saw him in the University Eleven, but in the Oxford and Cambridge matches during the four years in which he was at Oxford he was not particularly fortunate, and while unable to play in 1873, owing to a bad hand, his other scores were only small, amounting to 48 in four innings (one not out), with 43 as his last effort in 1874. Meanwhile, in 1870, he had played his first match for Kent (at Canterbury) *v.* Marylebone Club, and on the 23rd of November, 1872, the death of his father placed him in possession of the title by which he has been for years known to cricketers all over the globe. A dozen years ago Kentish cricket was not in the most flourishing condition, but during the four seasons in which he was at Oxford he did his best to assist the County, and in 1874, though he only figured in two out of five matches, in three innings he was able to claim an aggregate of 125 runs. On the retirement of Mr W. de Chair Baker, Lord Harris was induced to accept the Hon. Secretaryship of the Kent County Club, and the following year not only saw him serving on the Committee of the Marylebone Club, but acting in a triple capacity for Kent as Hon. Sec. and President of the County Club, and Captain of the County Eleven. His first appearance for the Gentlemen against the Players was at Lord's, on July 10th, 1875, and he fully justified his selection with an excellent second innings of 39 not out. From this year he fairly took Kentish cricket in hand, and in 1875 he took part in nine matches with an excellent aggregate of 565 runs fos sixteen innings, and an average of just over 40. The headquarters of the County Club during this year were at Catford Bridge, and his two best performances were on this Ground, to wit — his 94 v. Sussex and 92 v. Hants. In 1876 he was elected for the second time to represent the Gentlemen against the Players at the Oval, and the result of his 14 innings for Kent left him with the distinction of the highest aggregate, largest individual innings and best average of the year. Scores of 154 v. MCC, 84 not out v. Sussex, 82 v. Lancashire, and 79 v. Derby testify to his utility for Kent at this time, and in the following season of 1877, though he was second to that brilliant batsman, Mr Frank Penn, in the averages of the year, he was none the less successful with an aggregate of 533 for 23 innings. In 1878 he played in fourteen out of fifteen matches for Kent, and though Mr Frank Penn again enjoyed first place in the batting averages, Lord Harris had the highest aggregate with 655 as the result of 23 innings. His best show during 1878 was his 106 v. Derbyshire, but he was rarely unsuccessful, and among his other noteworthy scores were his 93 v. England at Canterbury, 88 v. Surrey, and 76 v. Sussex. In 1872 he had formed one of the team which visited America and Canada under the leadership of Mr R. A. Fitzgerald, and the winter of 1878 saw him on another cricket tour as captain of the fifth English team that had visited Australia. He was second in the batting averages to Mr

Hornby, but his return to England found him less successful, and in 1879 Messrs. F. Penn and W. Foord-Kelcey both headed him in the Kentish averages, though owing to the death of his father-in-law he was not able to take part in more than twelve innings. In 1880 he figured in all the thirteen matches played by Kent and with signal success. His best innings that year was 123 against Surrey, but he was also credited with 74 against the Gentlemen of England at Canterbury, and in all for 21 innings he had a fine aggregate of 689 runs. Absence from England deprived the Kentish eleven of Lord Harris's valuable services during a greater part of the season of 1881, but last season found him in even better form than he had yet shown, and his average of 41 runs for fifteen innings was a brilliant one. For Kent against Sussex at Gravesend, Lords Throwley (82) and Harris (176) made 208 runs for the first wicket, but the latter rarely failed to make a good score, and against Middlesex and Yorkshire he was particularly successful, scoring 72 out of 195, and 101 out of 188 against the former at Canterbury, 62 *v.* Yorkshire at Sheffield, and 51 and 54 at Gravesend.

His best performance of the present season has been his score of 118 *v.* Lancashire at Manchester, and the batting shown by him in conjunction with Mr R. S. Jones when 166 runs were added to the first total of Kent, was some of the best seen this year. Of his untiring energy in the cause of Kentish cricket too much cannot be written in praise. No one has laboured with greater devotion towards the promotion of genuine cricket, and the handsome testimonial presented to him during the course of last Canterbury week in recognition of his services for Kent might well have taken a wider scope in appreciation of the aid he has given to county cricket generally. As a batsman Lord Harris is in the very front rank. He hits very hard all-round, and always plays the game thoroughly under every kind of circumstances with the same pluck in losing as winning. In the field he is brilliant, being very safe, and in the out-field particularly smart, with a sharp return to the wicket. Lord Harris is a Captain in the East Kent Yeomanry Cavalry. He married in 1874 Hon. Lucy Ada Jervis, daughter of Viscount St Vincent.

Cricket 1883

31

Lord Hawke at Home

A Chat with the Captain of the Yorkshire Cricket Team

Owen Conway

One of the pleasantest interviews I have ever had was on the occasion of my recent visit to Lord Hawke, in his country house, Wighill Park, Tadcaster. My journey to York in the luxurious corridor train was speedy and comfortable: thence, after viewing the exquisite interior of York Minster, I took train to Thorp Arch. A rapid drive in the crisp morning air brought me at last to the home of the popular cricketer.

The Right Hon. Martin Bladen, seventh Baron Hawke, is the son of the late peer, whom he succeeded in 1887. He was born August 16, 1860, so is thirty-seven years of age. The first Baron, whose portrait has an honoured place in Lord Hawke's large collection, was the admiral who gained the great naval victory off Cape Finisterre in 1747, and twelve years later defeated Admiral Conflans off Belle Isle. Lord Hawke treasures especially a letter written on the eve of battle by his famous ancestor.

Yorkshiremen, or, for the matter of that, cricketers all over the world, need no pen-portrait of the subject of this article. The tall, stalwart figure, the genial face, the cheery voice of Lord Hawke are familiar to the countless thousands who have seen him play cricket in England, America, Australia, Africa, and India: and they know better than I would like to say all the good qualities which have made him so popular and esteemed a man. The county of sportsmen — as one may term Yorkshire — showed its regard for the triumphant captain of the cricket eleven by presenting Lord Hawke with a testimonial of over

£800. This handsome sum was spent in excellent portraits, by Mr Francis Williams, of the Dowager Lady Hawke and her distinguished son; a beautiful dressing-bag, fitted with silver-mounted contents; and a silver dessert-service of twenty-one pieces. I had the pleasure of seeing these tokens of regard and am certain they are greatly appreciated by their owner.

Our conversation took place, after lunch, in the billiard-room, which is decorated with ever so many photographs of well-known cricketers and the various teams which Lord Hawke has taken on tour. Near the fireplace I noticed a cricket-ball mounted in silver and asked its history.

'Oh, that was given me by Mr C. W. Wright to commemorate my startling success as a bowler once! It bears the inscription, "A. Z. Palmer. c. Ricketts. b. Hawke. Witness. Chawles! Ottawa, October 24, 1894." '

One could not, if one desired, talk of anything but the noble game of cricket in such a room where the faces of famous players glance from all the walls. There are framed prints of the Pavilion at Lords, crowded with familiar frequenters; portraits of the redoubtable W. G. Grace batting, of an Indian Thakore who patronizes the game, and group after group of cricketers whom Lord Hawke has captained. So I caught the inspiration of my environment and began a long and interesting conversation with my host.

'Of course you have been interested in the recent Test Matches?'

'Oh, yes! I have read the reports with great avidity and am as disappointed as can be at the failure of our Englishmen. But I know how difficult it is to play cricket in Australia under a burning sun, in a peculiar light, and amid altered conditions.'

'To what do you attribute the repeated defeats of Stoddart's team?'

'I think the Englishmen were outbowled from beginning to end. They relied too much, perhaps, on the expected success of Richardson and one or two other men. In my opinion Richardson was rather stale when he started, for he had been bowling practically all the season. His endurance is remarkable, but it is impossible for a great bowler to keep fresh under such a great and incessant strain. I shall never forget seeing Richardson bowling from three till nearly seven o'clock under a very hot sun and with undiminished effect all the while. He certainly is a most extraordinary man.'

'A good deal has been said about the cracked state of the ground in excuse for the defeat of Stoddart's men.'

'Yes, I have heard and read a good deal about that, but from my knowledge of Australian wickets I do not attribute much to that cause. It does not really affect the wickets so much as you would think. The heat is a serious factor for Englishmen. You see, when the Australians come over here, our hottest summer is only pleasant to them; but when we go over there, their ordinary summer is very trying to us. Darling has been playing wonderfully, and if he is persuaded to come to England with the next Australian team, he will be quite an attraction.'

'Do you approve of these matches being so protracted, Lord Hawke?'

'I must say personally that I do not hold with the constant adjournments of which we have read in the reports. I think it is a big mistake for the batsmen and the bowlers, just when each has got his eye in, to leave the wickets with the fieldsmen for an interval at tea-time. Of course, one must adjourn for lunch, but I have done my best to prevent the tea interval. Sometimes when it has been arranged for a brief interval, I have promised my men to have something sent out to them on the field to save them going into the pavilion. If I were not able to field from 2.15 till half-past six I should begin to suspect my strength. Then there is such a want of uniformity about these intervals, and that causes unfairness. Only last season, in a three days match, we wasted a lot of time the first two days over adjournments, and then on the third day had only three and a quarter hours in which to try and make 200 runs. The captain of the other side never suggested a tea interval on that day, for he was set upon getting us out. I can understand the bowlers want refreshment more than batsmen, for their work takes it out of them much more, but it would always be possible to have the refreshments sent out to the men instead of wasting the time which a retirement to the pavilion necessitates.'

'You are a great believer in these tours, I think?'

'Yes, for I am certain that a properly-arranged tour does a good deal for the spread of Imperial Federation. Wherever Englishmen go they take cricket with them, and it is pleasant for them, away from the home country to see cricketers once more. Besides, we spread a love of the game. I do not like the idea of tours being run for pecuniary benefit. In fact, the financial side of cricket is one on which I hold very strong views. There is a great danger of the game being spoiled by the money question, and I have done my best to keep the position of amateurs clear. At the same time, you know, I have also a great sympathy with professionals as long as they lead steady lives. A great many of them are first-rate fellows, and as pleasant on tour as anybody could be. There is nothing I value more than the beautiful gold cigarette-case which the Yorkshire professionals gave me not long ago as a token of their esteem. If a professional cricketer takes care of himself, he can make an excellent living, provided he is thrifty, and at the end of his career there is a benefit of perhaps a £1000 or £1500 as a nest-egg. Some people talk of amateur cricketers being better 'triers' than professionals, but I do not think so. Your amateur is quite as keen on his averages and his personal reputation as the professional making his living at the game, and both, if they are first-class men, are determined to win on every possible occasion. No one has any idea how mortifying it is to a cricketer if he fails to come off. To give you an instance: when Moorhouse was being slated by the press he was in dreadfully low spirits over it, and in every match he did his utmost to justify his inclusion in the eleven. The public ought to have a little more sympathy for us when we do not come off as well as when we do.

While I am talking about the game from the spectators' point of view, I should like to say that no cricketer likes a wet day, though you may imagine, from the behaviour of the crowd sometimes, that the elevens were revelling in enforced idleness. The moment the rain stops the public are ready to demand that we should go out into the field, forgetting that we have no ambition to be mudlarks. I think it is a little unfair that the onus of settling whether the wickets are fit for play should rest only upon the shoulders of the umpires. In the old days the captains decided on the matter, and if in doubt we abode by the judgement of the umpires. Now umpires have to bear the brunt of unpopularity, and sometimes a good deal of unpleasant hooting, in consequence of their decision. Spectators have still a great deal to learn as to fair play both in football and cricket. The treatment of referees, I may say in passing, is becoming a regular scandal. I am almost inclined to think nowadays that too much is made of individual success or failure. A nervous cricketer is affected by the barometer of his averages. Years ago it was more the question of winning the match than of pulling up your averages. Besides, averages are very misleading. I have read only this week an elaborate article with a view to proportioning the value rather than the total of the different scores a cricketer makes. For instance, a man may save a match by twenty-two runs and render a more important service than by making 150 on another occasion. Still, there is no possibility, I must admit, of taking circumstances into consideration when you are dealing with figures.'

'What is the most exciting match in which you have played?'

Lord Hawke leaned back in his chair, put his hands behind his head, and thought for a minute or two. Then he said, 'Well, that *is* a question! I think the most exciting time I ever had was when we lost the match against Essex by only one run. The game seemed so certainly ours that the result was all the more mortifying.'

'When did you begin to play cricket?'

'I can hardly tell you when I did not play cricket. My father was very keen on the game, and when I went to Hawtrey's School I soon began to be enthusiastic over it, too. Then I went to Eton, where I played in the eleven four or five times in 1876. I played for Eton *v.* Harrow, at Lord's, in 1878 and 1879. I went on to Cambridge, and in 1882 was in the eleven. At the end of the season I had the average of 24.3. Next year I was fourth in the batting averages with 25.4, which was fairly good, considering I had hurt my knee. I made 141 against England and played thirteen innings for Yorkshire County team. It seems strange but I am the only man in the county eleven who was playing for Yorkshire seventeen years ago. Perhaps you would be surprised to hear that I began as a left-hander. I urge boys at school to take up cricket rather than rowing, for you cannot make a river very easily, but you can usually make a cricket-field. As a kid I knew all about the cricketers of the day, Jupp, W. G. Grace and his two brothers, and the rest of them. I always had a good memory for names, so long as they are told me correctly at first, with the initials.'

Certainly Lord Hawke manifested in our conversation, lasting some hours, a most remarkable recollection of events, names and scores. He seemed never at a loss to give the exact figures of a match, however long ago it was played, or the name of anyone with whom he happened to have been associated. He has a kind word to say of nearly all the players of the day, and naturally waxes enthusiastic over the achievements of the Yorkshiremen. Every year he entertains the latter at Wighill Park, and the occasion is most enjoyable to host and guests. Lord Hawke's mother, sisters and brothers share his love of cricket, and follow the fortunes of the county with keen interest.

'Of course, Lord Hawke, you have especial acquaintance with the difficulties of captaincy?'

'Well, few people have any idea of the worry, work, and anxiety which belong to the captain of a county team, who of all the eleven is most subject to criticism. It is no use denying that most men do not enjoy criticism, however salutary it may be for them. I had a letter only the other day from a prominent editor saying that, as a public man, I ought to feel myself inured to criticism; but I am afraid I do not yet awhile. People won't believe that I am nervous, but I am horribly so: and criticism makes me more nervous. For instance, I was completely out of form for two or three years, as you may probably remember, and was perfectly willing to stand out of the eleven, especially in face of the continued carping as to why I was still playing for the county. Now, every criticism made me feel worse when I walked to the wickets, and took away my confidence. I have come to the conclusion that the secret of success for a captain is to give up trying to please everybody. Tact and good temper are quite as important as knowledge in a captain, and he has plenty of need of both. You cannot imagine the amount of letter-writing that is necessary in making the arrangements for a season or for a tour. Fortunately, I enjoy correspondence, and never have any difficulty, once I have a pen in my hand, in writing a score of letters. I have always endeavoured to keep up correspondence with any people who have been kind and hospitable to our teams abroad. Too often, I am afraid, we are inclined to taking these cases of generosity for granted, and imagine we are conferring a favour instead of receiving one. Some of the people who were good to me in India put themselves out of the way in entertaining me much more than English people would think of doing. I can tell you it is no joke to give hospitality in an out-of-the-way part of India to a band of ravenous English cricketers!'

'I believe you have taken out more tours than any other cricketer?'

'I have been on seven tours altogether, and look back on them with very pleasant memories. My visit to Australia in 1887 was unfortunately brief, owing to the death of my father, which caused me to return at once to England. We had a very nice tour in the West Indies, and, if you recollect, we went to South Africa, arriving just when the

Raid was about to take place. There was a question as to whether we should get any spectators at such an exciting time, but I may tell you that the people in South Africa took a great interest in our games, and I should like to return there some day. One thing always worries me on these tours. I do not think you will guess what it is, so I had better tell you; it is the amount of speechifying that is necessary. I have often said that I would rather make a duck before a large crowd than speak in public! To speak at each town on a tour is much more difficult than the casual speeches that one delivers at home, for there is nothing fresh that one can say about the merits of one's team. I recollect in India we were entertained by Lord Harris (then Governor of Bombay), and on that occasion we had suffered an unexpected defeat from the Parsees, Lord Harris began by saying that he had prepared a speech for a victorious team and was hampered by the unfortunate reverse we had sustained. When I responded, I began by saying that I also had prepared a very nice speech for a victorious captain to deliver, and that I was placed in a serious predicament by our friends the Parsees!'

And thus, with many an interesting reminiscence, our chat progressed till I took my leave for London. I said good-bye to Lord Hawke with a still stronger belief than I entertained before that he has done his country good and lasting service by devoting half his life to the game which all Englishmen love; and when, in process of time, he has to resign the willow, he will be qualified for holding any post where knowledge of men and true governing ability may be exercised on another field.

Windsor Magazine 1898

32

Captains Then and Now

Hon. Lionel Tennyson

We sat around, perhaps a dozen or more, some old-timers others moderately young, discussing as fellows will, men, matters and things in relation to life generally and, as might be supposed, cricket in particular. And inevitably there came to be held an inquest on captains, past and present, from Grace to Jardine.

The scope for striking contrasts was, of course, tremendous and necessarily there were sharp differences of opinion as to the worth of the various giants set on parade. Surprisingly, however, the skippers of long ago were not to a marked degree compared at the expense of the immediate generation. Which, to me at least, was refreshing.

I did venture to say, however, that Douglas Jardine would go down to posterity as one of the immortals, for though we have yet to have a full, complete and authentic story of all the happenings of the MCC tour of Australia, we already know enough to be sure that by personal example, courage, and iron determination he accomplished that which few, if indeed any, captains could have done. It is not possible for Jardine to be disturbed whatever the circumstances. He was meant to lead, to command and be obeyed.

His methods are peculiarly and severely his own. It is said, for instance (and I would give credence to the story) that before a ball is bowled he reduces the disposition of his field to the form of a diagram which he carries on to the field in his pocket, and consults from time to time.

Jardine has ever approached cricket with all the sternness of the Scot. He concedes nothing. I certainly could not imagine his budging an inch, not even under the heaviest pressure, nor yet the most biting criticism. He sets out to do his job though the heavens may fall.

His refusal to make any surrender has possibly made for misunderstandings. But if he does not tell of the poetry of cricket, it requires no profound student of psychology to see in him a born leader of men. His very masterfulness, his tenacity of purpose, inspires confidence. He is a type unto himself, for he seeks finality by ideas and ways of his own fashioning.

I feared that I had dropped a considerable brick when reminded by one of my North Country friends of Archie MacLaren, while another of a still older school inquired, with all the pointedness common to Lancashire, whether I had ever heard of A. N. Hornby. I would have it understood that while I hold up Jardine as a completely triumphant captain, Maclaren's greatness will be readily conceded by his contemporaries and all those steeped in the history of cricket. I dare say that those who can recall Surrey under Shuter and Key are quite decided that the county may never again enjoy such days. May be they are right. The past and the present necessarily have their heroes. Personally, I am quite sure that Percy Fender ranks with the greatest captains Surrey ever had. Which, of course, is meant as no disrespect to the most distinguished of his predecessors at the Oval.

I have ever been at a loss to understand why it was that at sometime or another Fender was not made captain of England, just as I am at a loss to know why Chapman was superseded by Wyatt in the last Test played against Australia in this country, and why, as I feel has often been inquired, I was ever made skipper. That, however, is the concern of the powers that be; and they must be free to do as they please.

My immediate business is to write about cricket captains generally and what, in my considered opinion, is demanded of them. It is elementary that a captain must have every member of his team pulling with him, and that is only possible by striking a human note. There should not, there can never be, any distinctions on the field. Sport in all its phases was intended to be, and is, the greatest of all levellers; but sport demands recognition of an accepted head and in that regard there are individual differences. That appreciated, the rest is up to the captain, the success of whom may never be appraised by his own personal scores or bowling analysis.

There is only one road to triumphant captaincy: that is by understanding every single member of one's side, so that he shall be as an open book, and by, at the same time, applying one's mind to the individual and collective strength of the opposition.

Captaincy by any rule of thumb is of no account. When I first saw Noble in charge of cricketing Australia, I was convinced that in some magical way he and not his bowlers or fieldsmen counted for most; and surely Warwick Armstrong was but little less great an Australian skipper for the reason that, like Noble, he had that penetrative mind which enabled him to assess values, and size up a situation to a nicety. The only difference between Noble and Armstrong was that one suggested a sphinx and the other a mountain of geniality. Actually both sought to arrive at the same conclusion by the same route – by drawing upon their intuition to the full. If I had to choose between the two I would declare Noble to be the greater captain, for the reason that he could the more surely employ his bowling to make that which was, in fact, moderate, appear to be positively deadly.

In the matter of the management of bowlers may I, without immodesty I hope, insist that oftener than not it is bad policy to keep on the two recognized best bowlers at the beginning of an innings for a given stretch. Not infrequently, whether a batsman is got out or not, A and B will be unchanged for three-quarters of an hour. Then a double change, and for the last quarter of an hour before luncheon, say, the original bowlers are called upon to resume the attack. That is wrong, if not wooden. I am all for ringing the changes. No matter how well a man is bowling, it is horse sense that if he is not getting wickets he should be asked to give way to another bowler, irrespective of the fact that his ability is not rated so highly.

The central idea of all games is to produce effect. I do not attach every importance to the fact that in point of reputation one of my bowlers is to be preferred to the other. Even with Alex Kennedy at his best, when he should have walked into his country's team (few bowlers in my time had such a sure command of length), I would not have hesitated to displace him by one of admittedly inferior quality if, though scarcely a run had been made off him, I was convinced that he was not likely to do more than keep the score down.

You younger captains than myself, take a tip from me! Do not be shy to exploit every available bowler whenever the tide is running against you. You may never know when you have a rod in pickle for the other fellow until you have exhausted your whole stock.

About bowlers may I explain this personal experience? I cannot recall an occasion when Tich Freeman has not left me all tied up in an impossible knot. It has almost invariably been when the great little man has set out to bowl that my number was up.

Illustrated Sporting and Dramatic News 1933

33

Great Cricket Captaincy

A Tribute to P. G. H. Fender

Neville Cardus

Since the war, cricket, by general consent, has been short of personality. There is no want of skill, of sheer efficiency. But there are few cricketers who capture the imagination by playing the game in a way entirely their own.

One cause of this scarcity of dominating characters is that through a variety of reasons — mainly economic — the amateur element has passed out of the county tournament considerably.

Now this eclipse in the skill of the amateur cricketer has had a serious and widespread influence on the game. It has lowered the status of the amateur, and consequently it has weakened the authority of captaincy. Your great captain needs to be a great player. Example is better than precept. The modern captain of cricket, being one of a class that cannot hold its own in terms of skill with the professionals, is bound to feel diffident when he is called upon to exercise the functions of leadership. A captain like MacLaren, or F. S. Jackson, had the most obvious right to go into the professionals' room and say, 'No more sitting on the splice, please. We must win this match — get busy with the boundaries.' Master was as good as his Jack in the bygone days.

At the present time, most captains may fairly be compared with the Duke of Plaza-Toro who 'led his regiment from behind — he found it less exciting.' But if county captains were strong enough to assert themselves, if county captains, when tossing for innings, made the vow that 'one side is going to win or lose this match' — well, there would be a quick end to dullness, and 'safety first', and the canny batsmanship at the wrong moment which now pervades the game.

Happily there are a few of the old Romans still with us — and one of these is P. G. H. Fender. If you were to ask any six professional cricketers, now in the game, to name the best of living captains, the vote would be for Fender every time by a majority of five to one.

In 1923, Sydney Pardon wrote the following words about Fender: 'By general consent, he is the best of county captains, never losing his grip of the game, and managing his side with a judgement seldom at fault.' Why is Fender a great captain? First of all, he is by character a strong man, a born leader of others. He has the quickest brain in modern cricket. Moreover, he has the courage to stand alone. Fender is not afraid of a splendid isolation. To say that he is not without enemies is to make compliment to his singlemindedness and to the power of his personality.

Next of Fender's assets is his technical skill. On his day, he will, with his own bat, win a match in a single hour, or with his own subtly spinning ball, will make a mess of the other side's best batsmen. But these splendid technical gifts of Fender would count for little if they were not directed by a mind that is always visualizing victory. He is constantly organizing his skill and the skill of the rest of the Surrey XI. Never is the Surrey XI allowed to drift on a hot day like a ship becalmed.

He has a superb aspect of the Machiavellian Prince in his lean aspect ('Let me have men about me that are fat,' said Caesar). It is one of the stimulating sights of modern cricket to see Fender during a long stand made by opponents of Surrey. Supposing Hearne and Hendren are set, putting together 186 for the third wicket, in 4 hours and twenty-five minutes. In such circumstances most of our captains quickly get resigned to Hearne and Hendren; they merely change the bowling in the sweet old routined way, and like so many Micawbers, they wait for something to turn up. Not so Fender! Hearne and Hendren in a long partnership bring the best out of him. Watch him at the close of every unsuccessful over. He walks from one end of the wicket to the other, as the slips change position, and his head is bent slightly his eyes cast downward. The sun shines on his high forehead, his temples of thought are obviously throbbing with cerebration. He is up to something! At any rate, the game is not in a state of drift.

It is likewise when he himself is taking active part in the attack. Each time he walks to his bowling place, his eyes, behind those bodeful spectacles, are plotting. Each time he takes that preparatory walk, he rolls up the sleeve of his left arm abstractedly — perhaps he doesn't know that he does so. His brain is trying to see a picture of

Hearne or Hendren somehow bowled out, caught out, run out. . . .

Fender is a hard fighter. He does not belong to the soft school of captaincy. Too many contemporary captains apparently imagine that cricket is honoured by the policy of 'Give your opponents *every* chance.' This is not chivalry; it is weakness which really does indignity to the greatest of games. A brave opponent is worthy of the most killing steel: he expects no quarter. Fender never gives anything away – and why should he? It would need an Australian with Old Nick himself inside him to get a new ball out of Fender – before the right and proper moment. And this is after the traditions of W. G. Grace himself, and cricket, after all, is not croquet.

In 1922 Surrey met Leicestershire at Leicester. Surrey won the toss, scored 501 for 8 and declared. Leicestershire got 334 and 316 for 5 by tea-time on the last day. The Leicestershire captain also declared, leaving Surrey with 150 to make for victory, in 80 minutes – on paper an impossible task. Surrey got the runs with 17 minutes to spare; Fender scored 91 out of 111, and hit two 6's and seventeen 4's.

Since the war Surrey's bowling has not been good: on the perfect Oval wickets it has often been poor indeed. Yet Fender has always seemed to marshal his attack to some purpose, offensive or defensive. He is a great saver of runs. A fine fieldsman himself, he is the cause of fine fielding in others. But he does not set his field so palpably that any fool can see the snares.

As captain and cricketer Fender is a glorious opportunist. He does not go into action with a preconceived strategy – danger lies there. He is a tactician before he is a strategist. His brain jumps to the situation as he sees it on the field. His bowling, too, has the note of opportunism. He is one of the few living spin bowlers. But frequently his full toss to leg is his most dangerous ball. A cricketer who lives in the game for all he is worth every minute; a cricketer who dignifies the game by expressing, as he plays it, the whole man that is in him. The game has been enriched in no small degree by his resolution, his courage, and his hatred of the soul-deadening compromise. Give us many Fenders in our time, O Lord.

Illustrated Sporting and Dramatic News 1928

34

A Cricketer of the Past

J. C. Masterman

Major E. G. Wynyard, DSO, or Teddy Wynyard as we came to call him when age had mellowed him, was born in 1861 and died in 1936. He was one of the heroes of my youth, for was he not the most brilliant cricketer whom the army had ever produced and did he not belong to that great period of amateur batsmen – Jackson, Ranjitsinhji, MacLaren, Fry, Jessop – and was he not the peer of them all? Yet who remembers him now?

I had the good fortune to play against him with some small success in 1913; he did not forget this and invited me to be one of the Free Forester side which he took to Canada in 1922. His devotion to cricket was boundless and he knew more about the game than anyone I had met up to that time. It is a lasting regret that I can only remember a tithe of the stories which he told me – stories which were by no means always about himself. He was by nature an autocrat, supremely confident in his own judgement, a fierce competitor and, like Sarah Battle, insistent on the full rigour of the game, sometimes cantankerous and irascible but always staunch towards his friends and always the leader in any group to which he belonged. He was, in fact, a good friend, but an awesome enemy. Can it be wondered at that he inspired admiration, respect and often affection among some and criticism and even hostility among others?

'Who was the best cricket captain?' I once asked him. The reply was immediate. 'Grace, of course. His authority was without question and his experience immense. I'll tell you about the last Test Match at the Oval in 1896. That was the match when all the professionals struck for higher pay, and when England would have been hard put to it to field eleven men if rain had not delayed the start. By the time it stopped all of them, except two, had given in. The wicket was a pig – England made 145 and Australia 119 in the first innings. At the end of the second day England had made 60 for five wickets – 86 runs on. I had batted for about twenty minutes and was not out and I assure you that I never batted better in my life – I was hoping to make a good score on the next day. On the next morning Grace pressed his great thumb several times on the wicket and then spoke to us. "I'm sorry for you, boys, for I know you'd like to make runs in a Test Match but you've all got to be out in half an hour. I must be bowling at them by twelve-thirty at the latest." Stoddart, who was not playing, protested in vain. "You can't do that, Doctor, you want every single run you can get." In the event England (all out for 84) took the field at about twelve-fifteen with Australia needing 91 to win. Tom Richardson bowled one over, and then J. T. Hearne and Peel bowled Australia out for 44. Yes, of course Grace was the greatest of all captains – though I never really understood why he gave Richardson that one over.' Certainly Richardson's analysis for an opening bowler in a Test Match is something of a curiosity. One over, one maiden, no runs, no wickets. *Wisden*, which cannot lie, records that Teddy Wynyard's score in the second innings was three, but it also records that in that year he was second in the first-class averages – and second only to the incomparable Ranji.

'Captains,' Teddy told me on another occasion, 'are sometimes a bit too clever.' In an early match on his first tour of the West Indies, Hawke's side was not doing too well against a side which bowled and fielded like demons. Hawke therefore hastily arranged a plot with his partner at the wicket. 'If I call "Yes" for a short run it means "No" and vice versa.' 'That was gamesmanship,' said Teddy, 'which I should not have allowed if I had been there.' The plan was wholly successful; bowlers and fielders alike were demoralized and overthrows advanced the score by leaps and bounds. In the evening Hawke – or 'de Lord' as he was always called in the islands – and his side were dining with the Governor. When Hawke signified that he would take champagne the West Indian butler firmly passed him by. It was not until 'de Lord' consented to say 'No, thank you' that his glass was filled. I sometimes think that some of our politicians have adopted Hawke's technique in their speeches.

It was something of a tragedy that Teddy never went with an English Test side to Australia. The first occasion on which he might have gone conceals a story which he did not tell me – and about which I should never have dared to ask him. Hampshire, Teddy's team, were playing Sussex and a fine bunch of hot-house grapes had been placed on the pavilion table for Teddy when he came in from the field. Unluckily Ranji, who was out after a good innings some time before the close of play, seeing the grapes and not knowing to whom they belonged, ate a few of them before going up to change. The horrid truth was told to Teddy when he came in from the field; his language was sulphurous and his wrath unquenchable, and soon, in spite of the courtesy of Ranji, a minor incident developed into a major altercation. Things went so far that fixtures between Hampshire and Sussex were cancelled for the following season. Then Stoddart took a hand. He pointed out that he had invited both Wynyard and Ranji to be members of his side for Australia and that he must cancel the invitation if Teddy did not apologize. Teddy had never apologized to anyone in his life and did not know how to do so, but some of his friends concocted a letter which, on a very liberal interpretation, could be construed as an apology, and this he was induced to sign. It was readily accepted, fixtures between the two counties were renewed and all was peace. Alas, the story had no happy ending, for the War Office informed Captain Wynyard that his military duties would not permit him to go to Australia.

The second occasion was equally unfortunate. In 1907 he was invited to captain the MCC (or England) side in Australia and was compelled to decline the honour for 'domestic reasons'. I do not know what these reasons were, but I have always thought that that tour might and ought to have been the crown of his cricket career. Had he been able to go, and had he been in form, he would, I think, be numbered among the cricket 'immortals'.

I take some pride in the thought that he seemed to like me and that, in his later life, he confided a good deal in me. Perhaps he had a sympathy for Oxford men, for he was Adjutant of the Oxford University Volunteers from 1899 to 1900. 'The Volunteers were not, when I arrived, a very warlike or efficient body of men,' he told me, 'and the work was not onerous, but it did bring me into one awkward predicament. I received information that the Volunteers would be inspected by the Duke of York and that I was to arrange things accordingly. How was I to put on a respectable show with only a small and motley band of partially trained undergraduates at my disposal? In such situations Oxford always plays up. I explained my trouble to the OUDS and the

Society produced an excellent band of enthusiastic actors whom I disguised as soldiers and who did not let me down. There was, however, a last-moment hitch. I had inquired at the War Office if it would be right to call for three cheers for the Duke at the end of the day's proceedings and received the answer that we were considering a military exercise and that, in consequence, cheers would be most improper. In the evening there was a ball in Christ Church Hall and before it began I was summoned to be presented to the Duke. "A very smart parade, Captain Wynyard; a good display of military efficiency — but I was surprised that you did not call for cheers for me at the close." I apologized as best I could for my omission and, of course, did not give away my superiors. My apologies were accepted with good nature. "Very well, we will forget it. Now you may dance with the Duchess." I was a worse than indifferent dancer, but protocol demanded that no one else should dance until the Duchess and I had circumnavigated the Hall. What an infernally big Hall it is!'

What a cricketer he was! In one match at Lord's between I Zingari and Gentlemen of England he was not out at lunch, but not satisfied with the way he was playing. Both sides went in to lunch, but Teddy ordered the three best bowlers on the ground staff to accompany him to the nets where he batted steadily throughout the interval. He told me that he went in to bat in the afternoon from the Nursery end, meeting his partner, who came from the Pavilion, at the wicket and that he made a century, but it may be that the story had grown in the telling. That it is founded on fact I do not doubt.

I did not see him play in his great days, but even in 1922 in Canada there were traces of greatness still to be seen. He played in only three or four of the matches, but in one of these he made a shot which few could have equalled. The bowler was medium or slow-medium and he delivered a half-volley just outside the leg stump. Ranji would have glanced the ball past fine leg with almost majestic contempt; Teddy treated it differently. He jumped off both feet and made a half-turn to his left in the air, and then, coming to ground exactly at the right moment, drove — yes, *drove* — the ball for six between fine and long leg. Surely a miracle of timing. Incredible, you might say, but I saw him do it — and he was sixty-one.

As a captain the word martinet is far too weak to express his dominant personality. Woe betide the young cricketer who was heard to murmur that his best place in the batting order was three or four. In his firm hand Teddy would write his name in the score-book number eleven. Once in a match between I Zingari and the Lords & Commons (played, I think, on the Hampstead ground) a strong wind was blowing down the ground. I Zingari had two opening fast bowlers in the side and they were engaged in a friendly discussion as to which deserved to have the wind to help him. The side went onto the field and Teddy opened the bowling himself with lobs and with the wind behind him. I wish I could finish that story by saying that he immediately took a wicket; I cannot, but it is true that he nearly — very nearly — bowled Lord Aberdare in his first over.

Off the field, as well as on, he demanded the best behaviour of all members of his side. Once, in Canada, I was instructed to go out to dinner with him to play bridge with two of his friends. (He was not a good player, but it was *lèse-majesté* to hint any criticism of his bids or his play.) We had an agreeable and remunerative evening and returned about midnight to our hotel. I was, therefore, very surprised when he fell upon me at breakfast next morning. 'You behaved very badly last night when we came home; in this country it is thought most discourteous to keep your hat on in the lift.' I felt a little ill-used, since the only occupant of the lift besides ourselves had been an elderly man, sitting on the floor, his clothing dishevelled, his head resting on his knees and, it seemed, sunk in a drunken slumber.

Towards the end of Teddy's life a major interest in cricket was the Jokers, a club of which he was Chief Joker. On the card informing one of election were written the three words 'Cricket, Golf, Curling'. The last came in, I suppose, because Teddy often visited Switzerland and had been at one time the Toboggan champion of Europe, but I do not know if the Jokers ever took their curling very seriously. Our cricket and golf matches were always referred to as 'Frolics' and frolics they sometimes were, although the rigour of the game was always insisted upon. I remember cricket matches at Victoria Barracks, Windsor, where a battalion of the Guards was always stationed. On the first occasion that I played there Teddy gave me the terse order: 'Go in first, and make a hundred.' Military bowling was not very formidable — but military umpiring was. I had made two or three (or was it even nought?) when a ball, well outside my leg stump, struck my pads and I returned unhappily to the pavilion. Teddy made no comment, but a year later on the same ground he won the toss. 'You were unlucky last time,' he said. 'Go in first and make that hundred you should have made last year.' I did not venture to disobey him twice.

The Victoria Barracks ground was long but very narrow, and troops, mostly 'other ranks', used to watch the game in considerable numbers and with loudly voiced comments. On one occasion Teddy put on Admiral Hickley, short, bearded and enthusiastic, to bowl lobs, and he took a wicket in his first over. Another Admiral, Sir Hugh Watson, was fielding on the boundary in front of the spectators and a guardsman beckoned to him 'Say, mister, who's that a-bowling?' 'That's Admiral Hickley.' 'Ah, a crafty old bugger, I should think.' I well remember with what glee a full Admiral ran up to the wicket to tell the other Admiral of the unusual bouquet he had received. Perhaps the crowd was larger than usual that year because, unexpectedly, Plum Warner was playing on the side of the soldiers.

Joker Frolics made a pleasing finish to what had been a most distinguished though sometimes stormy cricket career. What would Teddy have thought of the cricket of today? He would have been keenly appreciative of the skills of some of the masters, but I tremble to think what he would have thought and said of some of the innovations of recent years. What, for example, would have been his attitude if the spectators had invaded the sacred ground to shake his hand on reaching a century? I cannot tell, but I can guess with some confidence. Without a doubt murder would have been done, and it would not have been Major E. G. Wynyard, DSO, who was the corpse.

Blackwood's Magazine 1974

35

A Recollection of Great Hitters

Captain E. G. Wynyard

The treacherous wickets upon which batsmen have had to contend against bowlers up to the time of the first Test Match in the present season, and the enormous disadvantages at which the batsmen have been placed, lead one to pause and consider seriously whether two or three stout hitters in a team, who are prepared to take all risks, for the purpose of forcing the game and 'putting off' the deadly bowlers, would not be of infinitely more value to the side than correct players, on billiard table wickets, who are often ludicrously at sea when the pitch is a 'mud pie' caking under a drying sun. Apart from the enormous value of one or two of these stout hearts to the side, under difficult circumstances, there remains the fact that the cricket-loving public, without which cricket would not continue to exist, although they are perfectly capable of appreciating good innings played under disadvantageous and adverse circumstances, delight in seeing 'merry', 'lively' cricket, and, better than that, are exhilarated to boiling point by a daring, dashing, slashing smiter, and there can be no doubt that a few such dashing and delightful forcing players do more to keep the game popular with the public than many who accumulate runs laboriously with the assistance of leg play which, in cases, may be expedient but is certainly wearisome, and one cannot help thinking, in some cases, when carried to excess, has done much to kill enthusiasm for the game.

The case in which forcing play was probably best exemplified with successful results was on the occasion on which the Australians were playing the North of England at Old Trafford, in 1888. They had to get some 112 runs to win in the last innings, and I have it on reliable authority that P. S. McDonnell, the captain of the side, gave orders that a steady game was to be played; he himself hit so brilliantly and fearlessly that he made 82 out of 84 runs from the bat during his stay, and at the completion of his innings I am informed there were five men on the boundary. The Australians lost some seven wickets but won the match. As an example of brilliant hitting this, in my experience of cricket, stands alone.

Pride of place among great hitters, however, in comparatively modern times must be given to Mr C. I. Thornton. I had only the good fortune to see one of his very great innings, that of 110 in his second innings against Surrey when playing for Kent in 1869. Street and Southerton were bowling, and his huge drives were quite phenomenal. No man that I have seen had the extraordinary gift of 'timing' his hits in equal proportion. *Multi vixerunt ante Agamemnona*, no doubt, but shades of G. J. Bonnor, H. T. Hewett, J. J. Lyons, W. J. Ford, W. H. Fowler, H. H. Massie, and George Ulyett, yet were never quite as great. His hitting in this particular match can only be described as 'terrific'. Down near the present entrance gate of the Oval stood the old racquet court, and into that he repeatedly lobbed the ball. Gossip asserted that he had been backed to hit a ball, tossed to him from the field of play, over the New Pavilion at Lord's; that he never undertook the feat I know, but the new pavilion was not built until he had practically given up cricket; that he would have done it in match play when at the zenith of his power I do not for a moment doubt. The feat has yet to be accomplished. A. E. Trott was somewhat unfortunate not to accomplish it this season, as he had selected one of the highest points of the towers to drive at and just failed to clear it.

Taking the names of other great hitters in the order in which I have mentioned them above, I fancy G. J. Bonnor to have been an unequal hitter – gigantic, powerful, and with a wonderful reach, he was not a dashing hitter, nor was he a very good timer, but more to my mind a lunging player, and on many occasions seemed entirely unable to play a hitting game – and comparatively rarely, in spite of his undoubtedly great hitting powers, did he entirely demoralize the bowling side. At Scarborough, against a very fine eleven of I Zingari, he made some phenomenal hits, and one of his mightiest blows, it will be remembered, was caught by the late Mr G. F. Grace in the memorable Test Match at the Oval at the very edge of the far boundary from the Pavilion.

Next we come to Mr H. T. Hewett, the finest left-handed hitter of later days. Quite the reverse of Bonnor, he was a fearless, dashing, rollicking hitter, quite capable of knocking off any bowler on any wicket, and, strangely enough, the biggest hit I ever saw him make cost him his wicket — a wonderful on drive on the Southampton ground, which, but for a hurricane 'bringing it back', would have apparently finished somewhere in Southampton Water. It fell into the safe hands of H. W. R. Bencraft, the present secretary of the Hants County Club. The 'Colonel', as he is familiarly called, was one of the best beginners I ever saw, and started off the very first ball sent up to him as a rule. It was a great pity he and first-class cricket parted company as early as they did, but he can hit almost as hard and far now as formerly, even if he takes a little longer to 'get going'.

J. J. Lyons was a fast footed hitter. Huge and muscular, he would, once started, pulverize almost any bowling — probably more severe on Lohmann than any other batsman has been. The finest bit of hitting I ever saw him do was 99 in well under the hour at Lord's, and, seeing that Gunn was at his best in the long field and quite unable to prevent boundary after boundary, it is sufficient to show the pace at which he was able to make the ball travel. The biggest hit I saw Lyons make was in a Test Match at the Oval, when he just failed to hit Mold 'over' the old pavilion, the ball bounding off the back of the roof well down the road.

Of Messrs W. J. Ford and W. H. Fowler I speak only on hearsay. They hardly played sufficient first-class cricket to make their names household words. On the occasion that they did come off, however, their deeds created considerable sensation, and the former's best efforts appear to have been for Middlesex against Gloucestershire, while the latter gave the crowd merry moments when playing for Somersetshire. Each has imitators and understudies in his own family, for A. F. J. could hit right well and also bowl, while F. G. J. is still with us and at his best has only the rivalry of Darling and V. T. Hill, who plays now but seldom, to fear among left handers, while of the Fowler family, both Howard and Gerald are 'braw laddies wi' the willow'.

H. H. Massie was a very fine hitter. Perhaps his greatest shots were wrist shots played with enormous power. A stroke of his in front of cover point was wonderful. I have seldom seen anything like it. I remember Mr A. H. Evans describing it to me and saying that if the boundary were a brick wall the ball would be at the boundary and half way back before the fieldsman could realize it had been struck.

George Ulyett, 'the happy Jack' of Yorkshire, was a magnificent forcing player, his happy, genial temperament seemed embodied in his batting, and he made the most superb dives when at his best; coming at the ball with a swing and step, he struck with the body swing of a prize fighter, and nothing more inspiriting, at least from a spectator's viewpoint, could be desired than to see him play one of his great innings.

Another magnificent hitting performance, and certainly the best I ever saw accomplished, occurs to me. It was in a match between Hampshire and Somersetshire about the year 1887 — neither of the counties had then been promoted first-class. Mr S. M. J. Woods was then an almost unknown colt, and bowled probably faster than, or, at all events as fast as, at any later period of his career. Mr H. W. Forster, formerly in the Eton XI, going in late on the side hit up 80 runs in twenty-three minutes by the clock. The faster and shorter Mr Woods bowled, the harder Mr Forster hit.

In the above recollections attention has been mainly drawn to those who, alas, are hitters of a past era. There remains to add to them the names of some genii of smiting fortunately with us still. Of these, off-hand, occur the names of G. L. Jessop, F. G. J. Ford, C. B. Fry, A. E. Stoddart, Trott, *quondam* Australia now Middlesex, S. M. J. Woods, F. Sugg, Storer, E. Smith, of Oxford and Yorkshire fame, J. T. Brown, and of the present Australian team J. Darling, J. Worrall, E. Jones, and W. P. Howell; and in describing these fine hitters I shall be tempted to place them in two distinct classes — those of hitters with, and those of hitters without, a serious method. Each one in his own fashion is quite capable of turning the fortune of a game, but to some a reckless, blind, happy-go-lucky smiting has become a second nature, while with the remainder, hitting and hard punishing hitting is a finished art. Ideal hitters, to my mind, are Messrs C. B. Fry and A. E. Stoddart. A finer pair to begin an innings, saving always the presence of the great master of cricket, W. G. Grace, I cannot conceive. Their art is the mastery of placing their big hits, the pull, the hook, the big drive, all in addition to a big defence, always where no fielder can intercept and no danger from the out-fielder lurks. Their wickets are not to be recklessly sacrificed to the huge gallery drive, nor to the wile of the slow ball, but every big lunge is a masterpiece and a thought-out shot. Mr Fry's doings last year and this are indelibly stamped on every cricketer's mind.

Probably Mr Stoddart's greatest efforts in England were for his county against Lancashire. He appears to me to have had a special penchant for Mold, and some of his hook shots off some of that bowler's terrible body balls I have never seen equalled – and I expect that if Mold were invited to give his opinion as to which batsman he most feared to bowl to in the zenith of his career, the name he would give us would be Mr Stoddart's. Add to the names of these two giants those of Mr S. M. J. Woods, Storer, J. T. Brown and Mr F. G. J. Ford, and you have those of the English batsmen who hit with a method. I should doubt the actual defence of any of them being *very* great when compared with our foremost defensive batsmen, W. G. Grace, A. Shrewsbury, Gunn, F. S. Jackson, A. Ward, W. G. Quaife, *inter alios*, but they have a method in their striking, each in his distinctive style, and the power of turning offence into defence, or *vice versa*, which secures their success where others often fail. Hurricane hitters if you like are G. L. Jessop, A. E. Trott, F. Sugg and E. Smith, but one feels that it is to be hoped they will make the most of their time – and it must be admitted they generally do – otherwise their notches will probably be comparatively few. Now this may appear to be heresy, but judged dispassionately by results – when the glamour of an exceptional performance is put aside – the comparative number of failures to successes achieved by those named will bear out my theory. Yet I would be the last to detract from their actual value to a side, for each and every one of them is the hero of many notable performances, and these particular performances have done more in a very short period to *win* a match for their side than many a long-drawn innings of a master of defence.

Of the Australians above-mentioned, I hold the opinion that J. Darling and J. Worrall are their hitters with a good deal of method – and E. Jones and W. P. Howell, slap-dash, fearless hitters without much – and though none of the four can perhaps be put quite in the same class as their more famous predecessors, P. McDonnell, H. H. Massie, J. J. Lyons and G. J. Bonnor, yet each is a fine hitter.

Turning to University Cricket, we find that each has furnished the cricketing world with notable exponents of the forcing game, and while perhaps to Cambridge must be awarded the palm for the more famous roll, viz., Mr C. I. Thornton, F. C. Cobden, Hon. A. Lyttelton, M.P., F. Marchant, E. C. Streatfeild, S. M. J. Woods and G. L. Jessop, yet Oxford have a fine show of determined hitters also, viz., Rev. E. T. Drake, Mr W. H. Game, E. Smith, V. T. Hill, G. Fowler, H. Fowler, C. B. Fry, K. J. Key and B. J. T. Bosanquet.

In conclusion, I quote from one of the admirable paragraphs which 'Dux', of *The Sportsman*, gives us, and he calls attention to the fact that: 'Remaining at the wickets bat in hand is only a means to an end. The object of doing so is to make within an allotted time, more runs than the other side can make in an allotted time.' Alas, how often has this obvious maxim been lost sight of entirely! And many names will go down to posterity as those of great players who, however, have perpetually violated the simple principle of trying to *win* a match. If only into some of them could be instilled the spirit, and dash, even perhaps a little of the recklessness, of some of the heroes of the willow above-mentioned, I venture to predict that more matches would be played out, and also that cricket would in no way suffer.

Idler 1899

36

Great Reminiscences of Past Conflicts

George Giffen

What are 'The Ashes'? Nothing more nor less than the ashes of English cricket. A London paper immortalized them when the 1882 Australian Eleven defeated England at Kennington Oval; and ever since newspaper writers have alluded to Test Matches between representatives of England and Australia as the Fights for the Ashes. Until 1882 there were no Ashes. In 1877 an Australian Eleven defeated eleven representative English professionals at Sydney; but although that contest has always been regarded as the first of a series of half a hundred test matches, no one for a moment considered that Lillywhite's team thoroughly represented the Mother Country. England's supremacy was unquestioned, and continued so until the 1882 Eleven won so sensationally at the Oval. Since then there have been many gallant fights for the Ashes, and numbered amongst them are some of the greatest games recorded in the annals of cricket.

Who would ever have imagined twenty years ago that cricket matches, mere games, after all, would have excited such intense, such thrilling, such world-wide interest as we have seen in recent times when the representatives of the two countries have faced each other? The issue of a battle on which depended the fate of a dynasty could scarcely have been awaited with greater anxiety. Certainly its every phase would not have been described with greater attention to details. It has been my privilege to bear arms in many of these historical cricket battles, and as I have written these reminiscent pages, my blood has warmed within me at the recollection of some of the thrilling situations in which I have stood alongside my comrades.

The greatest match which had until that time been played – and for many years no other led to such sensational incidents; certainly there has never in an international contest been a more remarkable finish –

was the one Test to which the Australian Eleven of 1882 submitted. England placed a magnificent Eleven against us, at Kennington Oval, when the fateful day arrived. Just look at the array of cricketing giants – W. G. Grace, Hornby, Steel, Studd (who had the best batting average against the 1882 Eleven), Lucas, Alfred Lyttelton, Barlow, Barnes, Ulyett, Peate and Maurice Read. It is questionable whether at the time it would have been possible to materially strengthen that combination. We, however, suffered irreparable loss from the inability of George Palmer, through illness, to play, Sam Jones, who was the one unsuccessful player of the tour, being but an inefficient substitute for the Victorian bowler.

From the commencement of the game it was evident that we were in for a titanic struggle. The Englishmen who had been sent into the field bowled with splendid precision and fielded magnificently. Who could wish for finer all-round play than was seen when Peate and Barlow sent down more than a dozen successive maiden overs to Murdoch and Bannerman? Not a loose one from either of them, while the way the ball came back on the treacherous wicket put the batsman through a severe ordeal. Small wonder that we had 6 wickets down for 30. Blackham and Garrett then made 27 between them, and the total reached 63. Dicky Barlow's bowling was responsible for our downfall. We ought to have made at least 100. When Spoff yorked W.G.'s leg stump we were in a great feather, but good hitting by Ulyett and Maurice Read, and a clever innings by Steel, gave the Englishmen a lead of 38 on the first innings, which had been completed on the first day.

I am free to admit that Fortune smiled upon us on the Tuesday morning, when for a little while we had the wicket fairly easy, as the result of a shower of rain. This gave us a golden opportunity, and fortunately for us we had the man for the moment in Hugh Massie. Never on a slow wicket have I seen a batsman do a grander bit of hitting. Only for twenty minutes or so was the pitch really easy, but in that time Massie had got his eye in, so that when the ball did begin to bite he could bang away with as great certainty as before. It is worth noting that the only fair, genuine chance given during the great match came from Massie's bat, and it cost England 17 runs – 10 more than we won by. At last A. G. Steel came on and bowled Massie, but our hitter had given us a chance in the game. If one praises Massie's hitting, what can be said of Murdoch's batting, for long before he had completed the putting together of his 29 the wicket was as difficult as any bowler could wish? W.L.M. demonstrated then how great a batsman he really was, and I only once felt sorrier to see a man run out than I did when Murdoch, after seeing seven of us out, was run out through a bad call of Tom Garrett's.

England needed 85 runs to win. Would they get them? As we excitedly discussed our chances during the interval, Spofforth said they wouldn't. Spoff's faith in himself and Murdoch's cheery assurance inspired the rest of us, and we filed out of the dressing-room to make the effort of our lives. When the Demon had bowled Hornby and Barlow with only fifteen runs scored, we felt assured of victory; but the hitting of the Champion and Ulyett changed the complexion of the game, which then appeared to be gradually drifting away from us. Ulyett did not bat particularly well, but W.G.'s innings was a masterpiece. They were, however, separated at last, and with 53 up both had been sent to the right about.

Now began a tremendous struggle. Boyle maintained a grand length, Spofforth was well-nigh unplayable, and the fielding was perfect. The English batsmen were in the pickle Barlow and Peate had had us in on the previous day. Gradually we tightened our hold on the game; and the moment, I fancy, it was really clinched was when Steel was dismissed without scoring. So long as he remained we could not feel perfectly safe. The situation was one of those trying ones in which I think the batsmen invariably appeared at a disadvantage. A bit of fearless hitting might have snatched the game from us; but after Lyttelton and Lucas went, none of the great English batsmen could muster up the courage to have a bang, and, considering the magnificent way in which Spofforth was bowling, there was some excuse for them. Irresistible as an avalanche, he had bowled his last 11 overs for 2 runs and 4 wickets — the finest piece of bowling I have ever seen! Nevertheless, as I have said, the English batsmen were blamed, even ridiculed, and it was at this time that the London *Sporting Times* created the Ashes by publishing the following 'In Memoriam' notice:

IN AFFECTIONATE REMEMBRANCE
of
ENGLISH CRICKET
Which died at the Oval,
on
29th August, 1882.
Deeply lamented by a large circle
of sorrowing friends and acquaintances.
R.I.P.
N.B. – The body will be cremated, and the
ashes taken to Australia.

Punch congratulated us in the following lines:

> Well done, Cornstalks! Whipt us
> Fair and square,
> Was it luck that tript us?
> Was it scare?
> Kangaroo Land's 'Demon', or our own
> Want of 'devil', coolness, nerve, backbone?

It is not in the nature of Englishmen to smart under defeat without an effort at revenge. Accordingly, by the time the 1882 Eleven reached home, they found a strong English Eleven under the Hon. Ivo Bligh awaiting them. Of course, that team was not representative of England's strength with such giants as Grace, Ulyett and Peate away, yet it was a strong one, and the series of matches which followed were extremely well contested. The Hon. Ivo had been called 'St Ivo', and his tour had been alluded to as a pilgrimage after the Ashes, so that our matches were invested with something of the air of romance.

The 1882 Australian Eleven met the English team three times, but unfortunately each game was sadly interfered with by rain. In the first match we had the best of the wicket, and won by 9 wickets; in the second and third our opponents were favoured by the weather, and they won one game with an innings to spare, and the other by 69 runs.

Three splendid bowling performances are the only features worth recalling in connection with these three contests. Bates, that brilliant all-round Yorkshire player, was the hero of the first and best of them. It was in our first innings of the second trial of strength, and he not only secured 7 wickets for 28 runs, but accomplished the hat trick, the only such record, unless I am very much mistaken, in Test Matches. Percy McDonnell was his first victim, bowled; I was next, caught and bowled; and Bonnor, the third, caught by Walter Read. Bates's whole record for the match was 55 runs, and 14 wickets for 102 runs, and it says something for the generosity of the Australian crowd that for a visitor, who had been the principal instrument in defeating their own champions, they raised a collection of about £30.

Spofforth and Barlow were the bowling heroes of the last match, as they had been exactly five months before at the Oval. The wicket was a queer one, and the Demon, bowling throughout an innings of 123, captured 7 wickets for 44. This time it was our turn to have last innings, but with 153 runs between us and victory, we faced a practically impossible task. Barlow was unplayable, as an analysis of 7 for 40 indicates.

These three matches had aroused intense enthusiasm, and upon their conclusion a number of Australian ladies presented the English captain with a tiny urn containing ashes, upon the souvenir being inscribed, 'The Ashes of English Cricket'.

St Ivo was, however, not destined to take the Ashes back with him. Neither the Australian players nor the public were satisfied with the result of the games, for one thing, because the elements had played so unfortunate a part in them, and for another, because some of our men had shown that they were clean out of form. Therefore an extra match was arranged, and McDonnell, Massie and Garrett, who had done nothing, were replaced by Evans, Boyle and Midwinter. I give the names of our Eleven, because I consider it to have been the strongest Australia had until that time placed in the field: Murdoch, Bannerman, Horan, Spofforth, Blackham, Boyle, Palmer, Bonnor, Evans, Midwinter and myself.

We won the match by 4 wickets, after a curious mixture of poor and brilliant cricket, such as one has fortunately seldom seen repeated in a Test Match. The Englishmen got in first and made 263, of which Steel's share was 135 not out. He was missed before he had broken the ice, and three times more during the next hour, but after that his batting was perfect. Faulty as our fielding had been, what can be said of that of our opponents, who missed Bonnor no fewer than seven times! No wonder the Magog of cricketers made 87. We finished up one run to the bad. This prepared the way for an exciting finish, and we did indeed have one almost comparable with that when we won by seven runs.

The all-round play of each side in the second innings was of the finest description. Seven of the Englishmen reached double figures, yet the total was only 197. We had to make 199, and as the wicket had not worn any too well, the task was a serious one – so serious that Murdoch went in first himself with Alec Bannerman. The start was not encouraging. The bowling was so accurate, and the fielding so smart, that even Murdoch could not score, and with Alec stonewalling for all he was worth, maiden after maiden was bowled; in fact I have never seen slower scoring, from a pair of batsmen, for so prolonged a period. With three men, including Murdoch, out for 51, our chance was not a rosy one. Then I went in with a man to run for me, and Bannerman and I put on 56. At 107 Bannerman, who had latterly scored at a furious rate, was disposed of for 63. Blackham came in, and began to lay about him in his characteristic way. In the first innings he had made 57, and when he had got going again our hopes were raised. The bowling was splendid; but when he got a start on a hard wicket, our fearless wicket-keeper was always apt to make any bowling look simple. At 162 I was stumped, and as Evans was straightway caught, the chances were about even, as we had only Midwinter, Palmer, Spofforth and Boyle to come in. Sturdy, imperturbable Mid, the only cricketer who has played for both England and Australia in Test Matches, joined Blackham, and, cautiously defending his wicket, watched his partner knock off the runs, which he did without once faltering. Blackham carried out his bat for 58, and he himself was chaired to the pavilion on the broad shoulders of several of the delighted spectators – an experience probably unique in the annals of the Test Matches.

When in 1882 we had defeated All England, regret had been expressed that the players of the Old Country had not been given an opportunity to avenge their defeat, so that we of the 1884 team found three Test Matches arranged for us. When we arrived, we saw by the papers how keen Englishmen were for revenge. Of the three matches played, however, only one was finished, and England winning that one, regained the Ashes, although we had the best of the two drawn games.

In the initial game at Manchester there was some cricket of high quality on a slow wicket; the best individual performance was Boyle's 6 for 42 in England first innings.

We were outplayed in the return match at Lord's, and were beaten by an innings, after we had won the toss and gone in first. Our first innings realized only 229, and our second fewer still – 145 – Ulyett, on a worn wicket, on the last day, holding us at his mercy, and securing 7 wickets for 36 runs.

The catch with which Ulyett dismissed Bonnor I regard as one of the most brilliant I have seen. Bonnor was sent in third wicket down to knock off the dangerous Yorkshireman, and he tried hard to fulfil his mission. He got one fourer, then made a mighty drive. Everyone looked down the ground to see where the ball landed, and the spectators began to open a space in the ring, but the ball did not reach the crowd. Ulyett put up his hand, and meeting it with the right spot of his hand, held it. I was Bonnor's *vis-à-vis* at the time, and thoroughly appreciated the merit of that effort.

A. G. Steel was, however, the real hero on the English side. He went in when W.G., Lucas and Shrewbury were out for 90. Things might easily have turned against England had not a batsman of Steel's calibre barred our way. Before Palmer bowled him he had made 148, and the total was 379. This was the very best innings I saw Steel play, and one of the finest contributed against us in Test Matches.

The interest taken in the third 1884 match was tremendous. Having one game on the slate, England was determined not to lose her advantage, and to this end the team to oppose us was not chosen till the last moment. Then the following magnificent Eleven was put in the field: Lord Harris, the Hon. Alfred Lyttelton, W. G. Grace, A. G. Steel, W. W. Read, Barlow, Barnes, Shrewsbury, Peate, Ulyett and Scotton – the strongest side which, in my humble judgement, has ever represented England.

The weather being exceedingly hot was all in our favour. The cold English days have often seriously incommoded Australians, who have found their warm blood so chilled that they have been unable to enjoy fielding as it should be enjoyed, and mistakes otherwise unaccountable have been made. On August 11, 1884, however, we were in our element; it was so warm that several of the spectators fainted.

That first day was one of the most glorious Australian batsmen have had at the expense of English bowlers. The early dismissal of Bannerman did not augur well, but during the remainder of the afternoon only one wicket fell. The total when we adjourned was 363 for 2 wickets, and three men had made centuries — Murdoch, 145 not out; McDonnell, 103; and Scott, 101 not out. And this against Peate, Barlow, Barnes, Steel and Ulyett! Surely no other team ever had quite so hopeless an afternoon's work. There were mistakes in the field, but on the whole the batting was magnificent. Next day we concluded our innings for 551, of which Murdoch made 211, the highest individual score recorded in the whole series of Test Matches, and probably the masterpiece of Murdoch's brilliant career.

One of the interesting features of the innings was that every man on the English side had a try at the bowling crease, and a notable circumstance was that when all the cracks had failed Alfred Lyttelton went on, and with underhand lobs took 4 wickets for 19, which shows what wonders a change may accomplish.

With the wicket in such splendid order we entertained no real hope of getting England out twice; but so finely did Palmer bowl at a critical period of the first innings that for a short while we thought we might squeeze home, as eight wickets had fallen for 181. Then, however, Walter Read came in — as *tenth* man, mind — and knocked our bowling all over the field until he had made 117. Scotton, it will be remembered, played a grand defensive game, and 151 runs were put on for the ninth wicket.

Of course the game was drawn, but in our favour. Nevertheless, we had the satisfaction of knowing that we had demonstrated that an Australian Eleven could make a fight, on the best of wickets, with England's champions. This was eminently pleasing to us, because it had been said that we had no chance of defeating All England save on the sticky pitches whereon our Demon bowler was so deadly.

In 1884–5 a remarkably powerful professional team toured the Colonies, but with W.G. and Steel at home it was not an All England Eleven. Nevertheless there were several Test Matches.

The first was played at Adelaide against the returned 1884 Australian Eleven. McDonnell, Blackham and myself practised assiduously for a fortnight to get into form, but none of the others took the interest they should have in the match, and some of them played without having had more than a day's practice since they left England. Consequently only one double figure score was made by our men beyond those which the three of us who had practised contributed. Moreover, we were without Spofforth, who had not returned from England, so that it was not surprising that we were beaten by 8 wickets. For the Englishmen, Barnes, 134 and 28 not out, was in great form; while for us, Percy McDonnell batted beautifully for 124 and 83. Everyone who saw those two innings of Percy's agree to this day that they never saw prettier batting. He hit more brilliantly at Manchester in 1888, but at Adelaide he played perfectly true cricket, and the way he placed the ball was a treat to watch.

Four other games were played by Shaw's team against selected Elevens of Australia, but not one of the Australian Elevens was representative, owing to an unfortunate dispute with the visitors over money matters, which was prolonged further than it should have been. However, some of the 1884 team played in the last two matches. Of the four, England and Australia won two each.

Unquestionably the strongest of the four Elevens Australia placed in the field that season was the one which played in the third match, and won by 8 wickets, after our opponents had opened the contest with a score of 269. I bowled nearly throughout the innings, and secured 7 wickets, 6 clean bowled, for 117 runs. Bonnor, who made 128, hit magnificently when the chances seemed against us, and he and Jones put on 154 for the eighth wicket. A useful lead of 40 runs was thoroughly appreciated, for when rain came the Englishmen could only make 77.

Against a weaker team in the last match England won in grand style by an innings and 98 runs. Arthur Shrewsbury batted splendidly for 105 not out in a total of 386, while Ulyett took 7 wickets for 77 runs in the match.

I shall not attempt to go at length into the three Test Matches played in England by the 1886 Australian Eleven. The first we lost by 4 wickets, the second by an innings and 106 runs, and the third by an innings and 217 runs. In the first game we made a real good fight, inasmuch as, though England only had to make 106 runs in the second innings, the wickets of Grace, Scotton, Shrewsbury, Walter Read, Barlow and Ulyett were lost before the runs were hit off. In the other two games we were crushed.

Arthur Shrewsbury played a masterly innings for 164 at Lord's, undoubtedly the best though not the highest hit against our bowling during the tour. The wicket was none too clever. It was a fiery Lord's pitch, and most first-class batsmen know what that means; but his defence was perfect, and he played all the bowling as though it were simple as ABC.

This was Briggs's first Test Match in England, and he signalized the event by capturing 11 wickets for only 74 runs. Merry Johnny was then, and for many years afterwards, one of the most formidable of Australia's opponents, and had he been a more reliable batsman he would, to my mind, have ranked with Steel as an all-round player next to W.G. At his best he was a very fine bowler, one who was always worrying the batsman, and always had to be watched.

Just as we had been beaten at Lord's, mainly through the instrumentality of two men, so was it the case at the Oval; but here the players were different. Shrewsbury batted finely, but it was W.G. who made 170, a score which for nine years stood as an English record in Test Matches. Briggs again bowled well, but it was George Lohmann's bowling that upset us, his analyses being 7 for 36 and 5 for 68.

January 1, 1892, the opening day of the first Test Match with Lord Sheffield's team, may be regarded as the dawn of a new era in Australian cricket. While the ashes of Australian cricket were being scattered to the four winds in England, the critics had said that now that Murdoch, Spofforth, Boyle, Palmer and McDonnell had passed out of the arena, Australia could not replace them: they had been phenomenal. And this argument probably brought some consolation to Englishmen for the 1882 defeat. But in the era which began on New Year's Day at Melbourne six years ago we were to demonstrate that Australia had produced another generation of cricketers, who were worthy successors to the Tritons of former days.

The Australian Eleven, in the first match against Lord Sheffield's Eleven, comprised Blackham, Bannerman, Moses, Lyons, Turner, Bruce, G. H. S. Trott, R. McLeod, Donnan, Callaway and myself; so that there were only three of us — Blackham, Bannerman and myself — who had played in the sensational match at the Oval in 1882. Maurice Read was the solitary member of the Earl's Eleven who had played in that game.

Our 240 runs were earned by as fine batting as one could wish to see, for the bowling of Sharpe, Peel, Attewell and Lohmann was splendid, and the fielding perfect. The Englishmen scored faster than we did, and headed our score by 24. Then we replied with 236, and left them needing 213 to win. W.G. told me that he thought they would make the runs with the loss, at most, of six men, and when he and Stoddart had run up 60 for the first wicket, it appeared as though his prediction was going to be vindicated. Suddenly both were disposed of, and although Abel struggled manfully, the backbone of the team was gone, and in the end we won by 54.

I have said this was the most stubbornly fought game I had then played in. It ran into five days, and during that time, although the wicket was always first class, and some of the best batsmen in the world went to the wickets, the highest individual contribution was only 57. The fact of the matter was that directly a batsman gave a chance he was caught. Indeed, not a single chance that went to hand was missed, which can be written of very few matches. How differently games would result if the fielding were always so remarkable!

The batting of our men was the soundest all round we had ever exhibited. It had taken twenty years for the English batsmen to teach us that, on good wickets, matches were to be won by sound, rather than risky, batting. This match was the first great one in which Australian batsman after batsman put these precepts into practice, even Lyons and Bruce batting with remarkable patience. For once in a way the English batting was of the brilliant school, so that our victory was the triumph of the pupils over the masters. To give an idea of the different style of batting adopted by the two teams, I need only say that, although there was only 54 runs difference between us, the Englishmen bowled twice as many overs, and more than three times as many maidens, as we did. Many of the maidens were, however, accounted for by the presence in our team of a Bannerman — they had none. Alec scored 45 and 41, and batted in the respective innings three hours and a quarter and four hours.

And now we won the rubber. The return match was played at Sydney, and we were the favourites; even our opponents thought we would win with four or five wickets to spare. We started badly. The ground was drying after rain, and when Jack Blackham won the toss he was in a quandary. The wicket, though not a bad one, would help the bowlers slightly, and unless more rain fell it was bound to improve. However, the only game was to go in first. This we did, and our opponents got rid of us for 145, or, rather, George Lohmann did, for he secured 8 wickets for only 58 runs. The wicket assisted him a little, but really he bowled magnificently. He was at his best then, and on that day was unplayable. I had a great admiration for Lohmann's bowling. He was a bowler after my own heart. Seldom troubling to try to weary batsmen with off-theory, he preferred to out-manoeuvre them, and I doubt whether England has produced, in my time, a bowler of more resource and one who had greater command over the ball.

England responded with 307. Almost entirely to one man was a score of that magnitude due, and that one was Bobby Abel, who carried his bat through the innings – the only occasion, I believe, on which it has been done for England in a Test Match. His contribution was 132; the next score to his was 28! It was a perfect display, as fine a one as I have seen him give. Without taking the slightest risk, he met all the bowling with provoking confidence, and made some beautiful strokes.

Australia lost one – Trott's – wicket on the second day for one run, and, as Moses was incapacitated, our task seemed a hopeless one. But there was in store for us one of those marvellous innings which have made Australian hitters famous. Much as one admires and commends steady batting, one realizes that there are occasions when desperate remedies, when kill-or-cure hitting, alone can win a game. When Lyons joined Bannerman we were 162 runs in arrears; when he left we were 13 runs on. But in this innings Lyons did not hit in the ferocious manner which was to set England agog eighteen months later. He really played sound cricket, such as many had not dreamt him to be capable of, yet his strokes made the ball travel like a cannon-shot. It took him nearly three hours to compile his 134, which for him was slow scoring. Bannerman and I were not parted for some time, and at the close of the day we had 263 runs up, having during the afternoon scored 262 for the loss of two wickets.

Next day rain fell, and the innings closed at 391. Alec Bannerman was responsible for the odd 91. I shall never forget the sight of the field crowded around him as he stonewalled. There was W.G. at point, almost on the point of his bat; Lohmann a couple of yards away, at slip; Peel at silly point; Stoddart only a dozen yards away, at mid-off; and Briggs at silly mid-on. One gentleman remarked that it reminded him of the famous painting, 'Anguish', in which a bevy of crows is swarming round a dead lamb, over which the mother is watching. A barracker once called out, 'Look out, Alec, or W.G. will have his hand in your pocket'. But Alec stonewalled on, imperturbably blocking the straight ones, sardonically smiling at the off-theory, and judiciously tapping a rare loose one to leg. Suddenly he swished at an off ball, and cut it past W.G.'s ear to the boundary, and then what a yell rent the air! He was eventually caught by W.G. off Briggs, who had simply tossed the balls down slowly, with as much twizzle as possible on them, in the hope that he might lead Alec into an indiscretion. But the Englishmen had to wait seven and a half hours for that indiscretion! Truly, patience is a virtue.

Thinking the wicket would be worse on the morrow, W.G. sent in his batsmen in the usual order, and we got rid of him, Abel and Bean for 11 runs. The G.O.M. was blamed, afterwards, for not having sacrificed the tail end; but that was next day, when the wicket was found to roll out better than had been expected. Stoddart made a valiant effort, but we won by 72. And thus the English Ashes returned to Australia, and we regained possession of our own treasured emblems.

We were beaten at Adelaide in a third match with Lord Sheffield's team by an innings and 230 runs; but, inasmuch as the Englishmen completed their innings of 499 on a perfect wicket, and we had to bat twice after the pitch had been damaged by rain, we had no reason to feel ashamed of the result.

Not long were Australians allowed to remain in possession of the Ashes. They took them to England in 1893, and there they were compelled to leave them. The all-round cricket exhibited by our men in those matches was not worthy of their reputations; if our fielding had only been half as good as it had been in Australia in 1891–92, we might have come out of the ordeal in England with honours.

We had a wonderful chance in the first trial of skill at Lord's, where we met England without W.G. for the first time on English soil, an injured finger keeping the master-hand from operating upon us. The winning of the toss by Stoddart was of no advantage to him, on account of the dampness of the wicket on the opening day; but we threw away a golden chance by missing Shrewsbury and Jackson early in their innings, and both of them afterwards played magnificently – the one patient, the other brilliant. We had to face 334, at least 150 more than should have been the case. Then came Lockwood to upset our first batsmen, and we had five wickets down for 75. A plucky stand by Graham and Gregory saved us, and after all we were only 65 runs behind. The two famous Nottingham players, Shrewsbury and Gunn, wore down our bowling in the second innings, and the match ended in an unsatisfactory draw.

The second game was the only one finished, and it was a grand triumph for the Old Country, who massed the magnificent total of 483. Grace and Stoddart's 151 for the first wicket drove the first nail into our coffin, and Jackson sent a longer one home by hitting up 103. I conceived a great admiration for the young Cantab's batting from his displays in the 1893 Test Matches. He is certainly one of the finest, and at the same time most judicious, forcing batsmen England has produced for many a day.

Australia should have saved that game, considering that the Oval wicket remained in splendid run-getting order until the last ball was bowled. Wearied, however, by our long outing, we fell easy victims to Lockwood and Briggs, although weariness is not sufficient excuse for our first collapse for 91 runs. That we were capable of something better was demonstrated in the second innings, when we reached 349, Harry Trott batting grandly for 92. Still we could not avert the innings defeat.

As usual, we played better at Old Trafford than we had at either Lord's or the Oval. The game was the most stoutly contested of the trio, but was drawn slightly in favour of England. Here we faced Richardson for the first time in a Test Match, and he secured the fine analysis of 5 for 49. Once more a century was hit against us, so that we had had one in each of the Test Matches. On this occasion Gunn batted finely for 102 not out, at a time when it seemed on the cards that England would have been in arrears on the first innings.

Now one comes to that remarkable series of fights for the Ashes which took place during the tour of Stoddart's team in 1894-5. One may fairly say that Australians were the favourites, the prevailing notion being that, although Richardson had bowled so grandly in England in 1893, he would not be in the least deadly on the hard, true Australian wickets.

The first game was played at Sydney, and it will be a long time before its sensational incidents fade from one's memory. Probably a more remarkable match has never been played. The start was sensational enough in all conscience, for at 10 Richardson bowled Lyons off his pad, and at 21 clean beat Trott and Darling with successive balls. Then, however, came a long stand by Iredale and myself. Here I may say that I had trained specially for that season's play. During Lord Sheffield's tour, being unwell, I did not do myself justice, and there were plenty of critics who said that, though I could score in intercolonials, it was significant that I had not done so in the great Test Matches. Determined to vindicate myself, I went through a severe course of winter training, and began the season in as fine fettle as ever I was in. To resume, then, the thread of my narrative, Iredale, who batted perfectly, made 81, and helped me to put on 171, and then Syd Gregory and I added 139. When I had made 161, Ford caught me at slip. This I consider the best innings I have played. The score at the close of the first day was 346 for 5 wickets, and that after we had had three men out for 21! Gregory batted magnificently, and he and Blackham added 154 for the ninth wicket, which is a record for Test Matches, just heading Walter Read and Scotton's 151 at the Oval in 1884. Our total at Sydney was 586. Little Syd's was a wonderful innings, one of the most attractive I have ever seen. It roused the spectators — and there were nearly 30,000 of them — to such a pitch of enthusiasm that a collection of £103 was made for him.

With 586 runs on the slate we never for one second dreamt of losing the game. We were even sanguine of getting rid of the powerful lot of batsmen on the opposing side twice before they had reached our score. They, however, fought an uphill game with wonderful pluck and persistence; but an injury to Blackham in their first innings — an injury which closed his first-class career — seriously handicapped us. The Englishmen were 261 in arrears at the end of their first innings, and if we had had a wicket keeper, I doubt whether their second innings would have reached 300. One was, however, bound to admire the English batting in the second innings. One after the other the batsmen went in and played 'keeps', and gradually wore down the bowling, and in the end we were left with 177 to make.

Our task did not in the least appal us, because the wicket was as true as ever when we began our second innings; and when, at the close of the fifth day, we had scored 113 for 2 wickets, the match seemed as good as won. All of us thought so that night save Blackham, who feared rain. I know I turned in to rest with an easy mind on the subject. When I awoke next morning and found the glorious sun streaming into my room, I was in ecstasy. But the first man I met was Blackham, with a face as long as a coffee-pot. The explanation of his looks came with the remark, 'It has been pouring half the night, George.' Even then, so beautiful was the morning, it seemed difficult to realize that rain had fallen; but when we reached the ground, and found the wicket ruined, we knew we would have to battle for those 64 runs.

Did ever a team have such cruel luck? To make 586 and then be beaten by the wicket! Someone said the rain beat us, but Blackham was nearer the mark when he rejoined, 'No, it was the sun that did it.' However, we could not entirely begrudge our opponents their victory, for against tremendous odds they had fought magnificently.

The second game, played at Melbourne, led to another remarkable exhibition of cricket. One incident is specially noteworthy. We began on a Saturday upon a heavy wicket, and, as the weather prospects were good, Stoddart and I agreed, before we tossed, that at the close of the day's play we should have the wicket rolled out; otherwise the marks made by the feet in the soft turf would by Monday have hardened, and the wicket would have played badly. On the first day each side was disposed of, we leading by 48 runs.

Then, on the Monday, with the wicket perfect, began the struggle. The Englishmen became stonewallers. Even Stoddart completely discarded his usual tactics, and played almost as slowly as a Bannerman, until it was impossible to recognize in him the brilliant batsman who, going in first with W.G. in England in 1893, had slated our bowling so severely. But Stoddart was captain now, and he had to set his men an example. Nobly he accomplished his task, for he notched 173, and, by topping W.G.'s 170, gained an English Test Match record.

If the captain had batted patiently, what of Peel — three and a half hours for 53, and 37 of his runs were singles? Someone— an Australian, of course — remonstrated with him. 'I hope you are not going to develop into one of those wretched Scottons, Bobby!' to which he replied, 'Aye, aye, but I must play the game.'

We were set 428 in our second innings, and thought we had an outside chance. Bruce and Trott led off with 98 for the first wicket, and when, with 190 up, Trotty and I were still going, our prospects were really bright. But a sudden change came o'er the scene. Brockwell went on, and in half a dozen overs got rid of Trott, myself and Darling.

280

Thenceforward our opponents held the upper hand, and won by 94 runs.

We won the next two games at Adelaide by 382 runs, and at Sydney by an innings and 147, but each time we had the Englishmen at a disadvantage. At Adelaide the heat, at Sydney the rain, 'killed' them. Throughout the Adelaide engagement the thermometer registered from 102° to 105° in the shade! While most of us were in our element, the Englishmen were almost prostrated. Some of them took two or three shower-baths through the night, which, of course, was the worst thing they could have done. Next day Callaway and I dismissed them for 124.

Four of the younger generation of players distinguished themselves in that match: Iredale, who scored 7 and 140; Albert Trott, who knocked up 38 not out, 72 not out, and in the second innings captured 8 wickets for 43; Richardson, who captured 8 of our wickets, and was the only bowler to trouble us; and Callaway, who, besides making 41 and 11, secured 5 wickets for 37 in the first innings.

I doubt whether I ever felt greater admiration for Richardson than when he took 5 wickets for 75 in our first innings. With the broiling sun streaming on the back of his curly black hair, and the intense heat trying him severely, he bowled like a veritable demon. There is a good deal about the Surrey fast bowler to remind one of our own Demon of the 'eighties. Both are tall, and Richardson, like Spofforth, when he stands ready to make his run before delivering the ball, is the personification of determination. Other English bowlers are more subtle, but not one so deadly as Tom Richardson on a wicket which gives him the least assistance. England has not, to my way of thinking, had so deadly a bowler in my time.

Albert Trott's all-round performance must be ranked amongst the finest things done in Test Matches. Early in the season I had been commiserating with Harry Trott, who was at the time doing nothing. He replied, 'Don't mind me, but keep an eye on that young brother of mine. You'll find him a good one before the season is over.'

To secure his 8 wickets for 43, Albert bowled magnificently, with an off-break that was well-nigh unplayable, so quickly did it rise from the pitch. Thereby hangs a good tale. When he first came to Adelaide he did not take a wicket, and I made a fair score against the Victorians. Soon after his return to Melbourne, he erected three stumps, with a stout box in front of them, where a bat would be if a match were being played. Then he started to bowl, and with an occasional break-back, beat the box and hit the wicket. His brother Harry came along and asked what the box was for.

'Oh, that's George Giffen.'

'Easier to get past than George's bat, isn't it?' Harry suggested.

'That's just it, Harry. I found at Adelaide that straight stuff would never get him, so I am learning to bowl breaks.'

The Sydney match was spoilt by rain, and we had the best of the wicket. We had been sent in, and when 6 wickets were down for 51 it looked bad for us, but Graham and Darling tided us over until the stickiness left the pitch, and Albert Trott afterwards hitting up 85, we reached 284, after thinking we would be all out for under 100. Graham's 105 was the finest innings he has played, for until he had reached about 40 the wicket was a difficult one.

It was now our turn to have the Englishmen on toast, as they had had us a couple of months before, upon the same ground. Play had to be adjourned for a day on account of a record storm which raged at Sydney on the Saturday, and when resumed on the Monday the wicket was so bad that our opponents could only make 65 and 72. Peel, as in the Adelaide match, earned a pair of spectacles, and it is curious that in each innings at Sydney his score read, 'st Jarvis, b Turner, 0'.

With the record 'two all', the excitement during the month which elapsed prior to the conquering match was raised to fever heat. We had been chopping and changing our team throughout the series, and considerable interest was taken in the selection for the final struggle.

By the time the 1st of March came round, thousands of people had poured into Melbourne from all parts of the Colonies. Coasting steamers were crowded. Special trains brought human freight in hundreds from Sydney and Adelaide. What wonder, then, that during the five days over which that great game extended, 63,469 people paid for admission, and that the receipts amounted to £4003 14s. – records, not only for Australia, but for the world! The total attendance, including members, exceeded 100,000. The play which followed was worthy of the mammoth attendance.

The excitement extended to the players, and not the least to the captains. I know that when Stoddart and I went into the ring to toss and arrange preliminaries, he was as white as a sheet, and I have been told that the pallor of my own countenance matched his. It was a trying moment, for both knew that, with two such strong batting sides, much depended on the toss. I won it, and I felt as though a great burden had been lifted from my shoulders. Poor Stoddart gave me a despairing look, which said as plainly as words, 'I'm afraid it's all over, George.'

When we had made 414 we thought it was all right, and when we had Stoddart, Brown, Ward and Brockwell out for 166, it still looked good enough for us. Then came a great partnership by MacLaren and Peel, who added 162. They, however, were lucky. I missed MacLaren badly through an injury to the little finger of my right hand, which made it painful for me to hold the ball (a ball from Lockwood did it just before I got out in the first innings), and I may be pardoned for the egotism when I say that this accident to myself contributed materially to the English victory. Apart from the chances, MacLaren's batting was very fine, and Peel's scarcely less so. The total reached 385, and we were thus only 29 runs on.

In our second innings we expected to make at least 350, but a terrible dust storm on the fourth morning made the light bad, and a gale blowing across the ground caused Richardson's fast bowling to be very awkward. This was the only occasion during the season in which he bowled me (I pulled an off ball on to the wicket), although in England in 1893 there was only one innings in which I faced him that he did not bowl my wicket down. Under the circumstances, our 267 was not half bad.

The Englishmen were set 297, and, as everyone knows, they got them for the loss of four wickets. A mild Scotch mist made the wicket on the last day as easy as it had been at any time during the match, and Johnny Brown and Albert Ward did as they liked with our bowling, Brown especially playing with wonderful brilliance for his 140. We had one large slice of bad luck. Immediately upon resuming play after lunch on the last day, Jarvis caught Ward at the wicket; but the bowler got in the way of Jim Phillips, the umpire, who could not see the catch, and gave Albert in. There can be no question but that Ward touched the ball.

Of the last three matches played in England in 1896 I do not propose to say very much, because the events are so clear in the minds of those who follow the noble game. One could not help noticing that

W.G. and myself were the only pair who had taken part in the great struggle in 1882 who were still playing Test Matches.

Nothing can be said in extenuation of Australia's miserable batting failure at Lord's — a failure which, considering the excellence of the wicket, is a greater reproach to Australian batting than England's was at the Oval towards the close of the 1882 match. The magnificent batting of Trott and Gregory in the second innings gave us a second chance, which we threw away on the last morning by faulty fielding.

Grand as was Trott's batting at Lord's, one is fain to admit that it was eclipsed by Prince Ranjitsinhji's magnificent play at Old Trafford in the second match. The Prince's 154 not out was absolutely the finest innings I have seen. Just think of it! He made 154 and was unconquered, although the ten Englishmen, including W.G., Stoddart, Abel, Jackson, Brown and MacLaren, could only account for 151 between them. But then Ranji is the batting wonder of the age. His play was a revelation to us, with his marvellous cutting and his extraordinary hitting to leg. I have never seen anything to equal it.

That last wretched match played in the mud at the Oval was a farce. What seemed likely to be the game of games, the greatest ever known, was completely spoiled. England won by batting for over an hour on the first day, when the wicket was easy.

Of the matches which have been played by Mr Stoddart's team in Australia, lately, it would be superfluous to say anything, as the facts are fresh in all our memories.

What I should like to see, and I know it is scarcely possible, is five matches between the pick of the two great cricketing countries of the world, with wickets good throughout, and the matches played to a finish. One would confidently await the issue.

Windsor Magazine 1898

37

Some Cricket Yarns

Alfred Gibson

If we Englishmen were not quite so cold-blooded and so calculating we should have gone into hysterics by this time over the prospect of Stoddart's second team for Australia. Remember the unparalleled wave of enthusiasm that floated over England directly it became known on the last occasion that Stoddart's men had pulled the first international match out of the fire and gained a thrilling win by ten runs. That performance was enough to sustain excitement over the rest of the tour. For those few weeks there was a cricket fever in England. Politics went by the board. Nothing was saleable but Australian cricket, and the epidemic lasted until we had won the rubber, and had welcomed home the team as saviours of the honour of the old country.

But as I start out by saying, we are a cold-blooded people. We do not fatten on anticipation. Expectation is too fatiguing for your average Englishman; he knows that Stoddart's side will not be completed until the late autumn, and therefore his enthusiasm at present lies dormant.

I am, however, able to announce the names of a few players who have been invited to go to Australia; and for the rest – well, I think the average follower of the game will be able to make deductions. The fact of the matter is that the present season's form should have very little to do with Mr Stoddart's decisions, except in the way of confirming impressions. It was on late form that Lockwood and George Bean and O. G. Radcliffe were taken to Australia, and in each of these cases a mistake was made.

The player who has just failed at home is not at all unlikely to make his reputation in Australia. McKibbin was nothing in the Colonies, but he was useful enough over here; and in even greater degree the same can be said of Jones.

By the way, talking of Jones reminds me of a very funny experience at Eastbourne. I was talking to the fast bowler on the parade, and I was joined by a friend. The conversation turned to cricket, and my friend suddenly electrified both of us by asking: 'And do you think Jones, the Australian, throws?' I hurriedly said that it was a matter of opinion for the umpire, but Jones gravely ventured the theory that Jones *throws* every alternate ball. 'But,' he added, 'I have never seen him bowl. When I happen to play against him I will soon call the umpire's attention.' Subsequently I told my friend that he had been speaking to Jones, and he suddenly departed for another seaside.

The negotiations between Sussex and Jones fell through, but we are to have another Australian bowler in an English county team. I speak of Roche, the Victorian, who is qualifying for Middlesex. Roche has a physical pecularity. He is not, like Sharpe, the old Surreyite, minus an eye, but on his right hand he has only two fingers. And after that you will be surprised to learn that Roche is a right-hander. He both bowls and bats with that hand, and more curious still, he is a really fine player; indeed, a well-known Kent professional expressed the opinion to me that on anything like a broken wicket Roche would be the most dangerous bowler in the country.

The worst of talking cricket is that you are apt to wander. Now, I started out with the intention of discussing Stoddart's team, and I haven't said anything about it yet. Well, let me first of all put down Ranjitsinhji's name. The famous Indian is not only going, but a special Act of Parliament has been passed in Australia to enable him to arrive without the usual alien duties.

What Ranji will do on Australian wickets can only be conjectured. Having regard to the extent of his hitting on our own, it will be well to sympathize with the Australian bowlers forthwith and to expect some serious attacks on the world's batting records. By the way, I do hope that somebody will practise the old trick with Ranji. Do you remember that visit of his to Yorkshire while he was touring with the Cambridge Cassandra? The opposition side were secretly informed that Ranji knew not a word of English except 'How's that?' and 'Yes', and 'No'. The 'black chap' made a big score, and he was rather surprised at the open and rather embarrassing criticism of his play by the fieldsmen. One of them humorously suggested lynching, and when Ranji was struck by a rising ball the bowler audibly expressed the hope that that would knock some of the steam out of 'the darky'. At the subsequent luncheon Ranji made quite a long speech in giving a toast, and during this the faces of the opposition side were studies!

In the way of cricket yarns, however, I think that told me by George Lohmann to be the funniest. It was in an up-country match in Australia, of course – all the funny things happen there! – and Pilling finely stumped a batsman off a ball from George. To general amazement the umpire stentoriously gave 'Not out!' When asked whether he knew the game, he smiled sardonically. He said, 'Bowling I holds with, catching I holds with, but when it comes to bowling a man from behind – no, you don't catch Joe Robinson napping, even if you do come from England!'

Another member of Mr Stoddart's party is F. S. Jackson, who, by the way, has seriously been advised to wear a wig. 'Jigger' Jackson is of course the hero of a famous expression. When he came down to play at Lord's for Harrow against Eton, his father, the then Secretary for Ireland, promised him a sovereign for every wicket he took and a sovereign for every run he made. Jackson *fils* met with astonishing success, and was congratulated on his haul. But I must not repeat such a 'chestnut' as the retort, modest and effective, which was Jackson's reply.

Jackson has never been to Australia, and his visit will be keenly welcomed. The only thing that may stop him going will be a desire for political honours. It is a well known fact that Jackson wants to get into Parliament. Ranjitsinhji is another cricketer with like intentions. His constituency will be Brighton, and he will endeavour to wean the town out of its Conservative tendency. It is curious that this season at Lord's Capt. B. V. Wentworth, the present member for Brighton, and Ranjitsinhji should have been on opposite sides.

Archie MacLaren, the hero of the highest score, has been asked to repeat his visit, and is almost certain to go. MacLaren is one of the few men who scored a century on their first appearance for a county. Was it not he, by the way, who once having skied a ball declared the innings closed before the ball had fallen?

It is a pity that MacLaren cannot play regularly for Lancashire, for then the County Palatine would have a far better chance for the championship. He is, I think, one of the finest batsmen the world has produced.

Peel will go, as a matter of course. However fluctuating may be his success as a bowler, he is worth his place as a batsman and a fieldsman alone. I think it was Peel who told me that in an up-country match in Australia a batsman, whose off-stump he had knocked down, refused to go out because he 'always went by the majority'. Peel has a dry humour, and I strongly suspect that he invented that little joke.

Storer, of Derbyshire, has never been to Australia. He is a great cricketer, and he is not among those who overlook the fact; still, he should go to Australia. There is certainly not now a wicket-keeper — unless it be Lilley, of Warwickshire — who can claim to be so good a bat as Storer. The Derbyshire man is the only professional who has managed to hit up two distinct hundreds in one match.

Mention of records reminds me of a match I saw at Hamilton, when England were playing Canada in 1872. It had been agreed to finish the match on the evening in any circumstances. It got so dark that the ball could scarcely be seen, and I distinctly remember one of the Englishmen — A. N. Hornby I think it was (it would be just like him) — lighting a candle in the slips.

I don't suppose Gunn will be included in Mr Stoddart's team. He would not go on the last occasion, and I doubt whether he will be asked again. I often think of Gunn as the ideal batsman. What a perfect style he has! Indeed, he is the ideal on whom aspiring batsmen should model their play.

By the way, we were speaking of anecdotes. One that deserves a good place was told me by a Lancashire professional — you will surely guess his name? A match was played in a country district, and in an emergency a local farmer's boy was put in to keep the score, the duties being carefully explained to him. When the last man on the side had been caught, the fielders darted in to see the score, and they found — the book blank! That was the condition, too, of the 'scorer's' face. 'The truth is,' he said deliberately, 'I was sae eenteristed in the wee sport that I quite forgot tae mak' the crosses. But it disna matter — that wee laddie wi' the red face is the smartest runner amang ye!'

It is said that Jack Hearne, of Middlesex, may go to Australia with Stoddart's team. But a truce to these reflections. Let us to the field, gentlemen!

Windsor Magazine 1897

38

Cricket

Andrew Lang

'**D**oubtless Heaven might have made a better berry than the straw-berry, but certainly Heaven never did,' says the good English divine. Doubtless, we may alter the phrase — man might have developed a better game than cricket, but certainly man never did. This we say without regard to the feelings of tennis players. Their pastime is indeed 'the sport of princes', but for that every reason we cannot deem it 'the prince of games'. Tennis, like the Game Laws, private property in the land, the House of Lords, Covent Garden Market, and other notorious abuses, is a feudal survival of an exclusive and aristocratic chracter. The very disposition of the court, with its pent-house and grille, speaks of its origin in the court of the mediaeval castle. Now mediaeval castles have a notoriously bad character. 'Castelas he let wyrcean, and earme men swenete': 'castles he built, and made it rough for poor men', says the *Peterborough Chronicle*. While the villein was being sat upon by the baron, in a box half full of rough stones*, the baron's sons were playing tennis in the castle court. Thus tennis, like highway robbery, was the sport of princes such as Henry V, in his salad days; Henvy V, who received that famous present of tennis balls from the King of France. Even now there are probably not more than two or three hundred tennis players in England. It is a game of a closed-in court and a stuffy smoky *dedans*, and, with all its excellent qualities, can never be popular. Cricket, on the other hand, is the game of the people. Wherever you see two or three English boys with a ball and a stick, their amusement naturally takes the shape of a rude kind of cricket. In the parks the little street-boys pile their coats up to make a wicket, and show a fine natural tendency to hit to square leg. Even

* See Lingard, Freeman, Florence of Worcester, *The Peterborough Chronicle*, Thaddeus of Warsaw.

little girls make a wicket of a tree, in Kensington Gardens, and bowl slows with soft balls. Every open space has its own small match going on, and on all that is left of village greens you always see the worn marks of the wickets. I speak of the south of England, the north has kicking and other diversions — the north, that is, far from the influences of Sheffield and Manchester.

'How much are we to get by the hour for this?' said the Northumbrian swains, when their squire presented them with a ground, wickets, bats, balls, and an oration explanatory of the rules. But even in Northumberland cricket is being planted chiefly by curates. Even in the remote parts of Scotland, 'the country of the wild Scots', cricket is being introduced. Moral reformers hope that it will partially take the place of the favourite local pastime, 'to woo a bonnie lassie when the kye come hame', a diversion not found to elevate the character of the parish.

Granting, then, the popularity and pre-excellence of the noble game, what is its origin, and what its history? Of course no one invented cricket. Like almost everything else, cricket was evolved. We have but lately moved away from the state of mind of Herodotus, who tells us that the Lydians invented games during a famine to occupy their minds, and prevent them from feeling hungry. The Lydians could not have played cricket without having their meals regular. Look how the bowling always slackens before luncheon, and how, after luncheon, the bowlers, like men refreshed with beef and beer, mow down the wickets. Mr George Meredith is not wrong; cricket requires beer and beef for its noble nurture. The writers on this topic have usually had the sportsman's love of a bit of learning, of a bit of Latin, but they have not been really serious scholars. Scientific study has not bent itself to the question of the origin of cricket; and the weather is too warm, as Nimrod found 'the pace too good to inquire'. Certainly the Phaeacians described by Homer in his *Odyssey* did not know cricket. Had they known it they would not have diverted their guests by empty exhibitions of their dexterity in holding catches. No; they would have pitched the stumps, and displayed their address at cricket. Chapman, however, in his translations, shows that he imagined Homer to have known stool-ball, from which amusement I shall attempt to derive the origin of cricket. In truth, Homer only says that Nausicaa played at ball with her maidens, but Chapman puts it thus:

'Nausicaa
With other virgins did at stool-ball play,
Their shoulder-reaching head-tires laying by,
Nausicaa, with her wrists of ivory,
The liking stroke struck.'

Here 'the liking stroke' answers to our old 'trial ball', which is an exploded institution. Chapman goes on, 'The queen now for the upstroke struck the ball', a technicality of which the meaning escapes us. But before considering stool-ball in particular, let us notice the various natural species into which all sport with balls and bats differentiates itself. First the players may return the ball to each other across a barrier, such as a net. Hence comes tennis, and the 'tennis with chases' which the Spaniards found among the Aztecs, and *balloon*, and lawn tennis. Next, each side may endeavour to drive the ball to a goal guarded by the opposite party. Hence come hockey, *La Crosse*, the Red Indian game, the Persian *tsigan* (whence *chicane*), and our polo. Again, the game may be to see which party will drive the ball into certain holes, or through certain hoops, in the smallest number of strokes. Hence comes the old Jeu de Malle, or Pell Mell, and hence come golf, and the modern form of pell mell — croquet. Again, the object may be to strike the ball to such a distance as will enable the player to traverse a given space before the ball can be returned by the other party. If the ball be thrown or bowled to the striker, this game develops into rounders, base-ball, or the old stool-ball. A stool (which could be carried about and pitched anywhere in a moment) took the place of our wickets. I have played cricket with a camp-stool for wicket, I am sorry to say, in the market-place of Zug. It was excellent sport till a tremendous slog over the bowler's head went straight for the Burgomaster's windows. Again, if the ball be not thrown to the striker, but hit off the ground by himself, perhaps with the aid of some simple mechanism, we have the games of *knur and spell*, *trap, bat and ball*, or, substituting for the ball a short piece of wood, sharpened at the ends, we have tip-cat. Every one has seen tip-cat played in the streets. The street-boys are constantly hitting the cat into the eye of the wayfaring man.

Now, as far as we can ascertain, cricket seems to have been evolved out of stool-ball, and *tip-cat*, or as it was called, *cat and dog*. From stool-ball was borrowed the primitive wicket — a stool, or *cricket* —

which (perhaps) gave its name to the pastime. From stool-ball too, we have the custom of tossing or bowling the ball to the striker. From *cat and dog* we borrow that part of the game which consists in running between two fixed points while the ball (at *cat and dog* the cat, or piece of wood) is being fielded or returned, by the other side.

Cat and dog is in one sense a classical game. Bunyan tells us that he was playing at it, and was just about to strike the cat, when he heard a supernatural voice bidding him forbear. I remember reading this passage in childhood, and fancying that Bunyan was torturing a poor puss, and that his heart was suddenly wrung by a sense of his own cruelty. But Bunyan was merely affected by a consciousness of the wickedness of primitive cricket. It seems that in some districts, *cat and dog* was less like *knur and spell*, or *trap, bat and ball*, than I have supposed. The cat was not hit up and then knocked away by the player, as in *tip-cat*, but was thrown or bowled to him, as at cricket. *Cat and dog*, as played in Scotland of old, is thus described in Jamieson's *Dictionary*: 'Three play at this game, who are provided with clubs; they cut out two holes, each a foot in diameter and seven inches in depth The distance between them is twenty-six feet. One stands at each hole with a club; these clubs are called dogs. A piece of wood, called a cat, about four inches long, and one inch in diameter, is thrown from one hole to another by a third person. The object is to prevent the cat from getting into the hole. Every time that it enters the hole, he who stands at that hole loses the club, and he who threw the cat gets possession of the club. If the cat be struck, he who strikes it changes places with the person who holds the other club, and as often as these positions are changed one is counted in the game by the two who hold the clubs, and are viewed as partners.' This is simply double wicket cricket, with holes in place of stumps, and a bit of wood for a ball. As every one knows, there was a hole between the two primitive stumps at cricket, till the middle of the eighteenth century. The question rises, is *cat and dog* an economical Scotch debasement of cricket, or are the stumps and ball later improvements on the prehistoric cat and hole in the ground? It may be argued either way. The shoeblack in *Rarenshoe* played fives with a brass button. But fives did not begin with the use of brass buttons, and I fancy balls are older (the Phaeacians used them) than cats, and that cats were a rustic substitute for a better article. A ball and club appear in the often copied Bodleian MS. of 1344, quoted by

Strutt. However we settle this question, it is certain that 'cat and dog', and stool-ball, between them, have all the elements of cricket, except, perhaps, the 'catching out' of players. Stumping was certain to come in, for human nature, on the side of the cat-thrower, would rise up against the holder of the dog, when he ran in too far.

As to the antiquity of the name of cricket in application to a game, we know very little, and do not seem likely to learn more. The chief argument for the lateness of the game is the absence of reference to cricket in the lists of sports which, in old times, were formally recommended or prohibited. In the fortieth year of Elizabeth a piece of ground at Guildford was claimed as public property, because boys had always played cricket on it when it was not being used for bear-baiting. About 1630, it is recorded (by a Puritan) that Maidstone was 'formerly a very prophane town', where 'stool-ball, cricketts', and other games were practised on the Lord's Day. Thus, at that early date, a distinction was already taken, even by a Puritan who was no sportsman, between cricket and stool-ball. Then we hear, I really don't know on what evidence – but all the cricket books give the story – of 'crickitt' played by the crews of English ships at Antioch, about 1680. The annals of Warwick declare that a match was played there in 1715. Very early in the eighteenth century the Artillery Ground, in Middlesex, was a home of cricket, whence the sport migrated to the White Conduit Ground, the grandmother of the MCC. Pope, Gray, Walpole, are all familiar with cricket. Sir Horace Mann, Walpole's friend, was a distinguished bat. Walpole congratulates himself that, even in his boyhood, he can 'remember no finer things' than a game of cricket, or a battle with a bargee. The bargee would probably, like his successor in Collingsby, have 'liked wopping' young Horace. In 1743 an Ass wrote thus in the *Gentleman's Magazine* – his stupid wisdom is valuable because it proves that our noble game was by 1742 thoroughly recognized in the highest circles – 'Cricket is certainly a very innocent and wholesome exercise. Yet it may be abused if either great or little people make it their business. It is greatly abused when it is made the subject of public advertisements, to draw together great crowds of people who ought all of them to be somewhere else.' Why, where could they be better, than watching the cricket of that time, the huge carved bats, some of them five pounds in weight, the game which knew not of blocking, and the hitting 'blooming hard, blooming high, and blooming often'! But the thoughtful writer in the *Gentleman's Magazine* was right in one point. Cricket was then, like racing now, a medium of speculation. Big matches were always played for very high stakes, betting was general, matches were sold, professional players were corrupted, and the harmless cricket field was little better than the nefarious turf of to-day. The contemporary poet complained that

> 'Our well-bred heirs
> Gamesters and jockeys turn, and cricket players.'

The cricket of that date is best understood by aid of old pictures and prints. A fine full-length view of the bat may be got from the little portrait group after Downman of a boy with his sisters. Downman was a nomadic artist who used to visit the houses of the nobility and gentry, and sketch their children in the pleasant water-colour drawings of which there is a portfolio in the British Museum. A friend of my own once had an interview, a *tête-à-tête*, I may say, with a burglar, in awkward circumstances. The burglar, though only a provincial practitioner, was armed with a 'grievous crab-tree cudgel' like Bunyan's Giant Despair, whereas my friend had no weapon of any description. Looking round him for a tool, his eye fell on a bat, with which he gently but firmly induced the burglar to take his departure, and saw him off the premises. But he complained that a bat was really an awkward, unhandy sort of weapon, not to be trusted in an affair of arms by reason of the thinness of its handle. Now the bat in the sketch is as grievous a cudgel as a householder (who did not wish to 'give the point') could desire to have handy. Observe the gradual thickening from the handle through the curved pod to the lump at the end. Here are none of the well-marked neat shoulders of the modern bat. No fear that the handle of the bludgeon will yield. But what an extraordinary, obsolete style of play does this bat indicate! The curved blade is not meant to stop a length ball — using this instrument you could not play with a straight bat, the very essence of the modern game. Again, compare the bat with that in the hands of the hitter in the print from a picture by Hayman. This bat is even still more crooked at the end, in fact it is an exaggerated hockey stick. The inference is that the crook of the primitive bat was made for hitting a grounder, grub, sneak, or daisy cropper, a ball which rarely rose off the ground in its course from the bowler's hand to the wicket. Indeed we see that this kind of delivery is being offered by the bowler in the picture. Every one knows how easy it is to hit a ball lying on the ground with the crook of a stick, and how little can be done with the other end. Therefore we may infer from the oldest bats alone, if we had no other evidence, that sneaks were the only style of bowling in times past, and that the batter, with his crooked, heavy club, tried to punish the sneaks as hard as he possibly could, without thought of defence, which was scarcely possible in the circumstances. The picture we have been criticizing represents a single wicket affair among country fellows. The fields are probably set rather at random, as the artist heppened to prefer. Indeed we must not rely too much on the evidence of art. Even in popular modern periodicals, sketches of cricket are often drawn by men who manifestly know nothing of the sport.

There is much more method in a very fine picture by Hayman of the Royal Academy Club in Marylebone Fields, which was exhibited some years ago at Burlington House. Here, as in the sketch last noticed, we find that the old short two stumps and the single bail are still in use, though both pictures are subsequent to the date when the hole between the stumps became obsolete. As every one knows, the third stump was added about 1775, because it was observed that the straightest balls went between the wickets without removing the bail. This, people may say, would at once have occurred to the feeblest capacity. But mark the conservatism of the human mind, and the march of evolution. There was originally no middle stump, because the batter, when regaining his ground after a run, placed his bat in the hole between the stumps, itself a survival from *cat and dog*. The hole was filled up, and a crease (cut at first, not marked in whitewash, as at present) was substituted, to prevent the bat from coming down on the hands of the wicket-keeper, as he put down the wicket by placing the ball in the hole. Yet, though men had got rid of the hole, they did not at once add a third stick, custom and use were too strong for them, and we see the old unfair two stumps in both the designs before us. Indeed they appear as late as 1793, in a picture of a match between Lord Winchilsea and Lord Darnley for £1000 a side. Mark also the height of the wickets. Their lowness, like the shape of the contemporary bat, testifies to the habit of bowling grubs. A modern ball would rise high over these wickets, which could only be knocked down by a shooter or a yorker, or perhaps a half volley. Next observe the dispositions of the field. There is a man out in the long field on, a mid on, and a square leg far out. There is a wicket-keeper, long stop, point, third man, long hit off, mid off, and cover point. Apparently hard, straight driving on the off side was not expected. The bowler holds the ball to his eye, like the immortal trundler of Dingley Dell. The game, in spite of odd wickets, odd bats, and low underhand deliveries, required a disposition of the field not unlike that to which we are accustomed. The long stop, of course, would now be superfluous among good players. The quaint little cut of cricket at Harrow in the old times teaches us very little, as the boys are not engaged in a formal game, and the fielders are set anyhow. Modern cricket was well under way towards its present perfection when (1774) a committee of noblemen and gentlemen met at the Star and Garter in Pall Mall and settled the laws. The stumps were still but twenty-two inches high, and only one bail was used. Nothing is said in these early laws about lbw. Obstructing the ball's progress to the wicket with the leg is first heard of in the scoring sheets towards the close of the century.

Here is a queer rule: 'When the ball is struck up, either of the players may hinder the catch in his running ground, or if she is hit directly across the wickets the other player may place his body anywhere within swing of his bat so as to hinder the bowler from catching her, but he must neither strike at her nor touch her with his hands.' By way of a final lesson from the old engravings we should note, in our second illustration, the scorer sitting at point, a sufficiently dangerous position, and 'notching' each run with a knife on a bit of lath. No minute scores were then kept, and even in much later times, as when Byron played (with Shakspeare) for Harrow, the name of the bowler from whom catches were made is seldom given. Perhaps bowlers then rarely bowled for catches.

The great authority on the middle period of the game, between the age of 'sneaks' and curved bats, and the age of round-hand bowling, is Nyren, whose *Young Cricketers' Tutor* is a very amusing and instructive little volume. John Nyren was born in 1764, and died in 1837. His father was a Hampshire yeoman, a great player in the old Hambledon Club, and Nyren had practical knowledge of the game, as a looker on or player, from the time of Sir Horace Mann to the youth of George Parr. Nyren was not a highly educated man, but he had a natural gift of writing, a keen eye for character, and a love of whatever is honest, manly, and good humoured. 'I learned a little Latin when I was a boy, of a worthy old Jesuit', he says, 'but I was a better hand at the fiddle, and many a time have I taught the gipsies a tune during their annual visits to our village, thereby purchasing the security of our poultry yard.' To the historical novelist looking out for a singular characteristic figure of old England, one may recommend the yeoman's son, with his Jesuit tutor, his fiddle, and his gipsy friends. Nyren says vaguely, that the use of the straight bat, with all that it involves, came in 'some years after 1746', when Lord John Sackville captained Kent in a match against England. The scores were very small in these days, when Prince Charles was shaking the throne of the House of Hanover. Kent got 40 and 70, England 53 and 58. But we have seen even smaller scores made by good men on wet wickets, as when the Australians for the first time played MCC. Nyren well remembered the introduction of the third stump. A single-wicket match between the Hambledon Club and England was played on May 22, 1775, and Small went in, the last wicket, to get fourteen runs. These he knocked off, but Lumpy's balls several times passed between his stumps, and the absurdity of this led to the change. Many feared it would shorten the game, but Nyren said it would make the batter redouble his care, and would improve the defence. Why Nyren was 'consulted by the Hampshire gentlemen', when, on his own showing, he was but eleven years of age, it is difficult to guess. Probably the veteran's memory was a little confused. In any case he was right about the third stump. The year after its introduction, Aylward, going in last but one for Hambledon against England, made 167, then considered a prodigious score, against the bowling of the redoubtable Lumpy. Between 1746, then, and 1776, cricket became all that it could be without round-hand bowling. Nyren speaks of Tom Sueter, who would stump men even off 'the tremendous bowling' of Brett, and who was the first to 'leave the crease to meet the ball' when batting. 'He would get in at it, and hit it straight off, and straight on, and, egad! it went as if it had been fired.' Tom was 'the pet of all the neighbourhood; so honourable a heart that his word was never questioned by the gentlemen who associated with him, and a voice which, for sweetness, power, and purity of tone (a tenor), would with proper cultivation, have made him a handsome fortune.'

Hambledon must have been a pleasant place in the days of these old worthies, with their cricket, their fiddles, their tenor voices, and honourable hearts. The old 'Bat and Ball' tavern is there still; Nyren's house, the bricks are alive to testify to it; but where is the cricket, and where are the fiddles? 'Many a treat have I had,' says Nyren, 'in hearing Lear and Sueter join in a glee at the "Bat and Ball" on Broad Halfpenny,' the old cricket ground. Where is Broad Halfpenny now? 'Where's Troy? and where's the May Pole in the Strand?' When we think of these ancient times we must not suppose that all men played in cocked hats and yellow mankin tights, though Mr Budd, to the last, clung to these vestments, and disclaimed pads. No. White was the wear as much in the days of the Hambledon Club as in our own. What says the Rev Mr Cotton, of Winchester, in his essay, lauding Broad Halfpenny above the plains of Alpheus and the Cronian Hill?

> 'The parties are met and arrayed all in white;
> Famed Elis ne'er boasted so pleasing a sight;
> Each nymph looks askance at her favourite swain,
> And views him, half stript, both with pleasure
> and pain.'

This costume was more sensible than the tall hats and rolls of flannel which a famous writer, Miss Mitford, derided when she saw them clothing stiff middle-aged cricketers at Lord's. But what caused the emotions of pain in the breasts of the Hambledonian nymphs when they viewed their admirers? Probably they trembled for the manly shins exposed, without the protection of pads, to the tremendous bowling of Brett. In much later days Mr Budd played Mr Brand, the swift bowler, a single-wicket match. Budd was so hit about the legs that he twice knocked down his own wicket, lest his wounds should stiffen in the night, if the game were prolonged into the second day. Under-hand bowling can certainly be very fast, and the swiftest amateur I ever knew was even more dangerous to life and limb when he bowled under-hand than when he bowled round-hand. But there was little 'work' (except what came from accidents of ground) on the old bowling. Lambert, in his *Guide to Cricket*, gave directions for twisting the ball, but Nyren did not believe the twist could be communicated intentionally. He admitted, however, that Lambert possessed a twist 'just the reverse way from the off stump into the leg. He was the first, I remember, who introduced this deceitful and teasing style of delivering the ball.'

298

But it is time to turn from these old days, when Sir Horace Mann walked about the ground in great excitement, 'cutting the daisies with his stick', and when Lord Frederick 'dashed down his white hat in a rage', because he could not bowl Tom Walker. The said Tom Walker 'began the system of throwing instead of bowling, now so much the fashion'. Of course, Nyren thought that all was over with cricket, that the game would degenerate into horse-play, all slogging on one side, and all swift wide balls on the other. No doubt there was room for apprehension. Most young bowlers aimed only at pace. Length and spin were neglected. But time has proved the best judge. All the *a priori* arguments were against over-hand. All the facts are on its side. If we want proof that cricket is better than of old, look at the long scores, and look at the bowling and wicket-keeping. So straight is the swiftest bowling, and so good the wicket-keeping, that long-stop's occupation is gone, and he can be placed wherever he is wanted in the field. It must be admitted that the number of byes on this system is occasionally excessive. For example, in the dull weather-spoiled match between the Australians and England, played at Manchester on July 11 and 12, the byes were too many in the second innings of England, namely, 18 out of 180. But, in the 182 of the Australian innings, there were no byes at all. Considering that Ulyett was one of the bowlers, this speaks very highly for the wicket-keeping of Pilling. Tom Sueter, with his sweet tenor voice and honourable heart, could not have rivalled Pilling's performance, I presume. There were only five byes in the innings of 403, when Aylward made 167 for Hambledon against England, but then England must have had a long-stop; they never dreamed of playing without one. The great attention now paid to the state of the wicket, of course, makes the labours of the wicket-keeper more easy, and compels the bowler to get as much work as possible on to his balls. Nyren marvelled at Lambert's break back as a kind of miracle; now a bowler will often make the ball twist from either side at will, as Attewell did, with remarkable success, when the rain just saved the Australians from a prodigious beating at Huddersfield.

It is impossible to speak of the cricket of to-day without thinking at once of the Australians. They give the game an interest which it used to lack in most cases. Who cares very much whether Surrey beats Middlesex, or Middlesex beats Surrey! We are not depressed, such of us as bear the grand old name of gentleman, if the players lower the

299

proud banners of our Order at Lord's. But we do care, and we are depressed, when the Kangaroo defeats the British Lion, and drives him, as in the nursery rhyme, 'all through the town'; or, at least, all over the ground. Australia *v.* England is even more exciting than Oxford *v.* Cambridge, or Eton *v.* Harrow. I daresay the old boys who are designed here, and who occupy the best seats at the public school matches, would rather see their school defeated than their country vanquished. When one's University beats both Cambridge and the colonists, *then* a man can hold his head up. But, of the two, I would rather be beaten by Cambridge, if only England can cause wailing by the banks of the Yarra Yarra and the Murrumbidgee. The Australians this year seem to have begun by 'playing low'. Perhaps they did not quite get into their best and true form at once. At Oxford, and when so terribly defeated by MCC, they seemed to lose heart. 'There were eight captains in the field', and the batting was slovenly, when it was seen that the runs could not be made. At Huddersfield, too, when Scotton, Mr Hirst, Attewell and others hit so furiously, the Australians seem to have begun by taking matters too easily. But they quite recouped themselves when they beat the Gentlemen at the Oval. They won the match against the Players by the execrable fielding of the Professionals. But then the Colonists had lost the match against the North of England by their own bad fielding. You cannot give Mr Hornby six lives with impunity. The real strength of the Australians lies in a department where no labour will enable us to equal them. The bowler is born, not made, and the Australians are born bowlers. Bowling is in the air of the land of the spear and the boomerang, their native missile weapons. Englishmen who have played there say that a good style and plenty of twist are qualities common to all the bowlers, even in obscure country towns. These qualities, with endurance and hard work, are extremely remarkable in men like Mr Spofforth, Mr Palmer, Mr Giffen and Mr Boyle. We have nothing quite like them in England. Our amateur fast bowlers are seldom very difficult. Mr Christopherson, who is still very young, seems the best and most promising. Our professional fast bowlers have their day, but you never can depend so absolutely on them as on Mr Spofforth and Mr Palmer. Now we can no more make bowlers than we can make poets; to be sure our bowlers are better than our modern poets, but they are not quite good enough. Again, the Australians can all bat. Now if we except Mr Alfred

Lyttelton, who scarcely ever finds time to play, and Mr Kemp, what wicket-keeper have we to win a match by stubborn defence and hard hitting, as Mr Blackham can do? Can we expect a long score in an emergency from Pilling or Sherwin, or, among bowlers, from Peate, though none of these men are bad bats? Such are the advantages of the Australians. They have the pull in bowling, and in the universal power of run getting which pervades the team. In fielding they are nearly on our own level, certainly not better, though we naturally howl out when our own men drop catches, and only feel relieved when the Australians do so. In batting, I venture to think that our representatives excel. Their style is more finished. In Macdonnell and Bonnor the Australians have fine hitters; in Bannerman and Murdoch stubborn defence. Moreover, the hitters do not lack defence, nor the 'strikers' power to hit. But, for a brilliant combination of all a batsman's best points, with pluck and judgement, perhaps no Colonial player can equal Mr Steel, as we saw him in the second innings of the Gentlemen at Lord's; or Mr Grace, or Ulyett on his day, though that day, somehow, does not dawn when it is most desired.

However, the decisive matches between England and Australia have still to be played at the moment when these lines are written. Let us hope that England will show more pluck than in that hideous exhibition at Manchester, when the last five wickets only scored eight runs, and when Mr Lucas went in too late. Neither Flowers, Attewell, Mr C. T. Studd, nor Mr Alfred Lyttelton played on that occasion, nor has Mr J. G. Walker been tried, while many other names occur. We have about thirty excellent players after the first five or ten, and if we could only see, with the eye of prophecy, which is in his best form, we might easily beat the proud invader. But cricket must always be very much a game of chance, depending on weather, on umpire's decision, on the accidents of light and wind, of health and digestion. Accident, however, will not help a team to win three decisive matches, and let us hope that the draw at Manchester may be set aside, and the three great events played out after all. These are the things the country really and undeniably cares about; whether it cares very much about that other match between Lords and Commons we only learn on the authority of professional politicians. So let us say farewell to cricket in the words of the old song of the old Hambledon Club, a somewhat stoical and pagan song for a clergyman to have written:

'And when the game's o'er, and our fate shall draw nigh,
For the heroes of cricket, like others, must die,
Our bats we'll resign, neither troubled nor vexed,
And give up our wickets to those that come next.
          Derry down, &c.'

English Illustrated Magazine 1884

39

Recollections of Cricket

Frederick Gale

I was very cross for a moment with Mr Andrew Lang, as, on looking back to a number of this magazine – No. 12, September, 1884 – I found that in his charming article on cricket contained therein, the artist, doubtless at his suggestion, had reproduced my favourite picture at Lord's, *The Royal Academy Club in Marylebone Fields*, by F. Hayman, R.A., which I had in my eye for this article. To tell the truth, I was ignorant of the fact that Mr Lang had published a cricket article until it was pointed out to me, and my temper came back again when I read it through and found that I was wholly released from re-treading the oft-trodden ground of the earlier history of the game, a perfect compendium of which is contained in his writing. So I am free to write now of the many changes which I have seen during the last half century – and even a little before the beginning of it, as I saw in 1837, when fourteen years old, the first match ever played between Kent and Nottingham at Town Malling, which was the hot-bed of Kent Cricket; and as I played against Eton and Harrow at Lord's in 1841, and came to London in the following year, I am now doing my fiftieth year at Lord's. But I am a perfect boy in experience compared with my old friend Mr George Richmond, R.A., who finished his twenty-third year at Lord's as a spectator in 1890; or with Lord Verulam, a pretty regular attendant now, who played as a Harrow boy against Winchester and Eton in 1825, as did Cardinal Manning, who doubtless would be received with great honour if he visited the Pavilion to see Harrow play once more. Would not the boys cheer him just? I shall use Mr Lang's article and illustrations as one of those Consolidation Acts which are incorporated with a modern Act of Parliament. I shall venture to add one little thing to the many authorities which Mr Lang quotes in his article in illustration of the fact that many points in our

game of cricket spring from reports of the ancients, Greek and Roman
– or pre-historical, and it is as follows: In a note, 'Pila Velox' (*vide* Hor.
Sat. Lib. II. Sat. II. Line xi) it is written, 'Romana iuventus in Campo
Martio frequenter ludebat pila seu paganinaca seu trigonali; in qua
sinistrae usus praecipuus traditur magis quam dextrae; corporis autem
agilitas maxime valebat ut sciret apte pilam jacere atque excipere;
modo incurrere modo recurrere,' and in a previous note (*vide* Hor. *Sat*.
Lib. I. Sat. V. Pila), 'Trigonalis sive trigon. Nomen a triangulari situ
ludentium ternorum qui sibi invicem ita pilam reddebant, diligenter
caventes ne excederet manu, sive dextra sive sinistra.' Now if I was on a
cricket ground I should say, 'If this is *not* practising fielding I will eat
my hat!' But this would look rude in this magazine so I will substitute,
'I should be *much* surprised.' And as a first remark on cricket of to-day I
most heartily wish that many of the countless armies of cricketers who
think that 'practice' means simply going to the nets and batting,
would have a game of 'trigonalis' or 'paganica', and also try to learn a
little bowling, and to pitch a length, as their forefathers did, but
which they hire professionals to do.

If they would do this we should see fewer catches dropped in grand
matches, and more change bowling amongst amateurs. There is
another lesson to be learnt from two of the illustrations in Mr Lang's
article, namely *Cricket in 1743*, and that before alluded to – both of
which are to be seen in the pavilion at Lord's – which is, that in 1743
the scorer or 'notcher' is sitting where point *ought to* and *used* to be,
about seven or eight yards from the wicket, instead of fourteen yards
off, as point commonly now is; whereas in the picture of the Royal
Academy Club, which represents cricket of a date something like
thirty years later, the 'notchers' are sitting outside the watchers on the
off side from the striker, and the field are many of them placed on the
off side. This clearly proves that hard-off hitting came in between
1743 and thirty years later, as a man sitting down seven yards from the
striker 'notching' – as scoring was called – the scoring being done by
cutting notches in a stick – would not be alive for five minutes with a
modern hard-off hitter at the wicket. That picture of 1743 has been
reproduced so many times and even now may be seen done in tessel-
lated tiles in the lobby of some large taverns, that every cricketer must
know it.

A great-uncle of mine who was a Winchester boy in 1771 – which is probably about the date of the Royal Academy Club picture — told me that some of the boys played cricket, but it was by no means the prominent game in the school. At that date the two stumps, twenty-two inches high and six inches wide, with a single bail, existed, the third stump being added in 1775.

When the Badminton cricket volume was published the Editor did me the honour to ask me to write 'Country Cricket', and I taxed my memory hard to give a sketch of a village match — the first I ever saw — in 1830, mentioning the names and descriptions of some of the players; and curiously enough I was told by a gentleman at whose house I was staying in Kent last year that he heard the article criticized by one of the players mentioned in it — and who is alive now — and the verdict was that my description of a match now sixty years ago was quite accurate. For, shortly to epitomize, it was to the effect that the running, throwing, and catching were excellent; the under-arm bowling was well pitched and straight, and I distinctly remember the 'on-break'. Taking an era five years later on, when I went to a public school and began my cricket fagging in 1835, and daily for six years had the opportunity of seeing the Bishop of St Andrews, then the Rev. Charles Wordsworth, second master of Winchester, *aetat.* 28 (who played for Harrow in 1825), playing in College Meads, and being afterwards one of his cricket pupils when a big boy, I think the evidence is overwhelming that in the main points as regards hand, eye, pluck, courage and skill, the tradition of the game handed down by living memories must be true — that the game as a game was precisely as good seventy-five years ago as to-day. Of course the billiard table grounds and the fact of great players constantly meeting the same bowling have given facilities for advancing the science of the game. The Bishop of St Andrews was considered one of the finest fields, one of the best lob bowlers, and played with as straight a bat as any one could see. As regards boys I crave leave to repeat once more what I have often said in respect to fagging at sports, that when parents write to the papers and complain of their boys being compelled to join in or fag at manly sports, they are doing their sons an absolute wrong. These complaints come from those who never were at a public school, for if they had been they would have known that the whole making of a boy's character depends on his always being accountable for his time to the prefects, as it keeps him from coddling himself round the fire in the winter, or loafing at the pastrycook's, either of which is as bad for a boy as drinking and idling are for a man. Besides all this, he learns games which are a great amusement in after-life. Of course sometimes a prefect is a bully, just as there are bullies in every profession and calling in life.

One of the main differences between past and present cricket is that 'condition' was the *sine qua non* of a cricketer formerly. Many men had to walk several miles to a match and home; all runs had to be run out, and the ball had to be fetched home by the field unless hit out of the ground or into a hedge, or some other obstructor, where it could not be got out. Old John Bowyer, in the earlier part of this century, who played much at Lord's, used to walk from his house at Mitcham to Dorset Square — a fair eleven miles — and back every day in the summer *plus* a long day's cricket; and many others did the same. I knew the old man well from 1865 until 1880, when he died, *aetat*. 90, and he never had a day's illness, and I saw him in his coffin, and he was buried with a cricket bat screwed on to the lid. Then again it was expected of a cricketer not only to be able to run, throw, and catch, but constantly to practise all these things — as they did, as the Roman youth practised the 'trigonalis' and 'paganica'; and in a match a fieldsman would be expected to go where he was told — though more than often there was some special watch at which he was most useful; and he was also expected to relieve long stop on any change or emergency, for if he could not play long stop he could not field, and was out of place in the eleven. The fact was that cricketers had to learn every part of the game, bowling included, as there were few if any professionals. The bowling might not be first rate, but it did for practice, as, if it was easy and was punished, so much the better for those who were practising fielding. Boys also had to learn how to make a pitch on any ground with the aid of a five-pronged fork, a watering pot and a turf beater, in places like an open down where a roller was not available; and above all things how to lay out an eleven and cover the ground on downs and open spaces like Chatham lines, Woolwich Common or Blackheath, where a hard hit or a bye from a swift bowler would go for seven or even eight runs if it was not covered.

On reading a short pamphlet published by a player named Boxall in 1802, and dedicated to the Marylebone Club (and reproduced in *Cricket* at the commencement of this year) I found an absolute confirmation of a statement which I have often made to young England of to-day, and about which many are incredulous, and it is that an old-fashioned eleven in the field would stop half the boundary fourers which are so easily made to-day. And they would do it on the old plan, which was common in my earlier days, of shutting the batsman in by a set of fieldsmen much nearer the wicket than they stand now, and by having four fieldsmen deep out North, South, East and West, except when the batsman is a notorious striker, who never hits hard by. This arrangement enabled the in-fieldsmen to make a dash at every ball within reach, knowing that if they missed it an out-fieldsman who covered them would reduce the hit to a 'twoer', and the ball would not go away into space. This was Fuller Pilch's theory of 'you must give away "two notches",' as he called them, 'but keep them fourers off the slate.'

To sum up the whole matter in a few words, I think the older school used their in-field men more for harassing the batsmen than many captains of to-day, and never dreamt of leaving a large boundary open and undefended behind, or on any side of the wicket, and they relied most on bowling and fielding as their sheet anchors, leaving the batting — much of which was very excellent — to the chances of war, as no one can tell who will make runs on any given day, and you will generally see in modern scores that often two or three get most of the runs.

In the pamphlet which I quoted above I found an excellent maxim laid down which in my boyhood was much acted up to, as I well remember, which is a recommendation to young cricketers to have a wicket carefully pitched, and to practise bowling by trying to hit a feather or small paper mark placed in front of the wicket, at different distances for different styles of batting, and to practise at it constantly until the movement of hand, arm, feet and quickness of eye become almost mechanical. Alas! who practises bowling now amongst our amateurs? — I mean sheer earnest drill with the ball. Boys on village greens learn their cricket well by constant practice. George Yonge who played for Eton in 1841, and who bowled for years in Gentlemen v. Players, told me that when unexpectedly summoned to Lord's for that match he was in Wales, miles away from any cricket, and practised bowling in an orchard against an old apple tree, and came up in rare form to London.

There is a recent paper written by the Earl of Bessborough about the past. I remember him fifty years ago when the MCC entrusted him with getting up elevens of England or the Gentlemen's elevens at Lord's, and the captaincy of them. The paper appeared in Archdeacon Montgomery's book *Cricket and Cricketers*, 1890, last year. He sums the pith of his experience up in one sentence, i.e., 'that he never remembered the time when there were not many superior players'. This is the real truth. He was one of the most painstaking cricketers I ever saw, and he was much trusted by gentlemen and players. His attention was riveted on the game whether in the field, or when his side was in, and he was a very good cricketer as well. There were five splendid MCC umpires in those days whose names are now historical— W. Caldecourt, John Bailey of Mitcham, Tom Barker and Bartholomew Good, both of Notts; and Tom Sewell of Mitcham, all of whom were attached to Lord's, some of them from boyhood. Their decisions were never disputed. The bowling was not higher than the shoulder in those days, and the law of 'leg before wicket' was much more stringent against the batsman, as an equitable construction was put on the law, and the line of the ball was guessed from the bowler's hand in delivery to the wicket, so that the bowler saw all three stumps, and the batsman took guard to where the bowler's hand would be, and played 'the line of the ball', and knew exactly where he ought *not* to put his leg. And moreover after 'pads' were invented they were much smaller and much less closely stuffed than now, and were intended simply for protection against serious injury from bowling, much of which, ever since I can remember, was as quick as the quickest now, to wit that of Redgate, Alfred Mynn, 'the Lion of Kent', a grand and Herculean cricketer, and Sir Frederick Bathurst fifty years ago, of Harvey Fellows, Jackson the 'demon' of Notts, Tarrant and Wisden later on, down to the days of Spofforth, Demon number two, well known to all of this day. Before the days of— I will say— 'trespass on the popping crease', a batsman was struck on the pads once to every ten times of to-day, when the pad is looked on as a second defence by dishonest batsmen. However, public opinion and common sense have much abated this evil.

I listen very attentively and with some amusement when my old friend Mr George Richmond talks to me about the splendid play of Bill Beldham, who commenced his career with the MCC in 1787 on the site of Dorset Square, of Searle, Saunders and Mr Parry, and the heroes who shone soon after Waterloo. He is equally enthusiastic about 'the Doctor' and the Lytteltons and Walkers; and Alfred Shaw and Spofforth and Blackham, and all those whom he has seen since, and I *don't* call him a 'laudator temporis acti'. I put him in the same category as Lord Bessborough, as one who has had an enormous experience, and sees good in men of all ages. His lordship says that what strikes him is that the old-fashioned players were men who on more difficult grounds formerly had to study the great art of watching the ball and putting the face of the bat on it; and he says that he considers that the Doctor and A. G. Steel are the best exponents of what was the old game.

And now, having been asked, to give a few notes of my experiences; first explaining that I drop all prefixes for brevity's sake — distinguishing amateurs by their initials, calling players by their surnames only, and also calling the Australians by their surnames only (unless there are two of a name), just as we in talking of Oxford or Cambridge men or public school boys style them Jones, Brown or Robinson without a prefix.

Nets behind the wicket have been cruel enemies to cricket. Many of the best players, amateur and professional, learnt their first cricket as long stops and fags at school, or as grounds boys on public grounds, or as boys who lived on village greens and for a few halfpence would long stop or watch out all the afternoon — not forgetting little boys in the street who play their mimic game with a home-made bat out of a piece of board and a wooden ball. These early beginnings of cricket teach a boy to get a good sight, and to learn the run of a ball, and how to handle her and to find out that a 'cricket ball boldly faced never hurts'. The theory is admirable, though not perhaps quite true, but the exceptions prove the rule; but the fact is that any one who funks a ball is sure to get hurt.

It is never too late to mend. On change of residence from London to Mitcham in 1865 I found to my great joy that there was one of the finest village greens in England for good turf in Mitcham. It was late, at forty-two years of age, to begin again, but I did, and went on playing until I was sixty, and then my cross-sight went. I could see to bat well enough, but at point or short slip I could not see the ball after it had left the bat. So in 1865 I began again as long stop in practice on the green and found a regular 'new skin' coming on me, and with the aid of many professionals who lived there and thereabouts, and playing against good bowlers, with sixpence on the wicket, I picked up quite enough to give me many hours and days of enjoyment for many years, to say nothing of coaching up little boys of six years of age and onwards, and mixing much in the society of good old cricketers who 'minded the time when Squire Brown — the very best they ever saw', etc. etc. etc. You can supply the vacuum with reminiscences of old men's talk. Remember there were no boundaries on that green, and every ball had to be fetched home, and if we unfortunately lost a match the first thing which our critics looked at in the score was the list of 'extras'; and if there were few byes, etc., they were satisfied that we had done our best. But if, as captain, I had played a match without a boundary well guarded, and I had let byes and 'snicks' and 'tips' go for four or six runs, the whole crowd would have hooted at me. At school our bowling grew by the simple fact that all had to learn it as well as they could — some well, some indifferently; and at school, and as I observed later in life on Mitcham Green, boys got out with a ball and practised throwing and catching at odd times constantly. And in making out our elevens at school and in country villages, bowling and fielding, especially the latter, were the claims most urgently pressed.

Boys at school practised bowling at a single stump with one bail on the top, and pitched at a piece of paper or a feather, as above described. Many were attempting round arm the height of the shoulder, much of which was very erratic, but a large proportion practised round hand proper— which was allowed in 1828 by MCC law, *i.e.*, with the back of the hand uppermost and the arm extended about as high as the hip with the hand under the elbow; and many acquired great excellence, as regards pitch and break. Sir Frederick Bathurst, who was before my time at Winchester, never bowled in any other way, and he bowled more 'leg-shooters' than any one I ever saw, and formed one of the Gentlemen of England Eleven for a period extending over twenty-one years. During the few first years of his career as a Gentleman bowler, Harvey Fellows, who came out as an Eton boy in 1841, bowled much in the same style as Sir Frederick, and he was the terror of the professionals, but he raised his arm higher afterwards. Hillyer of Kent, one of the finest bowlers of any day, had a somewhat low delivery, as had Tom Adams of Kent (still alive), but all were below the shoulder, until Willsher of Kent and Southerton of Surrey (formerly of Sussex) 'went very much up stairs', as the crowd said; and within the last twenty years the 'very much up stairs' (which means carrying the bowling hand to any height) is the prevalent fashion. The thorough under-arm bowlers were Clarke of Notts, who came out very late in life and was forty-five years old when he was retained at Lord's and completely upset the tactics of the best batsmen in England; and later on, a little more than thirty years ago, V. E. Walker, the *only* V. E. Walker, followed suit, and with his slows, his wonderful fielding off his own bowling, his captaincy, and batting made him such a tower of strength to his side as we can hardly expect to see again. Good 'slows' now are very like the black swans, *rarae aves.* I always bracket V. E. Walker with C. G. Taylor of Sussex (one of the fifty years ago amateurs), A. G. Steel, and Alfred Lyttelton, as four amateurs who never *were* excelled by any four in any age— I must say as 'Cardinals', for of course W. G. Grace is the 'Pope', and has a chair quite to himself, as the eighth wonder of the world, and he is, I am happy to say, still to be seen alive and kicking.

Now there is very little room to do anything else except to speak of eras. Let us take 1840 as the date of my first regular introduction to the grand cricketers, when Kent, Sussex and Nottingham were the strongest counties in England. In those days Lillywhite (Sussex), Hillyer (Kent), and Cobbett (Surrey) brought round arm bowling the height of the shoulder, which was never surpassed. Alfred Shaw many years later on stood alone as the master of the same art. I told him, on his asking me at Lord's about the excellency of Lillywhite, Hillyer and Cobbett, when he prefaced his query by remarking that Lord Bessborough had spoken to him of their excellence — this namely, 'If a match was to be played for my life, and those three were alive, and in the form they used to be, and that you and Mr A. G. Steel and Peate were on the same side, all at your best, and you asked me who should bowl first, I should say, "Put the names into a bag and pull out two at a time; I don't care who bowls first of you six, for I never saw six better".' Redgate, Notts, and Alfred Mynn, Kent, were the terrific bowlers, the latter being also a grand batsman. Pilch was the pioneer of the splendid forward play, killing the ball in front of the crease and 'placing it' just as W. Grace does to-day; Wenman was a splendid back player, and Guy of Notts, and F. P. Fenner of Cambridge (now *aetat.* 80) were grand cricketers. Box and Wenman were pioneers of the brilliant wicket keeping of to-day. Charley Taylor, Sussex, was the A. G. Steel of his day, and so the story may run on truthfully. And now turning to 1850 onwards, and remembering that many of the lions of 1840 were still alive, there were William Nicholson, the MCC wicket-keeper and a good bat also; Charles Ridding, the best long-stop in England, without whom the Gentlemen could not bowl. Alfred Mynn and Harvey Fellows at Lord's; R. T. King and N. Felix, each 'king of points'; A. Haygarth the stone-waller who broke the heart of all the bowlers and was content with two or three runs an hour; the Hon. E. Grimston, Harrow and Oxford, and Parr (George) the finest leg hitter ever seen. In 1860 onwards the celebrated Surrey Eleven consisted of Surrey born cricketers captained by Fred Miller (a young amateur who supported the game loyally by hard work and money), and most of them young men from village greens, were carrying counties and even All England before them. V. E. Walker, captain, W. F. Maitland, R. A. H. Mitchell, C. G. Lyttelton (now Lord Lyttelton), Carpenter, Hayward, Tarrant, Jackson, Anderson, Daft and Parr (George) was not a bad England Eleven; and if I mistake not those names, or many of them, were to be found in V. E. Walker's English Eleven. Then in 1870 onwards there were the Walkers, Graces, Lubbocks, Lytteltons, the Shaws, Nottingham; Emmett, Freeman and Pinder of Yorkshire, etc., etc., etc. You see I write three 'et ceteras' because I shall not go on any more, and leave the last twenty years to be explained by those who saw all the play. Now please don't say, 'He has not mentioned blank or blank.' I am only giving samples. I must mention one of to-day whom we don't see very often, as he is engaged in his profession − W. H. Patterson of Kent, who throughout his career has been unsurpassed as a safe man for runs on a really bad, rough or wet wicket, and a grand field too. As to the late Hon. Robert Grimston, he may be summed up thus: 'A fearless batsman, not elegant in any other part of the game, but the noblest supporter of it amongst rich and poor ever known.' Lord Bessborough was I think perfectly right when he said that the Australians woke us out of a lethargic state as regarded fielding; and their visits have done a great deal of good, and most certainly they have shown us many brilliant performances. The mistake is that they try to do too much in the time, and when accidents occur their eleven get overtaxed sometimes. Our modern game is somewhat cramped owing to the enormous crowds. I should much like to see two modern elevens play on an open ground, and watch what the captains would do with their field, and how they would get on with no one behind wicket-keeper and a quick bowler on. Those 'fourer byes' are the blot on the game. The captain may do as he pleases and leave a whole side open and lose four after four — *that* is bad captaincy; but to play without anyone behind wicket-keeper *because he can only lose four*, and to leave on the score thirty or even forty byes or more, is rather a poor performance, according to the rules of Chivalry.

Well, cricket, after all, is only a game, but the noblest game in the world. It was not the tall hat of the past, which amuses young England so, which made cricket good or bad. What made it good was due to a quick eye under the tall hat, a big heart and good temper, and constant practice in every branch of the game. The grand matches of to-day are public tournaments, the funds for which are supplied by the gate-money; and when the weather is fine and the wicket like a billiard table, some of the exhibitions of batting by the batsmen much resemble one of Roberts's wonderful breaks at his favourite game. And it is on a wicket of this kind that one can test the powers of a bowler.

In days gone by gate money would not pay expenses as now, and the game was supported by lovers of it, just as in the case of those counties which some called 'second class' and 'minor counties'; and please pardon old-fashioned men, like the writer, for saying that our sympathies are *more* with those who by self-sacrifice of time and money and hard work do the best they can with the material which they have to hand to build up a County Eleven in a new district, than with those exhibition matches in populous cities: and my belief is that if all the great exhibition grounds and their staff and commanders were swept away tomorrow, it would make no difference in the love of the game, as cricket now is so indigenous to the soil in England and every country wherever Anglo-Saxons go, that nothing can root it out.

English Illustrated Magazine 1891

40

Cricketers I Have Met

C. B. Fry

Half the charm of playing cricket is that you knock up against men as they really are. There is something in the game that smothers pretence and affectation, and gives air to character. You cannot be a cricketer and stay in your shell, your inwardness must come out in your play. Most people devoted to the game have quite forgotten the use of their shells, if they ever had them. Cricket finds the truth even more surely than wine does: so it speaks well for human kind that no pleasanter fellow is to be met than the typical cricketer. Perhaps the game and its conditions give small scope for what is ungracious in man, or one may see the rosy side only of individuals in this connection. A nicer belief is that by playing cricket people save themselves from becoming what by nature they are not. An optimistic view? Well, optimism goes well with cricket. No one who can hit a fourer, bowl a yorker, or hold a swinging drive at long-on has any right to regard life otherwise than as desirable. Skill in cricket may not be the greatest good, but possessed even in a moderate degree, it can help more than many other possessions towards happiness. The game is full of fresh air and sunshine, internal as well as external. There is a generous life in it, simplicity and strength, freedom and enthusiasm, such as prevailed before things in general became quite as complex and conventional as nowadays. One gets from cricket a dim glimpse of the youth of the world. And cricket hurts nobody — it has even sufficient intrinsic nobility not to hurt itself. There is nothing in it that makes for what is mean or narrow. To have become deeply mixed up with money without deteriorating in the process is test enough of soundness and merit. A form of recreation free from all tendency to degrade either those who play or those who pay must have much to recommend it, if one may judge from what has happened elsewhere. There is no need to sigh for the good old days of cricket. Times are not so bad. People bat and bowl a bit better and know more of the game than they used to. Huge crowds congregate to amuse themselves looking on. There is money in the game and hosts of professionals — good luck to them! But the same old game is with us yet awhile to foster skill of hand and eye, suggest pleasant acquaintances, breed strong friendships and coin striking personalities.

What, then, has come out of cricket lately? The brightest figure is Kumar Shri Ranjitsinhji, whom we all love for his supple wrist, silk shirt, and genial ways. A volume might be written about him, for he contains much besides runs. Viewed as a cricketer, he is decidedly a subject for appreciation — except to bowlers. He makes enormous scores with the consistency so dear to the British heart, and makes them by such original methods. There is little of the old school about Ranji. But then he is a genius, and none the worse for it. There is that in his strokes which baffles the most confident analyst. One feels inclined to say with a certain profane cricketer, 'Come, Ranji, this isn't cricket, it's infernal juggling!' But fortunately it is cricket, and the very best. No one ever wants him to stop getting runs. It is so exciting to wonder what is coming next, and there is no waiting. Even bowlers find a sneaking pleasure in seeing him spoil their analyses. They want to discover how he does it. Fielders do not mind scouting-out, as W.G. calls it, for hours when Ranji is in. He provides fun and new sensations. As for the man in the crowd, he has come many miles for this, and is proportionately pleased. From the average batsman's point of view Ranji is a marvel and a despair. 'Yes, he can play,' said someone once: 'but he must have a lot of Satan in him.' Certainly one would not be surprised sometimes to see a brown curve burnt in the grass where one of his cuts has travelled, or blue flame shiver round his bat in the making of one of those leg-strokes. Yet there is nothing satanic about Ranji except his skill. He is mellow and kind and single-hearted, and has no spark of jealousy in his composition. No one has a keener eye for what is good in other people; the better they play the more he likes it. He is a cricketer to the tops of his slim fingers, an artist with an artist's eye for the game. With the stroke that scores four to leg when the ball was meant to go over the bowler's head he has no sympathy. He is very amusing on the subject of what he calls 'cuts-to-leg'. Apart from their value to his side, Ranji's big innings please him in proportion as each

315

stroke approaches perfection. He tries to make every stroke a thing of
beauty in itself, and he does mean so well by the ball while he is in. His
great success is partly due to this attitude of mind; but there are other
reasons why he is, on all but the stickiest of wickets, the best bat now
playing. He starts with one or two enormous advantages, which he has
pressed home. He has a wonderful power of sight which enables him to
judge the flight of a ball in the air an appreciable fraction of a second
sooner than any other batsman, and probably a trifle more accurately.
He can therefore decide in better time what stroke is wanted, and can
make sure of getting into the right position to make it. So he is rarely
caught, as most of us are, doing two things at once — moving into an
attitude and playing at the ball simultaneously. Even in cases where
body movement is part of the stroke he is the gainer, for besides
quickness of judgement he has an extraordinary quickness of execution. Practically he has no personal error. His desire to act and his
action seem to coincide. This enables him to make safely strokes that
for others to dream of attempting would be folly. But with far less
natural quickness Ranji would have been a great cricketer for the
simple reason that he is a great observer, with the faculty for digesting
observations and acting upon them. He takes nothing on trust. He sees
a thing, makes it his own and develops it. Many of his innumerable
strokes were originally learnt from other players, but in the process of
being thought out and practised, have improved past recognition.
This is due partly to his natural powers — eye, quickness and elasticity
— and partly to his hatred of leaving anything he takes up before
bringing it to the highest pitch of which he is capable. At present he is
engaged upon a new stroke that makes his friends' hair stand on end.
Before the season is over he will have scored many a hundred runs with
it. 'As if you hadn't enough strokes already!' sighs William Murdoch.
Ranji has made a science of taking liberties. One may fairly suspect
him of regarding Tom Richardson's best ball as bowled in the interest
of cutting and driving rather than with a view to hitting the sticks.
Not that he ever despises bowling, however cavalierly he may seem to
treat it. While at the wickets he takes it entirely under his own
management. It is a musical instrument upon which he plays, often
improvising; a block of stone which he carves into shape to his taste,
not with vague smashing blows, but with swift, firm, skilful strokes.
His work has a fine finish; there is nothing crude or amateurish about

it. And such a touch! It may be of interest to know that Ranji has worked very hard indeed at cricket. Some of his strokes have cost months of careful net-practice. He does nothing blindly. He thinks about the game, starts a theory, and proceeds to find out what use it is. Some of his strokes again were discovered by accident. For instance, his inimitable leg-play began thus: When a boy he started with the usual fault of running away from every fast ball that threatened to hit him. But instead of edging off towards square-leg, as most boys do, he used, with characteristic originality, to slip across the wicket towards point. Suddenly he found out that by moving the left leg across towards the off, keeping his bat on the leg side of it and facing the ball quite squarely with his body, he could watch the ball on to the bat and play it away to leg with a twist of the wrist. Nowadays he can place to leg within a foot of where he wishes almost any ball that pitches between wicket and wicket. His back play is as safe as a castle, and he scores with it repeatedly. His idea is that to be a good bat a mastery of both back and forward play is necessary, but that of the two the former is the more important. He has a slight prejudice against forward play for forcing strokes. There is a moment in a forward stroke when the ball is out of sight and the stroke is being played on faith, so that if the ball does anything unexpected, or the judgement is at all at fault it is mere chance whether the stroke be good or bad. This opinion is amply borne out by the fact that players who depend entirely upon forward strokes cannot make runs consistently except on true wickets. Why does he ever get out? Perhaps he knows himself. There may be reasons, but they are not apparent.

Perhaps Stanley Jackson would be a good authority to consult on the point. He knows most things about cricket, and would certainly not be at a loss for an answer. 'Jacker' is never at a loss in any circumstances. He and Lionel Palairet, two rival University captains of a year or two ago, stand out a head and shoulders above the younger generation of batsmen, with the exception of Ranjitsinhji and Archie MacLaren. Perhaps Ranjitsinhji is best left in a class by himself. Archie MacLaren is not able to play much till August, so he is somewhat handicapped. Jackson is undoubtedly the best all round cricketer of the day, and is probably the very best batsman on a sticky wicket, now that Arthur Shrewsbury has given up playing regularly. Some people might offer Hayward as a serious rival in all-round-man excellence,

317

but the Surrey professional is not quite as good a bat, and no better a bowler. Like Ranjitsinhji, Jackson is very safe in his back play, and can use it as a means of scoring as well as of defence. He is clever in placing the ball away to the on-side both with drives and wrist strokes. He does not use the ordinary forward style much, though he stops many difficult balls with a 'half-cock' stroke something between back and forward. His driving is exceptionally clean and fine. Few players score more rapidly than he, though his style is very safe. He always gives an impression of being all there, and having a very definite idea what ought to be done and how to do it. Nothing excites him much; nothing can put him off his guard. Yet there is much enthusiasm for cricket behind those somewhat cold blue eyes and that unruffled brow. By-the-bye, Jacker's eyes always look as if they must see clear and straight. He has many interests and much ambition — chiefly political. What is more, he is sure to succeed. The old story of his having replied to congratulations on a fine innings for Harrow with the remark, 'Yes, I'm glad I made some runs; it will give my governor a leg-up', bears repetition, though Jacker denies its authenticity. There is no need to. A run-getting son is worth a lot — nearly as much as a Derby winner.

Talking of race-horses suggests Lionel Palairet, who is without exception the most thorough-bred batsman now playing. His strokes are all 'blood'. As a pure stylist he is unsurpassed and few are more effective. He has not Ranjitsinhji's extraordinary versatility or inexpressible electric quality, nor does he watch the ball quite as closely and safely as Jackson, but there is infinite beauty and charm in all his movements. The only thing I have seen in athletics to equal his gracefulness was Reggie Rowe's rowing. It is as impossible for Lionel Palairet to make an ugly stroke as it is for a silver birch tree to swing in unharmonious curves. No one could watch him batting without catching the meaning of the poetry of motion. He seems to attain the maximum of power with the minimum of exertion. All his strokes are easy and unforced. Most of his runs come from off-drives. His treatment of good length balls on or outside the off-stump is masterly. The left leg goes well across, body, arms and bat swing easily to meet the ball close by the leg, and extra-cover scarcely sees the ball as it shoots to the boundary between himself and cover. The value of these off-strokes, now that the off-theory is universally adopted by bowlers, can readily be appreciated. Palairet has not cultivated strokes on the leg side to the same extent as those on the off, probably because his style was formed in early boyhood by home practice with such accurate bowlers as Attewell and Martin. Much of his perfection of style is the result of a very careful education. His methods were irreproachable before he went to school, and he has improved every year he has played. At one time he showed an inclination to go in for pure hitting, but he gave it up in favour of a forward style. He is nevertheless an exceptionally fine hitter, and plants as many balls as anyone into the churchyard that adjoins the Taunton ground. His hits fly like good golf drives. Nothing in cricket could be finer than some of his partnerships with H. T. Hewett. Pure style at one end, sheer force at the other, and a century or two on the board with no figures beneath. No wonder the West-countrymen like the cricket at Taunton. For even if Palairet fails to give them their money's worth, there is Sammy Woods coming in later on to upset all applecarts.

Sammy could upset anything, and looks the part. To begin with he is a giant. He seems big and strong in his clothes, but stripped his physique is even more striking. The power in his huge thighs, long back and knotted shoulders is colossal. He does not bowl as fast as he used to, nor quite as well. 'I have to pretend I'm bowling now,' he says. But he is a pretty good bowler still for all that, and will help the Gentlemen to get the Players out at Lord's for many years to come. If his bowling has deteriorated a bit his batting has improved to a corresponding extent. He maintains he was always as good a bat as now but did not have a chance. 'They condemned me to be a bowler,' he complains. Who 'they' may be is a mystery, for he has been captain of his own side much more often than not, and would certainly have persuaded anyone else to let him go in where he wanted. Sammy has wonderfully persuasive ways, with his soft voice, confiding smile and decisive chin. On foreign tours with Lord Hawke's team his innocent inquiry, 'Who's coming in first with me, Martin?' is as much an institution as the toss for choice of innings. And he is a rare good man to go in first, for if he stays an over or two he makes complete hay of the bowling. Not that he mows often. He keeps his bat very straight and hits with several horse-power from his heavy shoulders. He is the Ajax of the cricket field and would defy any lightning. He has not much wrist but makes up for the deficiency by forearm. Most of his strokes are drives, and genuine drives. He has a particular liking for the Surrey bowlers, generally managing to carve about eighty runs out of Lockwood's and Richardson's best stuff. It is always a solemn moment at the Oval when 'Greenheart', swelling with courage and pursing his lips into that child-like smile, comes from the pavilion to set right the failure of half his side. There is no better man than he to go in when the wicket is bad or things are going wrong, though he does sometimes play forward to a straight ball with his eyes turned full upon the square-leg umpire — a stroke he repudiates and never fails to use successfully once or twice an innings. As a man and a brother he is undefeated, and he is the best captain imaginable. No captain knows more of the game or uses his knowledge better. He has boundless enthusiasm, and the power of infusing a strong solution of it into others. What is more he tries every ounce and makes others try also. He thoroughly deserves his enormous popularity. It will be a shame if he ever goes back to Australia.

Woods' bowling mantle has fallen on a worthy successor, that is if it really has fallen, which is not certain. A fast bowler has risen among us who can bowl all day with consummate pleasure to himself and profit to his side — Tom Richardson. Tom may not have Woods' knowledge of the art of bowling nor his finished command of the ball, but he has a bigger break and more sheer pace, and he has equal energy and as large a heart, which is saying a good deal. There is a difference in their methods. Woods at his best used to get most of his wickets by his clever variations of pace and that deadly yorker. Richardson pegs away with the same good length ball, trusting his natural break to beat the bat. On the whole the latter has met with more success than the former ever did. But it must be remembered that the one has always had some strong bowlers to back him up, whereas the other has, times out of mind, had to do all the bowling for his side both in 'Varsity and county cricket. Some people consider Richardson to be the best fast bowler ever seen, and certainly his performances are enough to justify such an opinion. Personally I think Lockwood in his best form is rather more difficult, and Arthur Mold bowls a most unplayable ball at times. One is quite content to be fired out by any of the three. But Richardson is the most consistent and has the greater lasting power. And herein is his great merit and the secret of his success. He can bowl for hours without tiring or losing sting, and seems never to have an off-day. This is marvellous when the immense amount of work he has to get through during a season is taken into consideration. Of course he has magnificent physique and keeps himself in perfect condition. His arm is like the thong of a stock-whip and his leg as hard as oak. Most of his pace comes from the small of his back, which must have double-action Damascus-steel fittings. He is the cheeriest and heartiest of mortals and has a splendid appetite. They keep special steaks for him at the Oval. He needs them.

A greater contrast than between Tom Richardson and Bobby Abel it would be difficult to imagine. Look at them as they walk round outside the ropes together – a rare occurrence to begin with, because the 'Governor' is usually batting or sitting still thinking how he is going to bat. The bowler is nearly seven feet high, with black hair and eyes and a southern complexion, something between a Pyrenean brigand and a smiling Neapolitan, brimful of fire and nervous strength. The batsman stands scarcely five feet in his buckskins. His face is ruddy and wrinkled, and suggests premature age or many cares. He has the peculiar serious expression common to grooms and music-hall artistes; one is never quite certain whether he has just lost a dear relative or is on the point of saying something very funny. He never smiles even after he has passed his second century. But he has the reputation of being a jester of the first water. There are no two ways about his batting. He gathers runs like blackberries everywhere he goes, and is very popular on that account, and on the principle of 'go it, little un!' The average Cockney at the Oval suspects him of a wealth of cunning – 'ikey' little dodges for outwitting the bowlers and chuckles over all his strokes. As a matter of fact he is a conscientious player, with wonderful patience and perseverance, and a very good eye.

K. S. Ranjitsinhji, F. S. Jackson, L. C. H. Palairet, S. M. J. Woods, Richardson and Abel, form the nucleus of a grand side. Would W.G. be there? I hope so, for he is indispensable, an integral part of the game. When one writes on cricket W.G. is taken for granted.

Windsor Magazine 1898

41

The Oldest Living Cricketer

We publish this week a portrait of John Bowyer, the oldest living cricketer in England. John Bowyer was born at Mitcham on the 18th of June, 1790, and consequently has just entered on his eighty-ninth year. The first important match in which he appeared was Surrey *v*. Kent, at Lord's, July 16th, 1810. There were then still in their prime many famous members of the old Hambledon Club, and John Bowyer can boast of having played against William Beldham, Wells, Robinson, Thomas Walker, Fennex and Lambert (the 'Little Farmer'). Even in that age of cricket giants Bowyer was a celebrity. As a left-handed batsman he had no superior – he could hit hard, and was an obstinate sticker. He played in six of the unique matches, the B's *v*. England, when the B.s mustered such famous players as Lord Frederick Beauclerk, Mr E. H. Budd, Will Beldham, George Brown (of Brighton, the fastest bowler of his time), and Tom Beagley. Bowyer played his last match in 1838, and since then has resided at Mitcham, where until 1870 he used to stand umpire in the village matches, and was a cricket oracle to all the country-side. One who saw him eighteen years ago describes him as 'still of fresh and ruddy cheeks, great nimbleness of movement, and vivacity of eye'. And his eye kindled as he told of the days when he went 'cricketing with Lord Frederick Beauclerk, all round the country and in London, when we all put up together at the Green Man, in Oxford Street; wine and the best of beef wasn't too good for us, though those days soon cleaned out all the guineas paid for playing. Then that was the time for the Legs to come among us, buy us up and make the great matches safe enough to lay their hundreds on. But mark you this, sir, they didn't buy the same man twice. No; "once sold always sold" it was with them, for they would hold the threat over a man, that if he turned too particular he must expect to hear of the roguery he had done already.' The betting on cricket in those days was tremendous, and every effort was made to 'square' matches. Old Beldham used to tell of a single wicket match he played, which was a 'double-cross', one man being paid on each side to lose. Consequently at a critical point, one man would not bowl straight and the other would not hit, till the inevitable straight one came, and down went the wicket, to the disgust of the bowler. In an article from the well-known pen of 'F.G.', which appears this month in *Baily's Magazine*, the writer says, 'Old Bowyer told me a day or two before writing this, how in a match a noble lord drew himself in the guinea lottery for runs, and was in with him (Bowyer). He would not run any runs hardly but his own if he could help it, in order to get the lottery, "and," said old Bowyer, "Lord Ponsonby, who had drawn my name, promised me two guineas if I got most runs; but Lord —— went backwards and forwards to the scorers to count his notches and mine, and the end of it was that he got sixty-four and I only got sixty. Though," said the old man, "he did give me a guinea, Lord Ponsonby would have given me two, and I call that kind of thing which Lord —— did 'cheating' no more or less." '

Miss Mitford, in 'Our Village' has left us a picture of cricket in those days. She thus describes what she saw at Lord's: 'A set of ugly old men, white-headed and bald-headed, dressed in tight white jackets (the Apollo Belvidere could not bear the hideous disguise of a cricketing jacket), with neckcloths primly tied round their throats, fine japanned shoes, silk stockings and gloves, instead of our fine village lads, with their unbuttoned collars, their loose waistcoats, and the large shirt-sleeves, which give an air so picturesque and Italian to their glowing, bounding youthfulness; there they stand, railed in by themselves, silent, solemn, slow, playing for money, making a business of the thing, grave as judges, taciturn as chess-players, a sort of dancers without music, instead of the glee, the fun, the shouts, the laughter, the glorious confusion of the country game.'

Among such worthies did John Bowyer's lot fall, but it says much for him that in an age when an honest cricketer was something of a rarity he had a reputation for honesty which he never forfeited. They were a long-lived race, these cricketers of the 'good old times'. It is but recently that Mr Budd died at the age of over ninety years. Mr Felix still later passed away in a green old age. Bill Beldham died some fourteen years ago when he was well over ninety; and here is old John Bowyer in his eighty-ninth year. We wish we could say still hale and hearty, but he was taken seriously ill on the 14th of June last, and it was feared that the illness would prove fatal. That fear has, we are glad to say, not been realized, and old John Bowyer, we hope, may yet pull through, and for some years longer enjoy the honour and dignity of being the oldest living cricketer.

Illustrated Sporting and Dramatic News 1878

The Test match venues of Kennington Oval (top left), Trent Bridge (top right), Melbourne (below left) and Sydney (below right), as they looked at the turn of the century

above The England XI for the 1886 Test match *v.* Australia at The Oval. Left to right (standing) F. Farrands (umpire), George Ulyett, William Barnes, George Lohmann, Dick Barlow, C. K. Pullen (umpire); (sitting) Edmund Tylecote, Allan Steel, W. G. Grace (captain), Arthur Shrewsbury, Walter Read; (in front) William Scotten, Johnny Briggs

below A match of a rather different kind, Smokers *v.* non-Smokers, an interlude from the Anglo-Australian rivalry of the Victorian era. Left to right (standing) Jack Hearne, Alec Bannerman, Sir Timothy O'Brien, F. R. Spofforth, C. I. Thornton, George Giffen, George Palmer, Dick Pilling, W. Oscraft; (sitting) Dick Barlow, Stanley Christopherson, 'Tup' Scott, Billy Murdoch, W. G. Grace, Lord Harris, George Bonnor, E. M. Grace, Walter Wright; (in front) Billy Gunn, Ted Peate, C. C. Clarke, Percy McDonnell, Monty Bowden, Tom Emmett

THE SPHERE

AN ILLUSTRATED NEWSPAPER FOR THE HOME.

Volume VI. No. 78. [REGISTERED AT THE GENERAL POST OFFICE AS A NEWSPAPER] London, July 20, 1901. [WITH SUPPLEMENT] Price Sixpence.

above The traditional Eton *v.* Harrow match at Lord's, pictured on the front cover of
The Sphere of 1901
below 'Well Played!' A Sketch at a Ladies' Cricket match

'W.G.' stepping out to the Pot Pouri Lancers

42

A Veteran North-Country Cricketer

The characteristic portrait [in the illustration section] affords a vivid idea of one of the most remarkable veterans of the willow that ever made a score in the North Country. It is not enough to say that he is one of the old school of cricketers. The school to which Tommy Marshall belonged was old when Mynn, and Felix, and William Lillywhite, and old Clarke were in their zenith. To the best of our belief, he is the last living relic of the period when he made 'notches' — literally notches — on the banks of the Tees, on behalf of his native town, Stockton. In those days, the rare old boys, who played fierce matches, that began early and finished late, played, too, 'for a pound a man'; there were no enthusiastic historians to record their doughty deeds. It has come to us, however, on the wings of tradition that the battles between rival towns like Yarm and Stockton were unparalleled for intense excitement, and not seldom ended in contests of quite another character. Cricketing shoes were uninvented, and the matches were played by men who dared blisters and concomitant evils 'in their stocking-feet'. In the fullness of time, Tommy Marshall became groundkeeper, tutor, and umpire to the Stockton Club, then, and for many pleasant years afterwards, under the genial presidency of the late Doctor Richardson. It would fill a Court Gazette to name the number of good men and true who figured in the cricket arena during Marshall's *régime*. Bedale had a powerful club in those days. The two Mortons and George Anderson were members, and we rather think Roger Iddison. The annual matches out and home between Stockton and Bedale were properly regarded as the leading events in that line in the district. Bradford, too, was strong, and Harewood rising into power. Middlesbro' could scarcely be said to exist then, and the clubs on the Tyne and Wear — Durham, perhaps, excepted — were of comparatively little account. Thanks in a great measure to the unselfish exertions of 'the Doctor', who was a magnificent patron of the game, the Stockton club rapidly assumed a first-class position, and brought to the front a number of brilliant players, most of whom figured subsequently at Lord's and the Oval. The late Tom Darnton was one of these, together with Hornby, a left-handed bat with a wonderfully strong defence, Halton, a superior wicket-keeper (a great pet of poor Tom Lockyer's), and splendid bat, T. Robinson, a bowler who could 'send them down' as swiftly as Freeman himself, and Jonathan Joy. Besides, there were Mr T. Crosby, Lancaster, Mr Prince Stockdale, as powerful a hitter as Mr Thornton, the late Major Coates, and several others. Amongst the professionals who were engaged for several seasons were Rapley, the late T. Hayward, and Roger Iddison, the latter in those days a slim round-arm bowler and unequal bat, and George Atkinson. Barratt, who is now playing for Surrey, was one of Tommy Marshall's boys, but he belonged to a later period in the history of the famous club.

We have so far spoken of the club rather than of Marshall, because it is impossible to separate him therefrom. He is part and parcel of its history. He saw it rise to a position second to none in the North; and he has seen it fall during his more than eighty years' sojourn in the arena, into a state of comparative insignificance. The veteran is otherwise, we would add, a thorough Yorkshire sportsman. For years, during the hunting season he followed the Durham county hounds a-foot, and many a time and oft has he been in at the death. He used to be a clever trainer of greyhounds, and had all the mysteries of woodcraft at his fingers' ends. We believe it was he who sat, unconsciously, to the author of the 'Chronicles of Heatherthorpe', for one of the old boys in that north-country story. Old Tommy Marshall has seen many a hard tussle in the cricket field; but, perhaps, the most memorable that he ever assisted at was when the Stockton Eleven defeated the Eleven of all Scotland, on the Grange ground at Edinburgh. Five men were out for nine runs, but the sixth fell for ninety. It was Halton (59), and Robinson (34), who pulled that exciting match out of the fire. Major Dickins, who played for Scotland, must yet remember his day's leather-hunting. Dr Richardson's cheer on the conclusion of the battle must have been heard across the border! We have no space to mention the altogether 'historical' single-wicket matches in which the Stocktonians and Carpenter, Hayward and Tarrant took part. Tommy Marshall's well-known white hat was there, and at many another match besides. It is pleasant to know that the evening of the old man's days is being smoothed by the youngsters he nurtured and loved, and that the matches which are periodically got up in his behalf are 'benefits' in every sense of the term.

Illustrated Sporting and Dramatic News 1876

43

Robert Arthur Thoms

The lot of an umpire on the cricket field cannot, at the best, be a very happy one. It is human to err, and the most irreproachable of men must make mistakes in the occupation of a position which necessitates, above all things, promptitude and readiness of decision. In contrast, too, with the active cricketer who has all the excitement of actual participation in the play, the umpire's place is a dull round of routine work. His whole attention must be given to the game itself, the game, the whole game, and nothing but the game. Then, again, his decisions can not give satisfaction to everyone, and there are some few, very few we are thankful to say, who resent even the rulings of the most capable and conscientious arbiter whenever they do not happen to be in accordance with their own interests. At the same time the difficulties incidental to the post must be an additional incentive to fill it in a way to secure the general approval which those who do their duty honestly on the cricket field invariably earn. And, among those who have done real credit to the onerous position of the umpire, a very high place may fairly be awarded to Robert Thoms.

Born in Lisson Grove, St John's Wood, on May 19, 1825, his whole life has been spent within measurable distance of the headquarters of the game. His father, by trade a baker, was an intimate friend of Mr James Henry Dark, then the proprietor of Lord's Cricket Ground, and it was to this relation that Thoms owed his connection with the game. Mr Dark having called to borrow some weights to put on the roller, a very different article in those days from the ponderous machine now in use, took young Thoms, who then fifteen years old, had just left Willesden School, back with him in his gig to Lord's. Fitting him out with a new bat and ball Thoms, the younger, was planted in Knatchbull's corner to play with Mr Dark's nephews, and from that day forward his summers have been almost entirely spent on cricket grounds.

In the following year, when but sixteen, he became a member of the then popular St John's Wood Club, and as we gather from 'Scores and Biographies', the great work of Mr Arthur Haygarth, to whom Thoms was personally well-known, it was to that Club that he owed his *debut* on the classic soil of Lord's. He was just nineteen when he made his first appearance there in May, 1844, for St John's Wood Club against MCC and Ground, so that he may be said to have had an active and practical acquaintance with the headquarters of cricket for over forty years. For several seasons after this he was one of the most successful batsmen in matches against suburban and country clubs, and there were few better all-round cricketers at that time in the neighbourhood of London. His reputation among metropolitan players must have been high, for a few years later (in June, 1850), he was selected as one of the Fourteen of Middlesex to oppose the Marylebone Club and Ground, at Lord's. On this occasion he showed to great advantage with the bat, and he had the satisfaction of being the highest scorer with one and forty-three not out, the latter a performance of great merit, made as the runs were against such a formidable quartet of bowlers as Hillyer, Wisden, Lillywhite and Clarke. This innings so far established his name that he was chosen a month later to represent the Young against the Old of England, a great distinction, considering the combination of talent arrayed on the two sides. Here, again, his all-round cricket impressed the best judges most favourably, and his batting and fielding were alike so good that old Clarke, always on the look-out for a promising youngster, offered him an engagement to travel with the All-England eleven the following season. The opportunity for improving his cricket furnished by Clarke was eagerly seized by Thoms, and thus, like Richard Daft subsequently, he changed from the amateur to the professional.

The spring of 1851, though, found his luck as a batsman dead out in the few matches that he played, and though still shining as a fieldsman — for Clarke has handed it down that Thoms was as good a mid-wicket as he had ever seen — he was not satisfied that he was really doing justice to the All-England Eleven. As a consequence resigning his place he returned to London, where he was shortly afterwards called upon by his staunch friend in every sense of the word, Mr James Henry Dark, and offered an engagement to assist him in the management of Lord's, which did not pass till some years after into the hands of the Marylebone Club. There, however, he was not destined to remain very long. Having noted the rapid development of cricket in the neighbourhood of London, in conjunction with Humphrey Payne, his inseparable friend and companion, a good all-round cricketer, many years attached to the Old Copenhagen ground at Islington, Thoms entered into possession of the Eton and Middlesex ground, situate, as many *Cricket* readers will well remember, under the shadow of Primrose Hill. Under the joint guidance of Payne and Thoms cricket flourished there for twenty years, and in fact it was not till the land fell into the remorseless clutches of the builder that the enclosure, which had been admirably managed, ceased its existence as a cricket centre. But it is chiefly in his capacity as an umpire that Thoms' name will be handed down to posterity.

For a quarter of a century he has occupied, as we have already described it, a thankless position in a way to merit the highest respect of cricketers of all classes. When Middlesex was regenerated in 1864 and brought to the front by the united efforts of the celebrated brotherhood of the Walkers, he was retained by the County, and for seventeen years with hardly an exception Thoms was to be seen behind the sticks in their matches at Islington, Prince's, Lord's, the Oval, and on most of the County grounds of England. Nor was it only with Middlesex that he has been associated as an umpire. At the Oval, too, he has been in great request, and not a season has passed since the Surrey Eleven, under the leadership of the late Mr F. P. Miller, tackled England in which Thoms has not officiated in important matches. So universal, indeed, has been his popularity of late years that when the first match between England and Australia at the Oval was arranged in 1880, he was selected with H. H. Stephenson to umpire, as high a testimony to his efficiency as could have been given. No better proof of his impartiality can be adduced, it seems to us, than the readiness with which his appointment has always been received by the Australian teams, who, not as a rule tolerant in the matter of umpiring, have always shown a marked sense of Thoms' capabilities behind the sticks. Thoms' record as an umpire is one we should think without a parallel.

Some twenty-five years ago, when the Islington Albion was a power in the land round London, and Lovell and Wallace, two of the best bowlers of the day among metropolitan cricketers, led it to victory, Thoms was its trusted arbiter, and we believe we shall not be beyond the mark in saying that he stood in over two hundred matches for the old Albion without the shadow of an objection to his decisions. Since its very formation he has too been actively identified with the famous wandering club, the Incogniti, and certainly of late years there have been few Public School matches of any importance in which he has not been invited to stand. In 1878 in recognition of his long and faithful services the executive of the Middlesex County Club gave him a benefit match— Middlesex *v.* Notts at Lord's, the use of which had been kindly granted for the occasion by the Marylebone Club. The fixture itself was not only well supported, but Thoms' popularity was further proved by a substantial subscription list, to which the Australian cricketers, then on their first visit to England, were contributors.

Thoms, it may fairly be said, is an institution on the cricket-field. Thoroughly independent and never afraid of expressing his opinion, there is certainly no more conscientious umpire. With a complete knowledge of the game in every detail, a perfect acquaintance with the laws and their application, his decisions never fail to command respect. Always respectful without being obtrusive, full of humour with a cricket vocabulary of his own coining, Thoms is a cheery accompaniment to a cricket match, and we could fill pages, did space permit, with his quaint sayings and odd fancies. In his own fashion he is, too, a most amusing correspondent, as we ourselves can vouch. Full of cricket lore, he has innumerable reminiscences of cricket, and during the run of the interesting articles compiled by the late Mr G. M. Crawfurd entitled 'Cricket Notes and Notabilities' which appeared in the *Sporting Life* a few years ago, he was 'Gemse's' most valuable contributor with his anecdotal and characteristic sketches. Liberal to a degree, Thoms has always had a ready hand to help his brother professionals, and as we have ourselves had reason to know he is always among the first to assist to the best of his ability any case of necessity. In his way no one has done more to uphold the integrity of the game, or worked harder to advance the position of his brother professionals, none in fact deserved better of cricketers of all classes than Robert Thoms, the Middlesex Veteran.

Cricket 1885

44

The Umpire's Art

It is almost impossible to regard an umpire in the light of an ordinary fellow creature. The nature of his work forbids it. He may smoke really vile tobacco and have no soul for art or literature, but he becomes our lord and master when once we have asked him for 'two-leg'. We may sometimes sneer at his ruling, but we have to bow to his word. The sight of his broad forefinger pointing heavenwards is a sight as terrible to the batsman who has just played the ball with his pads as the sight of the approaching policeman to the detected burglar.

In private life the club umpire may be the most humble of individuals. There is nothing masterful or awesome about him as he packs furniture or cleans paint on Monday morning. Quite possibly he takes a bullying from his foreman with extreme meekness of spirit. At home he may even be sadly henpecked. But let him once be arrayed in the white coat of office and he is a being transformed. For a few hours he becomes the most absolute of monarchs. The power is his to make or mar your day. What he sees, or what he thinks he sees, may take all the sunshine out of your afternoon. His actions can transform the mildest of mortals into wild-eyed, moustache-chewing savages with homicidal tendencies; he can take a cheery optimist, and with one softly-spoken monosyllable turn him into a gloomy cynic.

It is scarcely humanly possible, then, to regard such a despot as a man and a brother. The tendency is to look upon him as a species of machine. But when he errs, as err he sometimes must, we are inclined to regard his slip as a piece of evil-minded villainy. When he is unkind to us we call him bitter names in the seclusion of the dressing-room. When he is perfectly satisfactory we take his wise decisions as a mere matter of course. We fear the umpire always; there are moments when we positively hate him; but we never admire him. It seldom strikes us that he does anything the least bit clever. That there are both bad and good umpires appears to be due only to the fact that some men have common sense while other men are fools.

There is nothing showy about an umpire's work, however well it may be done. No difficulties appear on the surface. It seems at first sight a perfectly simple matter to decide whether the ball hit the bat and to give some unfortunate beggar out. And who would say that it requires great mental capacity to count correctly up to six?

No, the superficial evidence of the umpire's task all suggests simplicity. That is why many bowlers go through life firm in the conviction that most umpires suffer from short sight, and why many batsmen suspect them of seeing optical illusions. But sometimes Nemesis overtakes one of those who hold umpires in such small esteem, and he finds himself umpiring in an amateur capacity. Then he quickly learns not a few sharp lessons.

Anyone who is umpiring for the first time since his schooldays deserves the pity of all charitable persons. You are hors-de-combat yourself, perhaps, and the regular umpire is mysteriously absent, so you light-heartedly consent to fill the breach with never a guess at the agony in store for you. Probably during the course of a chequered cricket career you have been guilty of occasional discourtesy to the man who seems to exist only to give you out. When his opinion has not coincided with your own on the subject of the position of your right leg at the moment of delivery, you may have shrieked 'What!!!' in a tone which clearly suggests that you consider him either a madman or a dipsomaniac; or you may have so far forgotten yourself as to bitterly remark, as you pass him on the way back to the pavilion, that the ball which has got you given out l.b.w. would have missed the off stump by exactly an inch and three-quarters. But, however far you may have offended against umpires in your time, you will assuredly meet with sufficient punishment when in an evil moment you consent to take on the job regardless of your lack of practice.

You make elaborate arrangements for counting the overs. The theory of how to avoid a mistake you understand to perfection. You hold six pennies in your hand, keep the hand in your pocket and carefully release a copper as each ball is delivered. When your hand is empty it logically follows that it is time to call 'over'. At least, that is the theory.

You begin quite brilliantly. The first ball is driven straight back to the bowler, and you decorously drop a penny. The second ball is returned by the wicket-keeper, and you release penny number two. The third ball——— 'By Jove! That was a ripping shot! Coming back six inches, and he glanced it like that! Wonder what he'll do with the next. O, good hit! If he goes on like this he'll——— hello, that was a close shave. A little less break and——— There he goes again. Only three this time, though. That chap at long-on has got some speed. Nicely, nicely cut! Why on earth don't they run? Plenty of time with third man so deep. Oh, my word, what a slice of luck! Second slip must have been quite asleep. Now, if———'

About this time mid-on timidly inquires whether it isn't nearly 'over', and you awake to the horrible fact that while you have been indulging in a detailed mental criticism of the game you have entirely forgotten your duties as an umpire. You also discover that although you distinctly remember several strokes, you still have four pennies in your hand. Silently praying that no one has noticed anything wrong, you murmur a defiant 'Over' and walk to square-leg with as much dignity as you can command.

With heroic self-control you keep your mind fixed on the work in hand for some time after this, and make several discoveries. You find that it is a physical impossibility, never having been taught to squint, to keep an eye on Smith's action – he being a noted chucker – and to watch the position of his feet at the same moment. You also find that the bowler greatly obscures your view of the batsman, and begin to dread an appeal for any sort of decision far more than you have ever dreaded 'a pair'.

A wicket falling, you have time for some bitter reflection, and begin to doubt whether you are altogether sound on the rules. All the ticklish points in the game that you have ever heard of rush quickly to your mind, and you feel utterly incompetent to give a sane ruling on any one of them. You wipe your fevered brow many times and pray for the best, but as a rule it is the worst that happens. When at length a bowler startles away your few remaining wits by bellowing 'Owzat!' within three inches of your ear, you realize that at the moment you were wondering who the lady could be in heliotrope at the extreme end of the ground, and you find yourself saying, 'Out; I mean, not out; that is to say –.' 'Well, what is it?' fiercely cry the fielding side like one man.

'I'm really awfully sorry,' you explain, 'but the fact is, I'm afraid I didn't quite see.' 'Didn't see!' shriek the fielding side, once more with one voice, and even more fiercely than before, and you gather by their tone and by their glances exactly what eleven men in the world think of your mental state. By the time you have five times been informed by the scorer that the bowler has sent down seven balls, and have shown an inclination to consult the square-leg umpire upon a question of l.b.w. your demoralization is complete and your character as an upright English gentleman lost for at least a month. When you leave the ground that night you are painfully aware that even your friends eye you with suspicion. But one thing you have discovered — that the average umpire is a much smarter, clearer-headed person than you had ever previously dreamed of. For the rest of your life you nurse the profound respect for all umpires — except, of course, when they give you out leg-before.

Considering how difficult is the umpire's task, the only wonder is that the standard of club umpiring is so uniformly high. The county umpire is engaged at the work nearly every day in the week. He does not suffer from lack of practice. To count the overs, to keep an eye on everything, becomes in time almost a mechanical occupation. But the club umpire often only dons the white coat on Saturdays. And in order to keep in the best form, practice is almost as necessary to an umpire as to a batsman or bowler. Then again the club umpire is generally the paid servant on one or other of the sides engaged in the match, which tends to render his position the more delicate. And at the best of times it is always extremely easy to make a mistake. The umpire cannot be in exactly the same line of vision as the bowler. Things happen very quickly, and sometimes distinct clicks are audible which have nothing to do with the bat.

Remember these things in the summer before you. The hardest thing to learn in the game of cricket is, however trying the circumstances, 'to abide by the umpire's decision and to go out smiling'. This is harder to learn than placing to leg a snorting off-break. And it is just as splendid.

Cricketer and Hockey Player 1907

45

The Cricket Jester

A Study of Craig, Cricket Rhymester

Radcliffe Martin

A lithe, slim figure, a sunburnt face surmounted by a shock of yellow hair, now turning grey, bright blue humorous eyes, the loose-hung jaw and large throat of the constant speaker — that is Craig, the Surrey Laureate, the Leno of the Cricket-field, the best-known man in London. Sometimes, when in reminiscent mood, Craig will tell the crowd the story of his life. 'I came down to London from Sheffield, gentlemen, with George Ulyett, more than twenty years ago. I took an excursion ticket, and I have not used the return half yet.' Nor will he, for in London he finds a better market for his ready wit than he would in the more serious North Country. He has made his way to the hearts of Londoners not by the quality of his poems (no one is better aware of that than Craig himself), but by the force of a genial personality. If he tried to sell his ode to Bobby Abel on scoring his fifth century, it would never be purchased on its merits. But when Craig, with a humorous twinkle in his eye, says: 'My latest rhymes, gentlemen, all four a penny'; then, taking his audience into his confidence — 'between ourselves a great deal more than they are worth', there is a hail of coppers, and trade is brisk at once. Every one likes to be humbugged so openly, so genially, and if Craig's poems are scarcely worth purchasing, still his audience is more than repaid by a flash or two of his characteristic repartee.

'Craig, you're making a lot of money. When are you going to open an hotel?'

'When you come and live next door to me, sir.'

Who can forget his artful little speech at Lord's when he saw some ecclesiastical dignitaries amongst his audience. 'Gentlemen, I do like addressing the people at Lord's, though I fear they are not all the Lord's people.' For the credit of the episcopal bench, one must add that the bishops were not backward in patronizing the poet.

Or his apt reply to the client who made a personal observation, 'Craig, you're getting rather grey.' 'As the hair grows whiter, sir, you will love me more.' Once when Yorkshire were playing at the Oval, Craig concluded a characteristic oration with the words, 'Yorkshire, my native county; Surrey, my adopted county.' 'That's very well, Craig,' cried a disgusted Essex supporter, 'but what will you say at the match at Leyton to-morrow?' 'Essex, my tip for the championship, sir.' And his Essex client beamed with gratification.

When a stonewalling batsman (I believe, Dr MacDonald, of Leicester) was tiring the Oval crowd, someone said to Craig, 'I say, Craig, you've made a lot of money out of us; when are you going to retire?' 'Gentlemen,' said Craig, 'I shall never desert you till – till – till Dr MacDonald has completed his innings.' Whilst Craig can give or take a joke with the best, the ill-bred person who thinks he can insult our writer of songs, soon finds that he has caught a Tartar. The rude interrupter will be withered by a few pungent phrases. It is curious to notice that when Craig stands on his dignity he lapses back to his old-time accent, and instead of the polished Londoner we hear the brusque Yorkshireman.

We all, in a way, regard Craig as our property. Strange legends pass round the Oval as to the money Craig has made from the public patronage. At one time or another every building (except the gasworks) within sight of Kennington Oval has been pointed out as the personal property of Craig. Doubtless rumour exaggerates, but the Oval crowd rejoices in the fortune of its favourite, and in a characteristic English manner respects the moneyed man. To do the British public justice, it does not care to muzzle the ox which treads out its chaff. The most wonderful thing about Craig is his memory. Make a remark to him at one match, and when he sees you six months later he will know you and recall it. Small wonder that he keeps his clients. Are we not all flattered to be borne in memory by a great public character? In addition to his marvellous memory for faces, Craig is a reservoir of cricket facts, an encyclopaedia of interesting cricketana, a veritable walking *Athletic News* handbook. At a critical point in a match, when some record is at stake, Craig will glide round the ground, not to sell his productions, but just to let the spectators know the exact facts about the last record. It is one of the delicate little attentions he pays his public. Or when the crowd is anxiously waiting to know who has won the toss, it is Craig who gets access to the pavilion (he can get anywhere in the cricket world), and runs round the ground with the news. Craig knows his public well, and is a sportsman. He will never trouble the crowd while the cricket is brilliant or the situation critical, but if there is a dreary stand and the crowd is weary of stone-walling, or if rain comes and the players take refuge in the pavilion, then Craig seizes his opportunity, and in five minutes the crowd in his neighbourhood has regained its good spirits. 'The rain will stop, gentlemen,' he will begin, 'directly I have sold these few copies of my new poem.' He is always sanguine and cheerful. The weather is always going to improve, England is always going to beat Australia, Hayward is always going to make another century. No one can better express the joys of victory or soften the pangs of defeat.

If there is a better known man than Craig in London we should like to see him. Perhaps another Oval habitué, John Burns, is his only rival. Once Bobby Abel (by the way, surely Craig will oblige with a poem on Abel's appearance in spectacles – 'His only pair') walked with Craig from the Oval to Westminster Bridge, and devoted his time in counting the persons who saluted the genial poet. The exact figures slip our memory, but considerably over a hundred people spoke to the Surrey Laureate. If Craig (far be it from us to suggest such a thing) were to stand for Parliament he would carry any working-class constituency in London, and we venture to say that his replies to awkward questions would be a treat for the gods and a model for all candidates. But we cannot spare Craig from his more important work. May he continue to prosper, and yet not be too prosperous. If he became a plutocrat he might be tempted to leave the Oval crowd sorrowing, and when Craig's innings comes to an end the gaiety of our cricket fields will be perceptibly diminished.

Cricket and Football Rhymes and Sketches
Athletic News 1904

46

Notts v. Surrey

The Oval,
August Bank Holiday, 1907

Respectfully dedicated to Lord Dalmeny,
Surrey's Popular Chieftain

A. Craig

Darling Old Oval, once again we meet,
One clan to triumph, one to bear defeat;
Notts, dear old Notts, appear in all their pride,
We greet them warmly to the 'Surrey Side';
Some old familiar faces are no more —
No Shrewsbury — as in happy days of yore;
No Alfred Shaw, a bright and leading star,
Immortal Walter Read, alas! has 'crossed the bar'
Their tasks are o'er, their 'spurs' they nobly won,
Rest follows toil, their hard day's work is done;
Lord Dalmeny is clad in bright array,
Cheers on his men to keep the foe at bay;
Seeks by his aid to raise his county higher —
A noble son of an Illustrious Sire;
The opposing captain, from beside the Trent —
Rare Jones — to Notts has oft proved heaven-sent;
He means to win or know the reason why,
Australia'll own his prowess by and by;
Old Surrey boasts a Hayward's matchless skill,
A gem of priceless worth and iron will;
A Holland, too, still on his conquering way,
When Yorkshire comes, our Fred shall have 'his day';
Tom Richardson is missed, and Lockwood too,

Gallants who did the tasks they sought to do;
England is poorer without men like these,
They left the ranks, but left us Walter Lees;
Wally, whose heart and soul is in the game,
His fire is quenchless, comrades catch the flame;
We glory in a Knox, whose lightning pace
Our sturdiest foe, good sportsmen, dread to face;
We claim a Crawford, Crawford honour'd name,
That makes more bright the annals of the game;
Yes, Surrey claims the only Ernie Hayes,
Hope never dies, so long as Ernie 'stays';
And patient Baker, watchful as of yore,
Science and tact combine to raise his score;
Has Davis ever yet been known to yield?
Safe as a batsman, brilliant in the field;
We laud Jack Hobbs, Tom Hayward's special choice,
His rare successes make our hearts rejoice;
Jack never, never thinks of looking back,
He keeps the path, young Hitch is on his track;
And Marshal has no other end and aim
Than to prove worthy of our kingly game;
Last, but not least, Bert Strudwick issues forth,
Another Pilling and of priceless worth;
Sound as a Stedman, fearless as a Wood.
He stands as stately as an Ajax stood;
Long may the Notts and Surrey favourites meet
In cordial fellowship each other greet;
And when the victors have been laurel crown'd,
May warm and kindly feeling still abound.

Cricket and Football Rhymes and Sketches
Athletic News 1904

47

County Cricket Grounds

George A. Wade

T he premier place amongst English county cricket grounds —
indeed, amongst those of the world — must be given to Lord's,
the famous ground of the Middlesex County Club. It is only fair
to say, however, that Lord's does not derive this pre-eminence from its
being the county ground, but from its being the ground of the MCC,
the recognized authority on modern cricket. Founded by one Thomas
Lord in the last century, and named after him, the enclosure at St
John's Wood is not only the oldest English first-class ground, but even
to-day it is still one of the most beautiful in its surroundings and
situation. Once inside the ground, you might easily suppose yourself
to be miles away from the bustling city, the trees and flowers giving
the whole place quite a country air.

Taken in its whole extent, Lord's is about the biggest of English
cricket grounds, covering an area of nearly sixteen acres; but only nine
of these form the real portion of the field of play on the occasion of
matches. Thus Lord's falls behind some other grounds in this particular. But it upholds its reputation in most other points. Its pavilion is
superb; no other cricket ground has one that is even its rival. In extent
it occupies nearly the whole of the Grove End Road side of the ground,
and is capitally designed and fitted for the various uses it has to serve.

One noticeable thing at the Middlesex county ground is the care and
comfort bestowed upon the spectators, as compared with many other
similar places that will be hereafter mentioned. Comfortable seats go
all round the ground, in most places covered by awnings which prove
equally serviceable in sunny or windy weather, to say nothing of wet.
And everybody can see; the field of play is not too great. As to the
wicket — well, it is nearly always in the best of condition, as, of course,
one expects from the MCC. But then they don't let Tom, Dick, and

Harry scamper over it on every available occasion, as so many other places do.

Lord's not only stands first in the matter of size, comfort and appearance amongst English cricket grounds, but naturally from its long career, its important position, and its relation to the MCC — more than to the Middlesex County Club — it boasts some of the noblest traditions and records of English cricket. It is the only ground where there is habitually a large attendance of the fair sex of the fashionable world; and such matches as Oxford v. Cambridge and Eton v. Harrow could not possibly be the same anywhere else as they are at Lord's. All the University matches since 1851 have been played here, and it is surprising how keenly some ladies follow the game, though from others the poor inferior male spectator often hears some curious cricket tit-bits. Thus, when Middlesex played Sussex here last August, the writer happened to be near a sweet young thing of twenty, whose cousin of twenty-five was acting as guide and *chaperon*; and when C. B. Fry hit Cunliffe for four, amidst applause, she innocently asked 'why they were clapping'. When the cousin replied kindly that it was a fine hit, she sweetly smiled and said, 'Yes, it *was* nice of that bowler to bowl him such a nice ball to hit so far, wasn't it?' And when all the men around grinned, the cousin looked as if he had made up his mind, and that it should be 'Never more!'

It was at Lord's in 1893 that Stoddart, for Middlesex v. Notts, scored over 100 in each innings, thus ranking among the noble half-dozen batsmen who have performed this feat. Barnes, the Nottingham man, for MCC v. Leicestershire, in 1882, scored 266; and this is the highest innings that has ever been scored at Lord's since 1820, when Mr Ward scored 278. On this ground Jesse Hide, for Sussex v. MCC, took four wickets with four consecutive balls in 1890. As may be gathered from its size and shape — Lord's is nearly square — boundary hits are not very long in some places, though diagonally they would allow, I believe, of a 'six' being run. W. G. Grace has hit a ball more than once clean out of the playing area, and struck the clock on the south side of the ground, but without breaking it. A similar feat was done during a match last season. Lord's has many glories and a great past. All true lovers of cricket will desire that its future may be equally glorious.

Lancashire's two great cricket grounds for county matches are the well-known Old Trafford at Manchester, and the Aigburth ground at

Liverpool. The former is by far the more important, since all the season's 'home' matches, except about three or so, take place on it. It was in 1864 that contests first took place here under the name of the 'County of Lancashire', and they have been continuous each season since.

The Old Trafford ground suffers, like that of Bramall Lane at Sheffield, from being in the centre of a large town. Like its Yorkshire rival, its wickets are not always as good as those on some other grounds, and like it, too, it has had a great and celebrated past. There is much similarity in another way between them. Just as the Yorkshire crowd most appreciate a contest with the Red Rose, so the Lancashirement prefer to watch a struggle at Old Trafford against their great rivals of the past. Thus it comes that as the record attendance on a Yorkshire ground was at a match against Lancashire, so that of the Old Trafford enclosure was for Lancs. *v.* Yorks in 1895, when 27,000 were present on the first day. The next record was at a similar contest in 1893, when 22,554 paid on the opening day.

The playing portion of Old Trafford is about seven acres in extent, so that in size the whole ground will bear comparison with most others. Of course Old Trafford boasts a spacious pavilion. Many great feats, including some records, are connected with the ground. Here were made both the smallest innings Lancashire ever totalled, 25 − *v.* Derbyshire, in 1871 − and also the smallest innings ever made against the county, viz., 17, singularly enough, by Derbyshire again, in 1888. At Old Trafford, in 1885, Mr V. E. Walker, for Middlesex, took all the ten Lancashire wickets in one innings; whilst in 1888 Briggs performed a very remarkable feat against Derbyshire, by taking no less than 13 wickets for 35 runs in the two innings. It would seem that Derbyshire matches at Old Trafford are always exciting for somebody or other! But the greatest feat in bowling, since it constitutes a record in first-class matches I believe, occurred at Old Trafford in 1882, when G. Nash, against Somersetshire, took *five* wickets with five successive balls!

A laughable incident occurred here at the refreshment rooms one year, when a party of young men, having ordered some eatables, monopolized the windows, which commanded a capital view of the game, and, after their meal, refused to move, though other customers were waiting. Although policemen were summoned, they could not be dislodged. But the proprietor hit on a happy expedient. Instead of using brute force, he simply engaged two men outside to whitewash the windows. The offending youths soon cleared out!

The Aigburth ground, at Liverpool — Lancashire's 'understudy' of a county enclosure — can boast of having, at any rate, one record to its credit. Here, in July, 1885, Briggs and Pilling scored 173 runs for the last wicket, this being a 'best on record'.

Ths ground has generally a good wicket, and, though not largely used for county matches, is often in use for Lancashire's contests with the Universities, and for first-class matches *v.* so-called 'Lancs' teams. It is somewhat surprising, considering the size of the county, that Lancashire's matches never go to the north or central portion of it. But so it is. Old Trafford is the traditional Lancashire cricket ground, as for many years it is likely to be.

Probably no ground in the world is better known than the Oval, which has since 1854 belonged exclusively to the Surrey County Cricket Club. The latter had been remodelled, so to speak, in 1845, and when the Montpelier Club, which had transformed what was an old kitchen garden into the cricket ground now known as 'The Oval', helped to form the new Surrey Club in 1854, the ground also was transferred to the County Club.

As everyone knows, the Oval is so called from its shape. It has an area of about eleven acres, and is situated in that portion of London known as Kennington, close to Kennington Church, and near Vauxhall Station. The Oval has always had a good reputation for its wickets, and a Surrey crowd, too, is a thing that has become famous. But the most enthusiastic Surreyite could not describe the ground as 'pretty', with those gasometers close by staring him in the face. The accommodation for the enormous crowds that gather here also leaves very much to be desired. Nor can the Oval be described as 'comfortable' for the spectator. There is about as much shade on a broiling summer day as there is on the Sahara.

The old pavilion has been replaced this year by a new erection, which is a matter for congratulation. Few crowds are more enthusiastic (when Surrey is doing well!) than those at the Oval, and it must be allowed that on few grounds have the spectators more often cause for enthusiasm, since this ground has been the scene of some of the most memorable events in modern cricket.

There have only been six cases of first-class county matches ending in a 'tie,' and, singular to say, all six have occurred at this cricket ground, five of them when the match was Surrey *v.* some other county, and the other Gentlemen *v.* Players in 1883. Here also was the largest attendance on record at any cricket match, viz., that of Surrey *v.* Notts, in August, 1892, when 63,763 persons paid for admission during the three days, of whom nearly half, 30,670, came on the first day. The Oval also holds the record of the highest score for the first wicket, Abel and Brockwell making, in August last year, 379 for Surrey *v.* Hampshire, thus beating by one run the Sheffield record of Brown and Tunnicliffe a few weeks earlier.

Amongst other notable feats performed on the Surrey ground may be mentioned the great Caffyn's bowling record in 1862, of 24 overs, against Kent, for 7 runs and 7 wickets; Marten's taking 6 wickets for 11 runs, in 1872, *v.* MCC; Lohmann's 8 for 18 runs, *v.* Hants, and Beaumont's 6 for 11 runs, *v.* Middlesex, both in 1885; and Richardson's bowling, *v.* Warwickshire, in 1893, when he took 4 wickets with 4 consecutive balls. In the season of 1868, Pooley the stumper, in the match Surrey *v.* Sussex, stumped 4 and caught 8, which is a record in first-class matches for the wicket-keeper; whilst in 1880, Surrey only made 16 in their first innings *v.* Notts, which score included no less than 7 'ducks'!

The Oval is a larger ground that many people would suppose on first seeing it, as its area given above will show; but this is further proved by the fact that only once has a ball ever been hit clean out of the ground by a batsman in a county match, and that feat was performed by Mr K. J. Key when playing for Surrey *v.* Kent in 1887. Hearne was the suffering bowler.

No mention of the Oval would be complete without noting the fact that here first appeared, in 1861, the covered scoring box and the telegraph board, of which Surrey were the pioneers. Surrey were also the first to give 'talent sovereigns', which used to be presented to the recipient at the close of his innings, on his returning to the pavilion; but as this often led to confusion, the later method was adopted. Only on two occasions has Surrey ever played 'home' matches away from the celebrated ground, viz., in 1854, when the Notts match took place at Godalming, and, in the same year, when both Sussex matches were at Brighton.

In leaving the glories of the famous Oval, one cannot but recall the figure of Craig, the Surrey poet, so well known to every *habitué* of the ground. He comes up smiling every time Surrey plays, and is as much a fixture as the rest of Surrey's property. His quips and sallies *re* Surrey's glories and Abel's triumphs cause endless mirth and laughter.

Yorkshire has in recent years, and with much success, adopted the method of Kent and Gloucestershire, and played its matches in various parts of the broad-acred shire rather than on one particular ground. Still most of its encounters, and all the more important ones, are always relegated to Sheffield, Leeds, or Bradford.

Bramall Lane ground, at Sheffield, was at one time the regular county venue of all Yorkshire's 'home' matches. But its turf has been wearing for years, and the sooty atmosphere of the cutlery town is not calculated to raise velvety turf on a ground surrounded by buildings on every side. For many seasons there has been reason to complain of the wicket there, and this, no doubt, aided in the development of other Yorkshire cricket grounds. But though some of its glories are departed, Bramall Lane will always be the classic ground of Yorkshire county cricket, for with it will ever be associated the names of Ulyett, Emmett, Ephraim Lockwood, and Freeman, and these will never die whilst cricket lives. It was at Bramall Lane, so the story goes, that George Ulyett, that terrific 'hitter', once drove a ball clean out of the ground, over the boundary street, over the row of houses, and into an attic window of a house in the next street, probably the biggest hit on record. This will impress one more after seeing Bramall Lane ground, which is not small by any means, the playing portion being over seven acres.

Here also Wootton, for All England *v.* Yorkshire in 1865, took all ten wickets in one innings; and here J. T. Brown and Tunnicliffe – the Yorkshire 'giant' and the Yorkshire 'little 'un' – made, *v.* Sussex last year, the enormous score of 378 for the first wicket, a record till the Surrey one of 379 a month or so later. Another record enjoyed by Yorkshire is that of the first three men in an innings each scoring over 100, which was done against Kent in 1887, by Hall, Ulyett and Lee.

The Bradford ground at Horton Park was the scene of the memorable benefits of Peel and Hunter. That of 'Bobby' holds the records amongst benefits, above £2000 being the amount handed over. Yet on the last day, owing to the early finish, only £65 was taken! Hunter's benefit here last year realized over £2000 for him, with subscriptions; for Yorkshire people seem to think that the acme of delight of a cricket match is to have a 'benefit', at the Bradford ground, for one of their 'pets', with Lancashire as the opponents. The Wars of the Roses are not over yet.

The Headingly ground, at Leeds, is now probably Yorkshire's finest ground, as well as one of the prettiest of county grpounds. The turf and wicket are always good, but a drawback to the ground – or at least batsmen think so – are the long boundary hits that are necessary in order to score four. This militates much against such big scores being made here as on some grounds. The area of the cricket ground is about eight acres, and there is a very fine pavilion. It is rather far from the centre of Leeds, and so somewhat inaccessible to the stranger, though there is a good service of trams, brakes, etc.

Owing to the few years that county matches have been played here, few very notable events are connected with it. One of the most striking is that of Yorkshire v. Gloucestershire in 1894, when 9 Yorkshire wickets had fallen for 19 runs in the second innings, and then, Yorkshire being only a few runs on, Hirst and Hunter went in for 'smiting' with such effect that they brought the total to 61. Gloucestershire, wanting only 78 to win, found this task utterly beyond them, owing to the magnificent bowling of Peel, Hirst & Co., and departed vanquished by 26!

Of minor Yorkshire grounds the most noted is Huddersfield, though its wicket is not at all perfect. Here Yorkshire v. Somerset, in 1894, was finished in a day; and here, in 1897, was the memorable match with Essex, where the latter won by 1 run, after Yorkshire had only wanted 16 with 3 wickets to fall.

Like Surrey's 'Craig', Yorkshire is not without its noted follower, and most of the Tykes know him. 'Now they're *num*bered on the *card* in the *order* of *go*ing in!' The beautiful cadence with which he sings this – accenting the syllables italicized – on all Yorkshire's grounds during county matches is a thing to be remembered. But, unlike Craig, he doesn't compose poetry: he attends strictly to business, with a jovial remark *re* 'Tunny', or 'Bobby', or 'J.T.', or 'Ted' thrown in now and again.

Few cricket grounds are more beloved by county cricketers than that of Sussex, which is known as the 'Hove' ground at Brighton. Sussex has another ground at Hastings, which has, on more than one occasion, been the scene of renowned encounters; but for all practical purposes the Brighton ground may be taken as being the regular venue where the southern county entertains its visitors. There are two things which endear this ground to the heart of every cricketer who has played on it; the first is its size— or rather its 'want of size'— since it has the record of being probably the smallest of any first-class cricket ground, certainly of county grounds. Hence 'boundary hits' are frequent, and the scoring naturally high. This tendency is increased by the second— the peculiarity of the ground, viz., its substratum of chalk, which makes the wicket dry rapidly, even in the wettest seasons. So that again points to high scores. Sussex has a first-class pavilion, splendidly fitted up, and the situation of the Hove ground, with the sea breezes fanning one, is probably as fine as any in England.

Naturally, with such aids to high scoring, no other cricket ground can show such a long array of big figures in that line. A full list of them would fill a page or two of this magazine. Only a few of the chief ones can be mentioned here. At Hove, in 1893, Notts made 674 in one innings against the home county, in which innings Shrewsbury scored 164, Gunn 156, and Barnes 102. In 1891 the match Cambridge University *v.* Sussex produced a 'record' aggregate of 1402 runs for a first-class match. Here, in 1892, George Brann joined the select band of those who have scored 'double hundreds', doing the trick in the match against Kent.

One of the most curious incidents here was when Surrey beat Sussex in 1887 by one wicket. Adams, the last Surrey man, was making his *début* for that county, and when he came in 7 runs were yet needed. Henderson, who was in with him, whispered to him to keep up his 'end' and leave the run-getting to him (Henderson); but Adams was ambitious to shine at this first attempt for Surrey, and letting go lustily, got all the 7 runs himself, amidst great laughter and excitement.

Like Surrey, Nottingham County Cricket Club can boast of its allegiance to its 'one' love, for since 1840, when the first county match took place at Trent Bridge ground, in Nottingham, almost all the 'home' fixtures of this famous cricketing county have been played there. There are many people who look upon Nottinghamshire as one of the original homes of the noble game, and hence to them Trent Bridge is a classic spot. It has, in any case, a great reputation. From its first opening, under the auspices of Mr W. Clarke, its wickets have been noted for their high state of 'goodness'. It is, as cricket grounds go, one of the larger size, covering an area of eleven acres. On one side it is bounded by the railway, and it is of this ground that the well-known story is told – whether true or not I do not venture to say – of how a batsman once hit a ball into the carriage of a passing train, which ball was not recovered for over an hour, during which time the batsmen had run some hundred runs or so, as the fielders could not cry 'Lost ball!' knowing perfectly well where it was!

The most striking object at Trent Bridge is the fine pavilion, which is only second to that of Lord's in its beauty and arrangement. The committee undertook to build one in 1871, at a cost of £1500, which was done. But Notts cricket so progressed that in 1886 a new one was built – the one now standing – at a cost of £5000. It is of red brick, with red tiles, and has ample balconies and vestibules, giving it altogether a most imposing appearance.

Trent Bridge cricket ground has never been famous for its large 'gates'. Curiously enough, the county which more than any other, except perhaps Yorkshire, has produced great cricketers from nearly every village green, and has a club in connection with every little Sunday-school, never seems to get up enough enthusiasm to rival the Oval, Manchester, or Bramall Lane in the matter of record gates. The Notts crowd is generally an average one of a few thousands, and, whilst strongly appreciative of the game, it takes the 'ups' and 'downs' of its favourites very quietly on the whole.

The 'record' gate of Trent Bridge was probably at R. Daft's benefit in 1876, and that is going far back. Daft got over £500, which is, however, small compared with Peel's at Bradford, or Maurice Read's at the Oval.

Yet Trent Bridge has seen great sights and wonderful things in cricket, though I question if it holds one single 'record'. It was in 1844 that Alfred Mynn, Fuller Pilch, and Hillyer – good gracious, what a trio! – played for All England v. Southwell District, for whom George Parr played. Parr hit a ball to long leg, the ball dropped on the canvas of the tent, and was caught by a fielder as it rolled down. Barker, the umpire, on being appealed to, gave Parr 'not out'. What the decision would be to-day is rather an interesting question. In 1862, Hayward, Carpenter, and Tarrant, of Cambridgeshire fame, played R. Daft,

Jackson, and Clarke a single wicket match, here. Truly a battle of giants! Jackson bowled the three cracks for 1 run, and Notts won by 11!

Ten years later occurred one of Nottinghamshire's most curious finishes. It was in the match with Surrey at Trent Bridge. It is thus described: 'The most violent storm ever known in Nottingham! To say it rained would be ridiculous; it came in torrents, and not only flooded the ground, but, aided by wind and lightning, tore down the refreshment (and other) tents and made them mere shreds as if they had been paper!' At the close of the third day, therefore, Notts had only three wickets down with the score at 180. It was in 1876 that Notts disposed of Surrey here for 26 runs. What a sensation that would cause to-day! But how much more if it was followed up by Yorkshire being dismissed – as Notts did then dismiss them – for 32!

One of the county's most anxious moments was in 1877, when Notts played Middlesex on this ground. When the last Nottingham man went in, there were still some twenty runs to get, and a few minutes to play. The batsmen managed to keep up their wickets and make a draw of it, though when time was called Notts were still 10 runs to the bad.

In bidding farewell to Trent Bridge we must recall Shacklock's performance *v.* Somerset, in 1893, of taking 4 wickets with 4 balls consecutively.

No county regularly plays its engagements on so many different grounds as Kent, unless we except Yorkshire. Kent may be said to have three very good grounds and two or three inferior ones. The chief grounds are those at Maidstone, Canterbury, and Gravesend; whilst occasionally the venue of county matches has been at Beckenham, Tonbridge, and Catford. Of the three latter grounds it is not necessary to say more than that the wickets have never been very good, the balls bumping up and down in most erratic style. If a really good wicket could be prepared at Beckenham, this ground might probably become an important one, since it is extremely charming in its surroundings, and is not too far from London to prevent many people going down there when a good match is on.

Of the three other grounds it is only necessary to speak in detail of that at Canterbury. There is little of importance to chronicle in connection with the other two; both are well situated, that of the 'Bat and Ball', at Gravesend, especially so. But Kent's chief ground is at Canterbury. Here takes place the festival of the 'Canterbury Week', when Kent plays its two matches, and all the county notables entertain their friends. Tents on the ground are as thick as possible. Cricket and afternoon tea are recognized institutions during the festival, and it is safe to say that no other cricket ground in England — saving Lord's during the Universities' or Public Schools' matches— can at all rival the brilliant scene displayed by the St Lawrence ground, at Canterbury, during this week. The ground is situated outside the town, and, as might be supposed, is exceedingly picturesque. Moreover, it is of fair size and provides good wickets. Certainly, if tents, and flags, and trees, and pretty dresses are aids to cricket, Kent should be unrivalled in its 'Canterbury Week'.

Of really great feats in cricket, Kentish grounds — especially when one recollects that Kent is one of our very oldest cricket centres— boast singularly few. Two of the most notable ones at Canterbury happened long ago. In 1862, Dr E. M. Grace took all the ten wickets in one innings for MCC v. Gentlemen of Kent; whilst in 1868, the great champion, 'W.G.', scored 100 twice during one match.

Gloucestershire is another county whose 'home' matches take place on many different grounds. Especially in use during the past season or two have been those at Bristol, Cheltenham, Clifton, and Gloucester. Matches are not now, and have not of late years been, played at Moreton-in-the-Marsh, though formerly several took place there. This is said to be due to the scanty attendance of the public, owing to the rural character of the district. It seems a pity, however, that matches were wholly dropped there, since the general opinion of the wicket, both by friends and opponents, was that it was a very good one. Indeed, on the celebrated occasion when Yorkshire defeated Gloucestershire here, the rival captains, Lord Hawke and 'W.G.', both specially complimented Mr Rouse, the secretary, on the splendid wicket he had obtained. The ground is of fine extent, not less than sixteen acres. In connection with the Moreton-in-the-Marsh ground two noteworthy matches must be noticed. The first one is that above, often known as 'Peate's match', since the noted Yorkshire bowler took 6 wickets in Gloucester's second innings for 13 runs! The 'home' county presented him with the ball, mounted in silver, as a tribute to his great prowess. The other match was one in which Kent were all

351

dismissed, on a wet wicket, for 27! Both these memorable matches were in 1884.

Many of Gloucestershire's matches now take place at Bristol. Here they have a ground of some sixteen acres, with a fine pavilion and grand stand. There is little, however, specially striking about the ground, which is not nearly so famous as those at Cheltenham and Clifton in the cricketing world. Both these are situated amidst lovely environment, and both provide excellent wickets. The Cheltenham ground strongly rivals Canterbury's in its fashionable 'cricket week', and the aspect and 'doings' are very similar, though probably there is less 'tea' and entertainment, and more — if possible — fashion and dress.

The Clifton ground has the unique record of being the spot where twice a batsman has made over 100 runs in each innings. Need we say it was the grand old Gloucester cricketer, in 1887, *v.* Kent, and, in 1888, *v.* Yorkshire. Thus 'W.G.' has the record — not likely to be broken yet — of doing this feat three times so far in his career.

After half an hour's travel from Liverpool Street Station, you arrive at the cricket ground of the Essex County Club, situated in one of the best parts of Leyton. It is a pretty ground on the whole, though not the prettiest in England, as some of its frequenters are so fond of believing. But the Essex County Club is to be congratulated on the way it has endeavoured to make its ground suitable for the game and comfortable for the spectators. Thanks to the raised seats all round the ground, a fine view of the game is everywhere obtainable, and as the playing area is not too large one can watch a match without straining the eyes, as one has to do at the Oval, or at the Leeds ground of Yorkshire. The wicket is generally in capital trim, and good scores are not uncommon on this ground.

The Essex County Club has had the ground since 1886, and it has persistently struggled, often against very great difficulties, in trying to improve both the position of the club amongst the other county clubs, and also the ground. In each case it has succeeded. The position of Essex on the Championship list of last year is a testimony to the one; the good attendance of the public at many matches here is a proof of the other. It was for a long time objected by some Essex supporters that the ground at Leyton was too far from London to ever become much patronized; but the persistency of the genial Essex secretary, Mr Borradaile, and the groundsman, Freeman, whose motto has been, 'If the public find we're worth coming to see, they'll come', has had its reward, as the three days' attendance of an aggregate of over 25,000 people to see Essex *v.* Lancashire last year amply proves.

The Leyton ground, though young as county grounds go, has had its noteworthy incidents. Here, when the Australians played some years ago, the giant Bonnor lifted a ball from the far wicket clean over the pavilion – a straight drive – and into the neighbouring road! Mr. E. C. Streatfeild on another occasion did ditto; whilst the late F. M. Lucas, a left-handed batsman, sent a ball out of the ground, over the road, over a garden, and into the red house that is so prominent a feature from the ground!

None of the 'new' first-class counties has tried harder during the last few years to bring itself well up to its rivals than Warwickshire, in all that pertains to the possession of a good team and a good ground. Warwickshire's county cricket ground is situated in that suburban district of Birmingham known as Edgbaston. It is one of our largest grounds, covering an area of quite twelve acres. But it has an even greater claim to notice than this, seeing that the wickets are almost always perfect. Authorities have long considered it probably the best 'wicket' in the country, or, at any rate, one of the best three. It is no wonder, then, that scoring rules very high on the Edgbaston ground; and, if anything like fine, dry weather prevails, the side losing the toss knows when its opponents go in, but doesn't know when they are coming out! For such teams as Lancashire, Yorkshire, or Surrey to get fairly set on this ground means something, as Warwickshire have found out to their cost before to-day.

It was here that in Yorkshire *v.* Warwickshire, in 1896, the first-named team made 887 runs, this being the 'record' score for any first-class match; whilst another record was made in the same encounter by four men on one side scoring over 100 each in one innings, viz., Jackson, Wainwright, Peel and Lord Hawke, whilst Hirst only fell a few runs short of this performance in the same innings. At Edgbaston, too, Shilton, for Warwickshire *v.* Leicestershire, in 1888, accomplished the unusual feat of taking 4 wickets with 4 consecutive balls. A crowd of 15,000 can be capitally accommodated here; in fact, that is the 'record' gate of the Edgbaston ground, when Warwickshire played the Australians in 1896. The pavilion has recently been enlarged, and is now one of the best arranged in the country. Besides all the usual rooms and offices, there is a capital dining-room which will seat 100; and in every way the Warwickshire committee has tried to make its ground an ideal one. To a very great extent it has succeeded.

The county ground of Somerset, at Taunton, carries the enviable reputation of being at the same time one of the prettiest of English cricket enclosures, and of having usually one of the very best wickets. It is bounded on one side by the River Tone, from which the town takes its name; and few more delightful views are available from any cricket ground than is here presented to the eye. As to its reputation for first-class wickets, it has good proof of this in the fact that on it was made the highest score ever totalled by one man in a first-class match, viz., the superb 424 of Mr A. C. MacLaren, for Lancashire *v.* Somerset, in 1895. Lancashire's innings on this occasion totalled up to 801, which is the largest that county ever made, and, though not a record, is well on the way towards Yorkshire's later total of 887.

Naturally, from the comparative smallness of Taunton, and the scattered nature of Somerset's population, there are not, and cannot be, the crowds at the Taunton ground that one sees in London or in the North of England. But the Taunton spectators wax great and enthusiastic sometimes, as when their county made a 'tie' with Middlesex, in 1890, after a severe fight. Somerset was not then a 'first-class' county. And later, when, in 1897, between the same counties, the last Somerset man going in with the score tremendously in arrears at twenty-five minutes to the 'drawing time', managed to play out time, though bowled by a 'no ball' some four minutes before the appointed hour, the scene was of that kind named 'indescribable'.

Yes, Somerset men are proud of the Taunton ground, as well they may be, for a more glorious turf is not to be found on any cricket field. It is, perhaps, worth noting that the ball is often hit out of the field by the terrible 'S. M. J.', Vernon Hill, and Mr Phillips. The latter, twice in one match last season, hit the ball not only out of the field, but clean across the River Tone!

One of the most memorable scenes on the Taunton ground was at last season's close, when Somerset managed to defeat Surrey for the second time that season, and robbed her of the County Championship, to Lancashire's great delight. Didn't the crowd line up! They might almost have been taught how to do it at the Oval!

There are three counties of whose cricket grounds, so far, nothing has been mentioned, but of which a few words must be said.

That of Derbyshire county, at Derby, has nothing specially significant about it beyond the usual appurtenances of a good cricket ground. Whilst usually well attended, it has never had the 'gates' that one would expect from an old cricket county like Derbyshire. The wicket is soon affected by rain; indeed, a few sharp showers during a match often make a world of difference in the cricket. It was on this ground, in 1881, that Lancashire's great cricketer, R. G. Barlow, took six wickets for three runs, doing the 'hat' trick in this performance. Probably this is a 'record' in county matches.

Leicestershire County Club has a good ground, nicely situated and well arranged, at Leicester. Here again the attendance is usually small. The ground is of average size, and the wicket is fast and true, fairly high scoring being the rule rather than the exception. Owing to the very recent inclusion of Leicestershire amongst first-class counties, however, there has scarcely yet been time for the Leicester ground to take that position and fame amongst its rivals that the play of some Leicester batsmen gives promise of in the future.

Most of Hampshire's 'home' matches take place on the Southampton cricket ground. Here, as a rule, scoring is good, and this is undoubtedly owing to the excellent wicket, for when a batsman can score 125 against such bowlers as Hirst, Wainwright and Peel, the wicket must be good. There is every hope that, as the county club progresses, the county ground will be further developed, until it becomes in reality one of England's 'first-class' grounds. As with that at Leicester, and one or two others, its comparatively recent attainment to that class has not yet given it the chance of being enrolled in the list of those grounds where the feats of the century have been performed.

Windsor Magazine 1898

48

Country Cricket

'W.P.'

There is a story told of a country umpire who, on being appealed to in a moment of doubt, unhesitatingly replied 'Out!' adding with a chuckle of profound simplicity, 'Hurray! I've won five bob!' — the same authority, I believe, who later in the day gave marked evidence of the wavering of his judgment by the following extraordinary decision, 'No ball — wide ball — no, by Jove! He's caught it! Out. Over.' To those accustomed to the game in its highest form at Lord's or the Oval, such an instance of venality and instability must appear in the highest degree incredible; but to any one whose powers do not entitle him to play for his county, and who has had experience of cricket in out-of-the-way provincial corners, nothing, however seemingly far-fetched, will be judged impossible, or even improbable. It was only the other day that in that remote spot, Bolesford, on the appearance for the first time of a noted University bat, who had the misfortune to place his leg in front of the wicket very early in his innings, Mr Baggs, the miller and umpire, gave it as his opinion with great firmness that it was not out, appending for the satisfaction of the astonished and angry field the explanation: 'I want to see the young gentleman bat.'

At Bolesford, on great match days, play begins at eleven o'clock, and long before that hour the geese are driven off the common, and the pegs driven in for the ladies' tent. Half-an-hour later the ostler of the Jolly Gardeners marks out the crease as near as may be, and the first stragglers put in their appearance; Mr Stebbings, the butcher, who bowls a desperate pace, Mr Brown, the saddler, much esteemed for his underhand, and Mr Stinch, the groom, especially renowned for the impartiality with which he whips all sorts of balls round to square-leg. At the Jolly Gardeners, on the edge of the common, preparations are being made on a large scale; the long room over the stable entrance has been swept for luncheon, and the tinkling piano dusted, the stone-china with the blue and white flowers descends from the shelves to the uses of common life once more, and in accordance with express request vast numbers of spring onions have been torn up for the cold beef, not without some observations, however, from the genteel Mr Brown, who warmly questions the propriety of eating onions with ladies so near in the tent at long-leg; an objection met by Mr Stinch in almost the precise words of a famous comedian, 'I don't care a dem for the ladies, I will have bread and inions!' By this time the rest of the eleven have arrived, and are engaged in a lively exchange of compliments with Annie, the barmaid, who, as she is in the habit of seeing most of them at least once a day, is familiar with all their weaknesses, and plays upon them with complete facility; even going to the length of opening and reading aloud a mysterious note pushed across the counter by Mr Gill, cab proprietor, in which (he himself being a notorious *gourmet*) the offer is made of his hand and a lobster salad. Punctually at the hour the opposing team selected by the local Member of Parliament to dispute the palm with Bolesford drive up in a waggonette from the house where they have been entertained at breakfast, and after much exchange of apparent jovial greeting an adjournment is made to the smoking-room to dress, and thence to the common to find fault with the wicket. Apparent jovial greeting only, for to the acute observer it is plain that the two elevens (this being the conquering match in a succession of six years) are profoundly jealous of each other, and will lose no opportunity that may arise for cheating, if it can be managed without any marked flagrancy, of which both are fully aware if only from the experience of past contests: and hence a certain tenderness in relations that otherwise seem frank and unconstrained.

The Member of Parliament's team consists principally of an auctioneer, a veterinary surgeon, and three or four clerks and young farmers, the rest being merely personal friends from London who are staying in the house, the Member of Parliament himself performing the office of captain. Each side has provided an umpire, who eye each other disparagingly apart; the one being a waiter, who assists at the neighbouring gentry's parties, and now appears in his evening trousers and a flannel jacket; the other the only constable of the district, with so complete a confidence in the honour of Bolesford to preserve the peace

357

in his absence that he stands with his tunic unbuttoned, and his helmet so arranged as to exclude the sun from his left eye.

'Play', calls the constable, on being assured that all the preliminaries, down even to a trial ball, have been observed, and Bolesford scores the first six runs by the ball bumping over the long stop's shoulder, and losing itself in a furze-bush covered with linen. For the first hour varying fortune attends the game, and by the time the ladies come down from the house the telegraph board marks that five Bolesford men have gone for forty runs, among them the schoolmaster, who, having been run out through want of judgement on the part of Mr Stebbings, the butcher, threw his spectacles on the ground and stamped on them. The scene is without doubt picturesque, and, to the ordinary observer who knows nothing of the passions seething beneath, eminently peaceful. South of the common runs the high road, along which passes the traffic of the district; the doctor's gig, the nobility's landau, and in long array hay carts and waggons containing sacks of barley and empty fruit baskets, on which in the hot sunshine lie stretched the drivers asleep in all the uncouthness of rustic slumber.

Further along, one or two carriages, full for the most part of children taking their morning drive, are drawn up to watch the game, and beyond them the tradesmen's carts, the occupants of which thus much delay the delivery of orders that they may report in the village how the Bolesford men are faring. Close by stand a row of ancient cottages, tumble-down and unwholesome, in strong contrast to the indigo merchant's new bright red house, shining with a broad glimmer of conservatory, under whose sheltering park walls sits the aged Brummles, who once hit a ball into Lord Nelson's carriage when he stopped to watch the game with Lady Hamilton, and who has missed no match or luncheon for sixty years. It is a pathetic sight to see him silently eating a scrap of cold meat among the noisy crowd in the long room of the Jolly Gardeners, and with trembling fingers filling and lighting his worn black pipe, few troubling themselves to notice the old man with the large hooked nose, the drawn mouth, and the fallen cheeks, who fought and was wounded at Badajoz.

At twelve o'clock the children come shouting out of school, and much increase the difficulties of those fielding out by tumbling up against their legs, and making unpleasant remarks when desired to retire behind the boundary flags. The majority have brought their luncheons of bread and meat and bread and jam, and these remain till half-past one; when, as the bell rings for their return, with a final whoop of derision they pull down the sheet behind the bowler's arm, and loosen the tent-ropes; not altogether with impunity, however, for the constable, discarding for the moment the character of umpire, swoops down upon them in retreat, and manages to capture a poor little mite with one eye, on whose blind side he made a dashing charge. By two o'clock Bolesford is despatched for eighty-three, not even the efforts of Mr Smith, who twice hit the ball amidst enthusiasm into his master's stable-yard, being successful in further raising the total. A move is now made for lunch; and, all taking off their cricket-shoes out of regard to the landlady's floor, the Member of Parliament carves the cold beef, and the schoolmaster carves the lamb.

At first complete silence prevails, broken only by irregular remarks fired from the length of the table at each other by the opposite heads, who differ considerably over the appearance of the hay-crop: but, as the sherry and the malt liquors flow, conversation increases in volume; and, when the veterinary surgeon has satisfied nature by twice to beef and gooseberry tart, he rises, in compliance with the general call, and, in a voice in which emotion and repletion struggle for the mastery, sings of 'the miller's daughter who has hair of golding hue'. To him succeeds a porter with a comic song, the burden of which we repeat, in the hope that he will remember the second verse: but, as he informs us, 'the line is locked' and his memory a blank, so he sits down to give place to a commercial traveller, who, with his hand in the bosom of his flannel shirt, gives us a Christy Minstrel ballad, with the fitful and melancholy chorus of 'Mother!' Even the Member himself obliges, in his best undergraduate manner, with 'Landlord, fill the flowing bowl'. And then, after a speech or two, the majority go out to smoke and throw at the coconuts balanced in front of a dirty cloth on a corner of the common. Some few of the more convivial are left to linger over the sherry, which they employ in patriotic toasts, until the Royal family and the bottle both being, fortunately, exhausted together, with three cheers for nobody in particular, they separate, or, in the more delicate phrase of William Meister, 'glide apart'.

It is not to be wondered at, therefore, if play for the next half hour is characterized by a certain wildness, or if the ball is thrown and hit with a hearty vagueness dangerous to all concerned; nor is any one

359

astonished when long slip falls, apparently with a hiccough, in the act of fielding, and long leg starts at a great pace in the opposite direction to the ball, in the firm belief that he is pursuing it. The ladies return to their tent to drink tea, without which, indeed, they would not have come near us, and at half past four the children come out of school again and resume their tactics of the morning. By this time there is round the ground what is known as a 'gallery', consisting of half-a-dozen carriages, a cart or two drawn up in front of the inn, a few haymakers asleep in the sun, and twenty or thirty quidnuncs on benches, who sneer and jeer at the catches occasionally dropped, or balls misfielded. For it must be confessed that the game is going badly for Bolesford, a young farmer being chiefly the cause, by the vigour with which he hits all sorts of balls, in all kinds of directions, with lusty impartiality; and, notwithstanding the gallant effort of the constable, who gives him run out, when it is plain to all (including the constable) that he is no such thing, the Bolesford total is passed, and the Bolesford flag is 'tore'.

Still, though the match is lost, all excitement has not evaporated, for the other umpire, burning with shame at, or with a desire to emulate, the constable's crime (of which he is perfectly well qualified to measure the enormity), triumphantly decides a point in the batsman's favour which it is quite clear should be against him, and aggravates the wrong by a wag of the head in the constable's direction, evidently to be interpreted 'You see there are others who can cheat besides you!' Then arise murmurs of discontent and cries of derision, which take articulate form from the lips of the schoolmaster, at point, who brands the offender with the fearful epithet of 'unconsholeable raskill!' a charge about to be repelled by force, did not the Member interfere on his man's behalf with the declaration that it was six of one and half-a-dozen of the other, and that now they were quits.

From that time to the drawing of stumps scarcely anything occurs worthy of notice; the only incident being the withdrawal of the ladies to dress for dinner, and the weariness of Bolesford, shown by the increasing lassitude with which they field, and the frequent inquiries as to the time. At seven o'clock the stumps are returned to the stable of the Jolly Gardeners, and the great match is over, Bolesford magnanimously surrounding the wagonette to cheer the victorious eleven, who return to the Member's house to supper. And thence they should have departed to their several homes, but two at least there were who somehow contrived to go astray; one, a young farmer, who was discovered by a shepherd at five o'clock in the morning fast asleep by the roadside, clasping his cricket bag, with his flannel trousers tied round his neck; the other the auctioneer, who knocked up half Bolesford, though, providentially, he omitted the constable, in search of his cousin, who, he declared, resided thereabouts, though, in fact, living many miles away, – a trifling obliviousness never forgotten by Bolesford, who, for some time afterwards, always received his appearance in the cricket-field with ironical cries of 'Have any of ye seen my coz.?'

The Graphic 1883

49

Village Cricket

'The Gaffer'

Village cricket – it is not pretentious; its scores trouble no printing machine save that of the parish magazine; a century is viewed as an earthquake; even a combined hundred is an exception; while its bowling is not great, and its pitches would disgrace the production of the LCC parks. Yet there is a peculiar fascination about it which is different from that of either county or good club cricket, though just as full of charm.

To begin with, there are its beautiful environments — and what could fail to be luring, if surrounded by miles of stretching fields losing themselves in blue-misted distance? Haymaking in busy progress all around in June, golden cornfields adding colour to the green glory of August — these things compensate for any annoyance caused through unevenness of ground and rabbit-holes in the outfield waiting for the unwary foot of the flying fieldsman.

Then there is the splendid mixed composition of the teams. The squire, the curate, the schoolmaster, the grocer, the blacksmith, the doctor, farmers, labourers, the groom and the butler from the hall, and probably in the holidays a few public school boys whose homes are in the district. This variety is found in most village teams, rendering them splendid mediums for the spread of Kropotkin ideals. But above all, what makes real village cricket so delightful is its humour, for which it is unequalled by any other class of cricket. County cricket has but little charm in this particular way. It is all seriousness on the first class or minor county field. A dog sometimes wanders out from the ring of spectators and causes laughter, sometimes a pig trespasses, as at Worcester; but for the rest, what laughter there is comes from a ballooning innings by the last man, a threatened tricky run on the part of, say, a Hayward, and such-like things that raise the muscles of the mouths of the earnestly-watching thousands. In good class club cricket, the wit is mostly confined to the clothes-huddled dressing rooms of the pavilion, and is usually foreign to the game, while in the lower order of club cricket, among the red capped, be-belted brigade of the hired pitch, the laughter is more often than not but the outcome of vulgarity. On the actual village ground, however, one is faced by humour everywhere, and laughter unconstrained renders many an otherwise dull innings a choice morsel to ruminate over at leisure, and recount again in the bar parlour. And hidden away behind the hills, lost among the grazing sheep, where the reporter does not deem it worth while to penetrate, are to be found hundreds of quaint happenings, worth the while of recording, every bit as much as the bare statistics of All-England matches.

Such is the case in 'Our Village' club, with its ground high up above a Salopian valley through which the Severn 'winds its gushing course'. It is but a rough, sloping field, with about an acre levelled for the wicket; yet it serves. Thistles abound in the outfield, scraggy, brambled hedges invite lost balls on two of its sides, and a long steep slope leading down to a coppice tempts the village hitters on the two other sides, and jolts the unfortunate fieldsmen as they endeavour to run swiftly but cautiously down in chase of the rolling ball, that naturally gathers speed in the course of its downward career, until perchance stopped by a tuft of grass, or the side of a browsing sheep. With the mention of a little wooden pavilion, a score or so of yokels squatting on the matted grass under the elms, the squire's daughter scoring under a large oak, and a small boy to alter the telegraph, our village cricket ground is placed before you.

There, as they play, pervaded by the great spirit of cricket that seems to have sprung from Nature herself, let us take a peep at them over the leaf-wrapped hedge.

A wicket has just fallen, and the squire, six feet three, grey, and capped with the brilliant colours of the MCC, is standing by his sticks waiting for the incoming batsman. A few claps, but more laughter, herald the fact that the new man has just left his seat and now approaches the wicket. A rough-hewn collier from the black burrows away beyond the distant wood-crested hills, he is. A weirdly-clothed man with a crinkled face, brown and hard like the polished root of a knotted briar. He goes to the pitch with a strange ungainly stride, his face all smiles, but his soul on fire. Not a ball bowled to him he allows to pass unsmote at. Hence the laughter from the handful of lookers on. A strange pair to play as partners; the one most of the rest of the week stripped to his coarsened hide, hewing away at the great black rocks, while the perspiration streams down his body and his veins stand out dark blue on the wrinkled brow; the other a gentleman; and each is the better for his game of village cricket once a week.

Lying full length just beneath our very noses is the occasional wicket-keeper, the village postmaster; a bad bat, a worse keeper. He is worth, however, passing notice; because of him it still lingers in the memory of all the club that he once stumped a man in a most remarkable manner, for when standing well back in his usual way, a high bumping flyer hit him on the chest, and rebounding with a drum-like sound, removed the bail of the scornful batsman, who was taking advantage of the wicket-keeper's inability. An extraordinary case of stumping surely!

But a few yards away is the greatest curiosity we have; a one-armed man! A true cricketer certainly. Not to be deprived of his game through the loss of a limb, he practised and practised more assiduously than ever after being deprived of the whole of his left arm by amputation, necessitated through the careless shot of a youthful sportsman. Originally a good batsman, he applied his energies to bowling as soon as he was fit to continue the daily round of his work as a farmer, and gradually began to be able to send down a very good ball, handicapped though he was by the unbalanced condition of his body. Then, longing still to feel the joy of having a knock, he schooled his remaining arm to keep the bat under control, and now, behold him as our best bowler, and though a long way down the list, not by three or four the worst bat. As a rule, indeed, he can be relied upon for a dozen, sometimes he gets even twenty — which is considered good on our wicket — mostly obtained through glances and snicks through the slips. A drive is, of course, practically out of the question, but straight balls he can keep from his sticks, and fast balls, outside the off-stump, he can cut square or place between the slips; so strong is he in his wrist. The strength, it seems, of his two arms has gone into the one, through exercise. And to see him loading hay faster than two ordinary labourers is a lesson to the lazy that might almost deserve a knighthood. To see him 'crupper' a horse with his teeth aiding his hand, or put a brake on a wagonette, holding the reins between his strong knees for the brief time that he takes to slip the lever, or master an unbroken colt are, too, sights for the gods. Thus, through all the feats of plucky strength and quickness performed in his daily work, he is surrounded by a certain glamour of interest that renders his inclusion in the team a matter of pride to us all. A curiosity we would not substitute for the local residence of W.G. himself.

A little way off, the curate, now with his many striped jacket, looking more like a jester than a priest, is discussing in terms of social equality with a one time private soldier — now the wheelwright's assistant — the latest doings of the Worcester eleven. The landlord of the 'Squirrel' Hotel, he, too, is sitting laughing, chatting, and exchanging tobacco with an old Sherborne boy. Again, one who was born and brought up in the county union is testing the bat of an owner of five hundred guinea Herefords. What a splendid thing, then, is this game of cricket as played on a country field; where there are no nets to practise in, where the marking of the creases is usually done, like the cutting and rolling of the pitch, by the early arrivals of the playing team, where all are amateurs, and the richest is as the poorest. A good influence, sowing the seed of real honest socialism faster than any philosophy, any creed, or religion. 'A mere game', say those who know not of the greatness of the 'glorious game with the beautiful name' — yet what a game!

It matters not if the scores are low, or if the Squire's partner leaves him waiting at the wicket again for the next man before another over is completed, nor that high risers are frequent, and black eyes by no means rare, nor that the players do not always put their legs together in fielding. It is the spirit that matters; the playing of the game for the love of it. The spirit that does not stake its whole desire on winning; the spirit that only the true cricketer understands; the spirit that brings a kindling light to every player's soul, leaves every man the better for it, and even throws a ray of youth back into the wrinkled face of old Mother Bantock, the carrier, while, leaving her donkey eating a choice thistle on the roadside, she gazes over the gate for a few brief moments on the village team at play.

Cricketer and Hockey Player 1907

50

The Private Test Match

Barry Wilson

Lionel Robinson was an Australian who tried hard to establish himself as a landed English gentleman. He never quite made it — he had the money but not quite the style. But he did carve a tiny niche in history for himself: he had a passion for cricket and he built an Australian cricket pitch on his isolated Norfolk estate; and in 1921 he staged what amounted to his own private Test Match in his own backyard, during the course of which England's greatest batsman played the finest innings of his career.

Lionel Robinson was born in Ceylon in 1866 but his parents returned to Melbourne when he was a few weeks old. His father became city editor of the *Melbourne Age*; Lionel himself dabbled in financial journalism before moving into stockbroking, where he prospered mightily. Before he was 35 burgeoning financial interests brought him to London and he became a powerful figure in the City.

To give substance to his new station in life he sought a suitable country seat. He found what he wanted in Norfolk, in the village of Old Buckenham, near Attleborough, 15 miles south of Norwich. The previous owner of the 2000-acre estate was the singular Indian antiquarian Freddy Duleep Singh (son of a deposed Sikh maharajah), who, like Robinson, also had problems in gaining full aristocratic acceptance in England (but for duskier colonial reasons; Duleep's more famous son gained another sort of acceptance when selected to play cricket for England in 1929–30).

Without delay the tough, swashbuckling Australian financier tore down the comfortable, elegant Duleep residence, and, in 1906, set about erecting an appropriate home for himself. It is reputed that, in all, he spent close to £1 million. Twice the building was pulled down and started again. At last he was happy with specially imported Dutch bricks and a style which could perhaps now be described as '1930's baroque'. The house had 14 bathrooms — a wondrous Australian novelty at that time.

He had Billy Smith, the local barber from Attleborough, cycle out to the hall every morning to shave him. He employed a superior butler, Royce, who ran the household.

But as a country gentleman he was neither genial, effortless nor stylish. He was obstinate and aggressive, and known for his abusive slanging matches with staff.

Increasingly, he turned his attention to his sporting interests. He built splendid stables and accumulated a fine and typically successful racing stud. The shooting was extensive. And at enormous expense he built the Old Buckenham Hall cricket ground in a clearing in the wood that surrounded the hall.

Robinson had been a regular spectator at the Melbourne Cricket Ground, and he had watched a lot of cricket in England. He was sick of the slow English pitches. He wanted to build a hard, fast Australian type of wicket, and he reckoned that in dry Norfolk (with rainfall half that in Melbourne) he at least had the right geography. He dredged a lagoon near the house for fine clay as foundation for the wicket area (and the soil mixture was reinforced with chicken netting). After the First World War, to further improve the pitch, he actually imported special turf from Australia.

The pitch proved as fast as Robinson hoped. Part of the original wicket area is still in use, known as the 'Australian end'. Present groundsman Billy Lancaster, who scored a century at Old Buckenham in 75 minutes in 1951, says: 'It's when we use the Australian end that the runs really come.'

Robinson soon made the cricket ground a focus for the sporting fraternity. In the early days the village team (which is now the only one using the Old Buckenham cricket ground) had to play on the village green: the ground at the hall had been reserved for the visiting toffs.

Robinson appointed as his personal cricket manager the somewhat boozy but still very shrewd A. C. MacLaren, who had been an outstanding bat for England. MacLaren had lived in a cottage on the Old Buckenham estate for many years.

It was in the first week of June 1921 that Robinson and MacLaren pulled off their small country coup. They persuaded the touring

Australian Test team — the finest to tour England since the war — to play the second match of their tour at Old Buckenham.

The teams for Robinson's Old Buckenham match were formed of nearly Test Match strength. For Australia: W. Bardsley, H. L. Collins, C. G. Macartney, J. M. Taylor, W. W. Armstrong (captain), J. M. Gregory, J. Ryder, H. L. Hendry, H. Carter (wicketkeeper), E. A. McDonald, A. A. Mailey.

For Mr Robinson's XI: J. B. Hobbs, D. J. Knight, V. W. C. Jupp, E. Hendren, A. P. F. Chapman, J. W. H. T. Douglas, P. G. H. Fender, A. C. MacLaren (captain), G. E. C. Wood (wicket-keeper), C. H. Gibson, J. C. White.

The Old Buckenham match, seen as a full dress-rehearsal for the 1921 Tests, got unusually extensive publicity. Just a few months earlier the Australians had drubbed England in Australia by five to nothing, which is a Test record still not equalled. Could Jack Hobbs, only just past the peak of his powers, cope with the new Australian fast bowlers Jack Gregory and Ted McDonald?

The Old Buckenham cricket ground was nearly four miles from Attleborough railway station. All hireable pony and traps worked to and fro for the duration of the three-day match. Bicycles, pedestrians, horse carts and motor-cars crammed the village roads. The Norwich *Eastern Daily Press* recorded: 'There was a great pilgrimage from all parts of Norfolk and the adjoining counties to Old Buckenham yesterday, and as the road traffic drew nearer the magnetic centre the country folk, all wide-eyed, no doubt wondered that a mere cricket match could cause so much commotion and stir . . . Never before had so many enthusiasts come from far and near.'

Even for this great occasion Mr Robinson did not depart from his practice of never charging entrance fees (although £163 was collected for the Norwich hospital). About 2000 people crowded the tiny ground on Wednesday, the first day, but it rained almost continuously. Only 15 minutes' play was possible, during which the Australians amassed 18 for no wicket.

The second day, by contrast, was bright, sunny and warm, and from the early morning all roads in the vicinity were thronged. Estimates of the crowd that day varied between 7000 and 10,000 — undoubtedly still the biggest crowd ever to watch a cricket match in East Anglia.

The *Eastern Daily Press* reported: 'This was one of the most wonderful days in the history of Norfolk cricket . . . Ranged behind the deep human wall were hundreds upon hundreds of motor-cars the roofs of which were converted into stands, and from these lofty perches distant views were obtained of the play. The park trees, now in their May glory of leaf, alone were sacred . . .'

For the English partisans the day was glorious in almost every respect; it was to be one of few such days that summer.

Astonishingly, the star-studded Australians were bowled out an hour after lunch for a feeble 136 (Douglas 6 for 64). This was the team's lowest score of the tour.

When the English team batted Knight was out in the second over. But then Hobbs and Jupp attacked the Australian bowling with a gusto unequalled since before the war. It was this onslaught that provoked Gregory and McDonald to resort to tactics that were to demoralize the Englishmen for the rest of the tour.

At the end of the tour, in which the Australians won the Tests three—nothing, and lost only two of their 38 games, Wisden selected both McDonald and Gregory among their Five Cricketers of the Year, and commented: 'This was maybe the finest Australian team we have ever seen, and it was the fast bowling that made the side so good. Never before have English batsmen been so demoralized by pace . . . Never were batsmen so obviously intimidated . . . McDonald was probably the finer bowler, but Gregory was far more alarming.'

At Old Buckenham Gregory and McDonald attacked Hobbs and Jupp with quite unprecedented ferocity, on a pitch that was remarkably fast. Both batsmen were hit several times. Both were eventually forced to retire hurt, Jupp with a broken thumb, Hobbs with a recurrence of a thigh strain that put him out of action for two months.

But before he was injured Hobbs showed what a difference he could have made. Several times he hoisted short pitched balls over the beech trees, at least 130 yards from the wicket. He scored 85 in just over 90 minutes. Years later, when asked on television which was the finest innings of his career, Sir Jack said: 'It was a minor match in Norfolk against the Australians in 1921. Always when I look back I think that was one of my best innings—if not *the* best. Everything went right that day; all my strokes came easily.'

All was anti-climax when Hobbs left the crease with the score at 125 for 1. J. W. H. T. ('Johnny Won't Hit Today') Douglas stonewalled characteristically, and old Archie MacLaren, going in last, reminded the crowd of his legendary hitting power before he closed the innings at 256 for 9. The match petered out in a draw when the rain returned.

Ill-luck now dogged Old Buckenham Hall. The next owner, Earnest Gates, a successful north country businessman, died two years after taking up residence, and his son Everard is remembered in the village for his wild parties, complete with what are still remembered darkly as 'chorus girls'. He sold up in 1937 and Old Buckenham boys' school was started. The Hall was gutted by fire in 1952, after which the school and the thatched cricket pavilion were moved to Brettenham in Suffolk. They're still there.

Today the isolated cricket ground, little more than a fenced off clearing with narrowing boundaries, is struggling to survive even as a village cricket ground.

Sunday Times 1977

51

Fashionable Cricket

Is it true that the last and most serious symptom of 'blue fever' is about to disappear from the list of engagements for the London season? Was the match played the other day at Lord's actually the last of the Eton and Harrow matches to be played in London? Is the institution about which so much sham enthusiasm is warmed up, and so much ridiculous rodomontade written, to be finally washed out by a steady downpour of rain? Perhaps. That is to say, if the persons — presumably old enough to know better — who write letters to the papers signed 'dark' or 'light' blue, do not prove too powerful for the authorities of Harrow. To judge by these letters, and the talk of the days of the Eton and Harrow match, the game of cricket is the noblest outcome of the thought and thews of man, and one to which other studies may worthily be set aside. For what chance, so far as popular renown is concerned, has a senior wrangler or a double-first against the stroke of the University boat or the captain of the University eleven? He may get on terms with the strong-armed and fleet-footed one later in life, but as a youth he is naught to the hero of the oar and bat. That this popular adoration of muscular feats is a reaction against the 'midnight oil' theory of existence is now clear enough, but whether the enthusiasm for cricket can be kept up to its present fever-heat is a little doubtful.

It is true that cricket appeals to the English people as a whole, and is, like fox-hunting, a truly democratic amusement. It goes through every stratum of that many-plied structure known as English society, and does under certain conditions admirable service in bringing various sorts and conditions of men together. What can be more pleasant than the evening game on the village-green, when the parson defends his wicket with might and main against that terrible bowler the village carpenter, who is always 'dead on' the wicket, or that insidious doctor, whose slow 'twisters' bewilder the batsman, who has only just escaped the heavy firing of his predecessor? What is more delightful than the home-and-home match between village and village, or between school and school? All those who come to see are interested in the game or the school, and there is a pleasant association about the meeting, such as that which made the day of the University boat-race once the pleasan-test of the year, instead of the aquatic Derby it now is, with every disagreeable feature of the Epsom kermess multiplied by ten. He would indeed be churlish who would grudge the lookers-on at really good cricket the pleasure of feeling themselves, in spirit at least, again exulting over a long drive, a clean cut, or a slashing if dangerous leg hit, and who would raise his eyebrows and shrug his shoulders at the grave college dons, who lose their gravity nowhere save on the cricket-field.

It is because we know good cricket when we see it, and sympathize both with players and appreciative onlookers, that the spectacle of Lord's during an Eton and Harrow match raises our ire. We know that of the assembled thousands not one in five either knows or cares anything about cricket, or has but the faintest connection with either of the competing schools. Lord's has been compared to a race-course, with peer and peasant anxiously watching the race, and feeling the pulse quicken as the leaders close at the half-distance and race home stride for stride; but we confess that we cannot see the aptness of the comparison. It will apply to the village match, but those who affect to see in Lord's a great democratic institution forget the gate-money, which effectually deprives it of any attraction for the masses. Moreover, the London masses do not care much for cricket, probably because they have very little chance of exercising any taste they may have for the noble game; but if they did, the half-crown gate-money would effectually keep them out. Public schools cricket at Lord's can, indeed, no more be regarded as a popular institution than the Sandown Club race-course, Hurlingham, Prince's, or the Orleans Club. In fact, the cricketing and scholastic aspects of the match have been so entirely overshadowed by the social and gastronomical importance of the event, that, except as affording opportunity for ill-timed applause and ill-bred censure, the two elevens might be dispensed with altogether, and much additional space gained for the accommodation of the carriages and their inhabitants. More tents for light refreshments could then be pitched; and, with the addition of a few marquees and all the musicians of the Household Brigade, a very good fashionable version of old Greenwich fair could be produced.

The change wrought by the last twenty years at Lord's has been gradual, but unchecked, as the advance of cricket itself in popular estimation. A century and a half ago cricket existed, it is true, but was classed with vulgar amusements, such as bull-baiting and boxing – not yet raised to the rank of a science. A nobleman who so far forgot himself as to consort with cricketers was denounced for his uncleanly living; aristocratic contempt going so far as to say that a gentleman who would play at cricket would eat black-puddings, whatever precise amount of turpitude may be promoted by that gastronomic feat. But in Opie's time, as is shown by his famous picture of the Red Boy holding the curiously curved bat of the period, the sons of peers played at cricket, and very funny they looked in the days when boys were dressed like men.

Let us imagine a boy keeping wicket in a cocked hat, red laced coat, breeches, shoes and buckles, like the tiny batsman painted by Opie. It seems odd, but perhaps not more so than the costume of I Zingari would have appeared to Sir Charles Grandison. Once taken up by the public schools, cricket, year by year, displaced the many sports of our grandfathers, to wit – bull-baiting, cock-fighting, badger-drawing, and boxing; but, so late as the day when Fuller Pilch batted, and Alfred Mynn bowled, in stove-pipe hats, braces, and the now extinct articles then known as 'white ducks', Lord's cricket-ground was not converted into a vast picnic. This object hardly entered into the calculations of the shrewd, hard-headed Scot, from whom the famous field takes its name.

The first home of cricket in London was the White Conduit-fields – at least that was the domain of the first cricket club. As the White Conduit district was built over, a cricket-ground was established on the place now occupied by Dorset Square, the original domicile of the Marylebone Cricket Club. Hence Lord's was driven by inexorably advancing bricks and mortar to a 'location' between North and South Bank. Then came the canal, driving him farther afield, till he secured the now well-known space north of the St John's Wood Road, not without difficulty, and a heavy whip of the Marylebone Club to acquire a long lease; for 'big money' was offered by the enterprising builders who have succeeded in covering a large part of St John's Wood with edifices equally fragile in structure and reputation. Lord's Cricket Ground was saved, and for many years was a delightful place of resort.

When first the public schools matches were played at Lord's, Winchester participating, not a score of carriages surrounded the ground, and the meeting of old college chums, and the excitement of the sisters and cousins of the boys, was very agreeable to witness. But all is changed, for now the preparations for the Eton and Harrow day assume gigantic proportions. There is a desperate struggle for stray members' tickets, and a noble ambition is shown to have, if not the best turn-out, yet the best luncheon on the ground. The same man who remarked that, if things go on at their present rate, the daily newspapers will be published at midnight, was, until doubt was thrown on the recurrence of the match, occupied in a calculation as to how early on the day preceding the Eton and Harrow picnic he ought to send his carriage, in order to secure what certain writers persist in calling a 'coign of vantage'.

It might have been thought that the fight for precedence could no farther go than the sending of a tenantless carriage to take up a good situation, but the Derby style of refreshment is not luxurious enough for the more ambitious matron. At whatever cost to others, she will have a tent, or, if not a tent, a table on terra firma, and her servants are hard at work in the morning unloading hampers, setting up tables and the rest, and making arrangements for heating soup; for your genuine girl of the period must have hot soup, or her luncheon is spoiled. In sober truth, the luncheon is the real event of the day, and the homage originally devoted to sinew is diverted to stomach. Previous to this supreme event, the Gainsborough hats pretend to take an interest in the match, although eighty per cent of them might, if they would, avow equal ignorance with that of the Russian lady who, at the conclusion of the first innings, enquired 'when the amusements were going to begin'.

When we hear the squeaky voice of a minor pipe out 'played' or 'bowled', our ears are tickled, for the little lad has some knowledge of what he is squeaking about, but what right has that too-radiantly-attired matron, Mrs McSpelter, to clap her hands and applaud every time a light blue hits the ball, whether he makes a run off or not? She knows nothing about either the game or the schools, and only wears light blue because it suits her complexion. Old McSpelter, who married her when he was already middle-aged, most assuredly never enjoyed the advantage of instruction at either Eton, Harrow, or — to judge by appearances — any school, public or otherwise. But Mrs Mac — as the worthy merchant designates her — hopes that her boys, yet young, may in time become of Eton or Harrow. This prospective enthusiasm is difficult to understand. That the young lady whose brother or cousin is at Eton, and has enjoyed the honour of being soundly thrashed by the younger brother of one of the eleven, should clothe herself, literally from top to toe, in the palest blue, is quite comprehensible. She is a pretty blonde to begin with, and impulsive withal — the sort of person capable of wearing papa's racing colours at Ascot, if — and this is a big 'if' — they became her. She knows the name of every one of the young barbarians at play, and would scream out 'bowled' and 'played' were she not restrained by a priggish brother, whose voice is as the sound of a flute, and who is suspected of writing for the Saturday Refrigerator. Not being much of a cricketer himself, the brother, who affects a clerical style of costume, although he is really a briefless barrister, occasionally permits a wintry smile to ripple over his face as a 'four' is scored, quite forgetting that in the playing-fields at Eton two would have been as much as the hit would have counted. But the flute-voiced one never was at Eton, and although he talks persistently of 'University men', never dwelt at either of the traditional seats of learning.

Outside the pavilion, the circle of carriages and the general picnic, circulates an army of loungers, for the most part arrayed like the lilies — Japanese lilies — of the field. There are pretty girls enough, with colour heightened, and eyes glistening with — but no, it cannot be that the champagne-cup, which cheers and inebriates, has been lifted once too often to the veritable arc de cupidon bent above that dimpled chin? There is the young man of the period too, tightly buttoned up in lengthy frock-coat of the M.B. style, or more gaily attired on the model of O'Barry of the War Office, who appears in a white hat, a pink shirt, a cravat of ambiguous blue, a green coat, and nether garments of moonlit grey. It is by no means difficult to those to the manner born, to separate the genuine public school men from the pretenders who vainly imagine that a patch of light or dark blue will in some way connect them with the contending schools. Among them is our old friend ''Arry'. ''Arf-a-crown' will not keep 'Arry — whose barber's shop yields a handsome yearly income — out of Lord's. By no means. He loves to be 'in it', as he says, to rub shoulders with those whom he calls the 'real swells', and he has been to Lord's so often that he talks of Eton and 'Arrow, both of which he attends professionally, as glibly as the best. 'Arry and O'Barry are, we must confess, a little too much for us, and we groan over the cockneyizing of an interesting struggle. Let, as the Harrow authorities properly insist, the boys attend before all to their studies, and if they must play public matches, let them be played away from the picnicking, the flirting, the eternal champagne-cup, the ogling and giggling, the vulgar noise and crush of Lord's.

In plain truth, the Eton and Harrow match, as it is now played, is a sham and a nuisance, crying aloud for abolition.

All the Year Round (conducted by Charles Dickens) 1877

52

Famous Cricket Families

Born Batsmen and Bowlers

There are certain names which suggest the cricket field just as surely as such names as Peel and Gladstone are associated with the House of Commons.

Whether cricket, like wooden legs, is hereditary, is a question with which this article is not concerned. Whatever the reason is, the fact remains that there are certain families every member of whom seems to have been born a batsman or a bowler, and sometimes both.

In any list of such families the Hearnes deserve a very high place indeed, not merely on account of their achievements, but for numerical reasons.

There are in all nine Hearnes who have more or less distinguished themselves in connection with our great national game. Oddly enough, the two most famous are the eldest and the youngest, to wit, 'Old Tom' and J. T. Hearne, the well-known Middlesex bowler.

As Tom Hearne is now seventy-three, his active cricket career, as may be imagined, has been terminated for some time. Thirty years ago he was one of the mainstays of Middlesex, and in 1866 earned the undying distinction of scoring a century − 122, to be exact − in the Gentlemen v. Players match at Lord's. When his days for active play were over, he was still, as head bowler at Lord's, for many years a familiar figure in the cricket world. From this post he retired last year on a well-deserved pension.

J. T. Hearne's exploits in the cricket field are so familiar to every lover of the game that there is no need to mention them here; but there is a story in connection with his first appearance for Middlesex, which, even if it has been told before, is good enough to bear reproduction.

At the time of his *début*, J. T. Hearne was comparatively unknown, and before the match, questions were put to old Tom by the *habitués* of the pavilion as to the precise relationship the new-comer bore to the rest of the famous family. Tom Hearne, who was always very jealous for the good name of his family, was not at all inclined to commit himself till he had seen something further of J.T.'s prowess. 'I don't rightly know,' he replied, 'but I am not sure whether he is any relation at all to us; anyhow, if he is a relation, it is a very distant one.' As the match progressed, and Jack Hearne showed himself to be a bowler of a very high class, old Tom seems to have looked more closely into the family tree; at any rate, at the end of the game he might have been seen arm-in-arm with the 'distant relation', and introducing him everywhere as 'my nephew'. 'He can bowl a bit, can't he?' continued the wily Tom, 'and so he ought, for I taught him.' As a matter of fact, J. T. Hearne is Tom's cousin once removed.

The other most famous members of the Hearne family are Alec, Walter, G.G., and Frank (J.T.'s brother), who have all played for Kent. Frank Hearne took up his abode in South Africa some years ago, where he has been devoting himself to teaching the young colonials how to shoot.

Everything connected with the Fords is on a grand scale. They are giants in height, powerful as smiters, while their initials are multitudinous. As on this last point considerable confusion arises, it may perhaps simplify matters to give a list of the renowned band of brothers, with their initials, and in order of age:—

W. J. Ford, F. W. J. Ford, A. F. J. Ford, H. J. Ford, W. A. J. Ford, L. G. J. Ford, F. G. J. Ford.

What the Lytteltons were to Eton, the Fords were to Repton. The whole of the seven were in the school eleven, and six of them were captains. In all, their name appears twenty-two times in the lists of the school elevens posted in the pavilion at Repton, and for a period of twenty years, without a break, Repton cricket was represented by a Ford. Six of the seven went to Cambridge. Three got blues and did not get a first class; three got a first class and did not get blues. The blues were W.J., A.F.J., and F.G.J.

The youthful enthusiast of to-day who has watched F. G. J. Ford smiting all sorts and conditions of bowling at Lord's and elsewhere, will feel inclined to doubt the statement that he is not the hardest hitter of the Ford family. Mighty hitter as F.G.J. is, his eldest brother, W.J., was mightier still. W. J. Ford, who at one time used to play regularly for Middlesex, bade farewell to county cricket in a characteristic fashion in 1896, when he smashed his triceps in making a colossal drive over the Members' Enclosure at Lord's.

A. F. J. Ford has retired for some time; but L. G. J., who is a parson and a master at Eton, is a shining light of the Windsor Home Park Club, and is quite good enough for first-class cricket if he cared to devote the necessary time to it. W. J. Ford, it should be added, writes about cricket almost as well as he plays it, and has for many years contributed to *Wisden* its annual criticism on public school cricketers.

If the Grace family has not been mentioned till now, it is only because there is nothing new to be told regarding the chief member of it. W. G. Grace is incomparably the greatest cricketer the world has ever seen or is likely to see. As Mr R. H. Lyttelton says, those whose memories don't carry them back to the days when Grace was king don't understand what cricket really is.

In his prime W.G. and ten second-class players would have been strong enough to tackle almost any eleven in the world, and to-day, when he is more than fifty years old, no English team would be quite representative without him. But though it is impossible to find anything fresh to say about W.G.'s superlative excellence, the careers of his brothers may not be so familiar to the younger readers of the *Harmsworth Magazine*.

For many years E. M. Grace was the second best cricketer in England, only because W.G. blocked the way to the first place. All his methods had the originality of genius, and he was the first player to reduce 'pulling' to a science. In minor matches he was probably the most prolific scorer that ever lived. He was a magnificent field at point, and could bowl very deadly lobs on occasions. 'The Coroner', as he is known down Glo'ster way, is seven years older than the Champion, and consequently, when he retired from county matches three years ago, he was by far the oldest player in first-class cricket.

The youngest of the trio of brothers, G. F. Grace, was also an exceptionally fine cricketer. He was only twenty-nine when he died in 1880. A fortnight before his death he had played for England against Australia, when, although he did not make many runs, his brilliant fielding was one of the features of the match. Poor Fred Grace's last match was for the United South of England against Twenty-two of

Stroud. After taking part in this match he slept at an inn where the sheets were damp, with the result that he caught a chill and died within a week.

Cricket seems an hereditary gift with the Graces. At any rate the Champion's uncle, Henry Grace, was a remarkably fine player, and the keenest of enthusiasts about the game. The third generation of cricket-playing Graces is represented in young W.G., the Champion's son, who, as everyone knows, got his blue at Cambridge, and occasionally plays for Gloucestershire.

It must not be supposed that Eton and Repton have it all to themselves in the nurturing of great cricketing families. Harrow can lay claim to two families who, though their members were not as numerous as the Lytteltons and the Fords, yet played a very conspicuous part in the cricket history of England. The Walkers were in their day among the most remarkable cricketers in the country.

There were four of them, all brothers – John, who died in 1885, V.E., R.D., and I.D., upon whom the fame of the family mainly rested. I.D., whose untimely death, it may be remembered, occurred last year just before the Harrow and Eton match, was the youngest and best known of the brothers. Although he did nothing very startling as a schoolboy, he developed into a batsman of the very highest class immediately after leaving Harrow. By playing an innings of 165 in the Gentlemen *v.* Players match, he enrolled his name among the immortals, though perhaps his really greatest feat was when he and Alfred Lyttelton, for Middlesex against Gloucester in 1883, put on 324 runs for the second wicket, and by some cyclonic hitting scored 226 runs in an hour and three-quarters.

But even if I. D. Walker had never scored a run his name would still deserve to be held in grateful remembrance for his services to Harrow cricket. For ten years before his death he acted as coach to the Harrow boys, and some of the results of his coaching can be seen at the present day in the persons of F. S. Jackson and A. C. MacLaren. I.D. and his three brothers all played for Middlesex; indeed it was mainly owing to the Walkers that the Middlesex County Club came into being.

Both John Walker and his brother R.D. played for Oxford, and an account of their fortunes in the 'Varsity match may prove a consolation to youthful blues who find their luck out on the day of the great match. John Walker, though for several years he represented the Gentlemen against the Players, could get no more than nineteen runs, or a haughty average of three, in the six innings he played against Cambridge; and R. D. Walker had an almost equally exhilarating experience in the 'Varsity match. Though he played for five years against Cambridge, the total of his runs amounted to no more than eighty-four, and forty-two of these he made in his first match. Yet during his last three years at Oxford he played for the Gentlemen *v.* Players and scored uncommonly well into the bargain. It is a somewhat remarkable fact that all the Walkers were underhand bowlers; in one match, England *v.* Surrey, V.E. took all the wickets in the first innings — a record no other lob bowler can boast of.

Another very famous name at Harrow is Hadow. Four Hadows played for Harrow against Eton, and subsequently appeared for Middlesex, but of the four brothers only one is alive at the present day. The early death of the three brothers is indeed almost a tragedy. W.H., the eldest, died last September when he was only forty-nine; A.A. died five years ago when he was barely forty, while the youngest, E.M., fell a victim to consumption at the early age of thirty-two. Another member of the family lost his life in the terrible accident on the Matterhorn.

Harrow suggests Eton, and Eton suggests the Studds and Lytteltons. As the doings of the Lytteltons were described in an article which appeared in the March number of the *Harmsworth Magazine*, it is not necessary to go over the same ground again; but the cricket history of the Studd family is writ large in the official score-books of Eton, Cambridge, and elsewhere.

No fewer than six Studds have played for Eton (E.B.T. of that ilk played last year for Harrow), and at one time there were three brothers in the eleven at once — a record only equalled by the Fords. The three were J.E.K., C.T., and G.B., and of these the greatest was C.T. He played for Cambridge, Middlesex, the Gentlemen, and England; but his cricket career was brief, as, shortly after leaving Cambridge, he went out as a missionary to China. He formed one of the English eleven that went down before the Australians in the sensational match at the Oval in 1882.

In that match his score in the second innings was 0, not out; and thereby hangs a tale. In England's second innings, as every cricketer remembers, only 85 were required to win; but Spofforth bowled so magnificently that nine runs were still required when Peate, the last man, came in. As Studd was at the wicket at the other end, there was still a chance of a victory for England; but Peate horrified the spectators by starting hitting at once, instead of merely trying to keep up his wicket, and leaving the scoring to Studd. He hit a two off the first ball he received, and was then clean bowled in trying to do the trick again. Peate's reply, when his captain remonstrated with him, was simply delicious. 'I had to hit,' he said, 'as I couldn't trust Mr Studd to stay in'! The point of the joke will be appreciated when it is remembered that Peate was no batsman, and was only playing in that match for his bowling, while Studd was one of the finest batsmen in the country, and had scored a century only a week previously.

In addition to his batting, Charles Studd was one of the best amateur bowlers of his time, and in the seasons of 1882 and 1883 took over a hundred wickets.

The fame of G. B. and J. E. K. Studd was somewhat dimmed by the brilliancy of C.T., but they were both cricketers far above the average. G.B. scored 120 in the 'Varsity match of 1882, and was generally allowed to be the finest fieldsman in England. What makes the Studds' record particularly noticeable is that they all retired from the game at an age when most cricketers begin to establish their reputation. After the above-mentioned trio, the two best known of the Studd family are H.W. and R.A., both of whom occasionally play for Hampshire.

The Steels, like the Studds, suffer somewhat from the overpowering excellence of one member of their family. A. G. Steel set such a high standard that it would be asking too much to expect all his brothers to live up to it. George Giffen, who may be supposed to know something, regards A. G. Steel as the second-best all-round cricketer the game has yet produced, which is generous of G.G., considering that he is a candidate for that position himself. Possibly, what impressed George Giffen was the contemptuous way A. G. Steel treated the Australian bowling.

In his account of the Australians in the Badminton Library, Mr Steel expresses the highest opinion of their skill as bowlers; but his practice didn't square with his theory, for no English batsman has scored more freely off the colonial trundlers, as the sporting reporters delight to term them. But then, A. G. Steel had a way of scoring freely off every 'trundler' — the home article, as well as the colonial. Though, in his first county match, A. G. Steel played an innings of 70, it was as a bowler that he first made his name, and while a 'fresher' at Cambridge he headed the first-class bowling averages. Unluckily for cricket, A. G. Steel has preferred the more solid honours of a barrister's career, and severed his connection with county cricket in 1888.

Three of his brothers — D.Q., H.B., and E.E. — have played for Lancashire. D.Q. was also in the Cambridge eleven at the same time as his brother, and H.B. still plays sometimes for the Liverpool Club; but the wiles of cricket could never induce any of the Steel family to regard it as anything more serious than a pastime.

If all the Lucases were gathered together, they could easily muster a full cricket eleven between them, though the team would have to include several of the name who are no relation to each other. F.M. and M.P. were brothers, but were no relation to either A.P. or R.S. The most renowned of all the Lucases is undoubtedly A.P., who was in the Cambridge eleven with A. G. Steel. He is a man of many counties, having represented Middlesex, Surrey, and Essex at various periods of his career. He has always been a bat of the instructive order; that is to say, he never made an ugly or 'agricultural' stroke in his life. But in his more youthful days his cricket, though it delighted the expert, was rather too slow to suit the tastes of the unscientific spectator. Once, when playing for Surrey, he carried his bat right through the innings for the portentous score of sixteen. But, slow or fast, A. P. Lucas has undoubtedly been one of the greatest batsmen that ever lived.

The Lucases have not devoted their allegiance to one county. R.S. played for Middlesex, while M.P. and F.M. clung to Sussex. F.M., who died of cholera in India when he was only twenty-seven, was for some time the most successful left-handed batsman in England, and, like R.S., was a tremendous hitter when occasion required.

No list of famous cricketers would be complete without some reference to the Gregorys. Syd Gregory, one of the members of the present Australian eleven, comes of a family of distinguished cricketers. He is a nephew of David Gregory, who captained the first Australian team that ever visited England, and his father, Ned Gregory, and two of his uncles, were among the best known Australian cricketers in the early 'seventies.

Harmsworth Magazine 1899

53

Cricket Surnames

A Competition on Novel Lines

'Historicus'

When the rain is pouring down pitilessly on what should be a fine summer day, or during a spare evening in the long winter months, the cricket enthusiast may pass many a pleasant hour in studying the surnames of players who have taken part in matches of note. The wider the net brought into action, the larger will naturally be the haul obtained. So far as this article is concerned, the term 'matches of note' includes, besides those ranking first-class, games played by any county team, the Gentlemen of a county, a well-known College or School, and good scratch sides; and, as all periods in the game's history are under review, the scope should be sufficiently comprehensive to satisfy the most exacting.

As the result of but little trouble, it is possible to arrange quite an interesting competition when two or more lovers of cricket are gathered together. All that is required is to decide on the nature of the games to be recalled, and for each person to write down all he can recollect so as to comply with the conditions agreed to. It might, for instance, be settled that only surnames which are also place-names — such as Windsor, Westmorland, Preston — should be recognized, or that the lists should be restricted to such as recall articles of furniture, machines, minerals — in fact, almost anything. One rule should be the necessity to place in brackets after the name the title of the side for which the person played, thus: 'Peach (Surrey).' In some cases it would be found that more than one man of the same surname was eligible for inclusion — Barnes and Tate are instances; and when that happens, every instance which can be remembered should be noted. The competition thus provides not only scope for ingenuity, but also a test of memory. It should be added that, so long as the pronunciation of the two words concerned agree, it is immaterial whether the spelling is identical, thus 'Rhodes' and 'roads' would pass.

After a little experience one will be surprised to find how readily once can recall names desired. To give some idea of this a few lists are appended, the first dealing with various branches of natural history. The reader may also like to associate the names with various teams, and, should he prove unable to complete the task, he could take the opportunity of testing the knowledge of the local cricket Solomon.

I. – Natural History.

First let it be stated that an Almond and a Raison have played for Essex, a Beet and a Root for Derbyshire, and a Bull and a Drake for Bucks.

(*a*) *Birds*. – Buzzard, Capon, Cockerell, Crane, Drake, Duck, Finch, Gull, Hawke, Martin, Nightingale, Partridge, Peacock, Raven, Robins, Rook, Sheldrake, Sparrow, Starling, Swallow, Swan, Swift, Teale, Wildgoose, Woodcock.

(*b*) *Beasts*. – Badger, Buck, Bugg, Bull, Bullock, Fox, Hare, Hind, Hogg, Hunter, Leech, Lyon, Mare, Mold, Pigg, Roe, Roebuck, Steer. (The names 'Barker' and 'Bruen', although suggestive, have not been included.)

(*c*) *Fishes*. – Dolphin, Fish, Herring, Otter, Pike, Salmon, Seal, Whale.

(*d*) *Trees, Shrubs, etc.* – Ash, Beech, Birch, Elms, Oakes, Barley, Bean, Berry, Brann, Budd, Burr, Cherry, Cobb, Figg, Flowers, Hay, Heather, Hedges, Lavender, Leaf, Leek, Leman, Lilley, Mace, Moss, Mustard, Nettle, Nutt, Oates, Orange, Peach, Peel, Pepper, Plant, Plum (surname), Reed, Rice, Root, Rose, Roseblade, Rye, Salt, Stocks, Straw, Thorne, Twigg, Vine.

(*e*) *Places*. – Brooks, Bush, Cliff, Common, Craig, Dale, Down, Dyke, Field, Forrest, Glen, Heath, Hill, Lake, Lane, Mead, Moor, Orchard, Pool, Quarry, Rhodes, Street, Vale, Waterfall, Weir, Wells, Woods.

(*f*) *Various*. – Clay, Cutbush, Dew, Frost, Gale, Mold, Nest, Weeding, Brown, and Breeze.

II. – The Church.

Beadle, Clark(e), Sexton.
Abbot, Bishop, Christian, Church, Creed, Crozier, Deacon, Fryer, Heaven, Kirk, Monk, Nunn, Parsons, Pope, Priestley, Prior, Sanctuary.

III. – Trades, Occupations and Professions.

Here again, kind readers (if any) will find considerable scope to test their knowledge either by supplying the names, with approximate dates, of the sides with which the players were associated, or by adding to the list set out:—

Baker, Barber, Brazier, Brewer, Butcher, Butler, Carpenter, Carter, Carver, Chancellor, Chandler, Collier, Constable, Cook, Cooper, Diver, Docker, Draper, Driver, Dyer, Farmer, Fisher, Forester, Fowler, Gardiner, Goldsmith, Groom, Hawker, Hewer, Hopper, Huntsman, Mason, Miller, Nutter, Ostler, Page, Painter, Piper, Plummer (no mate), Potter, Proctor, Rider, Sadler, Salter, Sellers, Seneschal, Sergeant, Shepherd, Shoesmith, Skinner, Skipper, Slater, Smith, Spicer, Stabler, Stoner, Tester, Thresher, Tinker, Tipper, Tyler, Usher, Warden, Washer, Weaver, Writer.

Perhaps Smoker and Walker might be added to the above.

IV. – Cricket Terms.

Bale, Ball, Bat (Gents v. Players, 1827), Bayles, Bowler, Chance, Colt, Creese, Field, Fielder, Fielding, Fluke, Gamble, Game, Greenfield, Grounds, Grubb, Light, Luck, Meadows, Mead, Over, Park, Player, Punchard and Scorer. Two other names possibly meriting mention are Kortright and Knox.

The writer does not expect to be believed, but it is a fact that at one time two maids in his employ were named Ball and Bowler. On going downstairs early one morning, whilst both of them were in the house, he met a sweep coming out of the dining-room. When asked what his name was, he replied: 'Over, sir.'

Whilst on the subject of names associated with play, it may be recorded that Raine, Showers, Sleat and Snow have all taken part in the game. Wade, too, recalls the conditions more than once of the Worcester County ground owing to the overflowing of the Severn.

V. – 'The Cup that Cheers.'

Bere, Champain, Port, Porter and Waters have all taken part in county cricket.

Other suggestive names are Bass, Buchanan, Burton, Guinness and Mumm. Victoria has produced a Drinkwater, and Winchester a Phillpotts.

There have also been Tod and Todd, but no Toddy.

Barrell, Butt and Tubb.

VI. – War, Ancient and Modern.

Notts have had three Gunns and a Shooter; Surrey one Gunn and two Shooters.

Archer, Bowman, Cannon (Victoria), Gunner and Lance.

VII. – Colours.

There have been many Blacks, Browns and Whites. Gray, Green and Pink have also appeared. For years, too, the name Dark has been associated with Lord's.

VIII. – Curious Names.

Bancalari, de Kerschendorf, Dracopoli, Hogsflesh, Hotchin, Rubegall, Rumbelow, Tarbox and Wildgoose.

Among wicket-keepers have been Wood and Stone – many batsmen have had to bow before them; Lilley, Oates and Straw.

IX. – Varia.

Abel and Cain; Adam, Eve and Eden; Abraham and Moses.

Day and Martin and Shine all played for Kent.

Anguish, Paine, Joy and Peace.

Bigg, Little, Broad, Short, Large, Small, Low, Long.

Evill, Faithful, Gentle, Good, Jolly, Nice, Noble, Perfect, Pretty, Proud, Tidy, Toogood, Valiant, Vane, Wild, Wise.

Bagge, Box, Case.

East, North, West.

Penny, Tanner, Twopenny.

Child, Doll, Kidd, Mann, Naumann, Suckling, Talboys.

Blunt, Round, Sharp.

Boddy, Brain, Foot, Hands, Head, Hide, Knee, Legge, Blood and Bone.

Boot (a Boots), Buckle, Capes, Coates, Cuff, Diamond, Hankey, Hatt, Rubie, Studd, Tye.

Boyle and Fry.

Young and Old.

Single and Batchelor.

King, Knight and Lord have played for Leicestershire, Duke for Kent, Earl for Derby, a Prince for four different counties, and two Squires.

Entries under this heading could be extended indefinitely. The pleasant task of doing so is left to the earnest student of the game.

The Cricketer 1926

54

Pursuit of Cricket under Difficulties

I know that we English are an angular and eccentric people — a people that the great flat-iron of civilization will take a long time smoothing all the puckers and wrinkles out of — but I was scarcely prepared for the following announcement that I saw the other day in a tobacconist's window near the Elephant and Castle:

On Saturday,
A Cricket Match will be played at the Rosemary
Branch, Peckham Rye,
between
Eleven One-armed Men and Eleven One-legged
Men.
The Match to begin at Eleven o'Clock a.m.

Well, I have heard of eccentric things in my time, thought I, but I think this beats them all. I know we are a robust, muscular people, who require vigorous exercise, so that we would rather be fighting than doing nothing. Our youth walk, run, shoot, fish, hunt (break their necks, even, in pursuit of health), tramp the world over, and leave their footprints in Arctic snows and Arabian sands. It is to this outward working of the inner fire that we owe our great circum-navigators, travellers, soldiers, and discoverers. Our English arms have built up half the railways in the world; our emigrants are on every sea; we are the harmless Norsemen of the nineteenth century. We can do (some of us) without working our brains much, but we Saxons must exert all our limbs; we pine if we are pent up at desks and ledgers. We are a race of walkers, sportsmen, travellers, and craftsmen. We are (by our arts and colonizing) the peaceful conquerors of the world. The days of the old red-handed conquest being now (as it is generally thought) gone by for ever, here these one-armed men go and caricature the national tendencies.

Such were my patriotic thoughts when I trudged down the Old Kent Road – chiefly remarkable, since the old coaching days, as the former residence of Mr Greenacre – and made my devious way to Peckham. Under swinging golden hams, golden gridirons, swaying concertinas (marked at a very low figure), past bundles of rusty fire-irons, dirty rolls of carpets, and corpulent dusty feather-beds – past deserted-looking horse-troughs and suburban-looking inns, I took my pilgrim way to the not very blooming Rye of Peckham.

Rows of brick boxes, called streets, half-isolated cottages, clung to by affectionate but dusty vines – eventually a canal, where boatmen smoked and had dreams of coming traffic – a sudden outburst of green fields, that made me think I was looking at streets with green spectacles on – brought me to the trim, neat public-house known by the pleasant aromatic name of 'The Rosemary Branch'.

A trim bar-woman, with, perhaps, rather too demonstrative a photographic brooch, stood in front of a row of glass barrels labelled respectively 'Shrub', 'Bitters', and *Sampson*', the latter, I have no doubt, a very strong beverage indeed. Nor did I fail to observe a portrait of the last winner of the Derby over the fireplace, and a little stuffed terrier pup above the glass door leading into the little parlour, where a very comfortable dinner was smoking.

I procured my ticket, and was shown through a deserted billiard-room, and down a back lane, to the cricket-field. I delivered up the blue slip to a very fat man with a child's voice who sat with an air of suffering at the entrance-wicket, and I was in the eccentric creatures' innocent field of battle.

There they were, the one-legged and the one-armed, encamped like two neighbouring armies.

Two potboys, girdled with tucked-up aprons white as the froth of bitter-beer, hurried past me as if to relieve the thirst of men wounded in war. After them came odd men carrying more benches for spectators of the one-armed men's prowess. The one-armed men were having their innings; the fielding of their one-legged adversaries, I could see in a moment, was something painfully wonderful and ludicrously horrible.

Totally indifferent to the mingled humour and horror of the day were the costermongers, who, grouped near the gate, threw a fair-day show over one section of the field. Those mere boys, with hard-lined pale faces and insinuating curls like large fish-hooks on each temple, were totally absorbed in drawing pence from the people of Peckham now that the bloom, so long expected, was undoubtedly on the Rye. There were boys shooting down an enormous tin telescope for nuts; there were men bowling clumsily at enormous wooden-headed nine-pins. But the crown of the amusements was the corduroy-sheathed lad who had, with true Derby-day alacrity, stuck four slender sticks into hampers of matted sand, and on those shivery columns poised hairy coco-nuts, gilt pincushions, and wooden boxes meretriciously covered. One, two — whiz — whirl; what beautiful illustrations of the force of gravity did those boxes and pincushions furnish at three throws a penny! With what an air of sagacious and triumphant foresight did the proprietor bundle up the cudgels under his arm and gingerly replace the glittering prizes!

But while I dally here the eccentric game proceeds; so, avoiding the cannon-shot of chance balls, I pass across the field to the little win-dowed shed where the scorer sits opposite to the signal-post that, with its 4−6−2 in large white figures, marks the progress of the game. Some boys are playing with a bundle of the large tin numerals that lie at the foot of the signboard-post. Inside the outer and open part of the shed sit a row of Peckham quidnuncs deeply interested in the game— a game which, if it were all innings, I hold would be almost perfect, but, as it is, I deem to be, on the whole, rather wearisome. I seated myself on a garden-roller kept to level the grass, and watched the game. A man driving two calves out of the way of the players informed me that the proceeds of the game were for the benefit of a one-armed man who was going in when the next wicket went down.

The players were not all Peckham men; that one-legged bowler, so deft and ready, I found was a well-known musical barber, a *great dancer*, and I believe a great fisherman, from a distant part of Essex.

The one-legged men were pretty well with the bat, but they were rather beaten when it came to fielding. There was a horrible Holbein-ish fun about the way they stumped, trotted, and jolted after the ball. A converging rank of crutches and wooden legs tore down upon the ball from all sides; while the one-armed men, wagging their hooks and stumps, rushed madly from wicket to wicket, fast for a 'oner', faster for 'a twoer'. A lean, droll, rather drunk fellow, in white trousers, was the wit of the one-leg party. 'Peggy' evidently rejoiced in the fact that he was the lamest man in the field, one leg being stiff from the hip downwards, and the wooden prop reaching far above the knee.

He did not treat the game so much as a matter of science as an affair of pure fun — of incongruous drollery, with which seriousness was altogether out of place. If there was a five minutes' lull for beer, when the 'over' was shouted, Peggy was sure to devote that interval to dancing a double-shuffle in the refreshment tent, where the plates were now being dealt round ready for some future edible game. When he took his place as slip or long-stop, he ran to his post while others walked; or delighted the boys by assuming an air of the intensest eagerness and watchfulness, putting a hand on either knee and bending forward, as if he had sworn that no ball should escape his vigilance; or when a ball did come, by blocking it with his wooden leg, throwing himself on it, or falling over it: an inevitable result, indeed, with nearly all the one-legged faction, as the slightest abruptness or jerk in movement had the result of throwing them off the perpendicular. I do not think that Peggy stopped a single ball unless it hit him; he generally fell over it and lost it until some comrade stumped up, swore at him, and picked the ball out from between his feet or under his arm.

The one-armed men had a much less invalid and veteran air about them. There was a shapely lad in a pink jersey, who, from having his hand off only at the wrist, merely looked at a distance like a stripling with his hand hidden by a long coat-cuff. But then, again, there was a thickset, sturdy fellow, in a blue cap, of the 'one-leg' party, who, though he had lost one foot, seemed to run and walk almost as well as ordinary people. Then, again, on the 'one-leg' side, there was an ostentatious amount of infirmity in the shape of one or two pale men with crutches, yet everybody appeared merry and good natured, and determined to enjoy the game to his heart's content; while every time a player made a run, before the dull beat of the bat had died away, there was a shout that made the Peckham welkin ring again, and all the crutches and wooden legs beat tattoos of pure joy and triumph. And when the musical and Terpsichorean barber rattled the wickets or made the bails fly, did not the very plates in the refreshment tent dance with pleasure!

Yet, really, Peggy's conduct was most reprehensible. In spite of his 'greyhound-in-the-leash' attitude, he was worse than useless; he kicked at the passing ball, he talked to it, he tumbled down to stop it, but for all the success he attained, he might as well have been away; why, Wilkins, with the long crutches and swinging legs, was three times as useful, though he was slow. I suppose, what with the beer, the heat of the day, the excess of zeal, and the fatigue, Peggy began at last to be pretty well aware that he was not doing much good, for he took to lying a good deal on his back, and to addressing the boys, who buzzed round him like flies, on the necessity of keeping a steady 'lookout' at cricket. I do not know what Peggy had been, but he looked like a waterman.

Now, a lad who lost his leg when a baby, as a bystander told me, took up the bat and went in with calm self-reliance, and the game went forward with the usual concomitants. Now come the tips, the misses, the by-balls, the leg hits, the swinging blows that intend so much and do nothing, the echoing swashing cuts, the lost balls, the stumpings-out, the blocks, the slow treacherous balls, and the spinning, bruising, roundhanders; not that our friends of the one leg and one arm swaddled themselves up in any timid paddings or bandages; they put on no india-rubber tubed gloves, no shelter-knuckles, they don no fluted leggings. What is a blow on the knuckles to a man who has lost a leg or an arm, who has felt the surgeon's saw and the keen double-edged knife? Yet all this time there was rather a ghastly reminder of suffering about the whole affair, to my mind. I could fancy the game played by out-patients in some outlying field of Guy's Hospital. I could believe it a party of convalescents in some field outside Sebastopol. Well, I suppose the fact is, that men don't think much of misfortunes when they are once irretrievable, and that these men felt a pleasure in doing an eccentric thing, in showing how bravely and easily they could overcome an infirmity that to some men appears terrible. After all, one thinks, after seeing such a game, one-legged and one-armed men are not so miserable as people imagine. Nature is kind to us in her compensations.

And all this time my eye was perpetually wandering to that blue bulbing dome and the two little pinnacles, that, though from here no larger than a chimney-piece ornament, is, I have reason to believe, Saint Paul's, some five miles distant as the crow flies. How delicate and clean cut its opaque sapphire – how pleasantly it crowns the horizon!

That view of Saint Paul's from the Peckham meadows I can strongly recommend to landscape painters as one of the best, because one of the nearest, suburban views of Saint Paul's. I know it, a little blue mushroom button from Banstead Downs, just cropping up above the grey rim of the horizon, where the dark brown cloud ever lingers to mark out London; I know it, a great palace of air from all the winding reaches of the Thames, But I think I never saw it before so beautiful, so unreal, so visionary, so sublime. It seemed more the presiding genius of the busy, turbulent, uneasy city. I felt quite a love for the old blue monster; the sight of him moved me as the sight of a great army moves me, or as the sight of a fleet beating out to sea, with their white wings set all one way.

And now looking again to the game — the excitement has become tremendous. A man with crutches is in; he props himself artfully up, while he strikes the ball feebly and with lacklustre stroke. A one-armed man with a wavering sleeve, bowls with his left hand, and makes a complicated business of it: the ball moving in a most eccentric orbit. At the opposite wicket Peggy is enthroned: his attitude is a study for Raphael — intense watchfulness, restless ambition, fond love of glory slightly dashed with inebriation, slightly marred by intoxication, visible in every motion. Alas! the first fell ball comes and damages his wicket. His perfect disbelief in the reality of such a catastrophe is sublime — it typifies the dogged constancy of a nation that never knows when it is beaten.

The one-arms are rudely exulting as Peggy stumps off, not that he ever made a run, but that the look of the man was so imposing. The *one-legs* droop, the *one-arms* throw up their caps, or dance 'break-downs', to give vent to their extreme joy. The outlying one-arms skip and trip, the one-legs put their heads together and mutter detracting observations on the one-armed bowling. 'There was no knowing what to make of them balls'; 'There was no telling where to have them balls'; 'They were a spiteful lot, the one-arms, so cheeky, so braggy;' 'But the one-legs knew what's what, and they are going to do the trick yet.'

Now the clatter of knives and forks and plates in the refreshment tent grew perfectly alarming; it was like a sale in a china-shop. The players, heedless of such poor sublunary things as boiled beef and greens and the smoke of flowery potatoes, played more like madmen than sober rational cricketers. St Paul's danced before my eyes as if I was playing cup and ball with it, so dazzled did I get with the flying red ball. The leaping catches were wonderful, the leg-hits admirable, the bowling geometrically wonderful, the tips singularly beautiful; the ball smashed at the palings, dashed into thorn bushes, lost itself, broke plates in the refreshment tent, nearly stunned the scorer, knocked down a boy, flew up in the air like a mad thing. As for Peggy's balustrade leg, had he not occasionally screwed it off to cool himself, it would have been shivered into a thousand pieces. You would have thought, indeed, that the bowler mistook his unfortunate 'stick leg' for the wicket, he let fly at it so often and so perversely. But in vain all skill and energy; the one-legs could not get at the ball quick enough, their fielding was not first-rate, the one-arms made a gigantic effort, forged fourteen runs ahead, and won. Peggy performed a pas seul expressive of hopeless despair, and stumped off for a pot of stout.

All the Year Round 1861

55

Curiosities of Cricket

C ricket itself is a curiosity to most foreigners. French, Spanish, and Portuguese writers, besides those of other countries, have described it with bewildering vagueness and misleading exaggeration. A Spaniard, who desired to make his fellow-countrymen familiar with the game, said: 'Two posts are placed at a great distance from one another. The player close to one of these posts throws a large ball to the other party, who awaits the ball, to send it far with a small stick with which he is armed; the other players then run to look for the ball, and while the search is going on, the party who struck it runs incessantly from post to post.' This is only part of the description; but the rest is much like it. If we did not know that cricket was the subject of the sketch, we should think the writer was explaining some game with which we are not familiar in this country.

But cricket has its curiosities, and scarcely a season passes without something happening which adds to the list of novelties. The frontispiece to Parry's *Second Voyage in Search of a North-west Passage* represents a cricket-match being played on the ice between the crews of the *Hecla* and the *Fury*. This was in March 1823, a month when it is not customary to play cricket in England. Cricket has also been played where grass would not grow, and where sand or gravel has been a substitute for the green turf which the cricketer loves. It must have been very hot in Hong Kong in October 1874, when, during a match, the middle stump was bowled out, but the two bails remained in their original position. The varnish had glued the bails together. This has happened even in milder latitudes.

Matches between women are not very common, but a number of them have been played. They have generally been either for sums of money or on behalf of public charities. In 1823, a match was played in

Norfolk between eleven married women and eleven single ones. The stakes were a pair of gloves each; and the married women won.

Among peculiar sides, the family Elevens may be mentioned. Some families are very famous for their cricketing abilities, but it does not often happen that eleven of their members are prepared to take the field against opponents. In 1867, eleven of Lord Lyttelton's family played the Bromsgrove Grammar School. The family was victorious by ten wickets. The Caesars, the Lubbocks, and others with well-known names, have played family matches.

At one time, the famous B. Eleven were able to meet the best of England. These players all had names which began with B. From 1805 to 1837 twelve matches were played by the Bs. Players came and players went, but the pre-eminence of the celebrated initial continued. Such names as Beauclerk, Budd, Beldham, Beagley, and Broadbridge, will suggest the strength of the side.

When matches were played for money, single wicket was far more common than it is now. Sometimes a celebrated player would have two or three opponents, and occasionally one man would play an Eleven. This happened in 1836 at Nottingham, when S. Redgate met and defeated eleven of the Kensington Club. Redgate made twenty-four in his two innings; but the other side made only ten.

There have been many expedients tried for the purpose of equalizing the chances of two sides, when one set of players was known to be superior to the others. Matches against odds are well known. At one time the All-England Eleven were constantly meeting eighteens and twenty-twos. This custom is fast passing away. County cricket is taking its place. In the year 1834, a novel expedient was tried at Nottingham. Eleven of that town met thirteen of Bingham. Nottingham won by eight wickets. It is said that this and the return match were the only ones ever played in which the odds were four innings to two.

Some years ago, there were two wandering Elevens consisting of one-armed and one-legged men. The first match between cricketers of this kind took place in 1811. It was for one thousand guineas, and all the men were pensioners of Greenwich Hospital. The one-arm side won. Their opponents were continually breaking or losing their wooden supports.

Sometimes the matches for money were genuine; but frequently the money was only pretended to be staked, in order to increase the interest in the public mind. Old advertisements of cricket-matches often state that a great deal of money depends upon the game. It was thought that players would be more likely to do their best if they were playing for money. This, however, was a great mistake. Matches are now contested as keenly as possible, when nothing but honour is played for.

At the present time, Left-arm would have a poor chance against the best Right-arm Eleven which could be put in the field. The Left-arm would do very well for bowling, but the batting would be weak. But the match has been played, and the full strength of the country has been divided between the two Elevens.

Another distinction between sides is Married and Single. The beginning of the alphabet has been pitted against the latter part— A to K against L to Z. During the last few years, a good match was made between Over thirty and Under thirty. In 1810, a similar match was played, but it was between Over thirty-eight and Under thirty-eight.

Single counties have played the rest of England; just as in the early days of cricket, a single club would hold its own against everybody else. Hambledon against England, with Hambledon victorious, is recorded in the early annals of cricket. The time has gone when any single county is strong enough to contend against all the others.

Some wonderful scores have been made at cricket; but in 1882 the Orleans Club beat all previous records. Against Rickling Green, they scored nine hundred and twenty in one innings. There are many cases known in which nothing has been scored in an innings; so that is a record which cannot be beaten. One of the highest individual innings ever played is that of Mr W. N. Roe, four hundred and fifteen for Emmanuel Long Vacation Club, against Caius Long Vacation Club, on July 12, 1881.

There are peculiar ways in which a man can be 'out' at cricket. In a match between England and Sussex, J. Broadbridge threw his bat at an off-ball; he hit the ball, and was caught. This is said to have lost the match for Sussex. Several times it has happened that batsmen have played the ball into their own pockets. Batsmen have been in as wonderfully as they have been out. The ball has been seen to go between the stumps without removing the bails, and yet when the ball has been placed between them, it has seemed impossible for this to happen. Bails have been known to be knocked off, and to have fallen back upon the wickets. But this is an event which very seldom happens.

A long list of extras does not look well in a cricket score. Some years ago, in a match between the Royal Engineers and The Establishment, there were one hundred and one extras. In 1842, the Gentlemen of Kent played the Gentlemen of England at Canterbury, and there were one hundred and fifty-nine extras in the match.

In Australia it is common to adjourn matches over Sunday, and play them out during the following week. This has seldom been done in England. In country matches there is sometimes an adjournment from Saturday to Saturday. But perhaps the longest adjournment ever known was at Stoke Down, in Hampshire. A match was commenced on July 23rd, and adjourned, after three days' playing, till June 28th of the following year. This was in the last century.

One of the most remarkable matches ever played took place at Shillinglee Park in 1843. On one side were the Earl of Winterton's Eleven, and thirty-seven labourers on the other. The Eleven won by five wickets. But this match was outdone three years after, when the same Eleven contended against fifty-six labourers. This time, however, the match was not finished.

Chambers's Journal 1883

56

Won by a Hat Trick

Married v. Bachelors

H. Graves

The town of Bundelpore was pre-eminently a sporting station. Athletics formed as essential a part of its social life as it does at either of our universities. A man of no use at sports was an outcast: the very natives regarded him with pitying smiles, and the 'smug' usually found it expedient to get himself exchanged into a more congenial sphere.

Bundelpore stuck pigs, shot all manner of strange beasts and fowl, and went into delirium at the long-desired advent of a tiger, for the king of the forest was scarce in the district. But notwithstanding the seductions of these fiercer forms of sport, cricket lay nearest to the heart of the station.

The reputation of the Bundelpore eleven had spread to the uttermost limits of the Indian empire, and its achievements even found a corner in Lillywhite. Nor was its prowess an ephemeral matter. The fame which came of strength bred fresh strength, and such Blues as filtered into India through the meshes of the Civil Service examinations looked to Bundelpore as the goal of promotion, and moved heaven and earth to get appointed to this Walhalla of cricket.

Under these circumstances the conduct of Augustus Jefferson was trebly presumptuous. It was bad enough that he should have forced himself upon unwilling Bundelpore, but that he should raise his eyes to Maud Burnett, the daughter of the Collector and the idol of every unmarried man in the place, was nothing short of sacrilege; for though Jefferson was in Bundelpore, he was not of it.

To begin with, he was *ex officio* an outsider – neither military flesh nor civilian fowl, nor even good medical red-herring. He was a young engineer engaged in constructing irrigation works on a rice plantation owned by a big company at home. He was not a public school man, but had exchanged the obscurity of a provincial grammar school for a desk in a surveyor's office, till at last a lucky chance put this Indian appointment within his grasp.

This, however, was a small matter, for Bundelpore was not inordinately snobbish. What annoyed Bundelpore was his colossal ignorance of sport. Indian life had perforce introduced him to horses, but he rode with marvellous awkwardness, and strictly as a method of locomotion.

Moreover, after he had riddled with shot the head-gear of the good-natured deputy magistrate, who had taken him out for a day's snipe-shooting, he was warned by in influential deputation that if he again appeared in public with a gun it would be confiscated, though in justice to Jefferson it should be added that his demeanour did not encourage volunteers to come forward to execute the sentence. But the worst of him was that in addition to the atrocious crime of being a duffer he opposed a taciturn reserve to the genial curiosity of young Bundelpore, which was genuinely anxious to discover in him, if possible, some saving grain of sporting ability.

But the bare toleration with which the station regarded him gave way to stronger feelings when he aspired to the affections of Maud Burnett, and she to all appearance did not resent it. What could she see in him — she, the fearless rider, the very Amazon of the cricket world? For had she not in the Bat *v.* Broomstick match contemptuously rejected the willow, and, choosing to be handicapped like her male opponents, triumphantly carried out her broomstick for fifty? So that her condescension to Jefferson was regarded with little short of horror: it was almost as bad as if she had been detected in a flirtation with a native.

Not the least astounded was the Collector himself, a Blue of prehistoric days, whose still respectable mastery of bat and ball, not less than his official position, well qualified him for the presidency of the cricket club.

Maud treated the hints of her friends and the objurgations of her father with equal disdain, while Jefferson showed for the present mood of Bundelpore no greater consideration than he had extended to its sporting susceptibilities.

But the love affairs of Miss Maud were forgotten by the station in the approach of the cricket season, to which this year unusual interest attached. An Oxford ex-captain, and one of the smartest of Cambridge batsmen, were among the recruits to the station, and Bundelpore was agog to see how they would acquit themselves.

Now, so immeasurable was the superiority of the home eleven to its neighbouring rivals, that matches with other stations aroused little attention. Bundelpore alone could furnish a worthy opponent for Bundelpore, and so it came about that only internecine conflicts among its own citizens stirred the interest of the station.

Chief among these was the great event of Married v. Single; for, though matches of this kind are, as a rule, scratch affairs, at Bundelpore the presence of a strong force of young married men decidedly altered the case. Last year, Married had won a hard-fought game, but the accession of the two new Blues had raised the hopes of the Bachelors, and correspondingly depressed those of the Benedicks, some of whose players, by reason of increasing girth and failing agility, were degenerating into a 'tail' of a pronounced type.

Amid the preparations for this great encounter came the amazing news that Jefferson was not only engaged to Miss Burnett, but to marry her within the month. The younger men talked darkly of lynching the prospective bridegroom: the elder addressed grave remonstrances to the president, to which he returned blandly evasive answers, an art in which he was exceptionally skilled.

However, there was nothing to be done: the opposition were powerless and the wedding was duly celebrated in the little iron church. The members of the cricket club vied with each other in shouting 'The Voice that breathed o'er Eden'. They explained that they regarded their action as the equivalent of ironical cheers.

Next day was destined for the great match. The Bachelors were confident of victory, the more so as their opponents had revealed the straits to which they were reduced by the inclusion in their team of 'A. N. Other', to the no small indignation of certain of the tubby brigade. Only the veteran president, who was himself captaining the Married side, retained his normal placidity, nor did he vouchsafe either to friend or foe the least inkling of his intentions. The married men wandered about the club making futile attempts to do a little hedging, and five to one was freely offered against their chances.

So Bundelpore went home to bed, to meet next day upon the cricket ground. All the world was there, and resplendent was the attire of its womankind, from the latest Parisian models, carefully kept back for this momentous day, to the gaudy bazaar shawls which graced the shoulders of the native women. Breathless was the excitement as the captains tossed for innings, and Smithson, the Single leader, winning the spin, elected to bat first.

Ten Married champions issued forth into the field, but still the question of the identity of 'A. N. Other' remained unsolved.

'Where's your eleventh man?' cried Smithson, as he walked, bat in hand, to the wicket.

'Here he is,' calmly replied the Collector from square leg, as Jefferson, than whom no man had been further from the thoughts of the crowd, emerged shyly from the pavilion, and made his way amidst amazed silence to the wicket at the Gasometer end. For Bundelpore had deliberately chosen a piece of ground adjacent to the gasworks. It seemed homelike, they said.

But more surprises were in store; Jefferson's first ball took Smithson's off stump. Next came the Oxonian, and landed his first ball into the hands of point, while his successor from Cambridge was hopelessly beaten by a fast ball with a peculiarly wicked break from the off. A captain of native cavalry who came next managed to block the two following deliveries, and the terrible over concluded. But the business was not to be stayed. The innings closed for 26, and Jefferson's analysis worked out at five wickets for 13 runs.

Married replied with 256, to which Jefferson, who came out strong as a stone-waller, contributed a patient 30. In the second innings of the Singles the Collector refused to put him on to bowl. 'We should be merciful to our enemies,' he explained, and he did not want unduly to curtail the match and lose a good day's cricket.

'How on earth did you find him out?' was the chorus that assailed the president at the club that night.

'Well, you see,' said the Collector, 'I was down by myself at the nets early one morning, when Jefferson strolled up, and asked if he could give me a ball or two. I let him try. He did the hat trick twice in twenty minutes.

'Afterwards I managed to get him to unfold a bit. He told me that he was considered a smart bowler at Puddletown Grammar School, but it was such a very minor seminary that it never got into the cricket almanacs. Besides, Loamshire is one of the lost counties, and doesn't run to a county team, so he didn't get any show that way. He simply wasted his talents on local hobbledehoys, and when he got to London he didn't manage to strike cricket circles. And, what's more, he never had any time to play.'

'But why didn't he tell us he could play cricket?'

'Well, for one thing he's one of those bashful chaps who don't trust themselves, but chiefly, I think, because he has a sense of the dramatic. I told him it was a pity he wasn't married, and he promptly offered to repair the omission. And really, when I thought it over, I didn't see why I should stand in the way. So between us we hatched our little conspiracy. I do hope, though, you wild young bachelors haven't been plunging on the match. Great mistake to get into the way of—— Ah, Smithson, five to one in fivers comes to——'

Harmsworth Magazine 1899

57

The 'Hat Trick' for a Wife

Alfred B. Cooper

Mr Job Eccles came stamping and fuming into his own drawing-room, where his pretty daughter, Gladys, was dispensing tea and cake to her afternoon callers. These were only two in number — Canon Horrox, the rector of Stanning, and May Sinclair, Gladys's special chum, and only sister of Jack, Fred, and Bob Sinclair, the three mainstays of the Pennerton Cricket Club.

Without this 'Varsity trio Pennerton would have been non-existent as far as the world of cricket is concerned, for it is one of the smallest places on the map, even if it appears there at all, but with the Sinclairs at home it was the joy and terror of Job Eccles's life — the joy, because he loved foemen worthy of his steel, or, to be exact, the steel of his famous cricket team: the terror, because Pennerton had given Stanning more serious frights than any other club in the district which they would stoop to play.

'Good afternoon, Mr Eccles,' said the Canon: 'no bad news, I hope?' for he saw the buff slip indicating a wire in the ironmaster's hand and noted his perturbed countenance.

'Read that,' said Mr Eccles, in his blunt way. The Canon took the wire and Gladys read it over his shoulder.

'New pro. ill — probable absentee. May have to play ten men Saturday — Sinclair.'

'Isn't it enough to make a saint swear, Canon?' said Mr Eccles, looking for ready sympathy.

'Well — I don't see — that it matters — very much.' said the Canon, looking up. 'You'll beat them all the easier, that's all.'

Mr Eccles looked too disgusted to explain further, and May Sinclair, who had picked up the wire, chimed in: 'Oh, it's from Jack! He's in London to-day. The new pro. ill? That's Plack, the man who was tried for Surrey last season. The boys say he's a treasure.'

'But — but — why can't they beg, borrow, or steal a man?' asked the Canon, still puzzled why Mr Eccles should take it so much to heart.

'Pon my word, Canon, you're not a bad sort for a parson,' broke in Mr Eccles, 'and you're a better sportsman than most of your cloth; but when it comes to seeing a point as plain as a pikestaff, or to choosing a curate' — this was a sly dig at the Canon's last failure — 'I give you up!' Then Mr Eccles slapped the Canon on the back and laughed uproariously, for at heart he greatly respected the genial Canon.

'You see, Canon Horrox, it's this way,' began Gladys.

'Yes, tell him, Gladys, there's a good girl. Now Gladys can see the point. She's a good sport, she is. I brought her up to it. When she brings a young fellow along I shall want to know if he's a good sportsman — none of your namby-pamby curate fellows. I believe that last milk-and-water failure of yours had a notion he might look her way. It's a good job he saw how the land lay and kept at a distance. Why, when he was playing cricket with the day-school team, do you know what he did, Canon? He went to the wicket to bat with one leg-guard on.'

'Well, I can't see anything very dreadful about that,' said the Canon.

'No; but he's a right-hand bat, and he put the pad on his right leg!' roared Mr Eccles. 'I'll tell you what, Canon; you should let me choose your curates for you. I've had some practice in spotting men, what with choosing hands for the works and cricketers for the club.'

'Much the same thing where you are concerned, Mr Eccles,' said the Canon, who knew that only cricketers need apply for the vacancies in the ironworks, which formed the only industry of the village of Stanning.

'Well, be that as it may,' resumed Mr Eccles, 'I know a man when I see him. Whether there are any men among the curate tribe I doubt, but if there should be one I guess I could spot him.'

The Canon knew it was not much use arguing this matter, so he turned to Gladys. 'You haven't explained the wire,' he said.

Gladys was thinking very hard about something, and started when the Canon appealed to her. 'Oh, it's quite simple,' she said. 'When Fred Sinclair was down south the other week he picked up a young fellow named Plack, a left-hand bat and left-hand medium-pace bowler. Jack told me in May's presence — May will corroborate — and I told dad, that Pennerton were going "to wipe the floor" with Stanning on Saturday.'

'Wipe the floor!' sneered Mr Eccles, making a cut for four at an imaginary ball with the Canon's ivory-handled walking-stick. 'We'd have given them "wipe the floor," even with the help of this wonderful Slack or Flack, or whatever he calls himself.'

'Well, don't you see,' went on Gladys, taking no notice of her father's interruption, 'the pater's in a rage because he won't have the chance of making Jack eat his words. Of course, as you say, they might beg, borrow, or steal a man, but Pennerton is a tiny place, and good cricketers are scarce anywhere.'

'Yes, sir, Gladys is right,' said Mr Eccles, who had just bowled and caught a man whose wicket was somewhere over beside the piano. 'Yes, sir, you can make parsons by the thousand, but good cricketers are born, sir – born – not made. And you'll find that a man who is a good cricketer has got his head screwed on all right. I find it so in the works. Why, if I were choosing a curate for you, Canon, I'd choose him on his cricket – ha! ha! ha!' And having made a final hit out of the ground he took his departure.

'Well, Gladys, you're coming to tennis to-morrow, of course?' inquired May. 'Oswald comes to stay with us to-night, and is preaching for Pa on Sunday. He wants to see as much as possible of you, at Pennerton, seeing that you won't hear of his coming here.'

'It would spoil the whole thing,' said Gladys, wistfully. 'He's a curate, you know, or going to be, and you've heard for yourself the way the pater talks.'

'Didn't you know that Oswald Rolles – I guess you're talking of him,' said the Canon, 'has applied for my vacant curacy?'

'No!' said Gladys, in horror. 'Oh, that would be fatal – unless – unless – we could get dad to nominate him.'

The Canon shook his head dolefully. 'I couldn't wish for a more delightful colleague, and if it depended solely upon me he should have it to-morrow, both for your sake and my own. But, as you say, it would be fatal to the course of true love.'

'Hurrah!' shouted Gladys, 'I've hit it. It's glorious! A splendid plan.'

'Well, don't keep all the fun to yourself,' said May; and then and there Gladys unfolded her little scheme, speaking in a whisper lest, perchance, the furniture might hear and tell Mr Eccles.

The next day she cycled over to Pennerton and — she must have given May the hint, surely — she was amazed to meet Oswald Rolles, when half-way there, coming to meet her on a bicycle he had borrowed from Fred Sinclair.

'You see, Oswald, it would be fatal to come to Stanning as the Canon's nominee,' said Gladys, a little later, as they pedalled together along the leafy lanes. 'Dad would be prejudiced in a minute, and never think anything of you ever after.'

'Then I suppose there's nothing for it but the curacy at Exeter,' said Oswald. 'It's ten pounds better and three hundred miles worse.'

'Oh, I certainly should, if I were you,' said Gladys, with infinite scorn. 'How beautifully love finds a way.'

Oswald stopped and jumped off his machine, expecting Gladys to do the same, but she rode on round the bend and out of sight, and Oswald mounted again, dolefully. But when he got round the corner he saw Gladys leaning against a gate.

'Forgive me!' he cried, as he propped his bike against hers. 'Wild horses and carts shall not drag me to Exeter.'

Oswald looked so earnest that Gladys laughed. 'Do you bowl left-handed?' she said.

'Why, yes. What's that to do with Exeter?'

'And do you bat left-handed?'

'I do that, also,' said Oswald; 'but I always do this right-handed,' and he put his arm round her.

'I thought so,' said Gladys, referring to the batting and bowling, and then she put her sweet lips to his ear and told him something which made him open his eyes wide and then smile and then laugh and then kiss her.

It was quite a big event when Stanning played Pennerton. Even the manufacturing town of Dartham sent forth its hundreds by road and rail, for, big town though it was, its cricket team was not a patch on Job Eccles's picked eleven, the very nursery of county cricket. Then, as for Pennerton, were not the Sinclairs all county players, and was not the new pro. coming — the redoubtable Plack, a left-hand batsman and bowler? Ah, they knew all about it.

So a big, excited crowd gathered round the field. They were mostly

Stanningites, because Stanning was a sort of chick of Dartham in the manufacturing line, and the bigger town was proud of the game young cockerel that could crow so lustily and use its spurs to boot.

The ironmaster won the toss, much to the crowd's delight, and to the much greater delight of Gladys. Indeed, she had almost extracted a promise from her stanch friend, Jack Sinclair, to take second innings in any case.

Mr Eccles was not much of a bat, but he always made it a point of going in first wicket down. He was morally worth any three men to his team, and he went in early as a sort of duty – the crowd expected it of him. Besides, he prided himself on keeping his wicket up while others made runs. He had been known to make a single in the course of a whole half-hour, and these workers were sportsmen and knew the value of patience.

But when Pennerton came out to field and only ten men appeared, there was a groan of disappointment from the spectators. Like Mr Eccles, they hated one-sided matches. They liked a fight to a finish, no advantage and no quarter.

'Why, t' new pro. hasna come'. 'They'n getten a soft thing on, hes Stanning, Aw reckon'. 'Aw would ne'er ha' bothered to come if Aw'd thowt Plack werena comin'.' Such were the comments of the ring.

The Pennerton bowlers tried all they knew on the first Stanning pair, but fifty runs were scored in as many minutes.

'By gum, t' fust pair'll win t' match', said the scornful Stanningites. 'Pennerton want a new bowler pretty bad, Aw reckon.'

At that moment a man in flannels, and a big Panama pulled well over his forehead, ran on to the field and went over to the captain, who shook hands with him.

'It's Plack, sure enuf,' said the ring. 'He's turned up unexpected. Sinclair'll put 'im on to bowl, yo'll see, pretty quick.'

They were right. Between the overs the newcomer took the pavilion end, sent down a few practice balls, and then prepared for the first ball of the over. The batsman had made thirty-five and seemed set. The bowler took a long run as though he were going to deliver an express, and there was a gasp of surprise when the ball was tossed as a child might toss it in play. It pitched to the off, and Barton stepped across his wicket to cut it fine, but the ball shot in behind his legs and took his off-stump.

Mr Eccles fairly jumped, and said something under his breath, as he pulled on his gloves preparatory to showing the ring how the new bowler should be played. He walked smartly to the wicket, took centre very carefully, patted down an imaginary 'spot' on the off-side, and stood up to face the second ball of the over.

It came curving high and slow, like the other one. He stepped out to meet it, changed his mind, stepped back quickly, with his bat held at an angle of forty-five, and, hearing an ominous rattle in his rear, turned round to see his stumps representing the majority of the remaining angles. The small Pennerton contingent cheered rapturously and the Stanningites said, 'By gum, he's stirrin' 'em, an' they lewk easy too.'

Mr Eccles walked right across the pitch and shook hands with the new bowler. 'I'm glad to meet you, Stack,' he said — he never could get names right — and walked hurriedly to the pavilion. Then everybody cheered.

The next man in was a mighty hitter. When he opened his shoulders, the next parish or the roof of the pavilion knew about it. The bowler's delivery was just the same, but the ball came at twice the speed. The smiter smote with all his might, fair and true — a straight, hard drive. Everybody looked to see it at the boundary in a flash, and thought they had lost sight of the ball because it was travelling so fast. But the bowler's left hand had shot out, and the crowd only realized that he had held the ball when he tossed it carelessly up. The new bowler had performed the 'hat trick' with his first three balls!

He took six wickets in all, and the innings closed for 111. As the players came off the field, Gladys, who was sitting at the front of the pavilion with Canon Horrox, gave no sign. But she saw her father, out of the corner of her eye, go forward to meet Jack Sinclair, who was walking with the new bowler.

'I congratulate you on your find, Jack,' he said. 'Plack's a bowler in a thousand.'

'Plack!' said the captain, with well-simulated astonishment. 'This is not Plack, the pro., but my cousin, Oswald Rolles.'

'I — I — I'm sure I'm very sorry,' stammered Mr Eccles. 'I thought — '

'Oh, it's all right,' laughed Jack. 'I only hope that Plack, when he comes, will do half as well.'

'You're all too flattering,' said Rolles, in his pleasant voice. 'The whole thing was a bit of sheer luck. But I'm glad I turned up in the nick of time, in response to Jack's invitation.'

'My dear,' said Mr Eccles, as they passed Gladys and the Canon – May Sinclair had stayed away for diplomatic reasons – 'let me introduce Mr Rolles to you – my daughter, Gladys. Ah, yes, our rector, Canon Horrox.'

'How d' do, Rolles?' said the Canon. 'Old friends, are we not? I knew you were all jumping to a wrong conclusion, but the joke was too good to spoil.'

'You sinner!' said Mr Eccles. 'Well, you got the pull of me this time, but I shall get my chance later – see if I don't!'

Oswald was to go in fifth wicket down, and, as he had been duly introduced, he saw no reason why he should not improve Miss Eccles's acquaintance. For total strangers they seemed to get on remarkably well.

'You must make some runs, Oswald,' said Gladys, 'so as to deepen the impression. You've done wonders, but he doesn't know you're a parson yet, and that might undo everything. Oh, dear! there goes Jack's wicket.'

The Pennerton captain was generally good for at least thirty, and his early dismissal was quite a disaster. But when Fred and Tom came and went for a total of thirty-nine the crowd chortled, and Pennerton began to look rather glum.

'Pennerton must win to-day,' said Gladys, as Rolles went to put his leg-guards on. 'Nothing could impress the pater more than a defeat. He'd simply covet you.'

The first ball Rolles received – the crowd still thought it was Plack, for did he not both bat and bowl left-handed – he touched to slip, who juggled with the ball like the clown at the circus and then dropped it! Gladys's heart had stopped, but it went on again at double the rate to make up for lost time.

The Canon, sitting beside Gladys, was almost as anxious as she. It was a match for a curate and a husband, but it must be confessed that the Canon's thoughts were not for himself. Gladys leaned forward and watched every ball as gamblers watch the roulette at Monte Carlo. Several times the ball missed the stumps by inches. But the fates were still propitious, and a miss is as good as a mile – especially in cricket.

Crash! That was the ball on the corrugated iron roof of the pavilion.

It rolled off at Gladys's feet, and if it had been a ball of pure gold she could not have regarded it more affectionately. She knew that every such hit was better than a division of artillery for beating down her father's fortifications of prejudice.

'He's gone!' cried the Canon, as the ball flew skyward and fell into cover-point's hands. But a groan escaped the crowd as cover-point, usually as safe as a tarpaulin sheet, let it slip through his fingers. But the next ball disposed of Oswald's partner, and two men followed for an addition of ten runs.

'Mr Rolles is in a hitting mood,' said Jack Sinclair to the professional, Hunt, who was going in next. 'Block every ball.'

But the first ball Hunt received was so tempting that he could not resist the impulse to 'have a go,' and he had to go! Mr Eccles caught him and looked pleased with himself.

The last man in was a bowler pure and simple. His average for the previous season had been 3.5. But this was Gladys's day, for the gods had so ordained. He hit at everything, and, what is more, he hit everything hard and often. The field was all round the rails watching the sky for catches. But the ball went a little too far, or fell a little short, or the sun was in the catcher's eyes — and the catches didn't come off.

'Two to tie, three to win!'

Rolles made a lovely drive all along the carpet. Gladys in her excitement stood up. Would it reach the boundary? No! The batsmen were running hard, but the ball was smartly fielded and thrown in just as Rolles called for a third run. The wicket-keeper had the ball when Rolles was three yards from home, but he fumbled it and missed the chance of a lifetime. Pennerton had just won on the post.

It was the next morning — Sunday — and Mr Job Eccles was strangely quiet over his breakfast.

'May Sinclair wants me to go over to Pennerton this morning, dad; will you come too?'

'Pennerton? No. Why should I go gadding about on a Sunday? What does she want with you to-day?'

'She wants me to hear Mr Rolles preach', said Gladys, with her heart in her mouth.

'Preach? Preach? Why, is he a parson?'

'Yes, dad — didn't you know?'

'Listen to the girl. How in the world should I know? Where's his church?'

'He hasn't one yet. He is just on the point of taking a curacy at Exeter, I hear.'

'Devon? A likely place for a cricketer! They haven't even a county team, have they?'

'Not a first-class one, but it's ten pounds better than the curate gets at Stanning, for instance, and he's not well off, I hear.'

'Ten pounds better! That old Canon you are so fond of is an old fool, Gladys — an old fool, I say. He knew this fellow Rolles — the only decent parson I ever struck — was wanting a place, and yet only last night he suggested some nincompoop that can't play croquet, let alone cricket. Why, Rolles would be the backbone of our team, and could qualify for the county.'

'Where are you going, dad? You've not had half a breakfast.'

'Going? Why, to the rectory, of course. I'll get my innings this time if I never did before. Ten pounds! I'll give fifty extra out of my own pocket to secure such a treasure.'

And he did; but six months later he willingly gave more — much more — the greatest treasure of his heart since his young wife's death twenty years ago — his fair daughter Gladys. The general hope is that they'll have a record partnership and make a long score.

Twenty-five Cricket Stories 1909

58

Eleven Maids Dressed All in White

Celia Davies

It was at a house-party at Nun Appleton, in Yorkshire, the home of Mr and Mrs Beckett, that the White Heather Cricket Club was formed by a group of ladies during the summer of 1887. One might be forgiven for thinking that cricket, as a game for women, was a revolutionary idea, a symptom of the age of 'The New Woman', but this was not so.

During the 18th century a great deal of cricket was played by girls and women, mostly in Sussex, Surrey and Hampshire. Their games were usually noisy, boisterous village affairs, often watched by large crowds. On one occasion at Harting, in Sussex, there were close on 3000 spectators. 'Married *v.* Single' was a favourite form of match, and the refreshments would consist of plum cake, a barrel of beer and a regale of tea. At a match played in 1745 an onlooker said that 'the girls bowled, batted, ran and catched as well as most men'. Yet another 18th-century women's match reported in the *Reading Mercury* was described as 'the greatest cricket match that ever was played in the south part of England . . . was played on Gosden Common near Guildford in Surrey, between eleven maids of Bramley and eleven maids of Hambledon, dressed all in white. The Bramley maids had blue ribbons and the Hambledon maids had red ribbons on their heads. The Bramley girls got 119 notches and the Hambledon girls 127.'

Cricket was not left entirely to village girls. The aristocracy also took part in this new sport, and in 1777 the Countess of Derby and 'other fashionable ladies' played a match at Sevenoaks. The players are wearing silk dresses with tight-fitting bodices and flowing skirts and beribboned hats perched on top of piled-up hair. The romping games of village cricket tended to die out at the end of the century. However, in 1811 Rowlandson caricatured a match played between the women of Hampshire and Surrey, which he called 'Cricket Match Extraordinary'. The stakes on this occasion were 500 guineas and it appears to have been a very unladylike affair.

A woman is credited with inventing round-arm bowling. At the end of the 18th century John Willes, an enthusiastic cricketer, practised batting with his sister Christina bowling to him. Her voluminous skirts made it impossible to bowl in the conventional under-arm manner. So she raised her arm and a new bowling style was born.

Early Victorian women were not much addicted to strenuous games, although many excelled in the hunting field. However, by the 1880s they were breaking with tradition and becoming more masculine in appearance. They still pinched in their waists and wore long skirts, but they favoured stiff collars and ties, and straw hats that differed little from a man's 'boater'. It is not surprising that cricket for women became fashionable once more.

The eight ladies who decided to form themselves into the White Heather Cricket Club were either closely related or intimate friends. They were the Hon. M. Brassey, the Hon. B. Brassey, Lady Milner, Lady Idina Nevill, Lady Henry Nevill, the Hon. M. Lawrence, Miss Chandos-Pole and Miss Street. Family ties were more closely forged 18 months later when Lady Idina Nevill married the Hon. Thomas Allnut Brassey. White heather was adopted as the club emblem, and the colours were to be pink, white and green. By 1891 the membership had risen to 50 and included many well-known names, such as the Viscountess Cantelupe, the Viscountess Dungan and the Hon. E. Gathorne-Hardy. Mrs Stanley Baldwin became a devoted member in 1892. She was an outstanding cricketer, at one time having a batting average of 62. She is reported to have convened a club meeting at No. 10 Downing Street in 1926 during the General Strike.

The first match entered in the score book took place at Nun Appleton in August, 1888. Lady Milner captained the home team and the visiting XI was captained by Miss Egerton, of Whitwell Hall, Malton. The match was described as follows:

'The ground . . . was in excellent condition and not too hard to be at all dangerous. Most of the players were got up in faultless cricketing costumes of white flannel, while some few preferred coloured dresses which, though not so workmanlike, added brightness to the scene.

The visitors arrived about noon and having won the toss went first to the wickets. In their first innings they succumbed rather too easily to the excellent bowling on behalf of the home team, no less than seven falling victims to Miss Whitehead's prowess with the ball and the total innings was only 28. Lady Milner's eleven then took their turn . . . They put together the very creditable total of 88, Lady Idina and Lady Henry Nevill, Miss Brassey and Miss Street making double figures. . . . After an adjournment for luncheon the visitors began their second innings and it was soon apparent that the welcome hospitality of Mr & Mrs Beckett had greatly invigorated their powers of defence.'

This must have been a lively match. It should be noted that although play did not begin until noon both sides had completed an innings before lunch. After lunch the visitors knocked up a total of 173; Mrs and Miss Fairfax batted together and 'mother and daughter put on runs very rapidly until, after a brilliant innings of 72, the latter had to succumb to one of Lady I. Nevill's undeniable shovellers and she returned amid the well-earned plaudits of the spectators'. There was one hour left for the home team to score 114 to win. However, 'thanks to the hard-hitting of Lady Milner, who made 41 not out', they won by four wickets.

Five months after this memorable match, in January 1889, the wedding of Lady Idina Nevill and the Hon. Thomas Brassey took place. The seven bridesmaids, who were all members of the White Heather Club, were 'suitably' dressed in white silk shirts, with the club tie, white flannel skirts and brown shoes and stockings. Their hard white straw hats were trimmed with the club colours, and they carried bouquets of white heather, pink carnations and green orchids.

The club continued to flourish with a full fixture card every season. Matches were played against girls' schools, boys' preparatory schools and ladies' XIs. Men took on the duty of umpiring, and in 1907 the following names were among those who helped in this way: Lord Nevill, Sir Frederick Milner and the Hon. T. A. Brassey. In 1913 Miss Georgie Waters, of Epping, became secretary and gave the club her unstinted services until her death in 1950. In 1921 she edited a booklet that gave an account of the formation of the club and included a list of past and present members. She conceived the idea of asking everyone to send a brief account of their activities during the non-cricketing years of 1914—18. This makes interesting reading, and for women who had been brought up in a society where any form of 'work' was considered unladylike, they put up a good record.

VAD work predominated. Miss T. Buxton went to Boulogne in September 1914 as a VAD organizer and was awarded the Mons medal; she was also mentioned in dispatches. Mrs Stanley Baldwin was Commandant of a Red Cross hospital and President of the Queen Mary Work Rooms and was awarded the OBE. Countess Brassey converted her Sussex home into a hospital of 85 beds, of which she was Commandant. Miss G. Hall and Miss Parker went farther afield, driving cars in Macedonia and Salonica with the Serbian Army, and Miss Parker was awarded the Order of St Sava. Mrs Coghill worked on a farm and 'did ploughing', while Lady Lowther was Acting Master of the Pytchley Fox Hounds during her husband's absence abroad.

With the return of peace the club became active once more and in 1939 there were over 70 members. Not much cricket was played after the second World War, but the members continued to meet one another at an annual dinner in London. In 1952 there were still 50 members, and the Viscountess Cantelupe was President. I have been unable to discover just when the club was disbanded, but I think it was during the 1950s. Did the members at their last meeting sing the song that, we may assume, had been composed by one who was a more accomplished cricketer than poet?

> 'The friendships we've formed in White Heather
> May they grow and lengthen each link,
> With a cheer "Here's cricket for ever"
> Neath the folds of white, green and pink.'

Country Life 1973

59

The Cricketers of Flanders

Cricket during War

The first to climb the parapet
With 'cricket-ball' in either hand;
The first to vanish in the smoke
Of God-forsaken No-Man's Land.
First at the wire and soonest through,
First at those red-mouthed hounds of hell
The Maxims, and the first to fall, —
They do their bit, and do it well.

Fully sixty yards I've seen them throw
With all that nicety of aim
They learned on British cricket-fields.
Ah! bombing is a Briton's game!
Shell-hole to shell-hole, trench to trench,
'Lobbing them over', with an eye
As true as though it *were* a game,
And friends were having tea close by.

Pull down some art-offending thing
Of carven stone, and in its stead
Let splendid bronze commemorate
These men, the living and the dead.
No figure of heroic size
Towering skyward like a god;
But just a lad who might have stepped
From any British bombing squad.

His shrapnel helmet set a-tilt,
His bombing waistcoat sagging low,

His rifle slung across his back:
Poised in the very act to throw.
And let some graven legend tell
Of those weird battles in the West
Wherein he put old skill to use
And played old games with sterner zest.

Thus should he stand, reminding those
In less believing days, perchance,
How Britain's fighting cricketers
Helped bomb the Germans out of France.
And other eyes than ours would see;
And other hearts than ours would thrill,
And others say, as we have said:
'A sportsman and a soldier still!'

ANON.

Modern Poetry (Ed. Guy N. Pocock) 1920

60

Cricket Won't Be Druv'

A Spectator Considers the Future

Edmund Blunden

Fragments of a conversation which was not intended to be especially private drifted across the snuggery, a night or two ago, and seemed to me to announce the shape of things to come. The speakers began with the question of cricket reform. This did not take them long, for when I next heard the words they went thus: 'Dr Grace . . . He was fifty-three when I saw him play. You remember he always fielded at point.' And so on; nothing astonishing, you may say, but I felt the presence of that quiet spectatorship, that steady enjoyment and exact appreciation which have belonged to the cricket crowds of my time. I meditated that the wise reformer would not venture on any strange experiment without thinking of such speakers, such onlookers.

Cricket has undergone many alterations in a long and rich history. As a spectator, or as a player, I do not think I should have liked it in its ancient form half as much as in its later growth. The days of the tremendously fast underarm bowling, and those when a bat had a crescent shape or thereabouts, even if you allow credit for the gay costumes then in favour, were not the prime of this enchanting game. It required rather more of science in the preparation and the equipment than it first had, in order that its beautiful possibilities might all come to bloom. But throughout all the alterations, the provision of the third stump, the invention of the cane-handled bat, the making of the 'perfect' pitch, some characteristics have remained, and when they depart a good many of the spectators will depart also – hoping to rediscover the cricket they once knew in a better land.

First undoubtedly there is the principle that cricket is a game. It would seem scarcely possible that it should be forgotten; it has been forgotten, in the old days of betting on matches and in the recent ones of international contests. Just now one might not believe a picture of the cricket world in dispute, only a few years ago, over a type of bowling; how angry we were, how serious in our wrath! Still, if it had been remembered all along that cricket is a game — no matter what teams play it, this peculiar vehemence and high tension would not have happened. If there is danger of matches in the future becoming a kind of battle, heated up with endless press gossip and philippic, then let us who would like to have our cricket call for reform — but simply the reform of an old principle re-established. We love great contests, we are never too aged to worship the splendid player, we desire 'the rigour of the game' — but before all else we want its music. It must be as harmonious as it is two-sided. Let it all be well-tempered.

Someone was telling me his pleasantest cricket memory: it has the light of the game in it. A. P. F. Chapman smote a ball from Tate for a glorious six. Tate grinned at him, and he at Tate. The bowler next sent down a really fast one, which shattered the batsman's wicket. Chapman grinned at Tate, and he at Chapman.

We of the crowd like our cricket to be well off in such personal touches. We are not in a hurry, we are not working out the averages, we like the differences and variations which arise within the limits of a game. Let cricketers never be so overcome by the occasion, or the economics of the game, as not to be individuals, characters, humorists, actors in some measure, doing things their own way. Far back in time there were records made, and figures were studied; but the appearance, the actions, the comments of the old players were quite as much a part of the cricket. Possibly we live in an age when character is less clearly demonstrated in the outward man; and yet it is not always so. A reading of Mr Robertson-Glasgow's inimitable description of Philip Mead settling himself at the crease (probably for a century) shows this, and shows what the cricket spectator enjoys. The golden reputation of Patsy Hendren was not founded merely in his magnificent force and audacity of batsmanship; it grew largely from the spirit he had, of generous and genial philosophy, at all states of the game. How charmingly he could make us all share it! I have quoted a simple story of bowler and batsman, and it reminds me of a day at Lord's when Bowley (of Sussex) was tossing up some of his slows to Hendren. So slow they were, that they amused both of the combatants, and Hendren (though watching them with all his powers) performed some little antics as if in a country dance. Again, a slight thing to record; but in memory it is the register of a true 'day in the sun'.

As to the nature of a cricketer's performance, it is our hope from behind the boundary pickets to see anything but uniformity. We read that so-and-so, if he would only curb his impatience to hit his first ball to the on boundary, would be a really fine batsman. We do not feel so eager for his redemption. He sometimes *does* hit the first ball where he intended. Equally, we do not demand that Blank shall be excommunicated because he never hits a four at all. He has a defence, which may be very useful this very afternoon when the slashing boys are all back in the pavilion; and there is a poetry in the placing of the ball. 'A most elegant craftsman,' said an old watcher to me the other day, speaking of Mr Palairet. I am afraid he had quite forgotten W. H. Ponsford. But his talk was not of batsmen only, for your true spectator is there to see the bowlers and the fieldsmen as well, and therein he has a range of fine sympathies, understandings, anticipations, restraints and ventures; it is all the play of the mind, and so far the game has not disappointed its votaries in out-cricket diversion. If bowlers prefer to deliver six balls an over rather than eight, that will not disturb, rather it will gratify the spectator, and you may call it reform if you please; but we cannot have any other change in the element of bowling.

Would we have faster cricket, and the rule of so many minutes for each batsman supposing he lasts so long? I doubt it. It is not the natural game, and we are not assembled to watch run-getting, though it can be brisk and blithe. We are prepared to see the genius of this or that player unfold itself without being forced. There are difficulties enough, in any case, closing round the best of players when they arrive at the crease. We wish the game which tests them with these and their nerves to permit of their building up their innings (should the day be right for them) according to their own art and character. Hitherto the three-day match has served this purpose well enough in an imperfect world. We would rather be limited ourselves to seeing only part of one day of it than have the rhythms and patterns blurred, or curtailed. And again be it noted, we come rather to see cricket than results. If it still means that cricket to be vivid must move for a result, we come rather to see one match than an item in the struggle for a championship. In that connection, one or two matches played by teams of thorough cricketers under captains who love the game, a little before the War, were held to be masterpieces excelling any of the Tests of the period. At the Mote, the contest of Kent and Gloucester, when the total innings was under 150 on an average of the four, was counted one of these glorious games. Who won? I could look it up, but it never mattered all that much.

Our appeal, then— if I read the minds of my fellow spectators right— is for much the same cricket arrangements as we have known, with more of the freedom of individuality, and with more of the county game unobscured by the international, and always more sunshine if the MCC can procure that. This may be accounted a very simple desire, but 'progress' in cricket is a very difficult one. The spectator on whose support the game can live is not coming to the summer greenness and the afternoon's tranquillity as one whose appetite demands rum and gunpowder; he is there to examine and ponder upon and sympathize in the subtleties of a very finely poised argument. If suddenly it changes to something dramatic, something capricious, something comical, he finds all welcome, but the essence of his cricket is still a leisured appreciation of qualities, a discussion of resource, reason, intention and circumstance. This, which the complex and ample game supplies so well, is a pleasure of the mind accompanied by the rest of the body in the charm of the scene; while we are about reform, let us ask for a few more trees on our cricket grounds, even if they overshadow deep square leg. Then all that is needed is the rise of new cricketers with personality as well as science and physique; and I need not name the half-dozen who in every county when this War ends, will still be young enough for years of wonderful cricket of the old sweetness.

Edmund Blunden: A Selection of his Poetry and Prose
(Ed. Rupert Hart-Davis) 1950

A Collection of Words on E.B. the Cricketer

John R. Hung

When once again he hears the umpire calling 'Play'
Needs must the veteran's heart rejoice
For on the turf a challenge to obey.
Half a century has he answered this call
Moving from county to county in rain or shine
With eleven jolly companions.
Into the village pub they would file
After a hard day's work;
Debating on who would win the Ashes
Or who would be the next County Champions.
Far into the night would they sit and talk
Before starting off for the next village.
'That's one way of seeing the country,' he said.

He played not in first class matches,
But enjoyed himself he certainly did
In care-free games where the nation
Was not at stake with one wrong move.
War stopped him not from playing;
A grassy patch found and enough men to play
Out would come stumps and bats from who knows where,
Twenty-two yards marked out and off they went
With enemy guns breathing smoke down their necks.
'If the Kaiser played cricket there wouldn't be any war',
They said.
Those were the days when cricket was to be enjoyed,
No politics were there in the sport then.

Now sheltered beneath a wide-brimmed hat

His spell at the nets done,
Eyes sparkling and with a boyish grin
He sits and gossips in the sun:
Of many a noble innings at the sticks
Fearless of the bowler's fiery bumpers
Or the wicket-keeper's guile,
Of catches missed and catches made,
Of bowling with a shineless ball —
No liberties would the batsmen take
When leg-breaks came off and balls cut through,
Praises he won and applause
In those ante-Test-match days.

Edmund Blunden, Sixty-five 1961

Index

Numbers in bold type refer to contributors